The Road to Abolition?

THE CHARLES HAMILTON HOUSTON INSTITUTE
SERIES ON RACE AND JUSTICE

The Charles Hamilton Houston Institute for Race and Justice at Harvard Law School seeks to further the vision of racial justice and equality through research, policy analysis, litigation, and scholarship, and will place a special emphasis on the issues of voting rights, the future of affirmative action, the criminal justice system, and related areas.

From Lynch Mobs to the Killing State:
Race and the Death Penalty in America
Edited by Charles J. Ogletree, Jr., and Austin Sarat

When Law Fails: Making Sense of Miscarriages of Justice
Edited by Charles J. Ogletree, Jr., and Austin Sarat

The Road to Abolition?
The Future of Capital Punishment in the United States
Edited by Charles J. Ogletree, Jr., and Austin Sarat

The Road to Abolition?

The Future of Capital Punishment in the United States

EDITED BY

Charles J. Ogletree, Jr., and Austin Sarat

NEW YORK UNIVERSITY PRESS

NEW YORK AND LONDON

NEW YORK UNIVERSITY PRESS
New York and London
www.nyupress.org

4/7 2991

Library of Congress Cataloging-in-Publication Data

The road to abolition? :
the future of capital punishment in the United States /
edited by Charles J. Ogletree, Jr., and Austin Sarat.
p. cm. —
(The Charles Hamilton Houston Institute series on race and justice)
Includes bibliographical references and index.
ISBN-13: 978–0–8147–6217–2 (cl : alk. paper)
ISBN-10: 0–8147–6217–4 (cl : alk. paper)
ISBN-13: 978–0–8147–6218–9 (pb : alk. paper)
ISBN-10: 0–8147–6218–2 (pb : alk. paper)
1. Capital punishment—United States.
I. Ogletree, Charles J. II. Sarat, Austin.
KF9227.C2R63   2009
364.660973—dc22   2009020633

New York University Press books are printed on acid-free paper,
and their binding materials are chosen for strength and durability.
We strive to use environmentally responsible suppliers and materials
to the greatest extent possible in publishing our books.

Manufactured in the United States of America
c   10 9 8 7 6 5 4 3 2 1
p   10 9 8 7 6 5 4 3 2 1

To my son, Ben (A. S.)

To my son, Chuck,
my daughter, Rashida,
and my wife, Pamela,
who have stood firmly with
me in their opposition to the
death penalty. (C. O.)

Contents

|||||||||||||||||||||||||||||||||||||||||||||||||||

Acknowledgments

The contributors to this book first came together at a workshop sponsored by the Charles Hamilton Houston Institute for Race and Justice at
Harvard Law School on February 15–16, 2008. We are grateful to the staff
of the Institute for their help and to our contributors for their good work
and enthusiasm for this project. We are grateful for the support of Amherst College's Dean of the Faculty, Greg Call.

This is the third book on which we have collaborated. Our collabora-
tion has been more stimulating, more fun, and more rewarding than we
could have imagined when we began.

Introduction

Toward and Beyond the Abolition of Capital Punishment

Charles J. Ogletree, Jr., and Austin Sarat

Civil societies have historically tried to distinguish the crime of murder from other offenses. Typically, murder has been subject to the most severe punishment and most intense public outcry. Countries with vastly different forms of government and systems of punishment find common ground on the seriousness of the crime committed by a person who causes another human being's death. The twentieth century, though, witnessed yet another kind of convergence around murder: nations of every political persuasion ended their use of death as a punishment for murder and other crimes.[1] They declared the death penalty to be unconstitutional, unacceptably cruel, or a violation of human rights (or all of them).

To take but one example, in a major decision by the new democratic court of the Republic of South Africa, the justices, citing various theories to support their conclusion to end capital punishment, abolished the penalty, despite growing concern about crime. Justice Arthur Chaskalson, writing for the court, stated:

> Constitutionalism in our country also arrives simultaneously with the achievement of equality and freedom, and of openness, accommodation and tolerance. . . . [T]he framers of our Constitution rejected not only the laws and practices that imposed domination and kept people apart, but those . . . that brutalized us as people and diminished our respect for life. Everyone, including the most abominable of human beings, has the right to life, and capital punishment is therefore unconstitutional.[2]

1

The emergent global consensus marked the United States, with its seemingly intractable attachment to capital punishment, as an outlier.

But what was unimaginable only a decade ago—namely, that the United States would join most of the rest of the world in abolishing capital punishment—seems within the horizon of possibility at the time of this writing. At the start of the twenty-first century, we are in the midst of a profound national reconsideration of the death penalty.

One of the most powerful and important touchstones for today's reconsideration of capital punishment is the U.S. Supreme Court's 1972 decision in *Furman v. Georgia*.[3] The *Furman* Court ruled that the way capital punishment was *then applied* violated the Eighth Amendment, and it imposed a moratorium on execution. At the time, Justices William Brennan and Thurgood Marshall wanted to go further and hold the death penalty to be cruel and unusual. Thus Marshall wrote:

> In striking down capital punishment, this Court does not malign our system of government. On the contrary it pays homage to it. . . . In recognizing the humanity of our fellow beings, we pay ourselves the highest tribute. We achieve "a major milestone in the long road up from barbarism" and join the approximately 70 other jurisdictions in the world which celebrate their regard for civilization and humanity by shunning capital punishment.[4]

Similarly, Brennan argued:

> The calculated killing of a human being by the State involves, by its very nature, a denial of the executed person's humanity. The contrast with the plight of a person punished by imprisonment is evident. An individual in prison does not lose "the right to have rights." A prisoner retains, for example, the constitutional rights to the free exercise of religion, to be free of cruel and unusual punishments, and to treatment as a "person" for purposes of due process of law and the equal protection of the laws. A prisoner remains a member of the human family. Moreover, he retains the right of access to the courts. His punishment is not irrevocable. Apart from the common charge, grounded upon the recognition of human fallibility, that the punishment of death must inevitably be inflicted upon innocent men, we know that death has been the lot of men whose convictions were unconstitutionally secured in view of later, retroactively applied, holdings of this Court. The punishment itself may have been unconstitutionally inflicted, yet the finality of death precludes relief. An executed person has indeed "lost the right to have rights."[5]

He concluded:

> Death is an unusually severe and degrading punishment; there is a strong
> probability that it is inflicted arbitrarily; its rejection by contemporary so-
> ciety is virtually total; and there is no reason to believe that it serves any
> penal purpose more effectively than the less severe punishment of impris-
> onment. The function of these principles is to enable a court to determine
> whether a punishment comports with human dignity. Death, quite simply,
> does not.[6]

Marshall and Brennan repeated their views consistently and unequivocally during their remaining years on the Court. Meanwhile, doubts about
capital punishment developed among other Justices. Just before his retirement from the Supreme Court, Justice Harry Blackmun, in the 1994
decision, *Callins v. Collins*,[7] determined that, despite the Court's efforts
over two decades to ensure its fairness and reliability, the death penalty
remained irretrievably flawed:

> From this day forward, I no longer shall tinker with the machinery of
> death. For more than 20 years I have endeavored—indeed, I have strug-
> gled—along with a majority of this Court, to develop procedural and sub-
> stantive rules that would lend more than the mere appearance of fairness
> to the death penalty endeavor. Rather than continue to coddle the Court's
> delusion that the desired level of fairness has been achieved and the need
> for regulation eviscerated, I feel morally and intellectually obligated simply
> to concede that the death penalty experiment has failed. It is virtually self
> evident to me now that no combination of procedural rules or substantive
> regulations ever can save the death penalty from its inherent constitutional
> deficiencies.[8]

In a 2001 speech at the David A. Clarke School of Law in Washington, D.C., Justice Ruth Bader Ginsburg observed, "In the United States,
the most daunting of those criminal matters currently are cases in which
death may be the punishment. (I have yet to see a death case, among the
dozens coming to the Supreme Court on eve of execution petitions, in
which the defendant was well represented at trial.)"[9]

That same year, Justice Sandra Day O'Connor described her own concerns about the application of the death penalty. Talking to a gathering of
the Minnesota Women Lawyers, she cited the fact that, at of the time of

her speech, 90 people had been exonerated from death row. She noted: "Serious questions are being raised about whether the death penalty is being fairly administered in this country. . . . Perhaps it's time to look at minimum standards for appointed counsel in death cases and adequate compensation for appointed counsel."[10]

In 2008, Justice John Paul Stevens used his concurrence in *Baze v. Rees*, a case about lethal injection, to register his unease with capital punishment:

> The thoughtful opinions written by THE CHIEF JUSTICE and by JUSTICE GINSBURG have persuaded me that current decisions by state legislatures, by the Congress of the United States, and by this Court to retain the death penalty as a part of our law are the product of habit and inattention rather than an acceptable deliberative process that weighs the costs and risks of administering that penalty against its identifiable benefits, and rest in part on a faulty assumption about the retributive force of the death penalty. . . . The time for a dispassionate, impartial comparison of the enormous costs that death penalty litigation imposes on society with the benefits that it produces has surely arrived.[11]

At the state level, where support for the death penalty historically has been strong, and where elected officials routinely have affirmed death penalty sentences, we see other evidence of increasing doubts. Governor George Ryan of Illinois, a long-time supporter of capital punishment, found himself facing an insurmountable dilemma when he examined the application of capital punishment in his state. Having learned through an investigation by journalists and others that several people had been wrongly convicted, Governor Ryan ordered a full-scale examination of capital punishment in Illinois, which resulted in his decision to commute the sentences of the 167 people who were on death row at the time he left office.[12] The Illinois case offers a stunning example of the way in which the legal system, with its ostensible procedural and substantive protections, failed to protect those accused of capital crimes. In further explanation of his decision, Ryan said:

> Thirty-three of the death row inmates were represented at trial by an attorney who had later been disbarred or at some point suspended from practicing law. Of the more than 160 death row inmates, 35 were African American defendants who had been convicted or condemned to die by all-white

juries. More than two-thirds of the inmates on death row were African American. Forty-six inmates were convicted on the basis of testimony from jailhouse informants. . . . That is an absolute embarrassment. Seventeen exonerated death row inmates is nothing short of a catastrophic failure.[13]

Other evidence of our entrance into a period of national reconsideration of capital punishment can be found in public opinion polls, which show that support for life without parole, as an alternative to the death penalty, has steadily increased to the point where the country is evenly split when people are asked whether they prefer the death penalty or life without parole as a punishment for murder. Moreover, politicians across the country are now willing to openly raise questions about capital punishment without fear that they will be labeled soft on crime. As a result, we have witnessed, among other things, a widespread moratorium movement and legislative abolition of the death penalty in New Jersey and New Mexico.

Indeed, supporters of capital punishment now seem to be on the defensive. To take but one example: in April 2005, then Massachusetts Governor Mitt Romney filed a long-awaited bill to reinstate the death penalty in his state. The bill, which Romney called "a model for the nation" and the "gold standard" for capital punishment legislation, limited death eligibility to a narrow set of crimes, including deadly acts of terrorism, killing sprees, murders involving torture, and the killing of law enforcement authorities. It excluded entire categories of crimes that many believe also warrant the death penalty, including the murders of children and the rape-murders of women. It also laid out a set of hurdles for meting out capital punishment sentences, in an effort to neutralize the kind of problems that have led to dozens of death-row exonerations across the nation in recent years. The measure called for verifiable scientific evidence, such as DNA, to be required before a defendant can be sentenced to death, as well as a tougher standard of "no doubt" of guilt (rather than the typical "guilty beyond a reasonable doubt" standard) for juries to sentence defendants to death. The limited nature of Romney's bill, which nonetheless ultimately was defeated in the Massachusetts legislature, provides a sign that the tide has turned in the national conversation about capital punishment.

Another key indicator is that the number of people being sentenced to death and executed in the United States has steadily declined in recent years. In 1998, some 302 people were sentenced to death; in 2008, just 111 were. The number of executions dropped from 98 in 1998 to 42 in 2007 and 37 in 2008.[14]

Fueling this changing sentiment is a growing awareness of the fallibility of the death penalty system. Exonerations from death row have become common. Since 1973, more than 125 people in 25 states have been released from death row with evidence of their innocence. These exonerations have had a great impact on the debate about the death penalty, leading to the imposition of moratoria on executions in some states. In addition, they have spurred the introduction of congressional legislation like the Innocence Protection Act, a comprehensive package of criminal justice reforms aimed at reducing the risk that innocent persons may be executed. Finally, approximately 80 percent of the American public now believes that an innocent person has been executed in the preceding 5 years.[15]

The specter of convicting the innocent has fueled the growth of a new abolitionist politics. Opposition to the death penalty traditionally has been expressed in several guises. For instance, some abolitionists traditionally have opposed the death penalty in the name of the sanctity of life. Even the most heinous criminals, they urge, are entitled to be treated with dignity. Other traditional abolitionists have emphasized the moral horror, the "evil," of the state's taking a life. Still others believe that death as a punishment is always cruel and thus incompatible with the Eighth Amendment's prohibition of cruel and unusual punishment.

New abolitionists, though, focus less on moral values and more on legal values. They use the familiar language of due process, equal treatment, fairness, and the incontrovertible proposition that the innocent should not be executed. They speak in the language of the "American mainstream"— of scrupulous, fair-minded people committed to the view that even in death cases, and perhaps especially in death cases, justice must be done justly. As Wisconsin Senator Russ Feingold put it, "The continued use of the death penalty demeans us. [It] is at odds with our best traditions."[16]

Meanwhile, the recent debate about lethal injection emphasizes another way by which the death penalty might be undermined. The Supreme Court in *Baze* affirmed the constitutionality of lethal injection, but did it in such a way that left the door open to continuing challenges. Until recently, lethal injection has been used in 35 of the 38 states that allow capital punishment and in the federal system. From hanging to electrocution, to lethal gas, to lethal injection, we have moved from one technology to another. And with each new invention of a killing technology—or, more precisely, with each new application of technology to killing—the law has proclaimed the previous methods either barbaric or archaic.

Today the legitimacy of capital punishment seems to hinge on the belief that we can execute in a humane way. If lethal injection were found deficient in this regard, might that threaten the viability of the death penalty?

Early in the twenty-first century, the road to abolition is paved with decisions by judges and legislators and growing public doubts about the wisdom of state killing. Each of the authors of the chapters that follow helps us understand where we are on that road. If the death penalty is to end, how will it happen? What factors will engender abolition?

In *The Road to Abolition?* we treat abolition as a historical, cultural, and political phenomenon and assess the state of our national reconsideration of the death penalty. We explore some of the factors propelling us toward abolition and look at the roadblocks in the way. Here we bring together distinguished scholars—some long-time experts in the study of the death penalty, others new to this field. We begin with a set of broad reflections on the recent history of the abolitionist movement and contrasting perspectives on the prospects for abolition, and then we consider the importance of the debate about lethal injection in that movement. We conclude by putting the debate about the abolition of capital punishment in a broader political and historical context, considering, first, the connections between our attitudes toward war and toward the death penalty and, second, how the progress of struggle against the death penalty in the United States depends on our success in "becoming modern."

Part I of the book, "Assessing the Prospects for Abolition," begins with Michael Radelet's optimistic view that abolition of the death penalty in the United States will be achieved within the next 25 years (chapter 1). Progress toward abolition, he suggests, has accelerated greatly in since the early 1980s. Rather than focus on the more visible victories of the moment, however, Radelet concentrates his analysis on more subtle changes in the discourse about executions. He claims that a shift in discourse and, subsequently, public opinion, is what accounts for the recent dramatic move toward abolition.

Radelet argues that empirical research (and a corresponding increase in the scrutiny of previous research methods which produced misleading results) has provided abolitionists with data discrediting traditional pro-death penalty arguments, such as deterrence, cost savings, and incapacitation. He contends that assertions that the death penalty can be applied fairly, without racial bias, and reliably, only to guilty parties, are similarly misguided.

In chapter 2, Simon Cole and Jay Aronson note that science has been, and will continue to be, essential to arguments for the abolition of the death penalty. They take up three key aspects of the recent abolitionist struggle: the "innocence revolution" brought about by DNA evidence and subsequent exonerations, the recent de facto moratorium on executions associated with the constitutional contestation surrounding lethal injection, and "incremental abolition"—the efforts to win Supreme Court judgments such as those prohibiting executions of juveniles based on diminished moral culpability. In each of these efforts and events, Cole and Aaronson contend, the "cultural authority of science" has played a key role.

Yet Cole and Aronson recognize that science alone is not enough; discourse based on science, like discourse based on morality, may lead to a stalemate because it can be interpreted differently and employed in arguments for both sides. In the end, science is a useful tool in the effort to shift public opinion against the death penalty because it may provide a discursive terrain on which a social consensus against capital punishment may coalesce.

The next three chapters turn from an assessment of the way knowledge practices shape the prospects for abolition and focus on the politics of, and strategies for, abolition. In chapter 3, Bernard Harcourt foresees the end of capital punishment in the United States by the middle of the twenty-first century. Harcourt does not expect support for the death penalty to wither away in the face of financial cost-benefit analysis or the cultural authority of scientific evidence. Instead, he asserts that abolition will be achieved because of the strength of moral opposition to the death penalty, specifically manifested in the forms of elite political leadership and ordinary acts of resistance, which will ultimately propel a federal constitutional ban on capital punishment.

Harcourt suggests that acts of resistance among ordinary people often occur in retentionist states when individuals who deal with capital punishment develop a certain level of disgust or discomfort with the practice. The deliberate stalling techniques employed by these men and women throw a metaphorical monkey wrench into the system and slow down the machinery of executing death-row inmates, thereby "erod[ing] the political support necessary for capital punishment to continue to function." It is these ordinary acts of resistance along with elite political leadership that will provide the momentum for swing states to embrace abolition, which, in turn, Harcourt notes, will result in a change of the political climate and shift public opinion strongly enough that, in his view, a federal constitutional ban on capital punishment will be in place by 2050.

In chapter 4, Carol Steiker and Jordan Steiker offer a more cautious optimism about the prospect of abolition in the United States. They assert that, should it happen, abolition will occur through a distinctive process. European abolition, for example, ultimately came from legislative action in the face of strong popular support for retention. Yet Steiker and Steiker argue that the differences between the European and American political systems are too great for the United States to follow the European path. Moreover, they disagree with Harcourt about the importance of elite political leadership, claiming that "European leaders are more likely to view themselves as leading rather than following public opinion," whereas in the United States, "the duty of political representatives to be responsive to the electorate is beyond question."

Steiker and Steiker highlight three different paths toward abolition, which they label (1) judicial abolition, (2) waiting and hoping "that capital punishment will become increasingly marginalized as an outlier practice in a few jurisdictions rather than attempt to stamp it out altogether," and (3) the relatively new practice of substantive regulation of capital processes in order to constrict the death penalty past the point of viability. In the end, whatever path is chosen, Steiker and Steiker believe that the United States is well on the road to abolition such that the end of capital punishment is in sight.

Michael McCann and David Johnson conclude this section in chapter 5, with a note of skepticism about the prospects of abolition. First, they argue that drastic changes in public policy often follow drastic "triggering events" and thus are hard to predict. Second, they assert that the present historical context—the chipping away at the machinery of death, which abolitionists have touted as the long fuse for the eventual explosion of nationwide prohibition of capital punishment—paradoxically has made it more difficult than ever to terminate the practice of state killing.

Like others in this book, McCann and Johnson emphasize the distinctive institutional structure of the United States and how its associated cultural norms matter in the debate between abolition and retention. They argue that variation in norms and subsequent changes in death penalty policy are contingent on subtle divergences in public discourse. McCann and Johnson analyze the potential for change in the historical contexts of post–World War II European abolition and the purported "near miss" abolition period in the United States in the 1960s and 1970s. They use these examples to show how unique institutional features of the United States (especially federalism) that have allowed for the decline of capital punishment in practice have also "fortified the endurance of capital punishment as a symbolic institution."

McCann and Johnson see two possible ways de jure abolition might be achieved in the United States. The first is a dramatic triggering event such as a high-profile miscarriage of justice. Yet the wrongful convictions in Illinois suggest that time unnecessarily spent in prison is not itself enough; a wrongful execution would likely be required, but this is unlikely, in their view, in this age of postconviction DNA testing during appeals. The second is a treaty obligation imposed by Europe at a time of American desperation on the international stage, which McCann and Johnson assert is also unlikely, given the history of American insensitivity in the international community.

Part II of this book, "Debating Lethal Injections," focuses on the significance of the ongoing debate about lethal injection. Deborah Denno, chapter 6, begins by taking up recent challenges to lethal injection methods and by analyzing how such challenges relate to debates about the death penalty in general. She argues that those challenges have been more successful than broader issues such as race and innocence in sidetracking the death penalty. Despite this success, she contends that "the oft-perceived link between execution methods litigation and the potential abolition of the death penalty is a double-edged sword" since that litigation distracts officials from paying attention to the nature of states' execution protocols.

Though lethal injection challenges may encourage "deeper reflection" about the death penalty in general, Denno worries that such reflection leads judges to uphold methods of execution, all the while criticizing execution itself. In *Baze v. Rees*, for example, Justice Stevens concurs with Chief Justice John Roberts's opinion upholding the constitutionality of Kentucky's execution protocols, despite including Stevens's declaration that he opposes the death penalty in general.

In chapter 7, Timothy Kaufman-Osborn contends that the Court's ruling in *Baze v. Rees*, in fact, was a setback for abolitionists. While he predicts that the lack of consensus in *Baze* will result in future methods suits, Kaufman-Osborn argues that Chief Justice Roberts's interpretation of the Eighth Amendment requiring a "demonstrated risk of severe pain" and a "readily available alternative" in order to declare current practices unconstitutional will make success in future challenges to lethal injection less likely.

Kaufman-Osborn situates *Baze* in the context of a long-standing search for the perfect execution. Like Denno, Kaufman-Osborn believes that the recent challenges to lethal injection provide an opportunity to consider whether it is wise to pursue abolition through legal challenges based on methods. To pursue methods challenges invites a response from the state that attempts to make us forget the violent elements of capital punishment; but to abandon them involves the risk of great suffering for the executed. In the end, he notes that, if abolitionists continue to pursue this strategy, the ideal of the perfect execution and its contradictory imperatives will continue to haunt attempts to abolish the death penalty.

In the final chapter of this section, chapter 8, Jürgen Martschukat suggests that it is not merely lethal injections that epitomize the push for perfection; rather, a more comprehensive movement underscores debates over technical procedures governing lethal injections. In general, Martschukat asserts that notions of speed and timing have been at the forefront of attempts to make executions "appear tolerable" by providing a "reliable, precise, and painless death" for the convicted.

In our search for a humane execution we are obsessed with speed and an aesthetic of death, which Martschukat says is "emblematic of a major delusion of modern cultures." In accord with Enlightenment thought, the guillotine was developed in order to kill without pain. The guillotine was accepted because it eliminated the risk of botched manual beheadings; mechanized executions were hailed as more rapid and reliable. Yet assertions that the head continued to live after being detached—supported by scientific experiments that registered blinking and grimacing after decapitation—led to a search for a new and improved execution procedure. In the late-nineteenth century, electricity was considered lightning fast and was presented as a neater and more dignified alternative to decapitation.

Martschukat argues that changes in execution methods have been prompted by the diagnosis of a "crisis" in execution procedures; people wanted state killings to be instantaneous and pain-free, and the replacement of one procedure by another after new technological innovations became inevitable. Thus, the expertise of medical professionals in anesthetization "seemed to offer the best of all solutions" for capital punishment procedures. By rendering the victim unconscious, this addition to the process was purported to eliminate the need for precise timing and speed because the condemned would no longer have any possibility of experiencing that crucial moment between the beginning of the execution and the end, or, more dramatically, between life and death. In addition to eliminating pain for the condemned, lethal injection became popular because it eliminated discomfort for witnesses.

Yet to achieve any progress on the road to abolition, those opposing the death penalty must reject the suggestion that the integration of experts and modification of execution procedures will ever provide a painless means of taking life. The perfect execution is an unattainable goal. Martschukat encourages abolitionists to stop debating how effectively executions are carried out and, instead, concentrate on the question of whether the practice of state killing should exist at all.

In Part III, "Putting the Death Penalty in Context," we are reminded that the debate about capital punishment provides a lens through which to view other pressing political, social, and cultural issues. In chapter 9, Robin Wagner-Pacifici focuses on connections between various modes of implementing state violence. She argues that torture, war, and capital punishment, though separate arenas of violence, collide in meaningful ways that have been previously overlooked. She claims that "debates in the United States about the death penalty and about torture ought to be connected" because they both revolve around shifting definitions of sovereignty and state violence.

To illuminate her arguments, Wagner-Pacifici examines the "war on terror." International public law, she argues, has demonstrated the quirky ability to undermine domestic law; specifically, the "war on terror" promotes "military necessity over humanitarian values." She parses state violence via degrees of risk, where war is a contest with roughly equal risk for both parties, torture is a contest in which the victim has little control, and the death penalty is "no contest at all."

Wagner-Pacifici demonstrates that almost every imaginable base has been invoked in the continuing search for a grounding of state violence, from the technological expertise of professionals to moral evolution and sovereign exceptionalism. She observes that, although all of these contexts are distinct, the very existence of so many areas of debate over one topic reflects a "resistance to settling into one order of justification." Thus contradictions and confusion abound as the public discourse flows in and out of various arenas attempting to assess various justifications for state killing. This confusion, she suggests, is itself a barrier to change.

Wagner-Pacifici ends her chapter by stating that "when the state engages its monopolized violence, it necessarily identifies and categorizes its targets and victims," and racism has always been present in the use of state violence in the United States. Racism, she argues, may be the link between the discursive frames around capital punishment, torture, and the "war on terror" in that racism has prompted a movement in state violence away from capital punishment and its bias against African Americans toward torture and its focus on Arabs during the present "war on terror." She also suggests that racism may be the strongest source of support for both practices in the public arenas. Thus, "the decline of the death penalty concomitant with [the] rise of (thinkable) torture against fundamentalist Islamicists (mostly Arabic) might not be an accidental contingency of separate historical frames but, rather, a reflection of a single mechanism." Making this connection explicit might be an essential prerequisite in the struggle to end state violence in any single domain, whether in the domain of capital punishment or elsewhere.

In chapter 10, Peter Fitzpatrick notes that the end-goal or "telos" of embarking on the road to abolition does not necessarily require that that road be straight and unswerving. There are contradictions inherent in modern political formations in which both sides of the argument about the death penalty can seem rational, and the challenge of resolving the contradictions "both sustains and counters the death penalty." Fitzpatrick argues that modernity disallows a "transcendent resolution," and he considers two opposing possibilities at the road's end: the first is an adoption of "hyperdeterminacy" and the resulting assumption of "a confident competence to deal death;" the second is acceptance of "responsiveness to life that is imperative for our being-together in modernity." He then suggests that, in order to be modern, we must abandon the former outcome for the latter; furthermore, since "modern political formation and the death penalty are incompatible," we must exclude the death penalty from our state practices. He laments that "the 'sovereign' affirmation of [the first] dimension embeds the death penalty and denies the modernity of the formation."

Fitzpatrick concludes that the road to abolition, like the path of modern political formation, is an open one; yet, "there were clear markers . . . indicating what direction the road takes in its orientation towards abolition . . . [and] the cumulation of these markers quite undermined that sovereignty still affirmed as the generative basis of the death penalty."

From debates about deterrence and the status of scientific evidence in considerations of the future of capital punishment to an examination of the linkages of capital punishment, torture, and war and of the conceptions of sovereign power that support capital punishment, charting where we are on the road to abolition is a complex and challenging enterprise. It is as much a project of understanding as of prediction, as much an enterprise open to the political theorist as the legal scholar. The perspectives of each are necessary if we are to unpack this moment of national reconsideration and chart its various possible trajectories.

As we move ever so carefully down the road to abolition, we must begin to consider the pragmatic compromises that might be required if we are to end capital punishment. Will we end the death penalty only to replace it with life in prison without parole? And thus, will life without the possibility of parole become, in essence, the new death penalty? For abolitionists, might that be a pyrrhic victory? In addition, we must consider what underlying, unstated, perhaps even unconscious impulses have helped justify the death penalty and, thus, could very well serve to justify whatever punishment might replace it.

In this regard, we need to think about the racial disparities within the system of punishment in the United States—in particular, in executions—that have been well documented for decades.[17] In the 1987 case, *McCleskey v. Kemp*,[18] which brought these disparities starkly to light in the case of Georgia's application of the death penalty, the Supreme Court, in a 5 to 4 decision, declared that such statistical realities, though indisputable, were not a violation of the Equal Protection Clause of the Fourteenth Amendment.

Writing for the Court, Justice Lewis Powell wrote that a decision in McCleskey's favor "taken to its logical conclusion, throws into serious question the principles that underlie the entire criminal justice system."[19] This, of course, was precisely the point that McCleskey's lawyers tried to make. The system, they maintained, was broken due to underlying racial bias that seemed to value white life over black. The death penalty was only the starkest, most severe manifestation of that bias.

More than two decades later, in, 2008, a black man was sentenced to death for the murder of a white policeman in New Hampshire.[20] It is the first time in 49 years that the state has sentenced a person to death. It is impossible to know whether or not racial bias played a role in this particular case. However, scholarly research clearly demonstrates that bias and stereotypes, albeit unintentional and unconscious, are likely factors in creating and perpetuating racial disparities within the entire criminal justice system. Ending capital punishment will not end those disparities. Taking honest account of this reality—the very thing that Powell said "throws into serious question the principles that underlie the entire criminal justice system"—may indeed be our most crucial work as we move toward abolition and even after we have achieved it.

Much remains to be done as we look to, and beyond, the end of capital punishment. The road before us is uncharted and uncertain. This is why the title of this book is posed as a question, not fact. Yet we take heart from the fact that, until very recently, no one could have predicted that today we would be as far as we are on the road to abolition.

NOTES

1. Death Penalty Information Center, at http://www.deathpenaltyinfo.org/article.php?scid=30&did=140.

2. *The State v. T Makwanyane and M Mchunu*, 1994, Constitutional Court Case no. CCT/3/94.

3. *Furman v. Georgia*, 408 U.S. 238 (1972).

4. Ibid. (Marshall, J., concurring), p. 371

5. Ibid. (Brennan, J., concurring), p. 290.

6. Ibid., p. 305.

7. *Callins v. Collins*, 510 U.S. 1141 (1994).

8. Ibid. (Blackmun, J., dissenting), p. 1145.

9. Ruth Bader Ginsburg, University of District of Columbia, David A. Clarke School of Law (April 9, 2001).

10. Sandra Day O'Connor, Minnesota Women Lawyers (July 3, 2001).

11. *Baze v. Rees*, No. 07-5439, U.S. Supreme Court (Stevens, J., concurring), p. 1547.

12. George Ryan's Commutation Announcement, Northwestern University, January 11, 2003. Available at http://www.law.northwestern.edu/depts/clinic/wrongful/RyanSpeech.htm (accessed November 19, 2007).

13. Ibid.

14. Death Penalty Information Center, at http://www.deathpenaltyinfo.org/executions-united-states-2008.

15. CNN/USA Today/Gallup Poll Release, June 30, 2000. Results summarized at http://www.njadp.org/forms/guessagain.html.

16. "Feingold Calls for Abolition of Federal Death Penalty to Mark the New Millenium," Available at www.truthinjustice.org/feingold.htm.

17. Amnesty International, "United States of America: Death by Discrimination—The Continuing Role of Race in Capital Cases," p. 3. Available at www.amnesty.org/en/library/info/AMRS51/046/2003. See also "Report of the Ohio Commission on Racial Fairness," commissioned by the Supreme Court of Ohio and the Ohio State Bar Association, 1999, p. 45. Available at www.sconet.state.oh.us/publications/fairness/fairness.pdf.

18. *McCleskey v. Kemp*, 481 U.S. 279 (1987).

19. Ibid. (Powell, J., concurring), p. 293.

20. Available at http://unionleader.com/article.aspx?headline=Jury%3a+Death+for+Addison&articleId=a52d3423-e67a-4f6f-aaae-5d1423ab0c86.

Part I

‖‖‖

Assessing the Prospects for Abolition

‖‖‖

The Executioner's Waning Defenses

Michael L. Radelet

Hugo Adam Bedau, my mentor, friend, and hero, turned 82 years old in 2008. I began research on capital punishment in 1979, when I was 28. If I am lucky enough to live as long as Hugo already has, I will have a 54-year career of death penalty work. Consequently, this essay is (more or less) my midway report and reflection on where we are on the road to abolition. My guess is that when I turn Hugo's age in 2032, the only scholars writing about "The Death Penalty in America"[1] will be historians.

How can that optimism be justified? After all, in the 31-year span encompassing 1977–2007 there were 1,099 executions in the United States. By May 2008, the death penalty was authorized by the federal government and by 36 states,[2] and there were some 3,400 inmates queued up to receive the executioners' services. On the other hand, if we step back from the trees and look at the forest, there can be absolutely no doubt that there has been dramatic progress toward worldwide abolition of the death penalty over the past three centuries and especially the past three decades. In July 1976, the U.S. Supreme Court decided *Gregg v. Georgia* and several companion cases,[3] thereby reinstituting the death penalty in the United States. At the time of *Gregg*, only 16 countries from around the world had abolished the death penalty. By May 2008, that figure stood at 92 countries that had total abolition and 137 countries that had abolished capital punishment in law or in practice.[4] In December 2007, the United Nations General Assembly called for a worldwide moratorium on the death penalty with a view toward abolishing executions. The vote was overwhelming: 104 of the U.N.'s member states supported the resolution, while only 54 opposed it and 29 abstained.[5]

The worldwide movement toward abolition is also occurring in the United States. For example, we all know about the commutation of 167 death sentences by former Illinois Governor George Ryan in 2003.[6] The day before the U.N.'s 2007 resolution, New Jersey Governor Jon S. Corzine signed a bill repealing New Jersey's death penalty, making New Jersey the first state to abolish the death penalty by legislative action and gubernatorial support since Iowa and West Virginia did so in 1965.[7] Just in the past 10 years, public support for the death penalty and the number of new death sentences has fallen, indisputable victories for death penalty opponents.[8]

These developments clearly show that those who oppose the death penalty are scoring significant victories that would have been unimaginable just a short time ago.[9] Furthermore, in addition to the above easily visible victories for abolitionists, more subtle changes are occurring that are more difficult to quantify, but in the long run they may be more long-lasting and important. Specifically, there have been dramatic changes in death penalty discourse that have taken place since the mid-1970s. Since *Gregg*, the ways in which Americans talk about and debate capital punishment have changed dramatically, and many of these changes resulted from important and irreversible victories by death penalty opponents. In the long run, these gradual changes in discourse are the key factors that are reducing the number of death sentences and increasing the social acceptance of citizens, jurors, and politicians who express discomfort with executions. It is no longer impolite to oppose the death penalty. In fact, there seems to be a national reconsideration of capital punishment, with proponents of executions increasingly on the defense.

In this essay, I share some thoughts on where we are on the road to abolishing the death penalty in America, how we have gotten there, and what battles lay ahead as we move further along the road. I do this by comparing justifications for the death penalty that were advanced at the time of *Furman* and *Gregg* with justifications used by friends of the executioner today. I argue that several pro-death penalty arguments of a generation ago have been discredited by empirical research. Included in this outdated list of claims are those that attempted to justify death on the basis of deterrence, cost savings, and the death penalty's supremacy of incapacitation. Similarly, the claims from death penalty supporters that the punishment could be applied equitably, without racial bias, and only to the guilty have been thoroughly discredited by empirical research. Even the most venerable pretext for the death penalty, retribution, changed dramatically by the end of the twentieth century, gradually shifting from a religious base (*lex talionis*) in the 1970s to an unadulterated version of vengeance in the late 1980s ("we want these folks to suffer because they deserve it") to a more utilitarian version today ("they need to suffer because it helps families of the victims"). I argue here that this latter incarnation of retributive thought, based primarily on the purported needs of families of homicide victims, will be unable to withstand empirical scrutiny over the next few years, leaving the executioner's tree with even fewer roots to hold it up.

Changes in Death Penalty Discourse

Public opinion polls on capital punishment are horribly misleading. The most frequently cited question simply asks if respondents favor the death penalty. In the abstract, answers to this question tell us nothing; it is a bit like asking people if they favor lower taxes, more ethics in government, or greater peace on earth. People may favor it only for Saddam Hussein, or only for anomalies like John Wayne Gacy or Timothy McVeigh, but not for the more typical scapegoats who find their way to the gurney. More commonly, respondents may oppose the death penalty given an option of natural death in prison. They may favor the death penalty in theory, but not with the arbitrariness, racial bias, and error that invariably accompanies it. Most importantly for today's arguments, we have no idea whether people would rather see millions of dollars invested in executions or spent on more direct and widespread efforts that can give some aid to families of homicide victims.[10]

Nonetheless, it is clear from polls that Americans are gradually and steadily moving away from executions, with more now favoring life-without-parole than the death penalty.[11] They are being joined by a growing number of political leaders who are also speaking out against the death penalty, or at least not exploiting the issue as a way to attract votes. In the early 1990s, New York Governor Mario Cuomo was all but alone among America's political elite in speaking out against the death penalty, a stand that helped defeat him at the polls in 1994. One of the turning points of the 1988 presidential election came in a debate when candidate Michael Dukakis badly fumbled a question on the death penalty.[12] Future president Bill Clinton was involved in that campaign and explained the past and future of politics to Susan Estrich, Dukakis's campaign manager, by taking out a sheet of paper and listing on it governors who supported and opposed the death penalty.[13] Running for president in 1992, Clinton left the New Hampshire campaign trail to return to Little Rock so he could preside over the execution of Ricky Rector, a severely brain-damaged prisoner.[14] By 2008, a list of "key issues" for presidential candidates included abortion, education, taxes, gun control, and a half-dozen other items, but capital punishment was a non-issue.[15] Indeed, instead of ordering the execution of a prisoner, Clinton's successor as governor of Arkansas, Mike Huckabee, while on the presidential campaign trail in Iowa, went hunting for pheasants.[16]

Erosion of Popular Death Penalty Arguments

DETERRENCE

In the mid-twentieth century and up through the time of the *Furman* decision in 1972, the top argument in favor of the death penalty was general deterrence.[17] However, this argument has never won much support from criminologists.[18] As Ruth Peterson and William Bailey concluded in their review of deterrence scholarship, "the evidence against capital punishment as an effective deterrent is extensive and cannot be dismissed as resulting from theoretical or methodological weaknesses."[19] In his review of relevant literature prepared for the United Nations, one of the world's leading criminologists, Roger Hood, concludes that the problems in deterrence studies "should lead any dispassionate analyst to conclude . . . that it is not prudent to accept the hypothesis that capital punishment deters murder to a marginally greater extent than does the threat and application of the supposedly lesser punishment of life imprisonment."[20] In November 1989, in part because "social science research has found no consistent evidence of crime deterrence through execution," the American Society of Criminology passed a resolution condemning the death penalty, one of only two public policy positions the organization has ever taken.[21] In 1996, Michael Radelet and Ronald Akers surveyed 70 leading American criminologists and asked their opinion about the empirical research on deterrence; they found that 85 percent of the experts agreed that the death penalty never has been, is not, and never could be superior to long prison sentences as a deterrent to criminal violence.[22] Similarly, a 1995 national survey of nearly 400 police chiefs and county sheriffs found that two-thirds did not believe the death penalty significantly lowered the number of murders.[23]

Of course, this does not mean that there are not significant pockets of death penalty supporters today who still claim to rest their position on the deterrence argument. Peterson and Bailey, for example, cite numerous examples of how deterrence has been mentioned as a justification for the death penalty in recent years by members of the Supreme Court.[24] In addition, several well-publicized econometric studies have been published since 2000 that purport to find a deterrent effect from executions, and these studies will no doubt be cited in the next few years by those who advocate the deterrence justification.[25] While preliminary analyses of these works has found that they suffer from abundant flaws,[26] and few (if any) attorneys or politicians have the ability to understand the complex mathematical models, their impact on public opinion remains to be seen. In the end, it could be that deterrence will remain as a "polite" argument for death penalty supporters—it is far more acceptable to tell friends that we support the death penalty only because we want to reduce homicide rates than it is to express our support on the grounds that we thoroughly hate the killers and want them to suffer and squirm far more than they would if they were "only" sentenced to life imprisonment without parole.

In the end, while some remnants of the deterrence argument remain, it is clear that the general public's support for the idea that the death penalty is a deterrent to murder had dropped precipitously by the end of the twentieth century. In a 1985 Gallup Poll, 62 percent of the respondents answered "yes" to the question "Do you feel that the death penalty acts as a deterrent to the commitment of murder, that it lowers the murder rate, or not?"[27] This fell to 35 percent in 2004, when the question was last asked. Conversely, the proportion of respondents who stated that the death penalty was *not* a deterrent doubled over the time period, from 31 to 62 percent.[28] This is a clear victory for death penalty opponents: what was once the executioner's top defense has all but evaporated.

INCAPACITATION

A generation ago, one of the strongest arguments in support of the death penalty was that those convicted of murder would be released from prison after serving a relatively short sentence and return to our communities where they would constitute a danger. According to this view, we need the death penalty to protect the public from recidivist murders. On its face, this is a simple and attractive position: no executed prisoner has ever killed again, and some convicted murderers will undoubtedly kill again if, instead of being executed, they are sentenced to prison terms.

After retribution, incapacitation is the most popular reason for favoring the death penalty. In a 1991 national poll, for example, 19 percent of death penalty supporters cited incapacitation as a reason for favoring the death penalty.[29] But since the 1990s, it has become clear that if citizens are convinced that convicted murderers will never be released from prison, support for the death penalty drops sharply.

Research addressing this issue has focused on calculating precise risks of prison homicides and recidivist murder. This work has found that the odds of repeat murder are small and people convicted of homicide tend to make better adjustments to prison than do other convicted felons. One study tracked down 558 of the 630 people on death row when all non-mandatory death sentences in the United States were invalidated by the Supreme Court in 1972. Contrary to the predictions of those who advocate the death penalty on the grounds of incapacitation, the researchers found that among those whose death sentences were commuted in 1972, only about 1 percent went on to kill again.[30] This figure is almost identical with the number of prisoners who were on death row in 1972 who were later found to be innocent. Interpreted another way, these figures suggest that 100 prisoners would have to be executed to incapacitate the one person who statistically might be expected to repeat. Arguably, today's more sophisticated prisons and the virtual elimination of parole have reduced the risks of repeat homicide even further.

When I was born, the fear of recidivist murderers in our communities had more justification than it enjoys today. One survey from the early 1950s found that most states had provisions for parole for inmates whose death sentences were commuted. Inmates whose death sentences were commuted were released from prison in an average of 10 years in Kentucky, 11 years in Texas, and 14 years in North Carolina.[31]

Those days are over, and with it there has been a concomitant decline in the argument that the death penalty is needed to make our communities safer from recidivist murderers. Today, 35 of the 36 states that retain the death penalty have a "life without parole" (LWOP) sentence available for those convicted of a capital crime but not sentenced to death.[32] When asked about support for the death penalty, given an alternative punishment of life without parole—a punishment with its own problems—support for the death penalty falls rapidly. Nationally, the May 2006 poll by the Gallup Organization found that 47 percent favored the death penalty and 48 percent favor life without parole—a vast difference from the "overwhelming support" that many erroneously believe the death penalty enjoys.[33] This underscores the point that asking people about their support for the death penalty in the abstract tells us very little—they may assume that if the offender is not executed, he or she will be given a short prison term. Whether one supports the death penalty depends on what the alternative is, and if that alternative is long imprisonment, support falls precipitously.

Finally, the widespread availability of LWOP has implications for the deterrence argument. We all know that the rate of shoplifting would go down if shoplifters were executed instead of being given minimal jail sentences. However, if shoplifters were already being sentenced to life imprisonment without parole, it is doubtful that any who are not deterred by such a severe punishment would be deterred by the threat of death. In short, the question of whether the death penalty is a deterrent is a question of whether the death penalty is a more effective deterrent than life in prison.

Rise of Conservative Arguments

Attitudes about the death penalty are strongly correlated with political ideology. A 2007 poll by the Pew Forum found that 14 percent of "conservative Republicans" opposed the death penalty, contrasted to 53 percent of "liberal Democrats."[34] Citizens might define themselves as "conservative" for all sorts of reasons, but among the strongest are support for religious values (e.g., prayer in school), belief in the foibles of big government, and support for fiscal integrity and lower taxes. Paradoxically, declines in death penalty support over the last generation can be traced to the increasing popularity of these conservative arguments.

CONSERVATIVE ARGUMENT ONE: RELIGION

While few formal religious denominations took a stand on capital punishment in 1976, today almost all the major denominations in America have found the death penalty to violate their evolving moral standards.[35] In the words of the late Robert Drinan, a Jesuit priest and member of Congress, "The amazing convergence of opinion on the death penalty among America's religious organizations is probably stronger, deeper, and broader than the consensus on any other topic in the religious community in America."[36] This increasing anti-death penalty activity has been fostered in part by the success of the book (and movie, play, and opera) *Dead Man Walking*, which presents the autobiographical "journey" of a Catholic nun, Sister Helen Prejean, who ministers both to inmates on Louisiana's death row and to families of homicide victims. Arguably, Prejean's account has become the most popular death penalty book in American history.[37]

While the leaders of most mainstream Christian and Jewish denominations are on record as opposing the death penalty, support for abolition is not universal among religious leaders. For example, a resolution was passed at the June 2000 meetings of the Southern Baptist Convention supporting "fair and equitable use of capital punishment by civil magistrates as a legitimate form of punishment for those guilty of murder."[38] Alternatively, some conservative religious leaders, such as televangelist Pat Robertson, have taken a stand opposing the death penalty, indicating that support of the death penalty by Christian evangelicals is not grounded in cement.[39] Clearly, while much progress has been made since *Gregg* in securing abolitionist statements from most religious denominations, there is still plenty of work for those opposing the death penalty to have that message accepted by those in the pews.

CONSERVATIVE ARGUMENT TWO:
GOVERNMENT IMPERFECTION AND THE ABSENCE OF FAIRNESS

Since the late 1970s, concern about the basic unfairness of capital punishment has grown markedly in the United States This concern rests largely on the allegation that those sentenced to death and executed are not the "worst of the worst" in terms of the heinousness of the crime, criminal intent, prior records, and a range of similar factors that are used (or not used) to decide who lives and who dies. Opinion polls documenting this concern are not difficult to find. In July 2000, some 63 percent of respondents in an NBC/*Wall Street Journal* poll favored a moratorium on executions until questions about its fairness could be studied.[40] In an opinion poll taken in October 2007, the Gallup organization found that 38 percent of the respondents thought that the death penalty was being applied "unfairly."[41] Conservative journalist George Will reminds us that "[c]apital punishment, like the rest of the criminal justice system, is a government program, so skepticism is in order."[42] One might question whether the same government that takes too long to deliver the mail or to fill potholes is a government that can be trusted to make life and death decisions. These imperfections lead to the question of whether the death penalty really is imposed on the worst of the worst.

Arbitrariness Arbitrariness occurs when there is no reliable basis for distinguishing between those who are sentenced to death and those who are not. This issue was raised by Justice Potter Stewart in *Furman*, who argued that death sentences were then being imposed in a way as capricious as being struck by lightning. Today we have a death penalty system where many scholars have found that the capriciousness condemned in *Furman* still exists.[43] It is easy to find cases where those accused of many murders are offered prison terms in exchange for guilty pleas (e.g., Ted Bundy and Gary Ridgeway[44]), or where only one of two equally culpable codefendants was sentenced to death, or where an inmate was spared execution only because she or he had an attorney who thought to raise an objection during the trial to what at the time seemed to be a minor point. With such a large role for Lady Luck to play, it is preposterous to claim that the death penalty is reserved for "the worst of the worst."

One problem that is increasingly being recognized is that, in many cases, whether one lives or dies seems more a function of the quality of the defendant's legal counsel than of any of the relevant characteristics of the crime, the offender, or the offender's prior record. Numerous cases can be cited where defendants who were sentenced to death were represented by attorneys who had drinking or drug problems or who, for a vast array of other problems, mounted little or no defense.[45]

For example, Calvin Burdine was sentenced to death in Texas in 1983 after his attorney fell asleep several times during his trial. In 2000, an appellate court affirmed the conviction with a finding that it had not been demonstrated that the parts of the trial during which the lawyer slept were important.[46] Finally in 2003, after spending 18 years on death row and once coming within minutes of being executed, Burdine was resentenced to three life sentences.[47]

Even the best death penalty attorneys occasionally have clients who are sentenced to death or even executed. Although the list of incompetent or ineffective defense attorneys is long, a larger problem is the lack of resources available to defense attorneys so that they can present credible defenses. For example, defense attorneys often lack funds that are needed for investigators, and experts who testify in death penalty cases (psychiatrists, serologists, etc.) often charge $100, $200, or more per hour.

Another indicator that death sentences are not always reserved for the worst crimes or criminals is the high rate of serious error that permeates death penalty cases. A comprehensive study that examined error rates in 4,578 capital cases during 1973–1995 found that 68 percent contained such serious error that appellate courts reversed the decisions.[48] This is particularly remarkable, given a political climate in most appellate courts that does not look with favor on motions from capital defendants. At retrials, more than 80 percent of these defendants were resentenced to prison terms. Clearly, these errors are not "small" or "harmless"; they lead to a system that hands out death sentences with an arbitrariness consistent with what Justice Stewart called in *Furman* "being struck by lightning."

An immense geographic disparity in American executions also undermines the argument that capital punishment is reserved for only the worst of the worst. Between 1972 and the end of 2007, at least 82 percent of all executions occurred in the South.[49] Overall, 128 dropped their appeals and asked to be executed (11.65 percent).[50] Of the 201 people executed outside of the South, 52 were volunteers (25.9 percent). Excluding volunteers, nearly 85 percent of executions in the United States since 1972 have taken place in the South (822 of 971). If we add Missouri to this total (admitted to the Union in 1821 as a slave-owning state), then 91 percent of the nonconsensual executions in the United States have been in the South (884 of 971). Even within individual states, such as Illinois and California, widespread geographical disparities in the probability of a death sentence have been documented.[51]

Racial Bias In addition to pure arbitrariness (or inability to predict who is sentenced to death), a plethora of studies have found that who is on death row can be predicted from legally impermissible factors, particularly the race of the victim. Those studies conducted before 1990 were reviewed by the General Accounting Agency; their report concluded that in 82 percent of the studies, "race of victim was found to influence the likelihood of being charged with capital murder or receiving the death penalty."[52] Since then, studies in Florida, Illinois, Maryland, and California, among others,[53] have also found that those who are suspected of killing whites are much more likely to be sentenced to death than those suspected of killing nonwhites.

Innocence Since 1976 we have learned quite a bit about how fallible our criminal justice system can be when determining guilt or innocence in homicide cases. A 1992 study documented over 400 twentieth-century cases in which innocent defendants were convicted of homicide.[54] Since *Furman*, more than 125 inmates have been released from America's death rows because of doubts about their guilt.[55] A common thread in almost all these cases is that the defendant was exonerated not because the "system" was working—the defendant was usually exonerated only because of *pure luck*. One can only speculate about how many equally innocent defendants were not so lucky and, instead, were wrongfully put to death. Indeed, the public is speculating: a May 2006 Gallup Poll found that 63 percent of the respondents believed that an innocent person had been executed in the preceding five years.[56]

Some researchers have claimed that concern about innocence has been the most important factor in causing a decline in death penalty support over the past several years.[57] Although I have been involved in research on innocence for 25 years, I would give less credit than many to the role of innocence in decreasing support for the death penalty.[58] Instead, innocence has become a window through which many larger flaws of the criminal justice system (in general) and capital punishment (in particular) can be seen. Once it was shown and definitely proved through DNA that we can put innocent people on death row, then a whole range of additional arguments about the flaws in the criminal justice system (e.g., arbitrariness, racial bias, quality of attorney, and the like) become more palatable. In the end, just as "deterrence" gives a polite pro-death penalty argument to those who may support the death penalty for a wide array of reasons, "innocence" is now a polite and socially acceptable argument that can be used by opponents, even if their opposition is attributable to a wide array of concerns. Again, the more encompassing message is a conservative one: the government is fallible.

CONSERVATIVE ARGUMENT THREE: CONTROL GOVERNMENT SPENDING

A third tenant of conservative thought is that we need to reduce government spending and cut taxes. One way to do this would be to eliminate the death penalty: both friend and foe of capital punishment agree that each execution costs millions of dollars more than the alternative punishment of life imprisonment.[59] Pretrial and trial costs in death penalty cases are high, and death sentences are actually imposed in only a small proportion of cases in which they are sought.[60] In the majority of cases in which a death sentence is imposed, a new trial or new sentencing is ordered by appellate courts, and so only a minority of those actually sentenced to death end up being executed.[61] The costs of a death sentence continue to grow in the 12–15 years that the average inmate spends on death row while his sentence is being appealed before he is executed.[62]

Two decades ago, the high costs of the death penalty were not widely recognized. Phoebe Ellsworth and Samuel Gross report, "In 1986 P. W. Harris found that 38% of those who favored a death penalty in all circumstances and 21% of those who favored it in some circumstances endorsed 'the high cost of imprisonment'" as one of their reasons.[63] A Gallup Poll in 1985 found that 10 percent of those who supported the death penalty did so because it was "costly to keep them in prison." This rose slightly to 13 percent in 1991.[64] Since then, we have learned how expensive death penalty cases are, and thus the argument that we need the death penalty to avoid the costs of long-term imprisonment no longer holds weight.

Of course, the executioners' strongest defenders would say that the costs of the death penalty, though high, are justified by its benefits. This suggests the need for a new type of public opinion polling where respondents are probed about what they see as the benefits of the death penalty, comparing lethal punishments with other ways to achieve the same benefit. If, for example, people support the death penalty because they believe that it will reduce crime, we need to know if they would still support spending millions of dollars on the death penalty instead of alternative policies that might achieve the same results, such as cutting drug abuse, restricting access to handguns, or hiring more police.

In sum, support for the death penalty two or three decades ago was justified by some as a means to reduce government spending. Unlike many other aspects of the death penalty debate, such as arguments over whether defendants "deserve" death, the cost issue is factual: since the 1980s, we have learned that those who support the death penalty because of fiscal constraints are factually mistaken.

The Executioner's Last Defense: Retribution

Although many of the death penalty's strongest justifications of a generation ago have fallen from popularity, retributive justifications remain and have perhaps even increased in importance. Here, pro-death penalty citizens argue that some murderers deserve even more punishment than life without parole sentences and that the suffering imposed by a death sentence is desirable. Retributive justifications for the death penalty have always been present,[65] but the way they have been articulated in death penalty discourse since *Gregg* has seen numerous changes.

Retributive justifications for the death penalty have often overlapped with religious and deterrent justifications. Throughout the nineteenth century and even up until the decision in *Gregg*, some religious leaders supported executions because of the biblical principle *lex talionis*, "an eye for an eye or a tooth for a tooth." The state was simply helping God by punishing people for their sins. Or, the prisoner's suffering was widely thought to increase the deterrent effects of the death penalty. To maximize the deterrent effects, executions were public events where citizens (including children) could come and have their criminal instincts restrained. Even the most ghastly punishments, such as burning at the stake, drawing and quartering, and sawing in half could be justified by their deterrent properties.[66] In more recent times, retributive and deterrent justifications for the death penalty are often intermixed: when Pedro Medina burned to death in Florida's electric chair in 1997, Florida Attorney General Bob Butterworth dismissed the cruelty as an added deterrent, stating, "People who wish to commit murder, they better not do it in the state of Florida because we may have a problem with our electric chair."[67]

As religious and deterrent justifications for the death penalty lost support in the 1980s, retribution became a goal in and of itself. No matter how much pain is imposed by the death penalty, it can be justified under the umbrella of "just deserts"—what the offender "deserves."[68] Retribution no longer needed a utilitarian pretext. Thus, at least in my experience from about 1980 until the mid-1990s, the death penalty was justified more and more on the grounds that the offender "deserved" all the punishment that the state could impose.

Nonetheless, retributive justifications are not without their internal contradictions.[69] To name some obvious flaws:

- Arguments based on just deserts invariably encounter the problem of how much of whatever sanction (whether it be reward or punishment) a given person (whether professional athlete, corporate executive, or mass murderer) "deserves."
- One might argue that life imprisonment is actually more retributive than the death penalty. Indeed, the fact that 128 of the last 1,099 executed in America dropped their appeals would support this contention. Countless others on death row—perhaps the majority— have grappled with the option of dropping their appeals, only to be convinced to fight on by fellow inmates, family, friends, ministers, and defense attorneys. Abolitionists need to be aware that paving the "road to abolition" with punishments that many in prison see as more punitive than death may not be "progress."
- At the same time that the death penalty has increasingly been justified on the grounds of retribution, the centuries-old search for a more "humane" way to execute has continued. Few would take seriously a plea from family members of homicide victims to burn the killer of their loved one at the stake. Even at the height of the era when retributive justifications were at their peak, Americans supported lethal injection by wide margins as the preferred patibulary method (56 percent in 1985 and 66 percent in 1991).[70]
- There has been a growing concern about "botched" executions, culminating in the 2007 moratorium on executions while the Supreme Court reviewed lethal injection methods[71] This presents an interesting contradiction: executions are justified on retributive grounds, but most want the executions to be "humane."[72]

In short, justifying the death penalty solely on retributive grounds has always been problematic. It is simply not polite to say that we need to execute prisoners only because of our unadulterated hatred for them.

A relatively new utilitarian justification for retribution emerged in the early-1990s: we need executions to help families of homicide victims.[73] While the families of victims have never been totally absent from death penalty debates, during the 1970s and 1980s there was a growing recognition that communities and the criminal justice system were not being responsive to their needs.[74] This has made prosecutors see themselves as the champion of victims' rights, lawyers for the individual victim rather than for the state, striving to win death penalty cases as a way to honor the deceased. As Franklin Zimring puts it: "The death penalty . . . is regarded as a policy intended to serve the interests of the victims of crime and those who love them, as a personal rather than a political concern, an undertaking of government to serve the needs of individual citizens for justice and psychological healing."[75] The death penalty has been symbolically transformed into a "victim-service program," and opposing it is depicted by its supporters as opposing help for families of homicide victims. Empirical studies of this impact are not needed because it is a justification based on faith.[76]

In the next few years, death penalty opponents will be challenged to counter this argument. Already the argument has been partially challenged by families of homicide victims who oppose the death penalty, such as Murder Victims' Families for Reconciliation and Murder Victims' Families for Human Rights.[77] While these voices have presented formidable challenges to the idea that executions can help survivors, they are limited by the counterargument that families of homicide victims are diverse, and although some families reject the idea that executions can bring healing, other families just as forcefully applaud it. In fact, while case studies of families of homicide victims are available,[78] there has been no systematic research on how executions actually affect the homicide victims' survivors.

Those who have argued that we have forgotten families of homicide victims are correct. However, whatever one's views on the death penalty, it could be argued that spending millions of dollars per case to send less than 1 percent of all murderers to execution chambers is not a cost-effective way to help the victims. Executions do little or nothing for the families of homicide victims in non-death penalty cases. My work with families of homicide victims since the 1980s has taught me that the single most important public policy that needs to be addressed is the falling number of cases that are resolved through identification or arrest of the suspected perpetrator. In 1961, the proportion of homicides cleared by arrests stood at 94 percent.[79] In 1976, at the dawn of the modern history of the death penalty, the clearance rate had dropped to 79 percent. By 1992, it had declined to 65 percent[80] In 2005, only 62.1 percent of murders in the United States were cleared by arrest or by exceptional means.[81]

Some Speculation about the Future

Any student of the death penalty quickly learns that its immediate future is nearly impossible to predict. Similarly, when the Dred Scott decision was announced in 1857, few would have predicted that it would be overturned in only 11 years by the passage of the Fourteenth Amendment. In 1989, when the Supreme Court ruled that the Constitution did not prohibit the execution of 16 and 17 year olds, few would have predicted that within 16 years the Court would reverse itself.[82] Also in 1989, the Court gave the green light to executing mentally retarded prisoners, but it reversed itself in 2005.[83] As recently as late 2006, no one would have predicted that executions would be halted—September 25, 2007, until May 6, 2008—because of concerns relating to lethal injection procedures.[84]

It is entirely possible, however, that in the next few years we will see several states follow the leads of the three states that have abolished the death penalty since 1972: Massachusetts and New York by judicial action, and New Jersey by the legislative and executive branches.[85] At the time of this writing in 2008, the most promising developments are occurring in states with relatively small death rows: Colorado, Connecticut, Maryland, Illinois, Montana, Nebraska, and New Mexico.[86] Each of these states has fewer than a dozen inmates on its death row, so abolition in one or another will not, in and of itself, save many lives.

How can abolitionists turn these isolated events into a chain reaction? In my opinion, those who oppose the death penalty should follow the advice of the kinfolk of *The Beverly Hillbillies*:

> Said Californy is the place you ought to be
> So they loaded up the truck and moved to Beverly.

Since 1991, Beverly Hills has been the site of the annual meeting and dinner of Death Penalty Focus, California's premier anti-death penalty group.[87] By hosting these strategy sessions, Beverly Hills is basically Ground Zero for the battle against the death penalty in California. In early 2008, there were 669 inmates on California's death row;[88] 250 more than any other state. Like the other states listed above where abolition in the near future is foreseeable, California rarely uses the death penalty. Between 1972 and (at least) mid-2008, only 13 people were executed in the state, and two of them had dropped their appeals. But, given its sheer numbers on death row and the state's reputation as a pacesetter, if (when) California abolishes the death penalty, other states will take notice. It is a bellwether state.

California's lack of success in executing prisoners is not because of any lack of effort. Friends and foes of the death penalty have few areas of agreement, but I suspect one of them is a collective belief that if any state could get an award for the most waste on capital punishment since 1975, California would easily win the prize. By any measure, their death penalty machinery is broken and dysfunctional.[89] In 1988, the *Sacramento Bee* estimated that California taxpayers spent some $90 million per year on the death penalty that would be saved if the maximum punishment was life imprisonment without parole.[90] In 2005, the *Los Angeles Times* increased that estimate to $114 million in added annual costs, or $250 million per execution.[91] In 2004, the legislature appointed a 25-member "Commission on the Fair Administration of Justice," which, among other things, is examining various proposals to reform the state's death penalty.[92] Because of trends discussed above, which indicate that the days of the death penalty are numbered, at least one commentator compares reform to rearranging the deck chairs on a sinking ship.[93] Abolition in California may be closer than many observers believe: we can only imagine what would happen if Governor Arnold Schwarzenegger (or one of his successors) suddenly proclaimed that the state could no longer afford the death penalty and sent their gurney to the scrapyard.

When California abolishes the death penalty, it is likely that the question of the morality of the death penalty will play only a minor role. Similarly, questions about the morality of the way that it is imposed—with arbitrariness, racial bias, the inevitability of error, and the like—will not be decisive factors. Instead, I believe that the ultimate questions will be about money. People will increasingly realize that the debate over the death penalty has basically come to a stalemate and whatever benefits the death penalty may bring are not worth all the fuss and all the cash. With governments increasingly interested in funding only "essential" services, political leaders may come to realize that resentencing inmates from death in prison by lethal injection to death in prison by natural causes will not save significant financial resources.[94] In short, the death penalty will die when its supporters realize that it is a luxury (from their perspectives) that we simply cannot afford. As such, instead of demanding a moratorium on executions or even the creation of a special panel to examine the death penalty's many flaws, abolitionists would make significant headway if they could obtain studies of the fiscal costs of the death penalty in various states. It is shocking that the death penalty is not subjected to the same cost scrutiny that most other government programs must undergo. Arguably, the lack of fiscal accountability may be one factor delaying the executioner's demise.

To be sure, in some states, the love for the executioner no doubt compares with the love of Mickey Mouse and Apple Pie, and the probability that their governors, legislators, or courts will abolish the death penalty in the next few decades is slim. Texas, with 37 percent of America's executions since 1977 and 60 percent of the nation's executions in 2007, leads the list of states with little hope for abolishing the death penalty on its own accord. The prospects for abolition in the near future in Virginia, Oklahoma, Missouri, Florida, and other states of the former Confederacy are also bleak. Nonetheless, even in states that continue to voice widespread support for capital punishment, abolitionist efforts will continue to reduce the numbers of people sentenced to death and the numbers of executions, and wholesale commutations by the executive branch are certainly not out of the question.

In the end, the Supreme Court may someday use much the same logic that it used in banning the death penalty for the mentally retarded and for juveniles to ban the death penalty completely in this country.[95] In those decisions, the Court looked at trends in which several states were moving away from executing juveniles and the mentally retarded. They considered international opinion, opinions of experts, and public opinion surveys. It is possible that continued shifts in public opinion and a movement away from the death penalty by several infrequently-executing states would compel Supreme Court action, regardless of the wishes or inaction of the Texas or Florida legislatures. This movement might well come from Supreme Court Justices appointed by Republican presidents: of the five Justices to speak out against the death penalty since *Gregg*, four were appointed by Republicans (William Brennan, Lewis Powell, Harry Blackmun, and John Paul Stevens) and only one by a Democrat (Thurgood Marshall).

With inevitable openings in the membership of the Court, this makes the 2008 presidential election especially crucial for the future direction of the death penalty. Our 82-year-old friend, Hugo Adam Bedau, may still see total abolition in his lifetime. Stay tuned.

NOTES

This essay was written while I was on sabbatical leave from the Department of Sociology and a guest at the University of Colorado Law School Legal Clinics. I thank Professors Deborah J. Cantrell and H. Patrick Furman of the University of Colorado Law School for their hospitality and inspiration. I also thank Hugo Adam Bedau, Samuel R. Gross, and the other contributors to this volume for helpful comments on earlier drafts of this chapter.

1. Hugo Adam Bedau, *The Death Penalty in America* (New York: Doubleday Anchor, 1964). A revised version was published in 1967; the third edition in 1982. Bedau further updated this seminal work in *The Death Penalty in America: Current Controversies* (New York: Oxford University Press, 1997).

2. The 14 states that do not authorize the death penalty include New York and New Jersey, which recently moved to the abolitionist column.

3. *Gregg v. Georgia*, 428 U.S. 153 (1976). Death penalty statutes were also approved for Florida and Texas. *Proffitt v. Florida*, 428 U.S. 242 (1976); *Jurek v. Texas*, 428 U.S. 262 (1976). At the same time, the Supreme Court struck down statutes that authorized a mandatory death penalty. *Woodson v. North Carolina*, 428 U.S. 280 (1976); *Roberts (Stanislaus) v. Louisiana*, 428 U.S. 325 (1976).

4. Amnesty International, "Death Penalty: Abolitionist and Retentionist Countries." Available at http://www.amnesty.org/en/death-penalty/abolitionist-and-retentionist-countries (last accessed May 15, 2008).

5. Edith M. Lederer, "U.N. Votes Solidly for Death-Penalty Moratorium," *Denver Post*, Dec. 19, 2007. Joining the United States in opposing the resolution were countries with some of the worst records in respecting human rights: China, Iran, Syria, North Korea, Sudan, and Iraq.

6. Jodi Wilgoren, "Citing Issue of Fairness, Governor Clears Out Death Row in Illinois," *New York Times*, Jan. 12, 2003. For the text of Governor Ryan's speech in which the commutations were announced, see "I Must Act," pp. 218–34 in Hugo Adam Bedau and Paul Cassell (eds.), *Debating the Death Penalty* (New York: Oxford University Press, 2004).

7. The Nebraska and New Hampshire legislatures also voted to abolish the death penalty, but these two bills were vetoed by their governors. In 1979, the Nebraska legislature voted 26–22 to repeal the death penalty, only to see the legislation vetoed by Governor Charlie Thone. In 1999, the same legislature passed a bill calling for a moratorium on the death penalty, but this time it was Governor Mike Johanns who vetoed the bill. Robynn Tysyer, "Death Penalty Study OK'd," *Omaha World Herald*, May 28, 1999, at 1. In 2000, the New Hampshire legislature voted to end the death penalty, but this bill, too, suffered a gubernatorial veto. John Kifner, "A State Votes to End Its Death Penalty," *New York Times*, May 19, 2000, at 16; John DiStaso, "Shaheen Vetoes Death Penalty in New Hampshire," *Manchester (N.H.) Union Leader*, May 20, 2000, at 1.

8. Death Penalty Information Center, "The Death Penalty in 2007: Year End Report (Dec. 2007)." Available at http://www.deathpenaltyinfo.org/2007YearEnd.pdf (last accessed May 15, 2008).

9. For a discussion of long-term trends toward abolition, see Bedau, *Death Penalty in America*, at 3–4; Hugo Adam Bedau, "The Death Penalty in America: Yesterday and Today," *Dickinson Law Review* 65 (1991): 759; Ronald J. Tabak, "Finality without Fairness: Why We Are Moving toward Moratoria on Executions, and the Potential Abolition of Capital Punishment," *Connecticut Law Review* 33

(2001): 733; Michael L. Radelet, "More Trends toward Moratoria on Executions," *Connecticut Law Review* 33 (2001): 845; Jeffrey L. Kirchmeier, "Another Place beyond Here: The Death Penalty Moratorium Movement in the United States," *Colorado Law Review* 73 (2002): 1.

10. This methodology, whereby support for one policy is measured relative to competing policy alternatives, is called "contingent valuation." Daniel S. Nagin, Alex R. Piquero, Elizabeth S. Scott, and Laurence Steinberg, "Public Preferences for Rehabilitation versus Incarceration of Juvenile Offenders: Evidence from a Contingent Valuation Survey," *Criminology and Public Policy* 5 (2006): 627–52.

11. The May 2006 Gallup Poll found that 48 percent of the respondents favored life without parole, while 47 percent favored the death penalty. Available at http://www.pollingreport.com/crime.htm (last accessed May 15, 2008).

12. Dukakis was asked, "If [his wife] were raped and murdered, would you favor an irrevocable death penalty for the killer?" Jack W. Germond and Jules Witcover, *Whose Broad Stripes and Bright Stars? The Trivial Pursuit of the Presidency 1988* (New York: Warner Books, 1989), 10, 16. The question was so important that the first chapter of their book is titled "A Killer Question."

13. Susan Estrich, *Getting Away with Murder* (Boston: Harvard University Press, 1998), at 69.

14. Marshall Frady, "Death in Arkansas," *New Yorker*, Feb. 23, 1993, at 105.

15. Associated Press, "Where They Stand: Presidential Candidates on Key Issues for 2008," *Denver Post*, Dec. 23, 2007.

16. Celeste Katz, "Huckabee Hunts for Votes," *New York Daily News*, Dec. 27, 2007.

17. As one criminologist wrote in 1952, "The most frequently advanced and widely accepted argument in favor of the death penalty is that the threat of its infliction deters people from committing capital offenses." Robert G. Caldwell, "Why Is the Death Penalty Retained," *Annual Review of American Academy of Political and Social Science* 284 (1952): 45–53. See also Ernest van den Haag, "On Deterrence and the Death Penalty," *Journal of Criminal Law, Criminology and Police Science* 60 (1969): 141–47, and the response to this paper by Hugo Adam Bedau, "Deterrence and the Death Penalty: A Reconsideration," *Journal of Criminal Law, Criminology and Police Science* 61 (1970): 539-48.

18. Some of the most prominent criminologists in American history have done research on the deterrent effect of the death penalty and concluded that such an effect does not exist. For example, Edwin H. Sutherland, "Murder and the Death Penalty," *Journal of Criminal Law and Criminology* 15 (1925): 522–36; Thorsten Sellin, *The Death Penalty* (Philadelphia: American Law Institute, 1959).

19. Ruth D. Peterson and William C. Bailey, "Is Capital Punishment an Effective Deterrent of Murder? An Examination of Social Science Research," pp. 251–282 in James R. Acker, Robert M. Bohm, and Charles S. Lanier (eds.), *America's*

Experiment with Capital Punishment, 2nd ed. (Durham, N.C.: Carolina Academic Press, 2003), at 275.

20. Roger Hood, *The Death Penalty: A Worldwide Perspective*, 3rd ed. (New York: Oxford University Press, 2002), at 230.

21. American Society of Criminology, "Policy Positions." Available at http://www.asc41.com/policyPositions.html (last accessed May 15, 2008).

22. Michael L. Radelet and Ronald L. Akers, "Deterrence and the Death Penalty: The Views of the Experts," *Journal of Criminal Law and Criminology* 87 (1996): 1–16.

23. Richard Dieter, *On the Front Line: Law Enforcement Views on the Death Penalty* (Feb. 1995). Available at http://www.deathpenaltyinfo.org/article.php?did=545&scid=45 (last accessed May 15, 2008).

24. Peterson and Bailey, "Is Capital Punishment an Effective Deterrent," at 275–76.

25. Robert Tanner, "Studies Say Death Penalty Deters Crime," *Washington Post*, June 11, 2007; Roy D. Adler and Michael Summers, "Capital Punishment Works," *Wall Street Journal*, Nov. 2, 2007; Adam Liptak, "Does Death Penalty Save Lives? A New Debate," *New York Times*, Nov. 18, 2007.

26. For example, Richard Berk, "New Claims about Executions and General Deterrence: Déjà vu All over Again?" *Journal of Empirical Legal Studies* 2 (2005): 303–30; John J. Donohue and Justin Wolfers, "Uses and Abuses of Empirical Evidence in the Death Penalty Debate," *Stanford Law Review* 58 (2005): 791–846; Jeffrey Fagan, "Death and Deterrence Redux: Science, Law and Causal Reasoning on Capital Punishment," *Ohio State Journal of Criminal Law* 4 (2006): 255–320; Ethan Cohen-Cole, Steven Durlauf, Jeffrey Fagan, and Daniel Nagin, "Model Uncertainty and the Deterrent Effect of Capital Punishment," forthcoming, *American Law and Economics Review*.

27. This question suffers from unusually poor wording. The death penalty might deter some murders, but it could also stimulate others. For example, William J. Bowers and Glenn L. Pierce, "Deterrence or Brutalization: What Is the Effect of Executions?" *Crime and Delinquency* 26 (1980): 453–84. Furthermore, the proper question for public policy is the death penalty's *marginal* deterrent effect—that is, whether it deters homicides over and above the deterrent effect of life imprisonment without parole.

28. David W. Moore, "Public Divided between Death Penalty and Life Imprisonment without Parole," *Gallup Organization*, June 2, 2004. Available at http://www.deathpenaltyinfo.org/article.php?scid=23&did=1029 (last accessed May 15, 2008).

29. Alec Gallup and Frank Newport, "Death Penalty Support Remains Strong," *Gallup Poll Monthly* 309 (June 1991), at 42.

30. James W. Marquart and Jonathan R. Sorensen, "A National Study of the *Furman*-Commuted Inmates: Assessing the Threat to Society from Capital

Offenders," *Loyola of Los Angeles Law Review* 23 (1989): 5. See also Joan Cheever, *Back from the Dead* (New York: Wiley, 2006).

31. G. I. Giardini and R. G. Farrow, "The Paroling of Capital Offenders," *Annals of the American Academy of Political and Social Science* 284 (1952): 85, 93.

32. Death Penalty Information Center, "Life without Parole." Available at http://www.deathpenaltyinfo.org/article.php?did=555&scid=59 (last accessed May 15, 2008). The lone exception is New Mexico. A generation ago, few states offered "life without parole" as an option to death sentences. Julian H. Wright, Jr., "Life-without-Parole: An Alternative to Death of Not Much of a Life at All?" *Vanderbilt Law Review* 43 (1990): 529–68.

33. Gallup Poll, May 2006. Available at http://pollingreport.com (last accessed May 15, 2008).

34. Reported in Robert Ruby and Allison Pond, "An Enduring Majority: Americans Continue to Support the Death Penalty," Dec. 19, 2007. Available at http://www.pewforum.org/docs/?DocID=272 (last accessed May 15, 2008).

35. American Friends Service Committee, *The Death Penalty: The Religious Community Calls for Abolition* (Philadelphia: American Friends Service Committee, 1998). This is an updated version; the compilation was first published in 1980.

36. Robert R. Drinan, *The Fractured Dream: America's Divisive Moral Choices* (New York: Crossroads, 1991), at 107.

37. Helen Prejean, *Dead Man Walking* (New York: Random House, 1993). Prejean's book was among the factors leading to the birth of "The Catholic Campaign to End the Use of the Death Penalty," sponsored by the U.S. Conference of Catholic Bishops. Available at http://www.usccb.org/sdwp/national/deathpenalty/ (last accessed May 15, 2008).

38. Southern Baptist Convention, "Resolution No. 5: On Capital Punishment." Available at http://www.sbcannualmeeting.org/sbc00/res.asp?ID=1295130452&page=0&num=10l (last accessed May 15, 2008). No study was ever conducted to ascertain whether the modern application of the death penalty by the United States is indeed "fair and equitable."

39. Dave Schleck, "Robertson Stuns Crowd by Favoring Moratorium," *Williamsburg (Va.) Daily Press*, Apr. 8, 2000.

40. NBC/*Wall Street Journal* poll, July 2000. Available at http://pollingreport.com/crime.htm#Death (last accessed May 15, 2008).

41. The exact question was "Generally speaking, do you believe the death penalty is applied fairly or unfairly in this country today?" Some 5 percent of the respondents had no opinion, and 57 percent responded that they believed it was being applied fairly. Frank Newport, "Sixty-Nine Percent of Americans Support the Death Penalty," *Gallup Poll*, Oct. 12, 2007. Available at http://www.gallup.com/poll/101863/Sixtynine-Percent-Americans-Support-Death-Penalty.aspx (last accessed May 15, 2008).

42. George F. Will, "Innocent on Death Row," *Washington Post*, Apr. 23, 2000, at A23.

43. For example, David C. Baldus, George G. Woodworth, and Charles A. Pulaski, Jr., *Equal Justice and the Death Penalty: A Legal and Empirical Analysis* (Boston: Northeastern University Press, 1990).

44. Bundy declined the plea bargain and was executed in 1989. Ridgeway, Washington State's "Green River Killer," was sentenced to life imprisonment in 2003 after confessing and pleading guilty to 48 counts of first-degree murder.

45. Stephen B. Bright, "Counsel for the Poor: The Death Sentence Not for the Worst Crime but for the Worst Lawyer," pp. 275–309 in Hugo Adam Bedau (ed.), *The Death Penalty in America: Current Controversies* (New York: Oxford University Press, 1997); Stephen B. Bright, "Neither Equal nor Just: The Rationing and Denial of Legal Services to the Poor When Life and Liberty Are at Stake," *Annual Survey of American Law* 4 (1997): 783–836.

46. *Burdine v. Johnson*, 231 F.3d 950 (2000).

47. Lisa Teachey, "Convicted Killer Avoids Death Row: Notorious 'Sleeping Lawyer' Case Ends in Plea Agreement," *Houston Chronicle*, June 20, 2003; Henry Weinstein, "Inmate in Texas Sleeping-Lawyer Case Pleads Guilty," *Los Angeles Times*, June 20, 2003.

48. James S. Liebman, Jeffrey Fagan, and Valerie West, *A Broken System: Error Rates in Capital Cases, 1973–1995*, June 2000. Available at http://www2.law.columbia.edu/instructionalservices/liebman/ (last accessed May 15, 2008).

49. This represents 901 of the 1,099 executions that had taken place, 1972 through 2007. According to the Bureau of Justice Statistics, there are 15 Southern states: Alabama, Arkansas, Delaware, Florida, Georgia, Kentucky, Louisiana, Maryland, Mississippi, North Carolina, Oklahoma, South Carolina, Tennessee, Texas, and Virginia.

50. A significant number of those who volunteer for execution have mental health disabilities. John Blume, "Killing the Willing: Volunteers, Suicide, and Competency," *Michigan Law Review* 103 (2005): 939, 989–96. According to the Death Penalty Information Center, of the 1,099 executions, 374 involved black defendants (34 percent). However, only 6 of the 128 volunteers were black (4.7 percent).

51. Glenn L. Pierce and Michael L. Radelet, "Race, Region, and Death Sentencing in Illinois, 1988–1997," *Oregon Law Review* 81 (2002): 39; Glenn L. Pierce and Michael L. Radelet, "The Impact of Legally Inappropriate Factors on Death Sentencing for California Homicides, 1990–1999," *Santa Clara Law Review* 46 (2005): 1.

52. U.S. General Accounting Office, *Death Penalty Sentencing: Research Indicates Pattern of Racial Disparities*, GAO/GGD.90-57 (1990), at 5.

53. Michael L. Radelet and Glenn L. Pierce, "Choosing Those Who Will Die: Race and the Death Penalty in Florida," *Florida Law Review* 43 (1991): 1; Pierce

and Radelet, "Race, Region, and Death Sentencing in Illinois, 1988–1997"; Raymond Paternoster, Robert Brame, Sarah Bacon, and Andrew Ditchfield, "Justice by Geography and Race: The Administration of the Death Penalty in Maryland, 1978–1999," *Margins* 4 (2004): 1; Pierce and Radelet, "The Impact of Legally Inappropriate Factors on Death Sentencing for California Homicides, 1990–1999." For a review, see David C. Baldus and George Woodworth, "Race Discrimination in the Administration of the Death Penalty: An Overview of the Empirical Research with Special Emphasis on the Post-1990 Research," *Criminal Law Bulletin* 39 (2003): 194.

54. Michael L. Radelet, Hugo Adam Bedau, and Constance Putnam, *In Spite of Innocence* (Boston: Northeastern University Press, 1992).

55. For descriptions of 68 of these cases, see Michael L. Radelet, William S. Lofquist, and Hugo Adam Bedau, "Prisoners Released from Death Rows Since 1970 because of Doubts about Their Guilt," *Cooley Law Review* 13 (1996): 907. The list of people released from death row because of innocence is regularly updated by the Death Penalty Information Center; available at http://www.deathpenalty-info.org/article.php?did=412&scid=6 (last accessed May 15, 2008).

56. Gallup Poll, May 2006. Available at http://pollingreport.com/crime. htm#Death (last accessed May 15, 2008).

57. For example, James D. Unnevar and Francis T. Cullen, "Executing the Innocent and Support for Capital Punishment: Implications for Public Policy," *Criminology and Public Policy* 4 (2005): 3–37; Frank Baumgartner, Suzanna L. DeBoef, and Amber E. Boydstun, *The Decline of the Death Penalty and the Discovery of Innocence* (New York: Cambridge University Press, 2008).

58. Michael L. Radelet, "The Role of the Innocence Argument in Contemporary Death Penalty Debates," *Texas Tech Law Review* 41(2008): 199–220.

59. The Death Penalty Information Center regularly updates its collection on studies of the cost of the death penalty. Available at http://www.deathpenaltyinfo. org/article.php?did=108&scid=7 (last accessed May 15, 2008).

60. For example, a recent Colorado study looked at all cases in which a death sentence was sought for homicides that occurred between January 1, 1980, and December 21, 1999. The death penalty was sought by prosecutors in 110 cases but imposed in only 13 cases. Of the 13, one was executed in Texas, and in Colorado one was executed and one remains on death row. Stephanie Hindson, Hillary Potter, and Michael L. Radelet, "Race, Gender, Region and Death Sentencing in Colorado, 1980–1999," *University of Colorado Law Review* 77 (2006): 549–94.

61. Liebman, Fagan, and West, *Broken System*.

62. The average time spent on death row by those executed in 2005 and 2006 was 146 months, or 12 years, 2 months. However, 13 of the 113 executed in these years dropped their appeals, lowering the average.

63. Phoebe C. Ellsworth and Samuel R. Gross, "Hardening of the Attitudes: Americans' Views on the Death Penalty," *Journal of Social Issues* 50 (1994): 19–52, at 30.

64. Alec Gallup and Frank Newport, "Death Penalty Support Remains Strong," *Gallup Poll Monthly* 309 (June 1991): 42.

65. Stuart Banner, *The Death Penalty: An American History* (Cambridge, Mass.: Harvard University Press, 2002), 116–23, 208–16.

66. Austin Sarat, "Killing Me Softly: Capital Punishment and the Technologies for Taking Life," pp. 43–70 in Austin Sarat (ed.), *Pain, Death, and the Law* (Ann Arbor: University of Michigan Press, 2001).

67. Quoted in "Condemned Man's Mask Bursts into Flame during Execution," *New York Times*, Mar. 26, 1997, at B9.

68. Walter Berns, *For Capital Punishment: Crime and the Morality of the Death Penalty* (New York: Basic Books, 1979).

69. Hugo Adam Bedau, "Retribution and the Theory of Punishment," *Journal of Philosophy* 75 (1978): 601–20.

70. Gallup and Newport, "Death Penalty Support Remains Strong." Before the recent revelations about its problems, lethal injection seemed to be the answer to the controversial search for a "humane" way to kill prisoners. In 2001, all 66 executions in the United States were by lethal injection, the first year in over a century where there were significant numbers of executions and all were performed by one method.

71. Michael L. Radelet, "Some Examples of Post-*Furman* Botched Executions." Available at http://www.deathpenaltyinfo.org/article.php?scid=8&did=478 (last accessed May 15, 2008).

72. Timothy V. Kaufman-Osborn, chap. 7 in this volume.

73. The following three paragraphs are slightly revised from Michael L. Radelet and Glenn L. Pierce, "Racial and Ethnic Disparities in Resolving Homicides," pp. 113–34 in Charles S. Lanier, William J. Bowers, and James R. Acker (eds.), *The Future of America's Death Penalty: An Agenda for the Next Generation of Capital Punishment Research* (Durham, N.C.: Carolina Academic Press, 2009).

74. James R. Acker and David R. Karp, *Wounds That Do Not Bind: Victim-Based Perspectives on the Death Penalty* (Durham, N.C.: Carolina Academic Press, 2006).

75. Franklin E. Zimring, *The Contradictions of American Capital Punishment* (New York: Oxford University Press, 2003), at 49.

76. Ibid., at 62, 63.

77. Information about these organizations is available online at http://www. mvfhr (Murder Victims' Families for Human Rights) and http://www.mvfr.org (Murder Victims' Families for Reconciliation) (last accessed May 15, 2008).

78. For example, Acker and Karp, *Wounds That Do Not Bind*.

79. Charles Wellford and James Cornin, "Clearing Up Homicide Clearance Rates," *National Institute of Justice Journal* (June 2000): 3–7.

80. U.S. Department of Justice, "Homicide Trends in the U.S.: Clearances," June 4, 2007. Available at http://www.ojp.usdoj.gov/bjs/homicide/cleared.htm (last accessed May 15, 2008).

81. U.S. Department of Justice, "Clearances," June 10, 2007. Available at http://www.fbi.gov/ucr/05cius/offenses/clearances/index.html#figure (last accessed May 15, 2008).

82. *Stanford v. Kentucky*, 492 U.S. 361 (1989), reversed in *Roper v. Simmons*, 543 U.S. 551 (2005).

83. *Penry v. Lynaugh* 492 U.S. 302 (1989), reversed in *Atkins v. Virginia*, 536 U.S. 304 (2002).

84. On September 25, 2007, the Supreme Court accepted certiorari in *Baze v. Rees*, No. 07-5439, a case that reviewed the constitutionality of procedures used in lethal injections in Kentucky. Linda Greenhouse, "Justices to Enter the Debate over Lethal Injection," *New York Times*, Sept. 26, 2007. The case was heard on January 7, 2008. Linda Greenhouse, "Justices Chilly to Bid to Alter Death Penalty," *New York Times*, Jan. 8, 2008. On April 16, 2008, the case was decided, giving states the green light to resume executions. Deborah W. Denno, chap. 8 in this volume.

85. Massachusetts has enacted two death penalty statutes since 1972. The first was passed in 1979 and struck down in *Suffolk Dist. v. Watson*, 381 Mass. 648,411 N.E. 2d 1274 (1980). The second was passed in 1982 and struck down in *Commonwealth v. Colon-Cruz,* 393 Mass. 150, 470 N.E.2d 116 (1984). See also in Massachusetts, "The Death Penalty in Massachusetts: Facts and History," available at http://www.nodp.org/ma/s1.html (last accessed May 15, 2008). In New York, see *People v. Stephen LaValle*, 3 N.Y.3d 88 (2004). In New Jersey, see Jeremy W. Peters, "Death Penalty Repealed in New Jersey," *New York Times,* December 17, 2007, available at http://www.nytimes.com/2007/12/17/nyregion/17cnd-jersey.html (last accessed March 7, 2009).

86. Colorado: In February 2007, the Judiciary Committee, Colorado House of Representatives, voted 7–4 to support a bill that would have abolished the death penalty and used the cost saved to fund "cold case squads" to investigate unsolved homicides. Alan Gathright, "House Panel Votes to Abolish Death Penalty," *Rocky Mountain News,* Feb. 8, 2007. Connecticut: Ken Dixon, "Connecticut's Death Penalty Will Follow New Jersey's," *Bridgeport Connecticut Post*, Dec. 15, 2007. Maryland: For example, on February 21, 2007, Maryland Governor Martin O'Malley published an op-ed in the *Washington Post* titled, "Why I Oppose the Death Penalty." Death penalty opponents in Maryland are optimistic about the chances for total abolition. Susan Goering, Richard Dowling, and Jane Henderson, "Repeal of Death Penalty Gaining Momentum," *Gaithersburg (Md.) Gazette*, Jan. 11, 2008. Illinois: Governor George Ryan halted executions in Illinois in 2000, and later Governor Rod Blagojevich continued the moratorium. Editorial, "Abolish the Death Penalty," *Chicago Tribune*, Mar. 25, 2007. Montana: In February 2007, the Montana Senate voted 27–21 to abolish the death penalty. Associated Press, "Montana Senate Votes for Abolishing the Death Penalty," Feb. 23, 2007. Available at http://www.msnbc.msn.com/id/17304006/ (last accessed

May 15, 2008). Nebraska: A bill to abolish the death penalty in Nebraska failed by one vote in Nebraska's unicameral legislature in March 2007. Leslie Reed, "Bill to Repeal Death Penalty Fails to Advance," *Omaha World-Herald*, Mar. 20, 2007. New Mexico: In February 2007, the New Mexico House of Representatives voted 41–28 in support of a bill to abolish the death penalty. Steve Terrell, "Death Penalty Repeal Passes State House," *Santa Fe New Mexican*, Feb. 12, 2007.

87. Death Penalty Focus was founded in 1988. The organization now has over 10,000 members and 10 local chapters throughout California. Available at http://www.deathpenalty.org/ (last accessed May 15, 2008).

88. California Department of Corrections, "Condemned Inmate Summary List," Feb. 11, 2008. Available at http://www.cdcr.ca.gov/Reports_Research/docs/CondemnedInmateSummary.pdf (last accessed May 15, 2008).

89. On January 10, 2008, the Chief Justice of the California Supreme Court, Ronald George, stated that the California Supreme Court spends 20 to 25 percent of its time just on death penalty cases: "The existing system for handling capital appeals in California is dysfunctional and needs reform. The current system is not functioning effectively." Crystal Carreon, "Death Penalty Cases Piling Up," *Sacramento Bee*, Jan. 11, 2008.

90. Stephen Magagnini, "Closing Death Row Would Save State $90 Million a Year," *Sacramento Bee*, Mar. 28, 1988.

91. Rone Tempest, "Death Row often Means a Long Life," *Los Angeles Times*, Mar. 6, 2005.

92. Commission on the Fair Administration of Justice. Available at http://www.ccfaj.org/ (last accessed May 15, 2008).

93. Michael C. McMahon, "Death Penalty Dysfunction," *Los Angeles Daily Journal*, Dec. 24, 2007.

94. Ian Urbina, "Citing Cost, States Consider End to Death Penalty," *New York Times,* February 25, 2009, available at http:www.nytimes.com/2009/02/25/us/25death.html (last accessed March 7, 2009).

95. Mentally retarded: *Atkins v. Virginia*, 536 U.S. 304 (2002). Juveniles: . *Roper v. Simmons*, 543 U.S. 551 (2005). For an overview, see Stacy L. Mallicoat and Michael L. Radelet, "The Growing Significance of Public Opinion for Death Penalty Jurisprudence," *Journal of Crime and Justice* 27 (2004): 119.

Blinded by Science on
the Road to Abolition?

Simon A. Cole and Jay D. Aronson

The central conceit of this essay is that the rhetorical invocation of science has been crucial to whatever recent progress the United States has made along the "road to abolition." Here we focus on three important milestones. First is what has been called the "innocence revolution," the harnessing of public awareness of wrongful convictions to stir up opposition to capital punishment based on the possibility of executing the innocent.[1] This trend has rested heavily on the "epistemological certainty" of DNA evidence.[2] Second was the recent (but temporary) de facto moratorium on executions generated by legal challenges to lethal injection protocols. Such challenges have rested heavily on appeals to medical knowledge about the possibility of causing unnecessary pain in the condemned. Third is the progress in what death penalty proponents suspect (and perhaps not without reason) is what Justice Antonin Scalia has called the "incremental abolition" of the death penalty, the winning of favorable Supreme Court judgments for categorical exemptions from the death penalty, thus chipping away at capital punishment.[3] Over the past several years, the Court has outlawed capital punishment for juveniles and the mentally retarded, and, to Scalia's consternation, these decisions are probably irreversible. Although the Court's opinions were not laden with scientific discourse in either case, the legal debates that led to these decisions drew heavily on scientific evidence to support claims of diminished moral culpability among these categories of offenders.

In this chapter, we examine three case studies of rhetorical appeals to the authority of science along the road to abolition. On innocence, we focus on the case *United States v. Quinones,* in which Federal District Judge

Jed Rakoff, before being overruled by the Second Circuit Court of Appeal, found for the first time that the possibility of innocence rose to the level of a constitutional violation in imposing the death penalty. Next, we discuss the use of medical knowledge in recent legal challenges to lethal injection protocols, especially the challenges by Michael Morales in California and the case *Baze v. Rees*. Finally, we discuss the appeal to neuroscientific evidence in support of the argument that juveniles have diminished culpability for impulsive violent acts. On this issue, we focus on the case *Roper v. Simmons,* in which the Supreme Court ruled the death penalty unconstitutional for individuals who were juveniles at the time they committed their crimes.[4]

What these three developments have in common, we suggest, is the rhetorical invocation of the cultural authority of science in legal attacks on capital punishment. Although these attacks met with limited legal success—only the attack on the juvenile death penalty was ultimately successful, and, even then, the neuroscientific evidence was apparently not crucial to the outcome—it may reasonably be argued that the attacks themselves have helped sow in the public consciousness the idea that capital punishment is somehow incompatible with science. We suggest that, taken together, these rhetorical appeals to science signal something new in abolitionist discourse. In place of moral or pragmatic arguments, the abolitionist movement has invoked the cold rationality of science.

The appeal of shifting toward the invocation of science is obvious. By the 1990s, capital punishment was on the rise. Although popular support for the death penalty could be eroded somewhat through the morally problematic strategy of embracing and promoting sentences of life without parole, the prospects for a major shift in American public opinion against capital punishment seemed grim.[5] Since the mid-1990s, however, what we might call "science-based" arguments against capital punishment began to gain traction: first, the innocence argument; then, categorical exemptions for the mentally retarded and juveniles; finally, challenges to lethal injection. Abolitionists began to see in these new arguments, especially innocence, the potential to significantly shift the balance of public opinion against capital punishment. Specifically, this might be done by reframing capital punishment in terms that would provoke revulsion among most citizens: the execution of the innocent, the punishment of purportedly less culpable individuals, or inhumane execution methods. As death penalty proponent Joshua Marquis complained in his testimony before the Senate Judiciary Committee in June 2000:

There is a concerted campaign in this country to shift the debate about capital punishment from a legitimate issue about the morality of the death penalty to framing the question as I am sure Mr. [Barry] Scheck [co-founder of the Innocence Project at Cardozo School of Law in New York City] will very ably do: well, OK, maybe you are for the death penalty, but surely you are not for executing innocent people. That is sort of like putting together a commission, frankly, to prevent kicking small children across the floor with steel-toed boots. No one is for that.[6]

More broadly, reframing capital punishment as inconsistent with modern science is important for at least three reasons. First, science is an institution with enormous cultural authority in modern American society. There is perhaps no more powerful rhetorical position to take than the position that "science says" a particular social decision should be made. Thus, if abolitionists can get the media to say things like "Science has shown that our death penalty system is deeply flawed," they may be able to effect a major shift in public opinion against capital punishment.[7] Second, science is presumed to be coldly objective. Rhetorical appeals to science offer the public a way to conceive a turn against capital punishment as an irresistible act of reason rather than a moral judgment. This allows members of the public to give up capital punishment, even while preserving their moral compass (i.e., "morally I believe that murderers deserve death, but science has shown that our system does not work"). (Consider, as an example of the converse, the statements of economist Naci Mocan, who says, though he is personally against capital punishment, "science" dictates that it has a deterrent effect.)[8] Third, the claim is consistent with the long-standing abolitionist theme of treating abolition as part of a "civilizing" process, through which modern societies discard barbarism.[9]

The turn to science has been noted in abolitionist circles, and many scholars have predicted that it may be the breakthrough issue that ends capital punishment in America (though some have been circumspect).[10] The abolitionist Richard Dieter states:

The issue of innocence, the presence of a number of innocent people who have been freed from Death Row and stories people have now heard—that convinced people outside of the usual opponents that there was something wrong. I don't think that people are being morally convinced that the death penalty is wrong. That's not what's changing. What's changing is a practical, fact-based concern about how the death penalty is applied. That's where the numbers are shifting.[11]

Stuart Banner notes, "The prospect of killing an innocent person seemed to be the one thing that could cause people to rethink their support for capital punishment." He goes on to suggest that "if any development had the potential to change" the popularity of the death penalty, "this was the one."[12] Robert J. Lifton and Greg Mitchell write, "every case of an innocent man freed from death row drives another stake into the heart of capital punishment."[13] Deborah Denno has written an article subtitled "How Medicine Has Dismantled the Death Penalty."[14] And Stephen Harper, a capital defense lawyer and activist in Miami, has argued that recent brain imaging studies have caused politicians and the general public to see the juvenile death penalty as "not just a matter of law and morality, but [one] of science and adolescent development."[15]

Here we bring a science and technology studies (STS) approach to bear on what we perceive as the "turn to science" in death penalty discourse— and, more specifically, in what Austin Sarat has called "the new abolitionism."[16] Methodologically, this means that we do not attempt to define "science" ourselves in terms of particular types of knowledge claims or empirical methods. Rather, we treat "science" as a rhetorical term, and we allow the social actors themselves to determine what counts as "scientific" fact or argument.[17]

Our goal here is to lay out the implications that an STS understanding of science as a rhetorical term has for the invocation of science in the death penalty debate, especially its invocation by abolitionists. We suggest that science alone is unlikely to have the power to break the deadlock on the death penalty that some abolitionists attribute to it. We suggest that this is for three reasons. First, science is subject to "bite-back effects."[18] To paraphrase James Liebman, what science giveth, science taketh away.[19] The same science invoked in the name of abolition may later be invoked in the name of retention. Second, the "scientific facts" are themselves often murky and open to multiple interpretations. Third, which of those interpretations wins out is at its core a social process. Thus, rather than using science to turn the public against capital punishment, it may be necessary to turn the public against capital punishment in order for the abolitionist view of the "scientific facts" to become the socially accepted one.

DNA and the Risk of Executing the Innocent

There is little doubt that we have entered a new phase in the centuries-old debate over the use of capital punishment in the United States, one that has been called an "age of innocence" or even an "innocence revolution."[20] After years of focus on moral and utilitarian issues, today perhaps the most resonant issue in the death penalty debate concerns the possibility of executing the innocent. Although many factors are involved, this shift is largely the result of several high-profile death-row exonerations brought about by postconviction DNA testing.[21] This development is itself something of a bite-back. Forensic DNA profiling, enthusiastically deployed as a law enforcement tool for developing leads and securing convictions, soon also become a lever for proving innocence in a small number of cases. (Indeed, even the earliest deployment of DNA technology in Leicestershire, England, unexpectedly became a tool for exoneration, as well as incrimination.)[22] The sanctity and authority of science is causing many members of the legal community and the general public to question for the first time the American criminal justice system's ability to deliver on the promise to convict the guilty and free the innocent.[23]

Science, in the form of DNA identification, has made the uncertainty of the legal system visible (and seemingly irrefutable) for all to see, and it has fundamentally altered the calculation of whether the risks of executing an innocent person outweigh the benefits of executing the guilty. In the pre-DNA era, when most people believed that the criminal justice system almost always achieved the correct verdict, innocence offered little ammunition to the anti-death penalty movement. But in an age in which DNA science suggests that the risk of executing an innocent person is much greater than was previously believed, innocence seems to have the potential to sway the death penalty debate.[24] At the least, it is clear that the scientific authority of this technique "has produced a massive shift in the terms of the national death-penalty debate,"[25] a shift "away from moral and procedural considerations, and toward the more substantive question of guilt and innocence."[26]

For example, the issue of innocence played a central role in the New York State legislature's failure to reinstate the death penalty after it was overturned on a constitutional violation.[27] Innocence was one of two principal reasons behind the American Bar Association's landmark call for a moratorium on capital punishment in 1997.[28] The issue of wrongful conviction (highlighted by several prominent DNA exonerations in the state) was given pride of place in Governor George Ryan's rationale for his historic clearing of Illinois' death row in 2003. Actual innocence, Sarat notes, was "the issue that drew his [Ryan's] most intense attention" and provided him with an entrée into other crucial issues, such as fairness.[29] To be sure, some abolitionists have prophesied endgames for capital punishment that do not invoke innocence.[30] But these are exceptions in a discourse with a heavy focus on actual innocence, DNA, the risk of error, and truth.

A significant sign of the rising importance of DNA-generated innocence in the death penalty debate was the short-lived federal court ruling in *United States v. Quinones,* which held that judicial knowledge about the near-execution of innocent persons rendered the death penalty unconstitutional. This was an extraordinary ruling, given the long-standing presumption of the constitutionality of American capital punishment. How was such a decision possible? The decision rested heavily on what Judge Rakoff called the "striking . . . results obtained through the use of post-conviction testing with" DNA. Specifically, Rakoff was referring to the fact that

> DNA testing has established the factual innocence of no fewer than 12 inmates on death row, some of whom came within days of being executed and all of whom have now been released. This alone strongly suggests that more than a few people have been executed in recent decades whose innocence, otherwise unapparent to either the executive or judicial branches, would have been conclusively established by DNA testing if it had been available in their cases.[31]

Rakoff begins with a premise with which virtually everyone agrees: that there have been at least 12 near-executions of factually innocent persons since around 1990, when postconviction DNA testing became available. It was the uncontroversial nature of this factual premise that makes that *Quinones* opinion possible. People differ as to what inference to draw from the premise. Rakoff infers that the occurrence of 12 *known* near-executions of factually innocent persons—and, crucially, the fortuity through which the factual innocence of those individuals became known to the legal system[32]—necessarily implies the occurrence of completed executions of individuals whose factual innocence remained *unknown* and that factually innocent persons remain housed on the nation's death rows. Proponents of capital punishment do not concur with Rakoff's inference, but they do not dispute his premise. Indeed, in its Brief in *Quinones*, the U.S. government conceded the factual innocence of the 12 individuals exonerated from death row but disputed Judge Rakoff's inference that this figure was relevant to the likelihood of a wrongful capital conviction of Quinones and co-defendants because they were being prosecuted at a different time in a different jurisdiction.[33]

The uncontroversial nature of the premise, in turn, rests on the conception of DNA evidence as science and on the cultural authority of science. Previous claims about the near-execution, or even the completed execution of innocents, were effectively stalemated by death penalty proponents, who were able to invoke radical skepticism to cast doubt on the factual innocence of alleged victims of wrongful conviction and execution.[34] Such moves have not been possible for postconviction DNA exonerations because they would require expressing skepticism about the epistemological certainty of DNA evidence. But, in an environment of scarce epistemological resources, the costs of disbelieving DNA evidence are too high. As Franklin Zimring observes, "DNA exonerations end the debate about whether a reversal or nonprosecution is really an exoneration. A broad public opinion accepts DNA findings as definitive, so there is no tactical advantage to prosecutors denying definitive DNA results as establishing innocence."[35] Thus, science in general and DNA evidence in particular have the power to break through the long-standing death penalty deadlock. DNA exonerations enjoy an "epistemological certainty"[36] that the non-DNA exonerations lack, making them impervious to the kinds of attacks mustered by those who doubt or deny innocence claims. Even an innocence skeptic like National District Attorneys Association Vice President Joshua Marquis conspicuously avoids challenging DNA-based exonerations even as he invokes radically skeptical views of non-DNA exonerations: he attacks the non-DNA exonerations but not, apparently, the DNA exonerations.[37] Thus, DNA has allowed abolitionists to say things like "we now have nearly irrefutable factual evidence that our past reliance on existing procedures to protect the innocent was misplaced. . . . One reason for this certainty that we convict innocents is DNA . . . that can, in some cases, be used by scientists to provide us with scientific answers to the question of guilt or innocence."[38]

However, as several commentators have noted, the privileging of science can be turned against the abolitionist movement. As Liebman puts it, "What DNA giveth the death penalty reform impulse . . . DNA reform can taketh away."[39] Such pronouncements refer to the use of DNA and the authority of science, not to undermine faith in the criminal justice but to bolster it, to make us not less but more confident in the criminal justice system. One may react to DNA's evidence of system failure in one of two ways. Pessimists may view the DNA exonerations as evidence of the untrustworthiness of all systems that purport to be able to sort guilt from innocence, and therefore they interpret DNA exonerations as good reasons to not even risk execution of the innocent. Optimists, in contrast, view DNA as a miraculous new technology that will make the system more trustworthy than it was before. Even if DNA shows that previous trust in the justice system was misplaced, optimists are unwilling to flinch from taking the leap again and placing renewed trust in a technologically renewed system. Senator Orrin Hatch illustrated the optimistic view in a 2001 congressional hearing on postconviction testing: "It is indisputable that advanced DNA testing lends support and credibility to the accuracy and integrity of capital verdicts. In short, we are in a better position than ever before to ensure that only the guilty are executed."[40]

In a sense, such a turn of events was a predictable outcome of the way in which innocence, DNA, and "science" were deployed in the death penalty debate. Indeed, in retrospect, it is possible to discern the seeds of this development even in the innocence argument's finest hour, Judge Rakoff's decision in *Quinones*. Rakoff's constitutional argument focused not merely on the epistemic certainty of the exonerees' innocence claims but also on their temporal nature—"that . . . convincing proof of their innocence often does not emerge until long after their convictions"—thus inviting risk of wrongful execution.[41] At times, Rakoff invokes the pessimistic position that postconviction DNA exonerations demonstrate the futility of trusting any system to sort innocent from guilty without risk of error. At other times, he seems to invoke the possibility that the real problem with DNA lies in its ability to make us aware of execution errors after the fact. This raises the disturbing possibility that wrongful execution might be acceptable as long as we don't know about it—that is, as long we don't anticipate inventing another "truth machine"[42] that will again provide the equivalent of a surprise inspection of the reliability of the criminal justice system.

By acknowledging the potential of DNA technology to "prevent future mistakes" at the same time that he pointed to its ability to "rectify past ones by releasing wrongfully-convicted persons," Rakoff effectively sunsetted his own constitutional claim.[43] In so doing, Rakoff endorsed the notion that social problems (in this case, wrongful conviction and execution) can be fully solved by technology and that the only real trouble consisted of the lag in bringing new technology to bear on the problem. This argument, of course, planted the seed for the argument that as soon as the point at which *preconviction* DNA typing became routine was reached, the "problem" that Rakoff believed constituted the constitutional violation would no longer be a problem. As Evan Mandery puts it, abolitionists "succumbed to the lure of innocence. . . . But now they've been called on it."[44]

Mandery was referring to the "guilty project." On September 23, 2003, Governor Mitt Romney's office issued a press release announcing his plans to reinstate the death penalty in Massachusetts, one of only 12 states at the time without capital punishment. Titled "Romney Takes Scientific Approach to Death Penalty," the press release stated that Romney hoped to rely on "the latest advances in forensic science" to ensure that the death penalty would be "narrowly applied and used in accordance with the highest standard of proof."[45]

Although the Massachusetts proposal is the clearest example, there are other instances of the ways in which abolitionists' deployment of innocence may be seen to have had "bite-back" effects.[46] Following Massachusetts, another abolitionist state, Wisconsin, recently introduced a nonbinding ballot measure asking whether the death penalty should be reinstated "if the conviction is supported by DNA evidence." The sponsor of the initiative said that he included the DNA clause "to defang opponents. 'It was my hope that this would dispel some of the fence-sitters from saying that the sky is falling and that someone is going to be wrongly convicted.'"[47] So, just as abolitionists hoped ironclad innocence, vouched for by "science," would sway the "center" in the death penalty debate, proponents of capital punishment are now hoping that ironclad guilt will sway the center the other way.

The tendency to characterize DNA as a "truth machine," fueled in part by the use of DNA to undermine trust in the death penalty itself, obscures the fact that DNA evidence is evidence, too, and therefore subject to error, misinterpretation, and uncertainty. One could also highlight recent discoveries of fraud and error in DNA laboratories around the country, most famously in the Houston Police Department's Crime Laboratory (which was closed down in 2002 after it was discovered that employees regularly fabricated DNA and other forensic evidence in their labs and lied in court about the results of their test),[48] but also at the FBI, where an analyst had been faking the quality control portion of her work for more than two years,[49] and in Washington State, North Carolina, Pennsylvania,

Nevada, and California, among many others.[50] To be sure, postconviction testing has not been immune from similar mistakes. In a highly publicized Virginia case, investigations associated with the postconviction exoneration of death-row inmate Earl Washington, Jr., led to the discovery that the State Division of Forensic Sciences Central Laboratory in Richmond, which long held a reputation as one of the nation's finest, had made numerous mistakes in the course of their 2000 review of Washington's 1983 conviction for rape and murder.[51] These factors are unlikely to be highlighted by abolitionists using DNA as an epistemological lever to undermine the death penalty.

Although other scholars have noted the moral and practical compromises entailed by the abolitionist embrace of innocence,[52] we emphasize here the way in which the nature of science itself renders this embrace problematic. The use of DNA-based innocence as an abolitionist argument strengthens the perceived epistemic authority of DNA evidence in ways that may ultimately hasten the execution of death-row inmates whose convictions rested on DNA evidence. Although DNA evidence is itself often subject to multiple interpretations, the abolitionist embrace of DNA-based innocence is likely to make that fact harder, not easier, for the public to accept. Finally, what inference to draw from the fact of DNA-based exonerations is not preordained. There will also be sufficient epistemological space for death penalty proponents to make the sorts of moves used by the government in *Quinones,* such as denying the applicability of the past to the present or one jurisdiction to another.

Anesthesiology and Lethal Injection

Between October 2007 and April 2008, the United States experienced a de facto moratorium on capital punishment. Such a moratorium is significant because many abolitionists have long held that the end of capital punishment will come about through a proverbial whimper, not a bang. It has been suggested that abolition in the United States, if it is to occur, is likely to occur as it has in most other countries, especially the western European counties. That is, capital punishment would not be legislated away but, rather, a moratorium that at the time its of inception seems temporary would gradually be extended until the will to reimpose capital punishment dissipated. Americans would learn they could live without the death penalty.[53]

Given this widely held belief among abolitionist scholars, any moratorium is significant because it could signal the eventual end of capital punishment in the United States. Since the late 1990s, abolitionists have held out some hope for such a moratorium, buoyed by the establishment of temporary de facto moratoria in some states, such as Illinois, Maryland, and North Carolina. Probably, most abolitionists expected the impetus for a national moratorium would be the innocence issue, discussed in the previous section. As it happens, though, the recent national moratorium was brought about by what only a few years ago might have been viewed by many abolitionists as a relatively hopeless cause: constitutional challenges to lethal injection as an execution method.

In the fall of 2007, the Supreme Court—by granting certiorari in the lethal injection challenge *Baze v. Rees*, and by granting stays requested for the purpose of delaying execution pending the Court's ruling in that case—imposed a de facto moratorium on capital punishment in the United States. The surprising rise of execution methods as another front in the death penalty battle appeared to many to be yet another sign of the weakening of American capital punishment. As Deborah Denno put it, "lethal injection is a crucial domino in the deck" of "the death penalty's slide."[54]

That scientific knowledge, once again, played a crucial role in this issue should come as no surprise. State executioners have long turned to science, technology, and medicine to provide ostensibly more humane methods of execution: from the invention of the guillotine to Edison and the electric chair to physicians and lethal injection.[55] As science, technology, and medicine have changed, execution methods that previously appeared scientifically or medically current have come to seem crude. In contemporary discourse, lethal injection appears to harness the most advanced available scientific knowledge in the service of bringing about a humane intentional death. As such, scientific knowledge itself lends a veneer of respectability to state-sponsored execution, even if it may, at the same time, provoke the familiar horror of enlisting science in the service of death, a horror familiar to us from popular reactions to such phenomena as chemical warfare and the gas chambers in World War II.

Although lethal injection was touted over the past several decades as harnessing medical knowledge in the service of humane executions,[56] we now know that the interface between medical knowledge and execution protocols was far more casual than most people believed.[57] Although a physician provided the basic outline of how known anesthetics might be used to bring about an intentional death and medical knowledge provided the rudiments of state execution protocols, we now know that execution protocols were as much penological as medical documents. In fact, as Denno notes, "State[s] adopted lethal injection without medical or scientific justification for the procedure."[58]

Executioners' rhetorical invocation of the cultural authority of "science" and "medicine" in defense of the purported humanity of lethal injection, while perhaps necessary to sustain public support for capital punishment after *Gregg*,[59] may also, in retrospect, turn out to have been a tactical error. To paraphrase Liebman again, what "science" giveth, "science" taketh away. Specifically, the invocation of "science" and "medicine" in defense of lethal injection protocols created an opportunity for abolitionists to invoke those same knowledges in arguing for the inhumanity of lethal injection. This was an all the more inviting strategy, given that, as Denno notes, there were essentially no scientific studies testifying to the purported humanity of lethal injection procedures. There was scientific rhetoric, but no scientific knowledge. The opportunity existed, therefore, to generate scientific knowledge that challenged the rhetorical claims of painlessness that surrounded lethal injection. Abolitionists and legal experts on lethal injection characterized medical evidence as a definitive refutation "by science" of the claims of painlessness advanced on behalf of lethal injection protocols. For example, the article by Denno, the leading legal scholar in this area, "The Lethal Injection Quandary," was subtitled, "How Medicine Has Dismantled the Death Penalty," suggesting that the superior epistemic authority of medicine had demolished legal claims to be enacting painless executions.

Our interest here is in these attempts to use scientific knowledge to undermine the claims of painlessness employed by defenders of lethal injection. We do not focus on other issues, such as ethical issues surrounding physician participation in executions. Perhaps the first attempt to bring medical knowledge to bear on states' claims that the three-drug protocol guaranteed a painless death was a study by anesthesiologists Koniaris et al. reporting disturbingly low concentrations of anesthetic from postmortem examinations of executed prisoners.[60] This study had some influence in early court cases, but it was quickly challenged in the medical literature. Critics charged that the postmortem samples were taken many hours after execution and that the anesthetic, sodium thiopental, had quickly dissipated into the tissues.[61] Thus, the low concentrations of thiopental found in the postmortem sample could not be construed as solid evidence that the concentration was low at the time of the injection of the third, potentially excruciatingly painful drug in the three-drug cocktail, potassium chloride. It turned out that no one had a good model for the dispersion of thiopental into the tissues because the subject was of no interest to normal (that is life-preserving rather than life-extinguishing) anesthesiology).[62] Further, research was hampered by the small number of postmortem biological samples and a general lack of information about when and from what tissue they were collected.

In the absence of either a convincing model or good data, a vociferous debate has ensued over how thiopental might behave by drawing analogies to other substances about whose dispersion more is known. In speculating about how thiopental might behave in the body, anesthesiologists hostile to the three-drug protocol have emphasized the lipophilic nature of thiopental, arguing that, since other lipophilic substances are known to concentrate after death, so might thiopental. If thiopental followed its lipophilic nature, this would suggest that the findings of low concentrations of thiopental many hours postmortem are fair estimations, or even overestimations, of the concentration at the time of the injection of potassium chloride.[63] Anesthesiologists supportive of the three-drug protocol, in contrast, emphasize the pH of thiopental, reasoning that it should behave like substances of similar pH. If this were the case, thiopental should dissipate after death.[64] This, in turn, would suggest that the findings of low concentration of thiopental many hours postmortem are no cause for alarm.

Perhaps because the postmortem concentration issue was stalemated, the challenge to lethal injection by Michael Morales, which as of this writing has now halted executions in California for more than three years pending the reform of lethal injection procedures, focused on more mundane signs of consciousness, albeit still vouched for by expert medical testimony, such as continued respiration and chest movement.[65] Medical knowledge was crucial in *Morales,* so much so that Denno has referred to it as "a showdown between law and medicine."[66] Of particular interest was the juxtaposition of two claims by two expert anesthesiologists. The state's witness, Mark Dershwitz, testified to a theoretical calculation that "over 99.999999999999 percent of the population would be unconscious within sixty seconds" under California's protocol. And yet, Morales's witness, Mark Heath, pointed to evidence from execution logs that the condemned appeared to be conscious in 6 out of 11 executions under the California protocol.[67] This glaring discrepancy between theory and practice was sufficient to convince Judge Jeremy Fogel to preclude the use of pancuronium bromide, which Morales contended would mask indications of consciousness, from Morales's execution, unless the execution were supervised by an anesthesiologist. Since the state was unwilling to proceed without pancuronium bromide and, as it turned out, unable to enlist anesthesiologists to supervise the execution, the ruling halted executions in California.

One possible reading of *Morales*, clearly, is that Morales successfully deployed medical knowledge, in the form of Heath's testimony, to demonstrate the scientific truth about California executions obscured in both the overblown claims of painless executions advanced by the state and Dershwitz's apparent lack of inclination to factor the possibility of operational error into his calculations. Similarly, it has been suggested that medical knowledge was crucial for lawyers litigating lethal injection challenges.[68]

However, it was also clear that lethal injection litigators would not be able to claim an undisputed scientific consensus against the three-drug protocol. The Koniaris study had been countered with its published rebuttals. Dr. Heath had been countered by Dr. Dershwitz. Thus, in *Baze v. Rees*, the defense explicitly disavowed any attempt to invoke a medical consensus against the three-drug protocol, declaring in its petition for certiorari that the case "is not a battle of the experts."[69] Instead, Baze's claim was centered around the existence of a safer alternative to the three-drug protocol, essentially the same one-drug massive barbiturate overdose permitted by Judge Fogel in *Morales,* and the legal argument that, if a safer, reasonable alternative existed, the three-drug protocol violated the Eighth Amendment. As it turned out, this argument was countered by a study of Dutch euthanasia, which found that many doctors viewed a massive overdose of thiopental as insufficient to ensure death and, in fact, often used pancoronium bromide, the very drug that comes under the most criticism in critiques of the three-drug protocol.[70]

Thus, in *Baze,* many of the disparate opinions were able to characterize the state of medical knowledge as unsettled and therefore an inappropriate basis for judicial action. The majority stated that Baze's proposed standard of review "would embroil the courts in ongoing scientific controversies beyond their expertise."[71] In his concurring opinion, Justice Samuel Alito argued that "an inmate should be required to do more than simply offer the testimony of a few experts or a few studies," disparaging the expert opinion against the three-drug protocol by expressing the number of experts as a raw number rather than as a proportion of all experts who had publicly declared a view on the question. "Instead," Alito suggested, "an inmate challenging a method of execution should point to a well-established scientific consensus." Alito then criticized the view of the single-drug protocol as effective for "not [being] universally accepted" and concluded that that choice of execution method "cannot be dictated by the testimony of an expert or two or by judicial findings of fact based on such testimony."[72] Similarly, Justice Clarence Thomas, in his concurring opinion, complained that *Baze*'s proposed standard would "require courts to resolve medical and scientific controversies that are largely beyond judicial ken."[73] And Justice Stephen Breyer, in his concurrence, dismissed the Koniaris study because it had been critiqued and invoked the Dutch study to conclude, "The literature . . . casts a shadow of uncertainty upon the ready availability of some of the alternatives to lethal injection methods."[74]

Thus, state executioners' characterization of lethal injection as a "scientific" execution method bit them back when opponents of lethal injection exposed the lack of scientific knowledge about the procedure. However, facing judicial demands for some sort of a "scientific consensus" that the states' procedures were either painful or, at least, inferior to a viable alternative, these opponents were stymied, not only by their inability to procure adequate information about the states' procedures[75] but also by the social nature of a "scientific consensus" itself.

Neuroscience and the Juvenile Death Penalty

On March 1, 2005, the U.S. Supreme Court banned the death penalty for offenders under the age of 18 years, reversing its 1989 decision in *Stanford v. Kentucky* that states had the right to decide whether or not to execute individuals who were 16 or 17 years old at the time they committed capital crimes. The case, *Roper v. Simmons*, revolved around the trial, sentencing, and petition for habeas corpus relief of Christopher Simmons, who murdered an elderly woman during the course of a burglary when he was 17 years old.[76]

The Court held that although the execution of juveniles was once considered acceptable in American society, a national consensus had emerged since *Stanford* that such a punishment was cruel and unusual and, thus, in violation of the Eighth Amendment. The majority argued that adolescents do not possess the emotional, intellectual, or biological maturity to be fully culpable for the violent acts that they commit. Although adolescents should not be excused from their crimes, they should not pay the ultimate price for impulses that they were unable to control. A key element of Simmons's argument was new brain-imaging evidence suggesting that the adolescent brain is not as well developed as the adult brain.

The 1999 Columbine High School shootings heightened American interest in the shortcomings of the teen brain as an explanation for violent and other inappropriate adolescent behavior.[77] Television documentaries, popular books, newspaper articles, and magazine features constantly promise to "revolutionize our view of the adolescent mind and explain its mystifying ways."[78] Teens are portrayed as unpredictable, rebellious, and messy; unable to properly analyze social situations or to take future consequences into consideration; and, most notably, excessively inclined to take risks. The articles point out that, although it used to be thought that these behaviors were caused by "raging hormones"[79] or by the need to assert one's individual identity through rebellion, their true source is now known: the evolving structure of the adolescent brain. For example, in a March 10, 2001, op-ed article that sought to explain why so many high school shootings had taken place in the preceding few years, Daniel R. Weinberger, director of the National Institutes of Health's Clinical Brain Disorders Laboratory, rejected cultural explanations such as violent entertainment and the failure to discipline teens for bad behavior. Instead, he argued, "To understand what goes wrong in the teenagers who fire the guns, you have to understand something about the biology of the teenage brain."[80]

Although brain-development studies have not yet been invoked as a legal defense (i.e., "my brain made me do it"), they are increasingly being used as evidence that teenagers are not yet adults and the legal system should therefore not treat them as such. This is exactly how brain-imaging evidence was used in *Roper*. Beyond the issue of whether criminal offenders under the age of 18 years should be put to death, *Roper* delved into the deeper question concerning the methods for determining whether a punishment is so disproportionate to the crime committed that it should be banned on constitutional grounds. The State of Missouri argued that it was the prerogative of state legislatures, not courts, to decide the age at which individuals became eligible for execution and it was up to juries and judges to decide only the culpability of individual defendants. In Roper's view, the only form of relevant, objective evidence that could be used to modify the definition of cruel and unusual punishment was democratic will, as expressed by state legislatures and jury decisions.

The respondent, Simmons, favored a categorical ban on the juvenile death penalty. In Simmons's view, a much wider range of evidence was relevant to the debate, specifically cutting-edge neuroscience research suggesting that the region of the human brain responsible for executive decision making and impulse control continued to develop well into adolescence and early adulthood. He contended that this biological limitation rendered the death penalty a cruel and unusual punishment because teens do not possess the brain structure necessary to fully control their actions.

The use of scientific evidence in *Roper* is of interest to us here for two main reasons. First, Simmons's legal team did not use brain images to make visible lesions or gross pathologies of the regions of the brain responsible for impulse control and decision making, which is how neuroscience has traditionally been invoked in the criminal justice system over the past two decades (e.g., in the case of John Hinkley).[81] Rather, they sought to narrow the legal category of culpability by constructing a model of a normal, mature adult brain that was capable of supporting the functions of a reasonable man and contrasting that model with one of a teenager's brain. They sought to have both anatomical and cognitive normalcy and pathology defined by age rather than by some diagnosable medical condition or mental state. Thus, Simmons sought to extend categorical exemptions to a group that had no obvious psychiatric diagnosis or medical problem.

Second, *Roper* highlighted the current, limited understanding about when individuals cross the threshold of brain development that makes it possible to know right from wrong and to make sound decisions in the heat of the moment. Recent neuroscientific studies have convincingly demonstrated that brains continue to develop well into the third decade of life, but the studies say almost nothing about when the brain can be considered developed enough to justify a determination of full legal culpability for a capital crime. A major problem lies in the fact that neuroscientific data are continuous (and highly variable from person to person), whereas determination of culpability in the context of the death penalty is binary—either a defendant is culpable enough to be put to death for a crime or he is not.[82]

In the death penalty debate, brain imaging has two functions. Most important, it provides biological confirmation of a part of America's shared folk knowledge about teens. As such, brain imaging was presented in *Roper* as relevant evidence supporting preconceived notions rather than as a revolutionary breakthrough. Its relevance trumped its scientific immaturity because the knowledge produced was intuitively correct. It was also presented as hard science that radically altered what used to be thought about brain development: development does not stop in childhood or adolescence but continues well into adulthood. Indeed, according to leading activist and Miami capital defense attorney Stephen Harper, neuroscientific evidence tends to be more convincing than the common sense and psychological perspectives that are now 20 or 30 years old, because psychological testimony is perceived as soft and subject to debilitating expert disagreement. Neuroscientific evidence, in contrast, "tends to be hard evidence. If you take an MRI and you can show that this part of the brain is active, and this part of the brain is not, it's hard science" that enables the finder of fact to make a fully informed and sound decision.[83]

This notion of neuroscientific evidence as "hard" is more a function of its visual appeal than its epistemological status. Many scientists, lawyers, and scholars recognize that brain images are not an unmediated portrait of the brain. As Joseph Dumit noted in his ethnographic account of the development and use of the PET scan in a wide variety of contexts, brain images are "expert images . . . objects produced with mechanical assistance that require help in interpreting even though they may appear to be legible to a layperson."[84] Similarly, sociologist Kelly Joyce noted that although the very power and authority of MRI images are gained from the seeming interchangeability of image and brain, in reality the image is a product of a complex set of techniques, subjective decisions, technical choices, and informed interpretations.[85]

Specifically, scientists and technicians must decide the level of detail at which they will scan the brain—for example, how thin or thick the slices should be, the degree of clarity they want, the contrast between different types of tissues, and how to filter signal from noise, to name just a few. At the level of study design, scientists and technicians must decide how many people need to be scanned to achieve adequate statistical power and what kinds of individuals to include in the test group—for example, in studies of mental illness, should they only scan people who have never been treated with medicine, or should they not even ask about treatment status? Should they only scan people who are currently in a state of illness, or should they include anyone who has had an episode in the past? Even more important, they must also decide how to construct the control population. This task is crucial because it allows scientists to determine which kinds of brain structure and function are normal and which kinds are pathological. In the case of fMRI (functional magnetic resource imaging), they must decide what types of tasks test subjects should perform and precisely how the experiment should be set up.[86]

In addition, despite claims that neuroscience produces hard data, the results of brain imaging are actually limited. For a variety of reasons, most neuroscientists and legal scholars are skeptical that brain-imaging techniques can diagnose mental conditions in individual offenders. Among other reasons, they cite the lack of in-depth knowledge of the range of variance in normal brain structure and function, the extent to which networks in the brain either compensate for or are affected by pathologies at any particular node, and the current deficiency of empirical evidence linking brain structure and in vitro function (i.e., performance on simple tasks while in the MRI machine) to specific behaviors in vivo (i.e., in real life). Critics of brain-imaging studies also cite flawed experimental design, with complaints ranging from the use of control groups that are not precisely matched to study groups to the failure to account for confounders in the study population and a willingness on the part of brain researchers to make scientifically indefensible interpretations of tenuous data.[87]

Although the juvenile death penalty debate has been settled on other grounds, *Roper v. Simmons* raised the possibility of extending the use of neuroscience in the juvenile justice context. In a recent presentation at the American Bar Association Center for Continuing Legal Education, for example, Simmie Baer of Seattle's Defender Association argued that, among other things, the notion of culpability was due for redefinition based on the findings in *Roper*. In her view, the old reasonable-man standard was no longer reasonable in light of "old soft and new hard" science. Instead, a new standard of the "reasonable adolescent" should be created on the basis of the scientific and sociological understanding of teen brain anatomy and behavior. She even went as far as to suggest that the legal system should consider adolescents to be in a "natural state" of diminished capacity on the basis of the new brain-imaging data and should treat them as such.[88]

Yet, as in the other cases, there is strong evidence to suggest that this might not be the optimal path to take by those who care about the treatment of juveniles in the legal system. As we have seen, science is subject to flexible interpretations and can "bite back." Put simply, there is no guarantee that further research will confirm the idea that juveniles as a class do not possess the necessary brain power to make adultlike decisions. While it is doubtful that such a conclusion will cause *Roper* to be overturned (because, as Scalia noted bitterly, it is unlikely that the Supreme Court will reinstate a practice it once deemed cruel and unusual), it may yet affect juvenile justice in new and unanticipated ways.

Conclusion

All three areas that we discuss in this chapter involve bringing scientific knowledge to bear on scientific questions that are, in some fundamental sense, unknowable: At what rate do we execute the innocent? How much do executed prisoners suffer? Are juveniles less morally culpable than adults? It would appear that appeals to science by abolitionists are no more capable of ending the death penalty debate than appeals to moral reasoning have been. In all three cases discussed here, "science" either has functioned, or potentially may function, as a double-edged sword: the science that supports abolition today may support retention tomorrow, or vice versa.

But we wish to make more than merely the mundane point that rhetoric can cut both ways. Rather, we want to emphasize the indeterminacy and social character of what we call "scientific knowledge" itself. The social value of "scientific facts" lies not, as is commonly supposed, in the fact that they are "fixed" by nature and, therefore, cannot be altered. Rather, their value lies in the fact that they are (always temporarily in principle, but often quite solidly) fixed by social consensus. This does not mean that abolitionists cannot be successful by getting the social actors to agree on such statements as "science shows that the death penalty is flawed," "science shows that juveniles are not as morally culpable as adults," and "science shows that lethal injection procedures are flawed." What it may mean is that, while science will not force people down the road to abolition, it may serve as the vehicle for those ready and willing to take the journey.

NOTES

This material is partially based on work supported by the National Science Foundation under Grant Nos. SES-0115305 and IIS-0527729 and the National Institutes of Health under Grant No. HG-03302. Any opinions, findings, and conclusions or recommendations expressed in this material are those of the authors and do not necessarily reflect the views of the National Science Foundation or the National Institutes of Health. We are grateful to Gavin Lee for expert research assistance and to Ty Alper, Jen Moreno, and the University of California Berkeley School of Law Death Penalty Clinic for assistance in getting access to primary source materials. We are grateful to Austin Sarat and Charles Ogletree for inviting us to participate in this project and to all the participants in the Road to Abolition workshop for helpful comments and suggestions and provocative discussions.

1. Carol S. Steiker and Jordan M. Steiker, "The Seduction of Innocence: The Attraction and Limitations of the Focus on Innocence in Capital Punishment Law and Advocacy," *Journal of Criminal Law and Criminology* 95 (2005): 613.

2. Seth F. Kreimer, "Truth Machines and Consequences: The Light and Dark Sides of 'Accuracy' in Criminal Justice," *New York University Annual Survey of American Law* 60 (2005): 655–74.

3. *Atkins v. Virginia*, 536 U.S. 304 (2002), at 353 (Scalia, J., dissenting).

4. *United States v. Quinones*, 196 F.Supp.2d 41 (2002); *United States v. Quinones*, 313 F.3d 49 (2002); *Morales v. Hickman*, 415 F. Supp. 2d 1037 (2006); *Baze v. Rees*, 128 S. Ct. 1520 (2008); *Roper v. Simmons*, 543 U.S. 551 (2005).

5. Samuel R. Gross and Phoebe C. Ellsworth, "Second Thoughts: Americans' Views on the Death Penalty at the Turn of the Century," pp. 7–57 in *Beyond Repair? America's Death Penalty*, ed. Stephen P. Garvey (Durham, N.C.: Duke University Press, 2003).

6. Committee on the Judiciary, *Post-Conviction DNA Testing: When Is Justice Served?*, United States Senate Hearing, June 13, 2000, 106. Available at http://frwebgate.access.gpo.gov/cgi-bin/getdoc.cgi?dbname=106_senate_hearings&docid=f:74753.pdf.

7. Philip Yam, "Science versus the Death Penalty," *Scientific American* (2006). Available at Scientific American (Sciam Observations Blog), January 5, 2006, http://science-community.sciam.com/blog-entry/Sciam-Observations/Science-Versus-Death-Penalty/300004159 (last accessed May 13, 2008).

8. Quoted in Robert Tanner, "Studies Create New Round of Death-Penalty Debates," *Associated Press*, June 14 2007.

9. Anthony G. Amsterdam, "Capital Punishment," in *The Death Penalty in America*, ed. Hugo Bedau (New York: Oxford University Press, 1982), 358. Interestingly, this article contains an early example of the phenomenon we discuss in this chapter, in which Amsterdam critiques "nonscientific proponents of capital punishment" (356).

10. Carol S. Steiker and Jordan M. Steiker, "Abolition in Our Times," *Ohio State Journal of Criminal Law* 1 (2003): 323–43; Steiker and Steiker, "Seduction of Innocence."

11. Quoted in Linda Lutton, "The End of Executions?" *In These Times*, Oct. 2000. Available at http://www.thirdworldtraveler.com/Justice/End_Executions.html.

12. Stuart Banner, *The Death Penalty* (Cambridge, Mass.: Harvard University Press, 2002), 304.

13. Robert Jay Lifton and Greg Mitchell, *Who Owns Death? Capital Punishment, the American Conscience, and the End of Executions* (New York: William Morrow, 2000), 246.

14. Deborah W. Denno, "The Lethal Injection Quandary: How Medicine Has Dismantled the Death Penalty," *Fordham Law Review* 76 (2007): 49–128.

15. Mark Moran, "Adolescent Brain Development Argues against Teen Executions," *American Psychiatric News* 38 (2003): 8.

16. Austin Sarat, *When the State Kills: Capital Punishment and the American Condition* (Princeton, N.J.: Princeton University Press, 2001), 258.

17. Steven Shapin and Simon Schaffer, *Leviathan and the Air Pump: Hobbes, Boyle and the Experimental Life* (Princeton, N.J.: Princeton University Press, 1985).

18. Edward Tenner, *Why Things Bite Back: Technology and the Revenge of Unintended Consequences* (New York: Knopf, 1996).

19. James S. Liebman, "The New Death Penalty Debate: What's DNA Got to Do with It?" *Columbia Human Rights Law Review* 33 (2002): 527–54.

20. Richard A. Rosen, "Reflections on Innocence," *Wisconsin Law Review* (2006), 237; Steiker and Steiker, "Seduction of Innocence," 613.

21. Peter Hodgkinson, "Capital Punishment: Improve It or Remove It?" in *Captial Punishment: Strategies for Abolition*, ed. Peter Hodgkinson and William A. Schabas (Cambridge: Cambridge University Press, 2004), 13.

22. Joseph Wambaugh, *The Blooding* (New York: Bantam, 1989).

23. Hugo Bedau, Michael Radelet, and Constance E. Putnam, "Convicting the Innocent in Capital Cases: Criteria, Evidence, and Inference," *Drake Law Review* 52 (2004): 603. 24. Ibid., 591–95; Frank R. Baumgartner, Suzanna L. De Boef, and Amber E. Boydstin, *The Decline of the Death Penalty and the Discovery of Innocence* (Cambridge: Cambridge University Press, 2008).

25. Joseph L. Hoffman, "Protecting the Innocent: The Massachusetts Governor's Council Report," *Journal of Criminal Law and Criminology* 95 (2005): 562.

26. Bradley R. Hall, "From William Henry Furman to Anthony Porter: The Changing Face of the Death Penalty Debate," *Journal of Criminal Law and Criminology* 95 (2005): 373.

27. Erin Duggan, "Death Penalty Foes Have Their Say," *Albany Times Union*, Jan. 26, 2005; Patrick D. Healy, "Death Penalty Is Blocked by Democrats," *New York Times*, Apr. 13 2005; Joseph Lentol, Helene Weinstein, and Jeffrion Aubry, *The Death Penalty in New York* (Albany: New York State Assembly, 2005); Joyce Purnick, "Temperature Seems to Cool on Death Law," *New York Times*, Dec. 20 2004.

28. American Bar Association, "Recommendation No. 107," 1997. Available at http://www.abanet.org/irr/rec107.html.

29. Austin Sarat, "The Rhetoric of Race in the 'New Abolitionism,'" in *From Lynch Mobs to the Killing State: Race and the Death Penalty in America*, ed. Charles J. Ogletree, Jr., and Austin Sarat (New York: New York University Press, 2006), 276, 275.

30. Steiker and Steiker, "Abolition in Our Times."

31. *United States v. Quinones*, 196 F.Supp.2d 416, 417 (2002).

32. Samuel R. Gross, Kirsten Jacoby, Dawel J. Matheson, Nicholas Mont-gomery, and Sujata Patel, "Exonerations in the United States 1989 through 2003," *Journal of Criminal Law and Criminology* 95 (2005): 523–60.

33. *United States v. Quinones, Brief for the United States of America*, 02-1403, 02-1405 (2002).

34. Hugo Bedau and Michael Radelet, "Miscarriages of Justice in Potentially Capital Cases," *Stanford Law Review* 40 (1987): 21–173; Stephen Markman and Paul Cassell, "Protecting the Innocent: A Response to the Bedau-Radelet Study," *Stanford Law Review* 41 (1988): 121–60.

35. Franklin E. Zimring, *The Contradictions of American Capital Punishment* (Oxford: Oxford University Press, 2003), 159.

36. Kreimer, "Truth Machines and Consequences," 658.

37. Joshua Marquis, "The Myth of Innocence," *Journal of Criminal Law and Criminology* 95 (2005): 501–21; Joshua Marquis, "Truth and Conse-quences: The Penalty of Death," pp. 117–51 in *Debating the Death Penalty*, ed. Hugo Bedau and Paul Cassell (Oxford: Oxford University Press, 2004); Barry Scheck, "Wrongful Convictions," *Drake Law Review* 54 (2006): 597–620.

38. Richard A. Rosen, "Innocence and Death," *North Carolina Law Review* 82 (2003): 68.

39. Liebman, "New Death Penalty Debate," 549.

40. Quoted in Committee on the Judiciary, *Post-Conviction DNA Testing*, 2.

41. *United States v. Quinones*, at 257.

42. Kreimer, "Truth Machines and Consequences."

43. *United States v. Quinones*, at 420.

44. Evan J. Mandery, "Massachusetts and the Changing Debate on the Death Penalty," *Criminal Law Bulletin* 40 (2004): 519.

45. Massachusetts Governor Mitt Romney's Office, "Romney Takes Scientific Approach to Death Penalty" (Boston: Governor's Office, 2003).

46. Tenner, *Why Things Bite Back*.

47. Doug Erickson, "Tying DNA to the Needle," in *madison. com* (2006). Available at http://www.madison.com/archives/read.php?/ ref=wsj/2006/10/22/0610210525.php.

48. Office of the Independent Investigator for the Houston Police Depart-ment Crime Laboratory and Property Room, "Independent Investigator Issues Fifth Report on Houston Police Department Crime Lab," May 11, 2006. Available at http://www.hpdlabinvestigation.org/pressrelease/060511pressrelease.pdf (ac-cessed May 14, 2008).

49. U.S. Department of Justice, Office of the Inspector General, *The FBI DNA Laboratory: A Review of Protocol and Practice Vulnerabilities* (Washington, D.C.: Office of the Inspector General, 2004).

50. Washington: "Errors in Evidence," *Seattle Post-Intelligencer,* Mar. 9, 2004; North Carolina: Phoebe Zerwick, "DNA Mislabeled in Murder Case," *Winston-Salem Journal,* Aug. 28, 2005; California: William C. Thompson, "Tarnish on the Gold Standard: Recent Problems in DNA Testing," *Champion,* Jan./Feb. (2006): 14–20.

51. ASCLAD-LAB, "ASCLD-LAB Limited Scope Interim Inspection Report: Commonwealth of Virigina Division of Forensic Science Central Laboratory," Apr. 9, 2005. Available at http://www.dfs.virginia.gov/services/forensicBiology/externalReviews.cfm (accessed May 13, 2008).

52. For example, Douglas A. Berman, *Sentencing Law and Policy* (Aspen, Colo.: Aspen, 2006); Angela Y. Davis, *Are Prisons Obsolete?* (New York: Seven Stories, 2003); Sarat, "Rhetoric of Race in the 'New Abolitionism'"; Steiker and Steiker, "Seduction of Innocence."

53. Lifton and Mitchell, *Who Owns Death?*; Zimring, *Contradictions of American Capital Punishment.*

54. Denno, "Lethal Injection Quandary," 61.

55. Mark Essig, *Edison and the Electric Chair: A Story of Light and Death* (New York: Walker, 2003); Jonathan I. Groner, "The Hippocratic Paradox: The Role of the Medical Profession in Capital Punishment in the United States," *Fordham Urban Law Journal* 35 (2008): 883–917; Richard Moran, *The Executioner's Current* (New York: Knopf, 2002).

56. Timothy V. Kaufman-Osborn, *From Noose to Needle: Capital Punishment and the Late Liberal State* (Ann Arbor: University of Michigan Press, 2002), 199.

57. Denno, "Lethal Injection Quandary," 118; Gavin Lee, "A Painless Cocktail? The Lethal Injection Controversy," pp. 95–111 in *The Death Penalty Today,* ed. Robert M. Bohm (Boca Raton, Fla.: CRC Press, 2008).

58. Denno, "Lethal Injection Quandary," 118.

59. Kaufman-Osborn, *From Noose to Needle,* 180.

60. Leonidas Koniaris et al., "Inadequate Anaesthesia in Lethal Injection for Execution," *Lancet* 365 (2005): 1412–14; Teresa A. Zimmers, Jonathan P. Sheldon, David A. Lubarsky, Francisco López-Muñoz, Richard Weisman, and Leonidas Koniaris, "Lethal Injection for Execution: Chemical Asphyxiation?" *PLoS (Public Library of Science) Medicine* 4 (2007): 646–53.

61. Jonathan I. Groner, "Inadequate Anaesthesia in Lethal Injection for Execution," *Lancet* 366 (2005): 1073; Mark J. S. Heath, Donald R. Stanski, and Derrick J. Pounder, "Inadequate Anaesthesia in Lethal Injection for Execution," *Lancet* 366 (2005): 1073–74; Robyn S. Weisman, Jeffrey N. Bernstein, and Richard S. Weisman, "Inadequate Anaesthesia in Lethal Injection for Execution," *Lancet* 366 (2005): 1074.

62. Mark Dershwitz and Thomas K. Henthorn, "The Pharmacokinetics and Pharmacodynamics of Thiopental as Used in Lethal Injection," *Fordham Urban Law Journal* 35 (2008): 931–56.

63. David A. Lubarsky, "Remarks at Session on the Lethal Injection Drugs Demystified," presented at conference on The Lethal Injection Debate: Law and Science, Fordham University School of Law, New York, 2008.

64. Dershwitz and Henthorn, "Pharmacokinetics and Pharmacodynamics of Thiopental."

65. *Morales v. Hickman*, 415 F. Supp. 2d 1037 (2006).

66. Denno, "Lethal Injection Quandary," 52.

67. *Morales v. Hickman*.

68. Henry Weinstein, "Lisa McCalmont, 49; Lawyer Challenged Execution by Injection," *Los Angeles Times*, Nov. 14 2007.

69. *Baze v. Rees, on Petition for a Writ of Certiorari to the Supreme Court of Kentucky*, 2007 WL 2781088 (2007).

70. Gerrit K. Kimsma, "Euthanasia and Euthanizing Drugs in the Netherlands," pp. 193–210 in *Drug Use in Assisted Suicide and Euthanasia*, ed. Margaret P. Battin and Arthur G. Lipman (New York: Pharmaceutical Products, 1996).

71. *Baze v. Rees*, 128 S. Ct. 1520 (2008), at 1523.

72. Ibid., at 1541–42.

73. Ibid. (Thomas, J., concurring), at 1562.

74. Ibid. (Breyer, J., concurring), at 1565.

75. Ty Alper, "What Do Lawyers Know about Lethal Injection?" *Harvard Law and Policy Review* 1 (2008). Available at http://www.hlpronline.com.

76. *Roper v. Simmons*, 543 U.S. 551 (2005).

77. For a sampling of magazine articles, see Sharon Begley, "Getting Inside a Teen Brain," *Newsweek* (Feb. 28, 2000), 58; Shannon Brownlee, Roberta Hotinski, Bellamy Pailthorp, Erin Ragan, and Kathleen Wong, "Inside the Teen Brain," *U.S. News and World Report* (Aug. 1, 1999), 44; Duncan Graham-Rowe, "Teen Angst Rooted in Busy Brain," *New Scientist* (Oct. 19, 2002), 16; Roberta Hotinski, "Were You Angry?" *U.S. News and World Report* (Aug. 9, 1999), 50; and Claudia Wallis and Kristina Dell, "What Makes Teens Tick?" *Time* (May 10, 2004), 56. For a sampling of newspaper articles, see Associated Press, "Teen Excesses Are Linked to Brain Growth: New Research Suggests That Hormones Are Not Cause of Adolescent Angst," *Saint Louis Post-Dispatch*, Dec. 31, 2000, B7; Matt Crenson, "Brain Changes Shed Light on Teen Behavior: Old Theory Shattered by New Technologies, New Information Gained about Brain Development," *New Orleans Times-Picayune*, Dec. 31, 2000, 18; Fran Henry, "Dealing with Your 'Crazy' Teens: Bad Behavior May Not Be Their Fault—or Yours, Psychologist Says," *Cleveland Plain Dealer*, Dec. 3, 2001, E1; Curt Suplee, "Key Brain Growth Goes On into Teens: Study Disputes Old Assumptions," *Washington Post*, Mar. 9, 2000, A01; and Shankar Vedantam, "Are Teens Just Wired That Way? Researchers Theorize Brain Changes Are Linked to Behavior," *Washington Post*, June 3, 2001, A01.

78. "Secrets of the Teen Brain," *Time* cover, May 10, 2004.

79. Begley, "Getting Inside a Teen Brain," 58

80. Daniel R. Weinberger, "A Brain Too Young for Good Judgment," *New York Times*, Mar. 10, 2001, A13.

81. Joseph Dumit, *Picturing Personhood: Brain Scans and Biomedical Identity* (Princeton, N.J.: Princeton University Press, 2004); Jennifer Kulynych, "Psychiatric Neuroimaging Evidence: A High Tech Crystal Ball?" *Stanford Law Review* 49 (1997): 1249–70.

82. This point was originally made by an anonymous reviewer of Jay D. Aronson, "Brain Imaging, Culpability, and the Juvenile Death Penalty," *Psychology, Public Policy, and Law* 13 (2007): 115–42.

83. Stephen Harper, personal communication with Jay Aronson, May 24, 2005.

84. Dumit, *Picturing Personhood*, 112.

85. Kelly Joyce, "Appealing Images: Magnetic Resonance Imaging and the Production of Authoritative Knowledge," *Social Studies of Science* 35 (2005): 437–62. See also Paul Rodriguez, "Talking Brains: A Cognitive Semantic Analysis of an Emerging Folk Neuropsychology," *Public Understanding of Science* 15 (2006): 301–30.

86. Dumit, *Picturing Personhood*.

87. David Cohen and Jonathan Leo, "An Update on ADHD Neuroimaging Research," *Journal of Mind and Behavior* 25 (2004): 161–66; Jonathan Leo and David Cohen, "Broken Brain or Flawed Studies? A Critical Review of ADHD Neuroimaging Research," *Journal of Mind and Behavior* 24 (2003): 29–56.

88. Simmie Baer (Speaker), Roper v. Simmons: *How Will This Case Change Practice in the Courtroom?* Teleconference conducted at the American Bar Association Center for Continuing Legal Education (June, 22 2005). Available at http://www.abanet.org/cle/clenow/roperreg.html (accessed May 14, 2008).

Abolition in the United States by 2050
On Political Capital and Ordinary Acts of Resistance

Bernard E. Harcourt

Is the United States on the road to abolition, and, if so, by when will it have abolished the death penalty? The federal structure of the United States complicates the answer to these questions; nevertheless, recent trends in the United States and within the larger international community suggest that the country is headed toward abolition of capital punishment. In all likelihood, a number of retentionist states will converge toward abolition over the course of the next 20 years. The combination of this domestic shift and the legal and political pressure of the international community will likely result in the U.S. Supreme Court imposing a federal constitutional ban on capital punishment, at the latest, by the mid-twenty-first century. It is entirely reasonable to believe that even before then—by 2035 or 2040—there will be no or very few executions in the United States.

Recent statistics are extremely revealing. The United States witnessed significantly decreasing numbers of executions and capital sentences during the first decade of the twenty-first century—despite a continuing political shift toward crime-control policies, as evidenced by the steadily increasing rate of incarceration throughout the country.[1] The historical trends are reflected in the following graphs. Figure 3.1 shows a steep decline in the number of executions in the first decade of the twenty-first century.

Of the 42 executions that were carried out in 2007, the state of Texas accounted for 26 (or 62 percent) of the total, and only nine other states participated in the statistic (Alabama and Oklahoma executing three inmates each; Indiana, Ohio, and Tennessee two inmates each; and Arizona, Georgia, South Carolina, and South Dakota one inmate each).[2] This reflects the fact that the death penalty in the United States has become predominantly a Texas phenomenon and that, putting aside Texas (and occasionally a few other outlier states like Alabama, Georgia, and Virginia), few executions are being carried out in the rest of the country.

The decrease in the annual number of executions has gone hand in hand with a similar decrease over the period in the number of persons sentenced to death in the United States, as reflected in figure 3.2. The declining trend in the imposition of capital sentences is not only true at the national, aggregated level but also at the individual state level. Even in a state like Texas, prosecutors and politicians have tempered their enthusiasm for death sentences.[3]

In addition, the number of abolitionist states has increased since the U.S. Supreme Court approved post-*Furman* capital statutes. Since then, Massachusetts, North Dakota, Rhode Island, New Jersey, New York, and Vermont joined the ranks of eight other abolitionist states (Alaska, Hawaii, Iowa, Maine, Michigan, Minnesota, West Virginia, and Wisconsin) that had never legalized capital punishment.[4] And on March 18, 2009, New Mexico abolished the death penalty. This trend is reflected in figure 3.3.

These graphs and the underlying data are merely the objective reflection of a series of unexpected developments, many of which are recounted in greater detail in the chapters of this book. New York State reinstated

FIGURE 3.1

Number of executions in the United States, 1999–2008

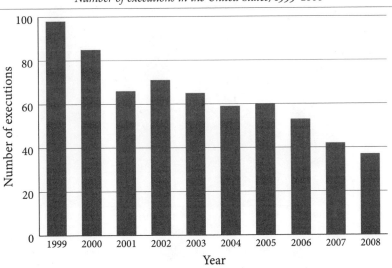

Data from U.S. Department of Justice, Bureau of Justice Statistics, 2007 (table 15).

FIGURE 3.2

Number of death sentences imposed in the United States, 1999–2007

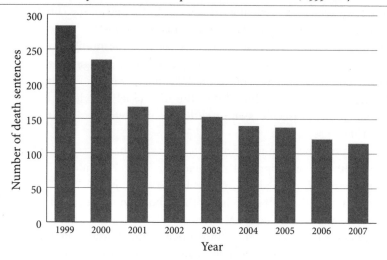

Data from U.S. Department of Justice, Bureau of Justice Statistics, 2007 (table 14).

FIGURE 3.3

*Number of abolitionist and retentionist states in
the United States, 1971–2009*

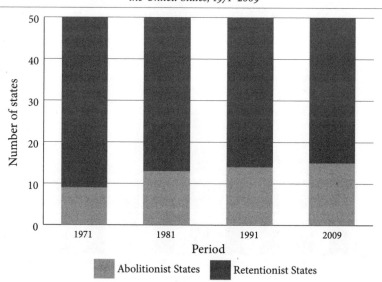

Data from Jacobs and Carmichael, 2002, and Death Penalty Information Center, 2008.

and flirted with the death penalty in the early 1990s but after several years ultimately rejected capital punishment. A Republican governor in Illinois, George Ryan, imposed a moratorium on the death penalty because of the mounting number of wrongful convictions and then commuted the death sentences of all inmates on Illinois' death row.[5] The Supreme Court over-turned its prior decisions and restricted the substantive scope of the death penalty, prohibiting its use in the case of juveniles and persons with men-tal retardation.[6] In over 125 cases, persons accused of capital crimes and sentenced to death were exonerated after an average of almost 10 years on death row.[7] In December 2007, Governor Jon Corzine of New Jersey signed a bill abolishing the state's death penalty. At about the same time, the Supreme Court effectively imposed a temporary moratorium on the death penalty while the justices considered the legality of lethal injection.[8] And, according to reliable reports, "In states like Maryland, . . . and South Dakota, legislative efforts to repeal the death penalty—once considered hopeless—now appear to be within a few votes of success. Blue-ribbon committees similar to the one in New Jersey have been appointed in places like Illinois, Tennessee, Maryland and Florida."[9]

These domestic shifts mirror the larger international trend toward abo-lition of the death penalty. As Roger Hood, William Schabas, and others have shown, there has been a global tendency toward abolition over the course of the twentieth and twenty-first centuries—a trend that grew in increasing proportion in the last decades of the twentieth.[10] Whether one considers countries that have abolished capital punishment for ordinary crimes only or for all crimes, the proportion of abolitionist countries has increased significantly. As Hood notes, "the annual average rate at which countries have abolished the death penalty trebled: from roughly one a year in the period 1965–88, to three a year over the years 1989–2000."[11] This is demonstrated in figure 3.4. It should be noted that the graph does not even include, in the category of abolitionist states, countries that have not executed anyone in the past 10 years—what are referred to as de facto abolitionist states. These numbered 18 states as of 2004.[12]

As a result of this global trend, Amnesty International reports that, at year end 2005, some 86 countries had abolished the death penalty for all crimes and another 36 countries were abolitionist in practice (either because they had abolished capital punishment for ordinary crimes, re-taining it only for military or other exceptional circumstances, or because they had not executed anyone in the preceding 10 years). In other words, 122 countries were effectively abolitionist.[13] This represents a significant

FIGURE 3.4

Twentieth-century global trend regarding abolition

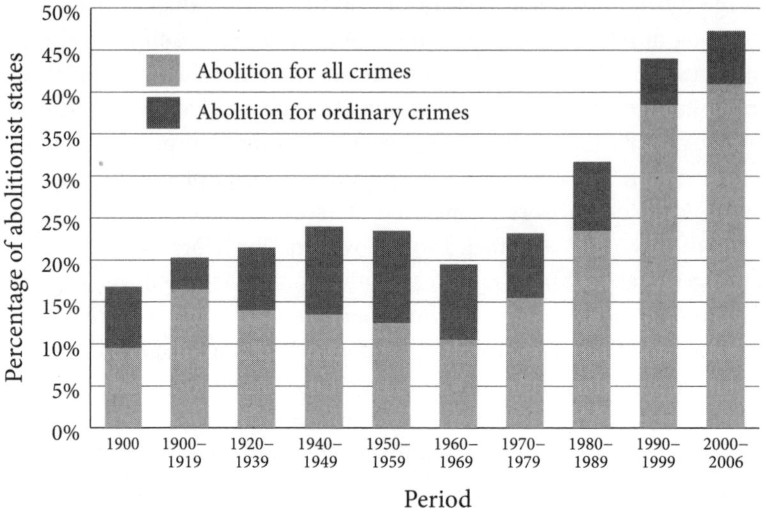

Data from Neumayer 2008 (tables 1 and 2).

majority of the countries in the world, over 60 percent. Only 71 countries retained the death penalty for ordinary crimes at the beginning of
the twenty-first century.[14]

Part of this trend is certainly attributable to Europe's militant opposition
to capital punishment and the requirement that states abolish the death
penalty in order to gain membership to the European Union. This influence
can be expected to continue for the next several decades. But the European
Union does not explain the depth of the global trend. Some of the countries
that have abolished the death penalty for all crimes since 2000 include, for
instance, the Philippines, Samoa, Mexico, Liberia, Côte d'Ivoire, and Bhu-
tan. The depth of the international sentiment is widely spread and reflected
well in the vote of the U.N. General Assembly in December 2007 calling
for a worldwide moratorium on executions. As Michael Radelet suggests,
"The vote was overwhelming: 104 of the U.N.'s member states supported
the resolution, while only 54 opposed it and 29 abstained."[15]

The most rigorous, quantitative, cross-national analyses of the global
trend toward abolition have identified a number of leading predictors, including, for instance, regional peer pressure and the level of democratization of a country. Along practically all of these predictor dimensions, the

United States as a whole should already be in the abolitionist camp—not just 14 of the 50 states plus the District of Columbia, but the whole country. To be sure, the fact that the United States as a whole does not now rank among abolitionist states may simply be the fortuitous and contingent result of the Supreme Court's near-miss decision in *Furman v. Georgia* in 1972.[16] It is also difficult to speak of the United States "as a whole"—putting aside the federal death penalty—given the unique federalist structure of the country in the area of penal administration. Regardless, it is likely that the political forces that have shaped these trends toward abolition at the international level will continue to exercise pressure on the United States and individual retentionist states in this country. Peer and regional international political pressure—combined with the overall decline in violent crime,[17] a more moderated public opinion when presented with the sentencing option of life imprisonment without parole,[18] and increased awareness of cases of innocence and wrongful convictions[19]—will likely push several other states from de facto abolitionist and retentionist ranks to the abolitionist camp over the course of the next two decades—barring, naturally, unforeseen global shifts or catastrophes. This is most likely to occur first in states such as Colorado, Connecticut, Idaho, Kansas, New Hampshire, South Dakota, and Wyoming, which have executed only one or no inmates since resumption of the death penalty in 1976, or in states such as Maryland, Illinois, and Tennessee, which are currently reviewing their capital punishment practices; but the political momentum created by these states likely will extend to other retentionist states.

The gradual convergence of a number of retentionist states toward abolition of the death penalty, in combination with the increased role of international legal and political opposition to capital punishment, in all probability will lead the U.S. Supreme Court to ban capital punishment as a federal constitutional matter. The numerical trend and political momentum toward abolition likely will play an important role in the decision, but so will the greater role of international law in the Supreme Court's interpretation of the Eighth Amendment's "evolving standard of moral decency."[20]

Though it is difficult to chart the likely path of abolition, it is probable that, within retentionist states, the transition to abolition will occur as a result of elite political leadership and ordinary acts of resistance. Experience has shown that abolition of the death penalty is rarely the result of loud and explicit democratic politics but, instead, is more often the product of slightly countermajoritarian, at times elite-driven, judicial or political maneuvers. Abolition most often occurs against the backdrop of mild popular support for the death penalty. As such, it often entails an *expenditure* of political capital: it is not an issue that *builds* political capital for emerging leaders but one that requires using *existing* political capital.

Another important but rarely discussed factor that promotes abolitionist reform is ordinary acts of resistance by those who are either knowingly or unconsciously uncomfortable with capital punishment or truly opposed to the ultimate punishment. These men and women—a clerk at the county courthouse, an employee at the local police department, a secretary in the prosecutor's office, sometimes even a judge or law clerk—gummy up the system and slow death penalty cases down, sometimes to a snail's pace. Texas, again, is the outlier here, but it is revealing precisely for that fact: the reason that many other states are far less efficient than Texas at executing death-row inmates is the product of ordinary, minor acts of resistance, sometimes conscious but often unconscious.

Neither of these two factors is an especially good topic for elaboration since both take place below visibility. Yet they both likely will play important roles and will push states at the cusp into the abolitionist camp, continuing the national and global trend toward greater abolition of the death penalty. In this chapter, I explore these less-visible dimensions of abolitionist reform, after first analyzing the leading indicators of abolition at the cross-national level.

Leading Cross-National Indicators of Abolition

The cross-national models confirm what recent trends show: in all likelihood, the United States will tend toward greater abolition. There are fewer such studies than one might expect, but two recent quantitative studies attempt to systematically assess the determinants of death penalty abolition using cross-national models.[21]

Eric Neumayer, a professor at the London School of Economics, has an excellent cross-national quantitative study of global abolition and finds that the foremost determinants of abolition are political factors—namely, democratization and regional peer pressure. In his study *Death Penalty: The Political Foundations of the Global Trend toward Abolition*, Neumayer tests a number of political, cultural, social, and economic explanations for the significant shift, over the past 50 years, toward abolition. His data, for the most part, span 50 years, from 1950 to 2002.

Neumayer tests six political factors, including (1) a measure of the democratic nature of the state; (2) an indicator of regime transition to democracy (or what Neumayer calls "democratization"); (3) whether the country has a left-wing political orientation, measured by the World Bank's assessment of whether the chief executive's party is considered left-wing; (4) the historical experience with armed political conflict or the country's history of warfare, which is expected to correlate positively with retention of capital punishment at least for treason; (5) western European pressure on eastern European countries; and (6) international pressure from regional peers and neighbor countries. Neumayer also includes in his models another five cultural, religious, economic, and social factors, including (1) whether the country's legal system is based on English common law, which is believed to have a retentionist influence; (2) whether the society is strongly Islamic, as measured by the fraction of the Muslim population; (3) economic inequality; (4) ethnic and racial fractionalization; and (5) lagged rates of violent crime and homicide.

Using a proportional hazards model, Neumayer finds that, with regard to abolition for all crimes, three political factors seem to be strongly related to abolition: the democratic nature of the state, transitions to democracy, and regional pressure. A fourth, participation in the Council of Europe, is also important but obviously less generalizable. Having a left-wing chief executive is also important, but the data for the model that includes this variable are limited and cover only 1975 to 2000 (n of 768 instead of n of 5,458 in the first model). The historical experience with armed political conflict is not significant. In contrast, three cultural, economic, and social factors seem to be associated with retention, and these are the greater degree of ethnic fractionalization, higher income inequality, and legal systems that are based on English common law. High homicide rates are also associated with retention, but here again the data are few and cover only the period 1975 to 2000.[22]

Neumayer's findings are mostly similar with regard to abolition for ordinary crimes, except that ethnic fractionalization, homicide rates, and economic inequality are no longer statistically significant. As a result, the key factors are predominantly political: "democracy, a regime transition toward democracy, membership in the Council of Europe, a higher share of abolitionist countries within the region as well as the left-wing orientation of the chief executive's party all raise the likelihood of abolition. A legal system built on English common law and a predominantly Muslim population have the opposite effect in some regressions with relatively large sample sizes."[23] Neumayer concludes that "the continuation of the abolitionist trend is contingent on a further spread of democracy around the world, on political pressure imposed on retentionist countries, on regional peer group effects and on the political balance between conservative and left-wing parties within countries."[24]

Neumayer decided to code the United States as retentionist; however, when he ran the analyses dropping the United States from the dataset, he found that this "hardly affects the results":

> Many talk about American exceptionalism since with Japan it is the only democratic and developed country still holding on to the death penalty. Discussing possible reasons for this exceptionalism is beyond the scope of this paper. Unfortunately, for statistical reasons it is not possible to include a dummy variable for the US into the estimations to see whether the retentionist status of the US can be explained sufficiently by the explanatory variables, in which case the dummy variable would be insignificant, or whether there is something truly exceptional about the US, in which case the dummy variable would be statistically significant. Loosely speaking this is because with the US being retentionist over the entire period, such a dummy variable would predict failure to abolish perfectly and therefore be dropped from the model. If we exclude the US, or the US and Japan together, from the estimations, then results are not much affected. This is not very surprising given that these represent just two out of a great many countries. If we include dummy variables for the regions of Western Europe as well as South America to account for the fact that countries from these regions were often frontrunners of abolition, then again our results are hardly affected. It is not simple regionalism that drives abolition.[25]

On the political factors, the United States should tend toward abolition: a strong democracy surrounded by two abolitionist countries, Canada and Mexico, with, at least occasionally, a center-left chief executive at the federal and state levels. The factors that would tend toward retention— setting aside the peculiarities of our federal system—would include the English common law tradition and the high incidence of violent crime and homicide. But the latter should be diminishing as a contributing factor, at least since the early 1990s. To be sure, as Neumayer notes, "The unique character of state-determined criminal law and substantial laymen participation and influence on the extent of punitiveness of the criminal sanction system might provide hints why many states in the U.S. maintain the death penalty and execute a great number of people."[26] But the political forces should still be at play and will likely influence the further trend toward abolition in the United States.

In their 2005 study on "Cross-National Variability in Capital Punishment," Terance Miethe, Hong Lu, and Gini Deibert explore the comparative sociopolitical conditions of 185 countries to determine the correlates for the legal retention or abolition of capital punishment. Their principal predictors include measures of economic development, political conditions, primary religion, location in world region, and the extent of extrajudicial executions. To be more specific, the measures of economic development are based on each nation's per capita gross domestic product (GDP) in 2000 (the authors reach similar results using per capita income, but, due to missing observations for infant mortality and literacy, were unable to use a human development index). The political condition variables measured two separate dimensions: first, an index of how much citizens are able to participate in the selection of governments ("voice and accountability") and, second, the perception of political stability and presence of political violence. Primary religion and world region are self-explanatory. The extent of extrajudicial executions were derived from a 1996 report from the Special Rapporteur of the U.N.'s Commission on Human Rights, augmented by annual reports of Amnesty International and Human Rights Watch.[27]

Simple bivariate patterns reveal that each one of these predictors is significantly associated with the legal status of capital punishment. Miethe, Lu, and Deibert find that the likelihood of retaining capital punishment is significantly higher for countries that (1) have lower economic development; (2) experience lower political voice and accountability; (3) have lower political stability; (4) are dominated by religions other than Christianity; (5) are located in the Middle East, Asia, or the Caribbean regions; and (6) have recent histories of extrajudicial killings.[28]

Multivariate logistic regression analysis reveals that the first three factors remain significant when all the variables are taken into consideration. The authors report that "[t]he association between increasing economic development and legal abolition remains statistically significant even after successive controls for the nation's primary religion, history of extrajudicial executions, and various measures of political conditions. . . . [U]nit increases in economic development decreased by about 50 percent the odds of legal retention of the death penalty after controlling for other variables."[29] There are exceptions, of course, and the United States and

Japan stand out as such among large industrialized nations. But the correlation is strong, and capital punishment remains much more highly associated with low economic development. As the authors note, "more than two thirds of the developing countries (i.e., defined by GDP per capita of less than US$4,000 in 2000) have retained the death penalty in law."[30]

The other two measures of political conditions—political voice and stability—also had "significant net effects on the legal status of capital punishment. Countries with greater political voice had substantially lower net risks of legal retention, whereas the conditional odds of retaining the death penalty were about 2.3 times higher among more than less politically stable countries."[31] Along most of these dimensions then, with the single exception of political stability, the United States is an outlier: the resulting model would suggest that the United States should rank among abolitionist states.

The authors also used qualitative comparative analyses to look at the joint or conjunctive effects of the different variables to determine which combinations of variables are more or less likely to result in retention of the death penalty. Here, too, the United States is an outlier, located in a cluster with a sociopolitical profile of predominantly abolitionist nations that includes, for instance, Australia, Canada, France, Italy, and Norway. This cluster—predominantly Christian nations with high political voice, high political stability, and high economic development—contains 22 nations, of which 91 percent are abolitionist. The United States is singled out, in the analysis, as one of the few examples of "exceptions to the dominant pattern."[32]

In sum, the two existing quantitative models intended to predict whether a jurisdiction should have the death penalty would suggest that the United States should have already abolished the ultimate penalty. In terms of highly industrialized large nations, the United States and Japan are the only countries that continue to use the death penalty. In terms of culturally and sociopolitically similar countries, such as the United Kingdom and Canada, the United States is the only country with a death penalty. Even when we narrow the comparison group to those "matching countries"—countries that have similar cultural values and histories, such as Great Britain and Canada or even, to expand a little more, Germany, Mexico, and Australia—the United States remains an outlier that should tend toward abolition.

Naturally, a host of cross-national cultural variables that are not as easily quantifiable have been offered to explain differences in death penalty regimes. Some are more convincing than others. At least in the U.S.-E.U. comparison, one of the important cultural factors should be the fact that the death penalty was used in a more politicized manner in eighteenth- and nineteenth-century Europe; as a result, the penalty itself had a differ- ent symbolic meaning. It was not so closely tied to crime and punishment but, instead, to the repression of political dissent. The repression of the Paris Commune in 1871, for instance, led to the execution of as many as 20,000 civilians—the number is contested, but in 2004, in "In the World-Shadow of Bismarck and Nobel," Benedict Anderson places the number at 20,000 and others have estimated it as high as 50,000. In the United States, the primary political connection to the death penalty is racism— the use of capital punishment as a way to repress the African American community. (To be sure, during the antebellum period, capital punishment of slaves was expensive to masters and therefore not used extensively. The death penalty and lynchings became more efficient tools of repression af- ter emancipation.) But I do not think that racism has the same resonance in the United States as political killings—whether of Communards, anti-Jacobins, or Resistance members—have on the European continent. An- other important cultural difference, again in the U.S.-E.U. context, is that the left in Europe is much further to the left than in the United States. However, as Carol Steiker demonstrates ably in her article "Capital Pun-ishment and American Exceptionalism," even the most convincing non-quantifiable cultural explanations leave a lot to be desired—which leaves us with the handful of quantitative predictors that predominantly point in the direction of abolition for the United States.

Domestic Political and Social Correlates of Abolition

Recent developments and these statistical analyses suggest strongly, then, that a number of retentionist states at the cusp will likely join abolitionist ranks, further pushing the United States to join its international abolition-ist peer group. The question this raises, naturally, concerns the mechanics of abolition. What political and social factors will lead retentionist states at the cusp to tilt toward repeal of their capital statutes?

In addressing this question, the quantitative research is somewhat less helpful. There are a number of studies that have tried to identify the *do-mestic* factors that predict whether an individual state is abolitionist or retentionist. The leading predictors in this set of studies tend to include measures of ethnic or racial diversity, of inequality, of political ideology, and of religious faith. The difficulty with the quantitative research here, though, is that it ultimately tends to map the different regional characteristics of the predominant death states, notably the "Death Belt" states. Moreover, although the studies identify likely predictors of variation between retentionist and abolitionist states, they do not necessarily indicate which *mechanisms* influence abolition.

David Jacobs and Jason Carmichael have tested the leading hypotheses that have been offered to explain retention versus abolition in a series of studies. In their first, published in 2002, "The Political Sociology of the Death Penalty," Jacobs and Carmichael test three different hypotheses using state-level panel data. The first hypothesis is that enhanced minority presence may intimidate or threaten the majority population, and the majority may respond by deploying more repressive penal measures. To test this theory, Jacobs and Carmichael rely on measures of ethnic or racial diversity as a proxy for this theory of racial threat and tension. These measures generally correspond, simply, to the proportion of the population consisting of African American or Hispanic persons. The underlying rationale of the second hypothesis is similar: namely, that political elites will use more repressive punitive methods when economic inequality, and therefore potential conflict, is greater. The authors rely on measures of economic inequality, here, also as a proxy for social and economic threat. The third hypothesis concerns the political strength of law-and-order conservative ideology in the population. Jacobs and Carmichael include other factors as well, such as the strength of the Republican Party.

In their 2002 study, Jacobs and Carmichael find that their state-level data support both the racial and economic threat explanations: "states with the largest black populations are more likely to retain capital punishment after the amount of violent crime and many other explanations are held constant, but we find no evidence that Hispanic presence matters." They also find "strong support for the less prominent economic version of threat theory."[33] Jacobs and Carmichael also find a positive correlation between Republican Party strength and the existence of capital punishment in cross-state comparisons. These findings are consistent with research in the broader area of punishment and incarceration. David Jacobs and Ronald Helms, in their 1997 study on the determinants of prison admission rates, for instance, find that the increased political strength of the Republican Party in a jurisdiction produces a subsequent growth in incarceration.[34] In their 2004 study, Jacobs and Carmichael find that greater numbers of death sentences correlate with states with greater membership in conservative churches, as well as states with higher violent crime rates.[35]

The difficulty, again, is that these models are static in the sense that they identify the factors that explain the difference between retentionist and abolitionist states, but they do not identify what dynamic changes occurred to move retentionist states into the abolitionist camp. To address this question, it is necessary to explore anecdotal evidence regarding the historical shifts that have taken place in the broader movement toward abolition.

On Political Capital

A review of the larger historical literature suggests that, within those states at the cusp, two political forces will likely play important roles. The first is elite political leadership—or what one might think of as political leadership from the top. The second consists in ordinary acts of resistance— or what one might think of as bottom-up political opposition. I address these in order.

Abolition of the death penalty is not a political issue that *creates* political capital, that *builds* political support, or that *makes* a political career. A young or emerging politician at the local or national level, especially in a retentionist state, will never attract a majority of political support by advocating abolition of the death penalty. That is simply not the kind of political issue that works on the campaign trail.

There are, in effect, two kinds of political issues in a democracy. There are political issues where the public is evenly divided. On these issues, it is possible to acquire political capital independently of the position advocated, based on oratory skill, charisma, or political ability. On these issues, even if the population is deeply emotionally invested, even if the issues raise deep cultural cleavages, it is possible to build political capital by changing a few votes. But there are other political issues—like the death penalty—where public sentiment is extremely lopsided. On those issues, a young politician cannot build political capital by taking the minority position. On the contrary, opposing the death penalty entails *expending* political capital. And the term "political capital" should be understood here literally: a politician will use up a portion of his or her popularity by advocating abolition, regardless of the fact that there may be, ultimately, a return on the investment. It may pay a political dividend in the future, but often it is a form of political recognition or admiration that has the quality of martyrdom rather than populism. The abolitionist political leader is viewed as someone who had moral conviction despite popular opposition; someone who went against the current of public opinion and who, in prevailing, acquired some moral status, recognition, or respect. These are the political leaders who are thought of as "just" or "righteous," though not necessarily as popular.

In this sense, abolitionist politics can produce a political aura but rarely political votes. This was true, for instance, with regard to François Mitterrand in France. Before the abolitionist reform, there was only a political debt to be paid—no votes to be had. Mitterrand and Robert Badinter, his justice minister, understood this well and tried to minimize the damage. During the 1974 electoral campaign between Valéry Giscard d'Estaing and Mitterrand, both candidates were hostile to the death penalty—Mitterrand far more than d'Estaing—yet neither of them mentioned the issue. Badinter writes that Mitterrand "would only make a rare reference to the issue [of the death penalty]. Announcing an unpopular measure is not the best way to win votes. And it was a victory in the ballot box that he had to achieve first. Abolition would follow by itself."[36]

This is not to suggest that abolitionist politicians should or do lie about their convictions. Again, taking the case of France, Mitterrand never lied about his position. Rather, he and others—d'Estaing and even Jacques Chirac in 1981[37]—did not raise the issue on their own and did not campaign as abolitionists. On two occasions, Mitterrand was asked about his position on the death penalty, and on both occasions he responded honestly. But he never sought out the question as a campaign strategy. And his responses were always from the heart. During the 1981 elections, for instance, Mitterrand was asked about his position on the death penalty, and he responded without hesitation:

> In my conscience, in the deepest recesses of my faith, I am opposed to the death penalty. . . . I don't need to read the opinion polls to know that a majority of the people favor the death penalty. I'm a candidate for President of the Republic. . . . I say what I think, what I sincerely believe, my deepest spiritual attachments, my faith, my concern for our civilization. I am not in favor of the death penalty.[38]

In this sense, abolition is not a political strategy. It is a political cost. The 2008 Democratic primaries in the United States were illustrative.

None of the three early Democratic front-runners was willing to stake out a clear position against the death penalty. Whenever they expressed support for the ultimate punishment, it was always qualified. Frankly, it was difficult to know where they really stood—in their conscience. Hillary Clinton appears not to have made any direct statements on the death penalty, but, according to some reports, she had difficulty with the issue.[39] In the 2004 debates, John Edwards cautiously supported the death penalty, noting that reforms were necessary: "I believe the death penalty is the most fitting punishment for the most heinous crimes, and I support it. But we need reforms in the death penalty to ensure that defendants receive fair trials, with zealous and competent lawyers, and with full access to DNA testing."[40] Barack Obama, in his book *The Audacity of Hope*, declared:

> While the evidence tells me that the death penalty does little to deter crime, I believe there are some crimes—mass murder, the rape and murder of a child—so heinous that the community is justified in expressing the full measure of its outrage by meting out the ultimate punishment. On the other hand, the way capital cases were tried in Illinois at the time was so rife with error, questionable police tactics, racial bias, and shoddy lawyering, that 13 death row inmates had been exonerated.[41]

Only marginal candidates—candidates with no hope of winning the primaries, such as Democrat Dennis Kucinich and Republican Ron Paul—expressed opposition to the death penalty.

At the national level and within most retentionist states, capital punishment is a litmus test issue, somewhat like abortion and gay marriage. Advocating abolition is perceived by the vast majority of citizens as being weak on crime, almost unpatriotic. As a result, it is only possible for an elected politician to effectively oppose the death penalty once he or she is already in a political position with excess political capital. Illinois Governor George Ryan's commutations are a good example of this. Ryan effectively *expended* political capital when he placed a moratorium on the death penalty. Ryan was a charismatic, populist Republican politician. He was a talented orator and had a gift with political audiences—and he had a lot of political capital. Ryan had a compelling, "man on the street" approach. In discussing the moratorium, he would explain that being governor in a state with the death penalty is just like being the CEO of an airline: if 12 flights make it to their destination, but 13 crash and burn, you simply have to stop outgoing flights to find out what is happening.[42] It was that simple. And, of course, in Illinois, since the state had reinstated executions in 1977, some 12 inmates had been executed while 13 had been exonerated. It was just good management to stop and inspect the planes. Ryan was extremely compelling and a formidable politician, but there was no question he was using up his political capital: what is clear from the historical record is that he used up a lot of political capital when he intervened in the capital punishment arena. In his case, the later commutations were shrouded in allegations of political corruption and he was accused of taking the moral high ground on the death penalty in order to whitewash his political shenanigans and dryclean his reputation. But notice that the moratorium and commutations will remain one of his principal political legacies—something he did out of conviction, despite the fact that it was not popular. It may bring him respect in some quarters, but it did not build political capital. It was only possible because he had political capital to spare.

Elite political leadership of this type has always been important in the shift toward abolition. As Roger Hood explains, "political leadership has been a potent factor." This was true in France and also in

> the former German Democratic Republic, which in 1987 declared that capital punishment was no longer essential to defend socialism from violent crimes or even the legacy of Nazi war crimes. Georgia abolished capital punishment on the initiative of its President Edouard Shevardnatze in 1997, two years before becoming a member of the Council of Europe in 1999. . . . In South Africa, where the abolitionist movement had been unable to make any headway, it was the influence of Nelson Mandela and his new government which encouraged the Constitutional Court, in the landmark judgment in *The State v. Makwanyane and Mchunu* handed down in June 1995, to declare that capital punishment was incompatible with the prohibition against "cruel, inhuman or degrading" punishment and with a "human rights culture," despite the heightened concerns about rising crime in that country.[43]

Abolition is simply not a democratic issue. As Neumayer remarks, "leadership by the political elite is important since in many countries abolition has been achieved against the majority opinion of the people."[44] Naturally, this raises an interesting question about the link Neumayer discovered between democracy and abolition. The answer, though, seems to revolve around the fact that democracies often leave room for elite politics. As Neumayer suggests:

> [A]ny positive link between democracy and abolition is not caused by the fact that democracies are more accountable to the will of the people. Rather, what matters is that in most (full) democracies the political elite is willing to grant inviolable rights to all individuals, even if they are criminals, and to ignore public opinion, which might at times remain in favor of the death penalty.[45]

Ordinary Acts of Resistance

Another important factor on the road to abolition—one that receives far less attention because it is so much less visible—is the minor acts of resistance that tend to delay, prolong, and generally disrupt death penalty cases. These are the actions of men and women in retentionist states who, sometimes consciously but even more often unconsciously, delay death penalty cases. Though not necessarily abolitionists themselves, they may find capital punishment unpleasant, uncomfortable, slightly disturbing, perhaps even a bit disgusting—something they would simply prefer not to deal with. The parallels in the debates over methods of execution and forms of torture—or, for that matter the similarities in the discourses of suffocation in the lethal injection and in the "waterboarding" controversies[46]—are hard to escape or ignore. They infiltrate and permeate our thoughts about the death penalty, even if unconsciously. They make many people uncomfortable with the death penalty, even if unknowingly. And the resulting denial, discomfort, suppression, or simple plain disregard for death penalty cases has a significant influence on the life course of these capital cases. These men and women, whether by unconsciously trying to suppress these thoughts or deliberately ignoring the cases, effectively gummy up the capital punishment system—they slow it down, they put it on hold, they create delay, often unknowingly or unconsciously.

Clerks in the back office, secretaries and administrative assistants, a police officer, an investigator, a prison guard, people who have had their own brushes with the law or whose family members have been incarcerated—and given the high rate of incarceration in the United States today, reaching 1 percent of the adult population, there are many such people—these people render the death penalty system inefficient and somewhat ineffectual. In several death penalty cases in which I have been involved as a litigator, I have encountered more than just inertia—more than just laziness or distraction. I have experienced almost intentional or deliberate delay by men and women in all categories of life who take it on themselves to stall a death penalty prosecution by ignoring it. It is these acts of resistance—one could say minor acts of sabotage—that render the death penalty simply ineffectual in many states. The deliberate resistance of doctors to participate in the mechanics of capital punishment is the conscious and public manifestation of such resistance, but the phenomenon tends to be far more unconscious and, as a result, pervasive.

The model to understand these acts is that of "everyday acts of resistance" developed by James C. Scott and notions of "moral economy" developed in the work of E. P. Thompson.[47] Everyday acts of resistance offer a model to understand the way that politically less-powerful groups achieve resistance to a dominant political framework. Through hidden transcripts and minor deviant acts, the less-powerful groups challenge the dominant regime and interfere with the system. Those same acts of resistance can also be understood through the lens of moral economy. In his essay "The Moral Economy of the English Crowd in the Eighteenth Century," Thompson discusses how actions that may otherwise be interpreted through more familiar lenses of delay, deviance, or even criminality may actually bear important political dimensions. Thompson argues, for instance, that acts traditionally described as simple vandalism are often forms of political expression, of political protest or resistance to a political economic system that may appear to the actor as oppressive, disgusting, alien, or morally wrong. He describes how the food "riot" in eighteenth-century England may not have been mere spasmodic and occasional social disturbances brought about by a bad harvest but actually politically engaged resistance to, at the time, a relatively new laissez-faire political economy. These acts, Thompson argues, were "a highly complex form of direct popular action . . . operat[ing] within a popular consensus as to what were legitimate and what were illegitimate practices in marketing, milling, baking, etc."[48] The food riots were not about hunger but about the perceived violation of a moral economy. The act of rioting was not about stealing food but about damaging the mills and machinery—acts that were counterproductive from a hunger perspective. The riots were a response to the perceived violation to the legitimate beliefs and moral order of the economy.

A traditional critique of resistance theories is that ordinary acts of resistance tend to serve as substitutes for more direct and significant reform, thereby impeding political change. This critique may be more powerful in other contexts, but in the death penalty arena it seems to operate differently. The minor acts of resistance here seem to be effective precisely because they tend to sap the capital punishment system of its moral legitimacy. The lengthy delays undermine the primary justifications for the death penalty—whether it is the deterrent effect of the sentence of death, the finality of the punishment, or the moral equivalence, the *jus talionis*, of the death sentence. This may reflect the unique ways in which sovereignty is constituted in the death penalty context.[49] But in this particular context, those minor acts of resistance seem to erode the political support necessary for capital punishment to continue to function.

Another sentiment, also frequent in the United States, tends to contribute to the everyday acts of resistance: rooting for the underdog. This, too, is a strong strain in American culture. Many ordinary citizens are willing to help someone condemned to death when they feel that the system is stacked against them. There need not always be moral opposition to the death penalty but simply a feeling that the scales are too heavily weighted in favor of the state. Naturally, these are not the dominant passions that are always encountered in death penalty cases. These are not the more public transcripts; they are the hidden ones. The majority of actors in death penalty cases are deliberately seeking to promote the execution of the sentence of death. But the small acts of resistance—and the sustaining acts of kindness—have an important effect on the capital punishment system.

Predicting Abolition in the United States

The empirical data reflect a clear trend toward abolition: in all probability, the United States, like the larger international community, will experience greater abolition of the death penalty during the first half of the twenty-first century. There is no reason to believe that the movement toward abolition will be especially rapid. There are important institutional impediments to abolition in the United States. There are numerous features unique to our federal system of criminal justice—such as localized elections, decentralized policing and corrections, and multiple and dispersed layers of appellate court review—that present obstacles to abolition in the individual states.[50] Nevertheless, the evidence pointing toward greater abolition has been steady and consistent, not only in the last quarter of the twentieth century but also in the first decade of the twenty-first. It may well take 20 more years for the momentum to reach a tipping point, but the direction of change favors abolition rather than retention.

It is unlikely that the momentum will start in the deepest corridors of the Death Belt—in Texas or Alabama. It is far more likely that states such as Kansas or New Hampshire (which have not executed anyone since the resumption of the death penalty in 1976) or states such as Colorado, Connecticut, Idaho, South Dakota, or Wyoming (which have only executed one inmate since 1976) will gravitate toward abolition first. But in the process, it is probable that the movement toward greater abolition will eventually bring about a federal constitutional ban on capital punishment in the United States. And it is likely that this will occur before 2050.

With the eventual abolition of capital punishment in the United States, it is entirely reasonable to expect that, by the mid-twenty-first century, capital punishment will have the same status as torture within the larger international community: an outlier practice, prohibited by international agreements and customary international law, practiced illicitly by rogue nations, and defended only by a handful of conservative academics seeking attention.

NOTES

I thank Charles Ogletree and Austin Sarat for organizing this collection of essays; Jay Aronson, Hugo Bedau, Simon Cole, Deborah Denno, Peter Fitzpatrick, Timothy Kaufman-Osborn, Jürgen Martschukat, Michael McCann, Michael Radelet, Carol Steiker, Jordan Steiker, and Robin Wagner-Pacifici for their incisive reading and critiques of my earlier draft; Andrew Dilts, Florence Bellivier, and Pascal Beauvais for extremely helpful comments on an earlier version; and Marylynne Hunt-Dorta and Stephanie Noble for outstanding research assistance.

1. Federal and state prison populations increased dramatically from under 200,000 persons in 1970 to more than 1.3 million in 2002. That year, our imprisonment rate rose above 600 inmates per 100,000 adults. With the inclusion of an additional 700,000 inmates in jail, the United States incarcerates more than 2 million people—resulting in the highest incarceration number and rate in the world, five times that of Britain and 12 times that of Japan. The numbers and rates have continued to increase during the first decade of the twenty-first century. Harcourt 2007.

2. Death Penalty Information Center 2008; NAACP LDF 2008.

3. Carol Steiker and Jordan Steiker, chap. 4 in this volume.

4. Jacobs and Carmichael 2002:115.

5. Michael Radelet, chap. 1 in this volume.

6. Steiker and Steiker, chap. 4 in this volume.

7. Death Penalty Information Center 2008 (available at http://www.deathpen-altyinfo.org/article.php?scid=6&did=110); of those, only 16 of the exonerations are based on DNA evidence. For a nuanced assessment of political influence of the DNA exonerations. see Simon Cole and Jay Aronson, chap. 2 in this volume.

8. Deborah Denno (chap. 6), Timothy Kaufman-Osborn (chap. 7), and Jür-gen Martschukat (chap. 8) in this volume. These authors disagree as to the likely impact of the lethal injection challenges, with Kaufman-Osborn expressing the most cautionary view. What is not contested, though, is that the temporary mor-atorium created by the Supreme Court's grant of certiorari on the lethal injection issue significantly reduced the number of persons executed in 2007 and 2008 and the temporary moratorium contributed to the downward trend in the num-ber of executions. Incidentally, the temporary moratorium also created a natural experiment that will afford social scientists an opportunity to test, once again, the deterrent effect of the death penalty—which will likely provide further fodder for both sides of the death penalty debates.

9. Von Drehle 2007. Available at ww.time.com/time/natina/arti-cle/0,8599,1695334,00.html.

10. Hood 2001; Schabas 2002; Neumayer 2006.

11. Hood 2001:333; see also Hood 2002.

12. Neumayer 2008:table 3.

13. Amnesty International 2006:17.

14. Hood 2001:350 (table 1). In December 2000, some 71 countries retained the death penalty for ordinary crimes.

15. Radelet, chap. 1 in this volume.

16. Steiker 2002.

17. Some commentators suggest that the "war on terrorism"—which has displaced the war on crime—will have the effect of reinvigorating the death pen-alty. I am skeptical of this argument and tend to believe that the terrorist acts of September 11, 2001, have, in fact, reduced the national appetite for capital pun-ishment in the context of ordinary crime. The contrast between terrorist acts and typical capital murders, from my observations, has undermined the strength of the death penalty appeal in cases of ordinary crime.

18. Radelet, chap. 1 in this volume. Naturally, there is significant debate in the United States whether life imprisonment without parole is more cruel a punish-ment than death. I will not address this normative question. As a factual matter, support for the death penalty decreases when respondents are presented with the alternative of life imprisonment without parole, and this sentencing option has been increasingly used in the United State since the late 1980s.

19. Cole and Aronson express reservation about the political influence of DNA and other scientific exonerations in chap. 2 in this volume. While I agree that the argument from science does not normatively resolve the death penalty

debate, I do believe that the fact of so many innocent persons having been sentenced to death has exerted a dampening effect on the national enthusiasm for the death penalty and will continue to do so.

20. Steiker and Steiker, chap. 4 in this volume.

21. A number of other comparative studies by criminologists and sociologists that do not use quantitative methods may also be insightful, but I focus here exclusively on those that use multiple regression analysis. Those other studies include Killias 1986; Wiechman, Kendall, and Bae 1990; and Neapolitan 2001.

22. This also seems unreliable because, as Neumayer observes, "a higher lagged homicide rate lowers the likelihood of abolition for all crimes, but not for ordinary crimes" (2008:264); yet one would think that the higher homicide rates should be more influential on abolition for ordinary crimes since homicide and violent crimes are ordinary crimes.

23. Ibid., 261.

24. Ibid., 242.

25. Ibid., 18, 261–62.

26. Ibid., 251.

27. Miethe, Lu, and Deibert 2005:121–22.

28. Ibid., 122.

29. Ibid., 123.

30. Ibid., 127.

31. Ibid., 123–24.

32. Ibid., 125.

33. Jacobs and Carmichael 2002:126.

34. Jacobs and Helms 1997.

35. Jacobs and Carmichael 2004.

36. Badinter 2000:24, 117.

37. Ibid., 228. Chirac, as presidential candidate in 1981, was personally opposed to the death penalty but did not make a big deal of his opposition. As a political matter, he proposed a referendum on the death penalty and stated that he would vote against it. But, again, he did not emphasize the death penalty issue.

38. Quoted in Badinter 2000:230.

39. Kengor 2007:81–82.

40. Quoted in "Policy Q&A: Death Penalty" 2004.

41. Obama 2006:58.

42. I recall participating at an event with Governor Ryan in Chicago after he had placed a moratorium on executions, and this was how he presented the matter.

43. Hood 2001:338.

44. Neumayer 2008:250.

45. Ibid.

46. Discussed so ably by Robin Wagner-Pacifici, chap. 9 in this volume.

47. Scott 1976, 1985, 1990; Thompson 1991.

48. Thompson 1991:188.

49. This question is raised poignantly by Peter Fitzpatrick, chap. 10 in this volume.

50. This point is ably discussed by Michael McCann and David Johnson, chap. 5 in this volume.

BIBLIOGRAPHY

Amnesty International. 2006. *April 2006 Report*. Available at http://web.amnesty. org (*AI Index ACT 50/005/2006*).

Anderson, Benedict. 2004. "In the World-Shadow of Bismarck and Nobel." *New Left Review* 28 (July–August 2004). Available at www.newleftreview. org/?view=2519.

Badinter, Robert. 2000. *L'Abolition*. Paris: Fayard.

Death Penalty Information Center. 2008. Available at www.deathpenaltyinfo.org

Drehle, David Von. 2007. "New Jersey: A Death Penalty Trend?" *Time*, Dec. 17, 2007.

Harcourt, Bernard E. 2007. "The Mentally Ill, Behind Bars." *New York Times*, Jan. 15, A15.

Hood, Roger. 2001. "Capital Punishment: A Global Perspective." *Punishment and Society* 3(3): 331–54.

Hood, Roger. 2002. *The Death Penalty: A Worldwide Perspective*. 3rd ed. Oxford: Oxford University Press, 2002.

Jacobs, David, and Jason T. Carmichael. 2002. "The Political Sociology of the Death Penalty: A Pooled Time-Series Analysis." *American Sociological Review* 67(1): 109–31.

Jacobs, David, and Jason T. Carmichael. 2004. "Ideology, Social Threat, and the Death Sentence: Capital Sentences across Time and Space." *Social Forces* 83(1): 249–78.

Jacobs, David, and Ronald Helms. 1997. "Testing Coercive Explanations for Order: The Determinants of Law Enforcement Strength over Time." *Social Forces* 75(4): 1361–92.

Kengor, Paul. 2007. *God and Hillary Clinton: A Spiritual Life*. New York: HarperCollins.

Killias, Martin. 1986. "Power Concentration, Legitimation Crisis and Penal Severity: A Comparative Perspective." *Annales Internationales de Criminologie* 24 (1986): 181–211.

Miethe, Terance D., Hong Lu, and Gini R. Deibert. 2005. "Cross-National Variability in Capital Punishment: Exploring the Sociopolitical Sources of Its Different Legal Status." *International Criminal Justice Review* 15(2): 115–30.

NAACP Legal Defense and Education Fund, Criminal Justice Project, *Death Row, U.S.A.* (winter 2008). Available at www.naacpidf.org/content/pdf/pubs/ drusa/DRUSA_winter_2008.pdf.

Neapolitan, Jerome L. 2001. "An Examination of Cross-National Variation in Punitiveness." *International Journal of Offender Therapy and Comparative Criminology* 45(6): 691–710.

Neumayer, Eric. 2008. "Death Penalty: The Political Foundations of the Global Trend toward Abolition." *Human Rights Review* 9(2): 241–68.

Obama, Barack. 2006. *The Audacity of Hope: Thoughts on Reclaiming the American Dream.* New York: Crown.

"Policy Q&A: Death Penalty." 2004. *Associated Press*, Jan. 25. Available at www.ontheissues.org/archive/AP_QA_2004-Crime.htm.

Sarat, Austin. 2001. *When the State Kills: Capital Punishment and the American Condition.* Princeton, N.J.: Princeton University Press.

Sarat, Austin, and Christian Boulanger (eds.). 2005. *The Cultural Lives of Capital Punishment: Comparative Perspectives.* Stanford, Calif.: Stanford University Press,.

Schabas, William A. 2002. *The Abolition of the Death Penalty in International Law.* 3rd ed. Cambridge: Cambridge University Press.

Scott, James C. 1976. *The Moral Economy of the Peasant: Subsistence and Rebellion in Southeast Asia.* New Haven, Conn.: Yale University Press.

Scott, James C. 1985. *Weapons of the Weak: Everyday Forms of Peasant Resistance.* New Haven, Conn.: Yale University Press.

Scott, James C. 1990. *Domination and the Arts of Resistance: The Hidden Transcript of Subordinate Groups.* New Haven, Conn.: Yale University Press.

Steiker, Carol S. 2002. "Capital Punishment and American Exceptionalism." *Oregon Law Review* 81 (2002): 97–130.

Thompson, E. P. 1991. *Customs in Common: Studies in Traditional Popular Culture.* New York: Penguin.

U.S. Department of Justice, Bureau of Justice Statistics. *Capital Punishment Statistics.* Available at www.ojp.usdoj.gov/bjs/cp.htm.

Wiechman, Dannies, Jerry Kendall, and Ronald Bae. 1990. "International Use of the Death Penalty." *International Journal of Comparative and Applied Criminal Justice* 14(2): 239–60.

Zimring, Franklin E. 2003. *The Contradictions of American Capital Punishment.* Oxford: Oxford University Press.

||||||||||||||||||||||||||||||||||||||||||||||||||||||

The Beginning of the End?

Carol S. Steiker and Jordan M. Steiker

Is nationwide abolition of capital punishment a realistic prospect in the United States? This question has taken on new urgency as the United States has become increasingly isolated in its retention and use of the death penalty. Most nations of the world—including many third-world countries—have abolished the death penalty, leaving the United States as the *only* Western industrialized nation in the world to formally retain the practice. Moreover, our retention is not merely formal: even recently, after death sentences and executions have declined for several years in a row, we have witnessed, on average, approximately one execution each week in the United States. The continued willingness of the United States to reject the growing consensus of the West that capital punishment constitutes a violation of human rights has transformed the death penalty from a dramatic but nonetheless tiny aspect of domestic criminal justice policy into a highly charged symbol of America's respect for its peer nations and for international human rights.

This new significance of America's death penalty practices is mirrored in recent decisions of the U.S. Supreme Court. In constitutionally outlawing the execution of offenders with mental retardation, the Court made pointed and controversial reference (albeit in a footnote) to the amicus brief filed on behalf of the European Union.[1] In its decision a few years later, outlawing the execution of juvenile offenders, the Court expanded on the significance of the actions of other constitutional democracies with respect to the death penalty.[2] Moreover, the Court noted that in the dozen years preceding its opinion, only six other countries had acknowledged executing juvenile offenders (the Democratic Republic of the Congo, Iran, Nigeria, Pakistan, Saudi Arabia, and Yemen) and that even *these* countries (hardly exemplars of constitutional democracy) had formally abandoned the practice, leaving the United States completely alone in the world.[3] The Court's legal analysis in these cases reflects what can no longer be denied as a political matter: our capital punishment practices now reach far beyond death row, affecting America's self-representation and moral authority in the world, at a time when that authority is already tarnished.

Perhaps in part because of these developments, the prospects for nationwide abolition have recently changed, looking brighter than they have at any time since the Supreme Court reinstated capital punishment in 1976,[4] after outlawing it (temporarily) in 1972 in its landmark decision in *Furman v. Georgia*.[5] A decade ago, in the waning years of the 1990s, had we been asked what the prospects were for nationwide abolition of the death penalty, our answer would have been clear and firm: not a chance. Not in our lifetimes or our children's lifetimes. Now, approaching 2010, our answer is different. We would not say that abolition is inevitable, but we *would* say that it is possible. In what follows, we explain our newfound cautious optimism about the prospects for nationwide abolition. We explain why abolition, if it occurs, will not follow the pattern that has been most common in the rest of the West. We then map what we believe is the most likely course that abolition would take in the United States. We conclude with consideration of the implications of our views for abolitionist lawyers and activists, including some reasons for trepidation about the possible road ahead.

The Road Less Traveled:
Why American Abolition Must Follow a Different Path

European abolition of capital punishment has been neither fast nor monolithic. Portugal and the Netherlands initiated nationwide abolition of the death penalty for ordinary crimes in the mid-nineteenth century, and the Scandinavian countries followed in the first few decades of the twentieth. Germany and Italy abolished capital punishment for ordinary crimes in their postwar constitutions after surrendering to the Allied powers in 1945. Most of Europe, however, had capital punishment on the books well into the second half of the twentieth century, though executions were generally on the decline. The phenomenon that we refer to as "European abolition" has largely been an accomplishment of the past 30–40 years, since the late 1960s. While there was often a gap between abolition for "ordinary" crimes and abolition for all crimes (including military crimes, treason, and the like), by the early 2000s virtually all of Europe had completely abolished the death penalty in all forms, and this abolition was almost always the consequence of legislative action (either through the passage or ordinary legislation or the legislature's approval of constitutional provisions). To be sure, in the vast majority of these moments of legislative abolition, there appeared to be strong popular support for *retention* of capital punishment, as there is in the United States today. How did Europe manage to abolish and retain its abolition in the face of such popular support for the death penalty? Perhaps there are lessons here for the United States to follow.

Unfortunately, the likely explanations for European abolition in the face of popular support for the death penalty offer few applicable lessons for the United States. First, European political institutions and political culture are more oriented toward technocratic expertise and less oriented toward populism than their American counterparts. European parliamentary democracies are more insulated against single-issue voters, and European leaders are more likely to view themselves as leading rather than following public opinion. The United States has both more populist political institutions (the primary system, as well as the tools of direct democracy such as referenda and initiatives) and more of a populist political culture, in which the duty of political representatives to be responsive to the electorate is beyond question, especially in the arena of criminal justice.

Second, Europe has created a regional method of preventing backsliding on the issue of capital punishment. The European Union (E.U.) requires all member states to adhere to Protocol No. 6 of the European Convention on Human Rights, abolishing the use of the death penalty in peacetime. This requirement has proven a powerful incentive for otherwise reluctant nations to abolish (Turkey, for example) and a powerful force against reinstatement. The rebuff by the E.U. of the Polish president's call for reinstatement of capital punishment is a recent case in point.[6]

In contrast, in the United States, the death penalty is often in play on the local, state, and even national level as a potent symbol of a candidate's "tough on crime" stance. In the late 1980s and early 1990s, candidates and potential candidates for president, especially Democrats, had to pay close attention to how their position on capital punishment would be perceived by the electorate (consider Michael Dukakis, Mario Cuomo, and Bill Clinton). Although recent presidential races have not emphasized capital punishment quite as much, it still remains a powerful symbol: in the most recent Republican primaries, Mike Huckabee ran an attack ad about Mitt Romney criticizing the Massachusetts governor for "new taxes" and "no executions."[7] The death penalty has been an equally or even more powerful issue in gubernatorial races, district attorney races, and the appointment of judges. Capital punishment has taken center stage in these various political arenas because of the high political salience that crime has had in American politics since at least 1968. The combination of the central importance of crime as a political issue and America's populist political culture has firmly established the death penalty as easily read shorthand for crime policy. Nothing even comes close to being as potent a symbol in this area.

To be sure, there are more than a handful of staunchly abolitionist states, which have mostly remained so during this more than three-decade period of law and order politics. Indeed, New York and New Jersey have recently joined the abolitionist club, bringing the total number of abolitionist states to 14—New York by failing to reinstate its death penalty after its highest court struck it down on (remediable) constitutional grounds and New Jersey by legislative abolition (the first since 1976). But it is clear that the very close votes that led to these results in New York and New Jersey would not be remotely close in states like Texas or Alabama (or many others); bills to abolish the death penalty in such jurisdictions are simply non-starters and will remain so for the foreseeable future.

It is this feature of American politics—our commitment to federalism, especially in the area of criminal justice—that most precludes the European path of legislative abolition. Other "federal" states, like Canada, Germany, and Australia, have abolished capital punishment, but the United States is unique in its ceding of complete sovereignty over local criminal justice matters to individual federal units. Moreover, within each state, local law enforcement officials—district attorneys popularly elected by county—exercise virtually complete autonomy in the bringing of capital charges. This diffusion of responsibility ensures that some local and state units will vociferously oppose abolition of capital punishment, essentially precluding *nationwide* abolition by legislation.

This is not to say that the use of capital punishment might not significantly diminish and become substantially more geographically marginalized, limited largely to a few active states or even to a few counties within those states. The strong regionalization of abolition and retention in the United States suggests that the abolitionist regions of the Northeast and West might influence the retentionist states within and near those regions to move toward abolition. But without a carrot or stick akin to member-ship in the European Union, regional influence will necessarily remain weak and always subject to the possibility that a high-profile murder will turn the tide the other way. Even staunchly abolitionist Massachusetts came within a single vote of reinstating the death penalty in 1997 when a 10-year-old boy was brutally sexually assaulted and murdered.[8] One need not believe that there is anything unique about American "violence" or "wild west culture" to see that European-style abolition—in which na-tional political elites abolished the death penalty for entire countries in one fell swoop, with the European Union serving as a backstop—is simply a road foreclosed by American politics.

Judicial Abolition Revisited:
Emerging Prospects for Constitutional Abolition of
the Death Penalty in the Modern Era

As argued in the preceding section, we believe that nationwide abolition of capital punishment in the United States is more likely to occur through constitutional litigation than through legislative decision. This is not to say that we regard judicial abolition as either imminent or inevitable. But the prospects for judicial abolition of the death penalty have increased enor-mously since the late 1990s. Recent Eighth Amendment decisions have substantially altered the Court's proportionality doctrine, and the newly emerging approach is more hospitable to a global assault against the death penalty than the relatively deferential framework that it replaced.

The shift in doctrine is attributable in part to substantial changes in practice and attitudes on the ground. In the wake of the "wrongful-con-viction" experience in Illinois, in which more than a dozen death-row in-mates were exonerated, the American death penalty has been subject to increased public scrutiny and criticism. Legislative energies have focused on preventing error in capital cases, and politicians and prosecutors have shown little enthusiasm for broadening the death penalty's reach. At the same time, the widespread (near-universal) adoption of life without pos-sibility of parole as an available punishment for murder has contributed to substantially fewer capital prosecutions and sentences. Executions have declined as well, as a result of a complicated interplay between judicial and political actors (a decline accelerated by the recent challenges to the prevailing protocol for lethal injections). Moreover, executions have been increasingly confined to a few outlier jurisdictions, notwithstanding large death-row populations throughout the country.

These changes on the ground have not gone unnoticed by the Supreme Court, and its recent decisions limiting the availability of the death penalty for persons with mental retardation and juveniles reflect a newfound skepticism about whether current capital statutes capture prevailing public attitudes.[9] Indeed, in both of those cases, the Court embraced the constitutional claim, despite the fact that more death penalty jurisdictions authorized than prohibited the challenged practice.[10] Moreover, the jurisprudential changes inspired by facts on the ground, in turn, give increased weight to those facts in assessing the constitutionality of the death penalty. In particular, the Court's emerging jurisprudence gives substantial and potentially decisive weight to nonlegislative indicia of contemporary support for the death penalty, including contemporary sentencing practices, elite opinion, and public polling data.[11] Recourse to such measures makes it plausible to argue that the death penalty is inconsistent with prevailing standards of decency, notwithstanding its widespread legislative authorization.

The increased prospects for judicial abolition of the death penalty are reflected not only in the Court's decisions altering its proportionality methodology but also in other recent opinions (though not majority decisions). Several Justices have voiced skepticism about the reliability of state death penalty practices—particularly in avoiding wrongful convictions[12]—as well as fear that current sentencing procedures do not ensure that the resulting death sentences reflect prevailing community values. These opinions show an unusual willingness to broaden the lens of scrutiny beyond the particular issues before the Court to the American death penalty itself. Several Justices have also indicated their willingness to address whether prolonged and seemingly indefinite incarceration on death row might separately violate the prohibition of cruel and unusual punishment.[13] Taken together, these opinions suggest that the prospect of judicial abolition is not solely a topic for academic journals but part of an ongoing conversation in the Court about the constitutional sustainability of capital punishment in the United States.

In this section, we discuss the "first-generation" global challenges to the death penalty advanced in *Furman* and rejected in subsequent cases. We then detail the stabilization of the death penalty as a constitutional matter in the quarter-century following *Furman* and turn to the current period of increased public and judicial scrutiny of capital punishment. In the following section, we look to the future and highlight the variables most salient to the possibility of judicial abolition.

First Generation of Constitutional Attacks on the American Death Penalty

The legal effort to end the death penalty began in the 1960s, as execution rates dropped and public support for the death penalty (as measured in public opinion polls) reached its all time low. Before the 1960s, judicial regulation of the death penalty was extraordinarily minimal. Apart from the Court's insistence in the Scottsboro cases that indigent capital defendants receive the benefit of counsel,[14] the Supreme Court had rarely found fault with state death penalty schemes. The Court's limited role in capital litigation was largely attributable to its limited role generally in policing state criminal processes. Before the Warren Court revolution constitutionalizing criminal procedure (by "incorporating" virtually all of the provisions in the Bill of Rights protecting criminal defendants and extending them to state criminal proceedings), federal judicial regulation of state criminal systems was limited to review of egregious due process violations, such as mob-dominated trials.[15]

Immediately after the Court incorporated and applied against the states the Eighth Amendment's prohibition against cruel and unusual punishment in 1962,[16] several Justices indicated their interest in addressing whether the penalty of death was excessive for the crime of rape.[17] Although the Court rejected the call for review, the dissent from denial of certiorari signaled an unprecedented willingness to view questions surrounding states' death penalty systems as *constitutional* ones.[18]

In part motivated by this signal, civil rights lawyers (there were few full-time death penalty lawyers at the time) began to attack the death penalty on multiple grounds. The center of activity was within the NAACP's Legal Defense Fund (LDF), which both represented death-sentenced inmates directly and provided resources and advice to local attorneys. For the LDF, a core concern about the death penalty was its racially discriminatory administration, particularly for the crime of rape (African Americans accounted for about 90 percent of the defendants executed nationwide for rape during the period 1930–1967, but for less than 50 percent of those executed for murder).[19] As part of its strategy, the LDF funded empirical research to document the influence of race in capital sentencing for rape. But the LDF also sought to attack the death penalty itself and launched a moratorium strategy to end executions in the country. As Michael Meltsner reflected in his account of LDF's larger strategy:

> The politics of abolition boiled down to this: for each year the United States went without executions, the more hollow would ring claims that the American people could not do without them; the longer death-row inmates waited, the greater their numbers, the more difficult it would be for the courts to permit the first execution. A successful moratorium strategy would create a death-row logjam.[20]

The most astonishing aspect of the moratorium strategy was that it worked—at least, measured against its goal of preventing executions. Just five years before the moratorium strategy was adopted, Alexander Bickel had lamented that the Court had not provided any foundation for invalidating the death penalty and that, as of the time of his writing, "barring spectacular extraneous events," the prospect of judicial abolition was "a generation or more away."[21] But in 1967, the moratorium strategy brought a temporary end to executions in the United States, inaugurating the longest period in American history (five months short of a decade) without state-sanctioned killings. As part of its moratorium strategy, LDF focused on inmates nearing execution (including white inmates) and raised all conceivable bases for challenging the underlying convictions and sentences. The Warren Court revolution provided ample ammunition for procedural claims unrelated to the death penalty, including the vast new reservoir of rights under the Fourth, Fifth, and Sixth Amendments now applicable against the states. But the LDF also pressed several distinctive claims relating solely to the implementation of the death penalty.

Those distinctive claims centered on the arbitrary and discriminatory application of the death penalty, as well as the absence of state safeguards to ensure even-handed and proportionate sentencing in capital cases. By the 1960s, only a fraction of persons convicted of death-eligible crimes (which often included murder, armed robbery, kidnapping, and rape) were sentenced to death. Moreover, virtually every state statute left the decision between death and imprisonment to the unbridled discretion of jurors. Despite the recommendation of the American Law Institute (via the Model Penal Code) to guide sentencer discretion in capital cases, typical capital jury instructions throughout the country simply invited jurors to decide whether to extend "mercy" in cases of conviction, without specifying the relevant considerations that either aggravated or mitigated the offense. Worse still, in most jurisdictions, the sentencing decision was made at the same time as the guilt-innocence verdict in a "unitary" proceeding. As a result, defendants were not able to make specific arguments going solely to the appropriate punishment, and jurors were often unaware of substantial mitigating facts at the time they determined the defendant's fate.

LDF lawyers argued that the rarity of death sentences and executions in light of broad death-eligibility under state statutes amounted to arbitrary punishment, especially given that there was no reason to believe—in the absence of any guidelines—that those sentenced to death and executed were truly the "worst" offenders. Along the same lines, LDF lawyers insisted that unitary proceedings prevented defendants from offering, and jurors from hearing, essential mitigating evidence that would make proportionate sentencing possible. Moreover, in jurisdictions where minority offenders were disproportionately represented on death row—the old South—the LDF sought to demonstrate that unbridled discretion was used in practice to punish African American defendants more severely. The LDF commissioned a study by Marvin Wolfgang and others to determine whether nonracial variables could account for the striking disparity in sentences between white and African American defendants convicted of rape in Arkansas over a 20-year period. On the basis of Wolfgang's finding that race almost certainly accounted for the disparity, the LDF challenged death sentences of African Americans sentenced to death for rape throughout the state.[22]

Two other legal challenges emerged from these same facts. First, death penalty opponents argued that prevailing death-qualification practices for capital jurors inappropriately skewed capital juries. In many states, jurors harboring any conscientious reservations about the death penalty could be struck for cause, with the result that jurors who served in capital cases were uncommonly pro-prosecution and pro-death penalty. This practice of culling jurors with reservations about the death penalty, it was argued, allowed for the death penalty to continue to be imposed even as public opinion drifted in the other direction. Second, more broadly and more fundamentally, the combined facts of death qualification and dwindling death sentences and executions offered a basis for arguing that the American death penalty no longer enjoyed popular support. Despite statutes authorizing imposition of the death penalty in most American states, and despite large (and growing) numbers of offenders eligible for it, few offenders were sentenced to death (or executed), and those few sentences were obtained by a selection process that insulated death verdicts from community values opposed to the punishment.

Within five years of the effective moratorium on the death penalty, all of these issues had made their way to the U.S. Supreme Court. In *Witherspoon v. Illinois*, the Court rejected stringent death-qualification rules, insisting that jurors with reservations about the death penalty could be struck for cause only if they were wholly unwilling to consider the death penalty as an available punishment.[23] In so doing, the Court left open whether death-qualification rules impermissibly bias determinations of guilt or innocence (on the ground that jurors without reservations about the death penalty are more prone to convict).

At the same time, in *Maxwell v. Bishop*, the Court declined to address the substantial claim of race discrimination based on Wolfgang's Arkansas study, even though it granted review in the case on other claims (relating to unguided discretion and the unitary determination of guilt and sentence) and despite an extensive opinion on the race discrimination issue in the Court of Appeals (authored by then-Circuit Judge Harry Blackmun).[24] The Court's refusal to address the race discrimination claim in *Maxwell* reflected the odd discord between the legal framework for evaluating the American death penalty and the political and cultural one. From LDF's perspective, the continuing availability of the death penalty for rape was unquestionably the product of racial discrimination. And yet when the dissent from denial in *Rudolph v. Alabama*[25] had raised the possibility that death was excessive punishment for rape (and thereby triggered federal constitutional regulation of the death penalty), it failed to mention race at all. Now, seven years later, the Court was willing to address the procedural defects of the death penalty—the absence of standards and the lack of bifurcated proceedings—but again was unwilling to confront its racial legacy, this time in the form of a statistical demonstration that the death penalty was available not for rape generally but only for the rape of a white victim by an African American defendant.

Thus, the LDF, dedicated to eradicating race-based inequality, was put in the position of attacking death penalty *procedures* instead of racially disproportionate outcomes, the existence of which no one seriously doubted. Indeed, six years after *Maxwell*, when the Court reviewed the new capital statutes enacted in the wake of *Furman*, the solicitor general of the United States, as it defended those statutes as an amicus, conceded that the Wolfgang study was "careful and comprehensive" and indicated that the U.S.

government did "not question its conclusion that during the 20 years in question, in southern states, there was discrimination in rape cases."[26]

Not only did the Court narrow the issues it would review in *Maxwell*, it ultimately refused to decide the standardless discretion and bifurcation claims in the case, even though fully briefed and argued, and, instead, reversed on *Witherspoon* grounds. The narrow basis of decision in *Maxwell* (the *Witherspoon* issue had not even been raised) suggested that the Court might be unwilling to insist on sweeping changes in states' administration of the death penalty. The Court avoided deciding yet another potentially broad issue when, in a case challenging the death penalty as disproportionate for armed robbery, the Court again reversed on a narrower ground (the failure of the trial court to inform the defendant of the consequences of his guilty plea).[27]

But the Court ultimately heard and decided the broader challenges to the American death penalty. The first results were not encouraging to the advocates of reform and abolition. In 1971, in *McGautha v. California*, the Court rejected the arguments (heard previously in *Maxwell*) that standardless discretion and unitary proceedings violated the Due Process Clause.[28] Surprisingly, though, the Court almost immediately agreed to rehear the standardless discretion claim under the Eighth Amendment's prohibition against cruel and unusual punishments. More fundamentally, the Court would also address the ultimate challenge—the claim that the death penalty was no longer consistent with American standards of decency and could therefore not be imposed under any circumstances. Both of these claims were captured by the common question in the four cases before the Court (all involving African American defendants and white victims): "Does the imposition and carrying out of the death penalty in these cases constitute cruel and unusual punishment in violation of the Eighth and Fourteenth Amendments?"[29]

As it addressed these claims in *Furman v. Georgia*, the Court was venturing into uncharted territory. As Bickel had observed a decade before, the Court had no significant body of doctrine supporting substantial restrictions on (much less abolition of) the American death penalty.[30] As radical as *Brown v. Board of Education* might have seemed when it was decided,[31] numerous decisions undermining the lawfulness of race-based decision-making in general and segregation in education in particular had been issued over several decades before the Court decisively rejected segregation in the public schools. As the Court approached these global challenges to the death penalty, it had never found the death penalty (or any term of

incarceration) disproportionate for a particular offense; it had never suggested that broadly embraced sentencing practices might be deemed cruel
or unusual; it had never questioned the power of states to include the death
penalty in their sentencing arsenals; and it had just rejected the notion that
due process requires standards in capital cases or bifurcated proceedings
to reduce the possibility of arbitrary sentencing. In the wake of the Court's
manifest reluctance to address substantial challenges to the death penalty,
its subsequent rejection of two such challenges in *McGautha* (a 6–3 decision) and changes to the composition of the Court that seemed unlikely to
advance the abolitionist cause (the replacement of Justices John Marshall
Harlan and Hugo Black by Justices William Rehnquist and Lewis Powell),
the prospects for judicial abolition of the death penalty seemed relatively
slim, notwithstanding the fact that the issue was on the Court's docket.

The resulting per curiam decision tersely offered an affirmative answer
to the question presented, concluding that "the imposition and carrying
out of the death penalty under the present statutes" constituted cruel and
unusual punishment.[32] The minimalism of the per curiam language reflected the absence of a consensus among the five Justices who joined the
result. All five wrote opinions explaining their rationale, and all seemed to
agree that the prevailing system was unconstitutionally arbitrary.[33] In light
of the breadth of death-eligibility in state capital schemes, the rarity of
death sentences and executions, and the lack of guidance to capital decisionmakers, the Court believed that the few offenders caught in the death
penalty net were not fairly selected but, instead, unfortunate winners in a
"ghoulish national lottery."[34] The Court did not find the punishment itself
constitutionally problematic but, rather, its rare and indiscriminate use
(indeed, few pages of the massive decision addressed fears of its *discriminatory*, or race-based, use).

That conclusion, though, presented a significant puzzle. If the Due
Process Clause did not require states to provide standards in capital cases,
how could the resulting (perhaps arbitrary) distribution or rare imposition of the death penalty violate the Eighth Amendment? Equally puzzling was the reluctance of any of the Justices in the majority (even the
two who had joined *McGautha*) to clarify the relation between *McGautha*
and *Furman*. In some respects, *Furman* seemed to suggest that the Eighth
Amendment demanded nonarbitrary *results* even though the Due Process
Clause commanded no particular set of capital *procedures*.

Viewed in this way, *Furman* could well have been the final word on
capital punishment. At the time of decision, the death penalty appeared

to be a dwindling practice. By invalidating virtually all then-existing schemes—which cast the death penalty net widely and afforded unbridled discretion to capital decisionmakers—the Court seemed to write the last chapter on the American death penalty. The Justices in the majority did not take the additional step of declaring the death penalty inconsistent with prevailing standards of decency; only Justices William Brennan and Thurgood Marshall were willing to defend that proposition in the face of widespread legislative authorization for the punishment.[35] But the Court seemed to adopt a narrow basis for decision that would have the broadest possible effect: it would disrupt the status quo, cast aside prevailing capital statutes, and shift to those states committed to the punishment the burden of solving a constitutional violation whose contours were difficult to discern in light of the lengthy, conflicting opinions of the Court.

Stabilization of American Death Penalty Law and Practice

When 35 states responded with new capital statutes, the Court was forced to clarify the reach of *Furman*. States had sought to resolve the problem of standardless discretion in two ways—either by removing sentencer discretion entirely (mandatory statutes) or by providing guidelines in the form of aggravating and mitigating circumstances. In some respects, the mandatory statutes held out greater promise of solving the problems *Furman* had identified, because they promised to increase the number of death sentences and executions, thus removing the concern that the sheer rarity of death sentences and executions rendered its few applications unnecessary and therefore cruel. Justice Byron White had made this argument most forcefully in *Furman*, stating that the death penalty could not be retained if it was used so rarely that it could not possibly achieve any of the penological purposes (deterrence or retribution) it purported to serve.[36]

The Court, though, rejected the mandatory statutes on the ground that they denied offenders individualized treatment, precluded sentencers from considering relevant mitigating factors, and departed significantly from long-standing American practices.[37] Having rejected prevailing death penalty schemes in the belief that the death penalty had essentially run its course in the United States, the Court was not willing to approve a "solution" to the problems it had identified that would radically expand the death penalty's scope and diminish protections for capital defendants. At the same time, in *Gregg v. Georgia*, the Court upheld the "guided

discretion" statutes on the ground that they held out the possibility of reducing arbitrariness in the administration of the death penalty.[38]

Gregg transformed *Furman* from a substantive decision to a procedural
one. At the time *Gregg* was decided, the Court had little empirical basis
for concluding that the death penalty was being administered in a nonarbitrary manner (in the intervening four years between *Furman* and *Gregg*)
or that sufficient death sentences and executions would be imposed to
ensure that those sentenced to death were not among a freakishly small
group. Instead, the intervening period had demolished the assumption in
Furman that prevailing death penalty statutes were the byproduct of an
outdated morality (and that the American people, if put to the choice,
were ready to abandon the punishment). Now that the states had adopted
the standards that had been sought (but rejected) in *McGautha*, the Court
was willing to allow state capital schemes to go forward. Whereas *Furman*
had condemned a *system* of capital punishment in light of its indefensible
structure and results, *Gregg* treated the constitutional question as relating
to the facial constitutionality of several statutes.

The Court's shift in focus is likely attributable to its miscalculation of
public sentiment at the time of *Furman*. The decline in public support for
the death penalty that had been captured in the 1966 Gallup Poll turned
out to be a short-lived phenomenon, and the rise in violent crime rates
and the resulting politicization of criminal justice issues over the next decade triggered a backlash to the Court's intervention. Rather than abolishing the death penalty, *Furman* in the end merely required a firm declaration of purpose and a revamping of sentencing instructions as precondi-
tions to the resumption of death sentencing and executions.

Over the next quarter-century, the American death penalty expanded
and its legal regulation stabilized. Executions resumed in 1977, and, despite extensive litigation surrounding state capital procedures, the Court
gave little indication that the practice of capital punishment was itself in
any constitutional jeopardy. Indeed, the Court seemed particularly skeptical of claims that specific capital practices were contrary to evolving standards of decency. In its first proportionality decision, the Court rejected
the death penalty for the crime of raping an adult women, but it did so
only because, at the time of the decision, Georgia was the sole jurisdiction
in the country that continued to permit such punishment for that crime.[39]
The Court made clear that its own role in proportionality cases should be
limited, emphasizing that "Eighth Amendment judgments should not be,
or appear to be, merely the subjective views of individual Justices" and

that "judgment should be informed by objective factors to the maximum possible extent."[40] Even though Georgia stood alone in permitting death for the crime of raping an adult woman, three Justices still would have rejected a blanket proportionality rule finding such punishment excessive.[41] Interestingly, the Court again said nothing about the racial taint of capital rape prosecutions and chose a case involving a white defendant to declare the practice unconstitutional.

Subsequent decisions confirmed the narrowness of proportionality protections. In the realm of noncapital offenses, the Court upheld a sentence of life imprisonment imposed against a nonviolent recidivist who had promised but failed to repair a refrigerator and had thereby obtained $120.75 by "false pretenses."[42] The Court also summarily reversed a lower court decision that had found constitutionally excessive a 40-year sentence imposed for possession with intent to distribute nine ounces of marijuana.[43] Although the Court found a life sentence without possibility of parole excessive as applied to a nonviolent recidivist who had written a "no account check,"[44] that decision turned out to be the sole noncapital case in which the Court has ever found a term of imprisonment to be constitutionally excessive. Indeed, the Court came close to adopting a blanket rule eliminating proportionality review of noncapital sentencing and, instead, adopted a highly deferential approach that will not even examine and compare state practices if, as a threshold matter, the Court does not regard the challenged punishment as "grossly excessive" in relation to the crime.[45]

On the capital side, the Court briefly extended constitutional protection to nontriggermen, holding that the death penalty could not be applied to a defendant who had neither killed, nor attempted to kill, nor intended to kill.[46] But the Court retreated from the holding only five years later, permitting nontriggermen to be eligible for death as long as they could be deemed substantial participants in a dangerous felony.[47] As a result, despite the Court's professed commitment to ensuring that the death penalty is reserved for the most culpable offenders, the Court refused to curtail states' efforts to hold offenders vicariously liable for killings they neither directly caused nor intended.

The most significant proportionality decisions, though, issued simultaneously in 1989, rejected limits on the execution of juveniles and persons with mental retardation. At the time of *Stanford v. Kentucky*, the decision involving juveniles, only 30 offenders were on death row for crimes committed under the age of 18 (just over 1 percent of the death row population), despite the large number of minors who commit homicides, including capital murder.[48] Elite, professional, and religious opinion overwhelmingly opposed the death penalty for juveniles, and dozens of political and social organizations filed briefs opposing the practice. Given the relatively low number of capital verdicts in relation to capital crimes, a strong argument supported the claim that prosecutors and juries rejected the punishment in practice, despite its statutory availability in 25 of the 37 death penalty states.

Justice Antonin Scalia's majority opinion, though, adopted a quite narrow approach to proportionality. In deciding whether the practice was so marginalized as to be deemed contrary to prevailing standards of decency, the Court conducted its "head count" of the states and suggested that no national consensus against a capital practice should be found where a majority of death penalty states embrace it statutorily.[49] The Court refused to include in its count of states opposed to the practice the 13 states without the death penalty on the ground that their opposition to the death penalty said nothing about their views concerning the *juvenile* death penalty.[50] The majority opinion also placed little weight on the infrequency of juvenile death sentences, suggesting that such infrequency reflected at most a societal consensus that the juvenile death penalty should *rarely* be imposed—not that it was in all cases excessive. Finally, the majority dismissed as irrelevant the sentencing practices of other countries, insisting that "it is *American* conceptions of decency that are dispositive" to constitutional analysis.[51]

In other parts of his opinion, writing for only a plurality, Scalia rejected the notion that Eighth Amendment analysis should include consideration of public opinion polls or professional and elite opinion.[52] According to him, recourse to such factors pulled the Court away from "objective" indicia of evolving standards, which he viewed as limited to statutes and jury determinations. Moreover, Scalia emphatically rejected that the Court had any independent role, apart from assessing objective criteria, in bringing its own judgment to bear on the proportionality of executing particular classes of offenders based on their reduced culpability. In his view, either "society has set its face against" a practice or it has not, and "[t]he audience for these arguments . . . is not this Court but the citizenry of the United States."[53]

In Justice Sandra Day O'Connor's decision upholding the death penalty for persons with mental retardation, *Penry v. Lynaugh*, the Court was wary of creating a bright-line exemption because of the varying degrees of mental retardation and "the diverse capacities and life experiences of mentally retarded persons."[54] The legislative support for the exemption was much weaker than in *Stanford*, because only two death penalty states (and the federal government) forbade the practice at the time.[55]

Taken together, these opinions represented a dramatic rejection of significant federal judicial regulation of the death penalty. The decisions upheld marginal practices and refused to connect the Court's proportionality doctrine to the larger concerns of its regulation of the death penalty— particularly its goal of narrowing the class of death-eligible offenders to ensure that the few offenders sentenced to death are truly more deserving than the much larger group of offenders who are spared. The Court also embraced a methodological approach to proportionality that requires enormous deference to state statutes, even in the absence of other evidence of broad popular support for the challenged practices.

The Court's reluctance to impose substantive limits on the death penalty was equally evident in its rejection of the most serious challenge to the death penalty post-*Furman*—the claim in *McCleskey v. Kemp* that the racially discriminatory imposition of the death penalty violated both the Eighth Amendment and the guarantee of equal protection.[56] Revisiting the strategy it had taken pre-*Furman* with the Wolfgang study, the LDF had commissioned a new study of capital cases in Georgia during the post-*Furman* period. The goal was to demonstrate that the statutory changes wrought by *Furman* had not removed the influence of race in capital decisionmaking. The resulting Baldus study, employing a rigorous multivariate regression analysis, concluded that race—particularly the race of the victim—played a powerful role in capital sentencing. Indeed, according to the study, cases involving white victims were over four times more likely to generate death sentences than ones with minority victims, and cases involving minority offenders and white victims were treated much more severely than any other racial combinations (controlling for nonracial variables).[57]

Warren McCleskey, an African American defendant in Georgia who had been convicted and sentenced to death for the murder of a white police officer, sought postconviction relief based on the Baldus study's finding of pervasive race discrimination in the administration of Georgia's death penalty. The Court assumed for purposes of the decision that the Baldus study was methodologically sound and that race appeared to influence some outcomes in capital cases. But the Court denied that such statistical evidence could support a finding of constitutional error or provide a basis for a constitutional remedy.

The Court rejected the equal protection claim on the ground that McCleskey was required to show that the decisionmakers in his case had acted with a racially discriminatory purpose, and it refused to shift the burden to the state on the basis of the Baldus findings.[58] More significantly, on the Eighth Amendment side, the Court appeared to reject McCleskey's claim precisely because it called into question the sustainability of the death penalty.[59] According to the Court, discretionary sentencing in capital cases is constitutionally required, and one possible, perhaps inevitable, consequence of such discretion is race-based decisionmaking.[60] But the Court was not prepared to insist that states eliminate any demonstrable influence of race, because to do so would doom capital punishment. Quoting from *Gregg*, the Court insisted that, as it interpreted the Eighth Amendment obligations of states regarding the death penalty, it must be guided by the principle that the "Constitution does not place totally unrealistic conditions on its use."[61] Whereas *Furman* had invalidated prevailing schemes because of its fear of arbitrary sentencing, *McCleskey* rejected the Eighth Amendment claim despite seeming proof of something worse— invidious race-based discrimination.

McCleskey seemed like the death knell to global challenges to the death penalty, particularly challenges rooted in claims of its arbitrary or discriminatory administration. Like *Gregg*, *McCleskey* read *Furman* to require *procedural* safeguards aimed at preventing arbitrary outcomes but not to prohibit those outcomes themselves. Moreover, *McCleskey* made clear that if a constitutional claim and the continued implementation of the death penalty could not be reconciled, it was the claim and not the death penalty that must be rejected.

In the decade after *McCleskey*, the death penalty became increasingly entrenched as a national practice. Executions climbed from about 20 per year (nationwide) in the late 1980s to about 80 per year in the late 1990s. Notwithstanding the increase in executions, the national death-row population doubled between the years 1985 (1,591) and 1996 (3,219). Death-sentencing rates increased as well, as the per capita rate for death sentences reached its modern-era high in the mid-1990s. There were few signs of popular discontent with capital punishment, and the most significant legislative development during this period was federal statutory reform of federal habeas corpus. In response to the bombing in Oklahoma City, Congress coupled antiterrorism initiatives with unprecedented restrictions on the right of state prisoners to litigate federal constitutional claims in federal court.[62] Although the legislation applied to inmates convicted of both capital and noncapital crimes, federal habeas litigation had become increasingly focused on capital cases, in part because only death-sentenced inmates are entitled to counsel as a matter of right. The avowed goal of the legislation, reflected in its title "The Antiterrorism and Effective Death Penalty Act," was to reduce the time between capital sentences and executions, and death penalty opponents feared that executions would accelerate considerably over the ensuing decade. Moreover, with the retirements of Justices Brennan, Marshall, and Blackmun, the Court lost its three most reliable opponents to the death penalty (with Justice Blackmun announcing, just before his retirement, that he would no longer "tinker with the machinery of death" and thus would follow the practice of Justices Brennan and Marshall in voting to reverse all death sentences coming to the Court).[63]

At this moment in U.S. history, the prospect of abolition of the death penalty, either politically or constitutionally, seemed extraordinarily remote. The last global challenges to the punishment appeared to have been set aside, death sentences and executions were on the rise, and the political climate favored less rather than more regulation of the death penalty process. Like Bickel 35 years earlier, informed observers would have looked at this landscape and undoubtedly concluded that judicial abolition was at least a generation or more away—with Bickel's prescient caveat—"barring spectacular extraneous events."[64]

A New Era of Public and Judicial Scrutiny of Capital Punishment

The second reformist moment in the modern era was triggered by just the sort of spectacular extraneous event Bickel might have imagined: the discovery of numerous wrongfully convicted inmates on a state's death row. The issue emerged as the efforts of defense lawyers and journalists uncovered numerous innocents who had been erroneously sentenced to death in Illinois. The sheer number of innocent inmates discovered—13—was striking enough, especially in light of the fact that Illinois had executed only 12 inmates in the modern era. But as the story unfolded, it became apparent that the Illinois death penalty system was seriously malfunctioning. Prosecutors had engaged in misconduct in several of the cases, and the trial representation afforded many of the inmates had been abysmal. In one case, the death-sentenced inmate (Anthony Porter) had come perilously close to execution before he received a stay of execution unrelated to his claim of actual innocence; journalism students from Northwestern University subsequently discovered the actual perpetrator, who confessed to the crime.[65]

Governor George Ryan of Illinois, a Republican who had long supported the death penalty, became a national figure as he insisted that these events required exhaustive scrutiny of the Illinois capital system. Ryan issued a moratorium on executions pending the outcome of such study, and ultimately he commuted the sentences of all 167 death-row inmates.[66] At the same time, more sophisticated techniques for analyzing DNA evidence were employed to review convictions in many capital and noncapital cases throughout the country.[67] These efforts led to numerous exonerations and to a greater appreciation of the fallibility of our criminal justice system. Although the public was likely aware in the abstract of the imperfections of human institutions of justice, the experience in Illinois and the DNA revolution attached scores of faces and stories to the underlying problems.

As the number of exonerated death-sentenced inmates both within and outside Illinois grew, the public mood toward capital punishment palpably shifted. Legislative energies shifted from expanding the death penalty and speeding executions to avoiding error. In many death penalty states, particularly outside of the South, the death penalty had served a primarily symbolic function, and even as the death penalty stabilized during the 1980s and 1990s, these jurisdictions appeared to have little appetite for actual executions.[68] In light of the events in Illinois and nationally, many of these jurisdictions began to critically examine their death penalty practices, and issues which had long disappeared from national dialogue—such as race discrimination, quality of counsel in capital cases, the need for moratoria on executions pending further study, and even abolition—emerged as genuine topics of discussion.

Two years after Ryan imposed a moratorium on executions in Illinois, a major proportionality challenge returned to the Court—whether the Eighth Amendment forbids the execution of persons with mental retardation.[69] The decision of the Court in *Atkins* to revisit its 1989 *Penry* decision within such a relatively short period (13 years) seemed unusual, but the case was strengthened by the flurry of legislative activity in the wake of that decision. Sixteen additional states banned the execution of persons with mental retardation. Together with Georgia and Maryland, which had banned the practice just before the decision in *Penry*, now 18 states statutorily prohibited executing persons with mental retardation.[70] The legislative activity pre- and post-*Penry* gave the strong impression that when legislators focused on the issue, they were unwilling to endorse the practice. No statutes explicitly authorized the practice, and few states or politicians seemed adamant in their support. Indeed, in Texas, the governor had even denied that the state allowed the practice, despite the fact that Texas led the nation in the number of persons with mental retardation it had executed in the modern era (his quote appeared in a footnote to the Court's opinion).[71] The fact that many of the prohibiting states were active death penalty states—including Georgia, Arkansas, Florida, and Missouri—further suggested that there was little genuine support for the practice, as well as the fact that only five such executions had occurred nationwide since *Penry*.[72]

In light of these unusual circumstances, the resulting 6–3 decision invalidating the death penalty for persons with mental retardation might seem relatively modest. Although a majority of death penalty states had not yet abolished the practice, the Court emphasized that it was not relying on the sheer number of prohibiting states (18) as much as the "consistency of the direction of change."[73] The Court also explicitly cast doubt on whether its reversal of *Penry* justified revisiting its decision upholding the death penalty for juveniles. Although the number of prohibiting states was almost identical in each context, the "shift" apparent with respect to mental retardation was not evident with juveniles, because only two states had raised the threshold age for execution during the same 13-year period.[74]

But the opinion seemed to collide with the Court's prior methodological approach in proportionality cases, particularly the approach announced and defended by Justice Scalia in *Stanford*. In a lengthy footnote supporting its conclusion of a national consensus, the Court referred to expert opinion (citing amicus briefs filed by the American Psychological Association and the American Association for Mental Retardation), religious opinion (citing an amicus brief filed on behalf of diverse religious communities), and world opinion (citing an amicus brief filed by the European Union).[75] The Court also cited polling data showing "a widespread consensus among Americans" rejecting the practice.[76]

Without the footnote, the decision could have been viewed as an unusual but perhaps defensible read of legislative opinion, in which the Court was unwilling to defer to a majority of death penalty states because there was little to suggest that they had truly considered the issue. On this view, the recent prohibiting states, though a numerical minority, counted more than the permissive states, given that few of the permissive states had actually engaged in the practice or explicitly endorsed it.

The footnote, though, suggested something far more radical: that state statutes might not provide the best window into prevailing standards of decency. Such an approach would give the Court more latitude to reject practices that are widely authorized by states as unconstitutional under the Eighth Amendment. Public, elite, and world opinion will not always prevail in state legislative chambers, and the Court's willingness to treat such opinions as probative or perhaps dispositive in gauging emerging values would considerably broaden the Court's Eighth Amendment enforcement role. Indeed, by privileging elite, world, and public opinion over prevailing statutes, it is not difficult to construct a decision abolishing the death penalty altogether (especially if public opinion is gauged in part by willingness to sentence offenders to death and to carry out executions).

The dissenting Justices immediately recognized the potential importance of the footnote and chastised the majority for consulting such sources in its proportionality analysis. Chief Justice Rehnquist, although dissatisfied with the Court's reading of the state statutes, wrote separately "to call attention to the defects in the Court's decision to place weight on foreign laws, the views of professional and religious organizations, and opinion polls in reaching its conclusion."[77] Justice Scalia likewise rejected the Court's analysis of state legislation (particularly the decision to elevate a recent trend into a permanent rule)[78] but also devoted his most pointed responses to the potential shift in methodology. Scalia had previously argued that the Eighth Amendment does not contain a proportionality guarantee at all and that Eighth Amendment analysis should be limited to whether particular punishments are invariably cruel rather than whether a permissible punishment is inappropriate for certain offenses or offenders. On this ground, he would have dissented from the two decisions, *Coker v. Georgia* and *Enmund v. Florida*,[79] finding the death penalty disproportionate for rapists and nontriggermen. But he regarded the Court's reasoning in *Atkins* as beyond the pale, to the point of bestowing a new award for the analysis in the footnote: "[T]he Prize for the Court's Most Feeble Effort to fabricate 'national consensus' must go to its appeal (deservedly relegated to a footnote) to the views of assorted professional and religious organizations, members of the so-called 'world community,' and respondents to opinion polls."[80] Looking at the Court's death penalty jurisprudence more broadly, Scalia lamented the increased role for the Court in policing its reach, even as he distanced himself somewhat from the death penalty itself: "There is something to be said for popular abolition of the death penalty; there is nothing to be said for its incremental abolition by this Court."[81]

By itself, *Atkins* seemed a modest decision with potentially destabilizing language. But several other opinions have suggested a new level of critical scrutiny of the American death penalty. Just four days after *At-kins*, the Court held in *Ring v. Arizona* that jurors—not judges—must find the facts that render defendants eligible for death.[82] The ruling itself was unsurprising—it was the logical consequence of the Court's newfound dedication to jury-sentencing rights under the Sixth Amendment inaugurated by *Apprendi v. New Jersey*.[83] Although *Apprendi* had caused extraordinary disruption in the noncapital context by calling into question judge-administered sentencing guideline schemes, *Ring* would affect only a small number of death penalty jurisdictions. The surprise in *Ring* was Justice Stephen Breyer's concurring opinion. Breyer, who had helped draft the Federal Sentencing Guidelines and dissented in *Apprendi*, wrote separately in support of a broader jury right in capital cases—a right not only to a jury determination of facts relating to death-eligibility crimes but also to a jury determination of the ultimate question whether an offender lives or dies.[84]

Breyer's little-noted opinion offers an encompassing critique of the American death penalty. He notes at the outset that deterrence and incapacitation rationales for the death penalty are difficult to support in light of available empirical evidence.[85] He then observes the "continued division of opinion as to whether capital punishment is in all circumstances, as currently administered, 'cruel and unusual.'"[86] In light of these substantial doubts about the appropriateness of the death penalty, Breyer insists that there must be a continuing connection between public values and death verdicts. In his view, a process that permits "a single governmental official"—a judge—to make the ultimate death penalty decision inappropriately severs that connection.[87]

The most striking aspect of Breyer's opinion is his catalogue of the perceived flaws of the American death penalty—its lack of reliability (citing the events in Illinois), its arbitrary and discriminatory imposition (citing the Baldus study), its cruelty in the delays between sentence and execution, and the inadequacy of defense counsel in capital cases.[88] He also notes that other nations increasingly have abandoned the death penalty altogether.[89]

Breyer's effort to connect the Sixth Amendment jury question to the broader sustainability of capital punishment undermines the stability of the death penalty under the Court's Eighth Amendment jurisprudence. It treats the Eighth Amendment question regarding the constitutionality of the American death penalty as an open and contingent one—depending on its "current administration"—and it provides reasons to believe that the prevailing implementation is deeply flawed. Together with *Atkins*, Breyer's opinion strongly suggests that the constitutionality of the death penalty will not turn solely on whether the punishment remains available on the books.

Despite the footnote in *Atkins* distinguishing the controversy surrounding the execution of juvenile offenders, just three Terms later, in *Roper v. Simmons*, the Court decided to revisit *Stanford*.[90] As that footnote had suggested, the problem for the claim was that little had changed legislatively during the intervening 15 years. At the time of *Stanford*, 12 states and the federal government rejected the death penalty for persons under the age of 18. By 2005, only five of the permissive states had since prohibited the practice (four by legislation, one through judicial decision). Thus, a majority of death penalty jurisdictions still authorized the execution of juveniles, and there was no overwhelming or impressive shift toward prohibition comparable to *Atkins*.

Nonetheless, the Court in *Simmons* invalidated the death penalty for juveniles and in so doing prominently embraced the methodological changes to proportionality analysis that been relegated to a footnote in *Atkins*. Whereas *Stanford* had insisted on a limited role for the Court in discerning evolving standards of decency, in *Simmons* the Court affirmed the importance of exercising its "own independent judgment" as to proportionality.[91] As it exercised this judgment, the Court relied heavily on expert opinion regarding the mental and emotional development of juveniles, including their underdeveloped sense of responsibility, their vulnerability to negative influences, and their fluid personality traits.[92] This science supported the Court's view of the invariably diminished culpability of juvenile offenders. The Court also found "confirmation" for its judgment in the fact that the United States was alone among nations in the world in giving official sanction to the execution of juveniles.[93] The offhand reference to world opinion (within a footnote) in *Atkins* became a separate full section of the opinion in *Simmons*—equal in length to its discussion of state legislative and sentencing practice. The Court also explicitly defended its canvassing of international opinion and practice, on the ground that "the express affirmation of certain fundamental rights by other nations and peoples" underscores the "centrality" of those rights within our own culture.[94]

Like *Atkins*, *Simmons* invalidated a death penalty practice notwithstanding its authorization by a majority of death penalty states. It focused less on what states declared legislatively and more on what states actually did; the Court highlighted the infrequency of the practice—with only six states executing juveniles during the post-*Stanford* interval and only three states doing so in the 10 years before its decision.[95]

More generally, *Simmons*'s amplification of *Atkins* provides a blueprint for the judicial abolition of capital punishment in the United States. It privileges nonlegislative criteria that overwhelmingly cut against the continued use of the death penalty. The increasing rarity of death sentences and executions supports the claim that the statutes on the books do not reflect genuine public support for the punishment (especially in light of the broad net of death-eligibility crimes cast in the post-*Furman* statutes). Elite and professional opinion—from prominent religious groups, the American Bar Association, criminologists, and others—generally rejects the notion that the death penalty serves any important penological purposes, especially compared with the alternative of lengthy incarceration. World opinion increasingly condemns the death penalty as contrary to basic human rights.

Like all blueprints, though, the one in *Simmons* does not ensure that the (abolitionist) house will be built. *Simmons* was decided by the narrowest of margins, and its own author, Justice Anthony Kennedy, surely did not regard his opinion as casting doubt on the death penalty generally. The execution of juveniles, like the execution of individuals with mental retardation, was a more marginal practice than the American death penalty as a whole. Popular support for capital punishment as a general practice still remains strong, though perhaps not as strong or unconflicted as it was a decade ago.

But the fact that Justice Kennedy did not intend to initiate a discussion of the broader constitutionality of the death penalty does not mean that all of his colleagues are similarly disinclined. The most recent judicial attention to the death penalty emerged in the most unlikely of cases. In 2006, in *Kansas v. Marsh*,[96] the Court agreed to decide a highly technical issue from a relatively unimportant death penalty state—whether Kansas's death penalty statute inappropriately required the jury to impose death when aggravating and mitigating factors were in equipoise (instead of requiring aggravating factors to affirmatively "outweigh" mitigating ones).[97] At the time the case reached the Court, Kansas had a death-row population less than 10 and had not executed any inmates in over 40 years. Moreover, given that the Kansas Supreme Court had ruled in favor of the death-sentenced inmate, the Court was in the unusual position of deciding whether a state court was unnecessarily stringent in restricting the state's own death penalty apparatus.

The Court's resulting majority opinion was unremarkable. Justice Clarence Thomas, writing for the Court, relied on previous cases that permit the death penalty to be imposed absent an affirmative declaration by the jury that the defendant deserves to die. But Justice David Souter's dissent, joined by three other Justices, offers a remarkable and sustained critique of the American death penalty[98]—a critique only tangentially related to the narrow doctrinal issue presented in the case. Souter argues that the uncovering of pervasive error in capital cases—particularly in Illinois—amounts to "a new body of fact [that] must be accounted for in deciding what, in practical terms, the Eighth Amendment guarantees should tolerate."[99] His dissent recounts the experience in Illinois, discusses the role of DNA in identifying innocents on death row, and offers statistics about the number of "exonerated" inmates in recent years.[100] In light of this newfound error in the nation's system of capital punishment, Souter urges the Court to reject state capital procedures, such as the Kansas rule permitting the imposition of death in close cases, which unnecessarily increase the risk of error in capital cases. According to Souter, the events in Illinois and elsewhere have ushered in a "period of new empirical argument about how 'death is different.'"[101]

Souter's opinion seems self-consciously designed to bring the public debate about the reliability of the U.S. death penalty into the Court's jurisprudence. Along with three other Justices, Souter appears to travel down the same path, though not as far, that led Blackmun to declare that he would no longer tinker with the machinery of death. Instead of declaring the American death penalty doomed, these four Justices would shift the burden of proof to the states, requiring states to abandon procedures (previously embraced) that could potentially lead to additional wrongful convictions.

Perhaps most tellingly, Justice Souter's opinion declares, in Mark Anthony fashion, that "it is far too soon for any generalization about the soundness of capital sentencing across the country."[102] The need to disclaim any *immediate* need for this larger inquiry serves to highlight that such an inquiry could well become necessary at some future time. In this respect, the *Marsh* dissent is no less an invitation to future global challenges to the death penalty than the opinion of three Justices, more than 40 years before, lamenting the Court's refusal to decide whether the death penalty was disproportionate for the crime of rape. It signals that a substantial portion of the Court has increasingly grave doubts about the constitutionality of the death penalty and that they are willing—indeed, inclined—to evaluate specific claims identifying defects in state schemes in light of the broader goals and commitments of the federal constitutional regulation of the death penalty.

Like the footnote from *Atkins*, the dissenting opinion in *Marsh* received considerable attention from Justice Scalia, who recognized its far-reaching implications and wrote separately in response. Relying on the work of others, Scalia challenges the empirical claim about the extensiveness of error in capital cases. In his view, the number of "true" exonerations (where the defendant was actually "innocent" as opposed to "not guilty" or freed by legal error) is much smaller than Justice Souter's sources claim.[103] Moreover, Justice Scalia finds comfort in the exoneration of many innocents *before* execution, suggesting that the discovery of error coupled with the absence of any demonstrable wrongful execution in the modern era indicates the health rather than the pathology of the current system.[104]

But Scalia's main concern is that the *Marsh* dissent is part of a larger project to impugn the American death penalty before the world. Despite the absence of any citation to world opinion or practice in the dissent, Scalia uses his response to criticize international opponents of the death penalty in the United States, accusing them of "sanctimonious criticism" because "most of the countries to which these finger-waggers belong had the death penalty themselves until recently—and indeed, many of them would still have it if the democratic will prevailed."[105] Justice Scalia's opinion, with its gratuitous reference to international opponents of the death penalty, suggests that the members of the Court view themselves as caught in a larger debate about the wisdom and sustainability of capital punishment. In the wake of *Atkins* and *Simmons*, Scalia is also acutely aware that the fate of the U.S. death penalty might turn on U.S. responsiveness to international (particularly European) pressure. More fundamentally, that the Court could erupt so violently in a case about a mundane Kansas sentencing instruction indicates that the period of stabilization has ended and that the future chapters of the federal constitutional regulation of the death penalty remain to be written.

The most recent call for global reconsideration of the death penalty in the United States emerged in response to litigation over the administration of lethal injection. Starting in the early 2000s, numerous defendants in more than a dozen states challenged prevailing lethal injection protocols on the ground that they entailed an unnecessary risk of pain. Virtually every state adopted lethal injection as the central mode of execution since the early 1980s, and most of these states unreflectively embraced the three-drug protocol developed in Oklahoma in 1977. The major objection

to the protocol concerns the possibility that a defendant will be insuf-
ficiently sedated, a concern heightened by the unwillingness of medical
professionals to participate in executions; moreover, the frequency of
insufficient sedation is hard to establish because the second drug in the
standard protocol—pancuronium bromide—paralyzes the muscles of the
condemned and thereby masks any symptoms of pain. Over the past five
years, lower state and federal courts had responded quite differently to
the federal constitutional challenges spawned by these concerns, with the
result that executions halted in some states but continued without inter-
ruption in others. The Supreme Court agreed to hear the challenge and
effectively imposed a nationwide moratorium on executions during the
almost seven-month interval between its grant of certiorari in September
2007 and its decision in *Baze v. Rees* rejecting the claim in the context of a
challenge to Kentucky's execution protocol.

Although the execution-method challenge in *Baze* appeared modest in
its own terms—the petitioners sought not the end of lethal injection but
additional safeguards in the administration of lethal injection—the case
attracted widespread attention because of its broader practical and symbolic importance. On the practical level, the Court's decision to hear the
claim ushered in the longest period without executions in more than two
decades, and this moratorium naturally invited reflections about the current status and future prospects of the U.S. death penalty, especially given
the noticeable decline in death sentences and executions since 1999. The
case also brought to light some of the prevailing, though often obscured,
contradictions surrounding American capital punishment. In particular,
the case highlighted the difficulty of retaining the retributivist roots of the
death penalty—which tolerate and may even celebrate significant suffering
on the part of the offender to fulfill the penalty's retributivist purpose—
while also embracing a more modern aversion to the visible destruction
of the body or the purposeful infliction of physical pain.

The Court's rejection of the claim was as modest as the claim itself.
Writing for a plurality, Chief Justice Roberts did not disclaim any right
of inmates to avoid severe pain but concluded only that the petitioners
had not carried their burden of establishing an intolerable risk of serious
harm or the availability of a feasible, readily implementable alternative to
the challenged protocol that substantially decreased the prevailing risk.

Justice Stevens, in a stunning concurrence, declared that "instead
of ending the controversy" over lethal injection methods, the case "will

generate debate not only about the constitutionality of the three-drug protocol . . . but also about the justification for the death penalty itself." Stevens, who had coauthored the opinion reviving the death penalty in *Gregg* 22 years before, then declared his opposition to the death penalty as currently administered in the United States. Like Breyer in *Ring*, Stevens pointed to the troubling persistence of discrimination and arbitrariness in the implementation of the death penalty. Like Souter in *Marsh*, Stevens emphasized the risk of wrongful convictions. Stevens also found few social gains achieved under our current system. He found the retributive value weakened by our countervailing societal commitment to reducing pain; he cited the absence of any compelling proof of a deterrent effect (above and beyond the threat of lengthy imprisonment); and he saw little incapacitation value given the widespread availability of life without possibility of parole as an alternative to death. Ultimately, Stevens borrowed the words of White, who had declared in *Furman* that the death penalty was unconstitutional because it had ceased to serve the social purposes it was designed to achieve:

> I have relied on my own experience in reaching the conclusion that the imposition of the death penalty represents "the pointless and needless extinction of life with only marginal contributions to any discernible social or public purposes. A penalty with such negligible returns to the State is patently excessive and cruel and unusual punishment violative of the Eighth Amendment."[106]

Notwithstanding this conclusion, Stevens did not believe his newly declared view regarding the constitutionality of the death penalty justified a "refusal to respect precedents that remain part of our law."[107] But he also indicated his belief that the current embrace of the death penalty by states, Congress, and the Court, is attributable to "habit and inattention" rather than a thorough assessment of its true costs and benefits.[108] In this respect he has obviously left open the door to joining a decision revisiting the constitutionality of the death penalty. And while Blackmun declared his opposition to the death penalty at a time when it had become constitutionally stable, Stevens has done so at a time of increasing public scrutiny and while sitting on a Court that includes three other Justices who have voiced comparable, though not as emphatic, concerns about the sustainability of capital punishment.

Implications and Anxieties

The recent changes detailed in this chapter—in the Supreme Court's Eighth Amendment jurisprudence, the views of a substantial minority of the Justices, and public attitudes more generally—create a moment of possibility for constitutional change in the status of capital punishment. This moment bears some resemblance to the period preceding *Furman*: public attitudes about the death penalty are more skeptical than they have been in years, the use of capital punishment has been steadily declining for close to a decade, international attitudes are turning against the practice, and the Supreme Court seems willing to at least consider sweeping constitutional challenges. "Similar" is not the same as "identical": public support for the death penalty in the abstract remains stronger today than it was in the 1960s, and it seems unlikely that executions will reach the zero mark maintained for more than five years by the moratorium strategy of the LDF lawyers in the late 1960s and early 1970s. But today, international attitudes and practices are much more heavily weighted and passionately aligned against capital punishment, and the Supreme Court has more clearly marked the criteria relevant to its constitutional methodology.

The breadth of these criteria suggests that a much wider array of data is now relevant to the death penalty's constitutional future and that some combination of various forms of movement toward abolition might be held to constitute a new consensus against the practice, even while a majority of states still officially authorize it. On the most "objective" end of the scale—which used to include only legislative enactments and jury verdicts—the Court now will consider legislative "movement" that does not result in formal law-making. For example, in support of its finding of a new consensus, the *Atkins* Court noted one state in which the legislature had acted to exempt those with mental retardation from execution even though the bill was vetoed by the governor, and two other states in which such bills passed a single house of a bicameral legislature.[109] Similar activity has occurred in recent years on the abolitionist front: the New Hampshire legislature passed legislation to abolish the death penalty in 2000, only to have it vetoed by Governor Jeanne Shaheen,[110] and the New York legislature failed to reinstate the death penalty after it was invalidated (on technical, easily rectified grounds) by the state's highest court.[111] Other possible measures of legislative "movement" toward abolition are surely possible, such as the approval of abolitionist legislation by a legislative committee (or rejection of reinstatement). One could count how close legislative votes are (and compare the relative counts over time). A recent news article stressed that an abolitionist bill in (retentionist) Maryland failed by a single vote in a key legislative committee,[112] while in (abolitionist) Massachusetts the full legislative vote against reinstating the death moved from being as close as a single vote in 1997 to an overwhelming majority (99–53) against Governor Romney's "foolproof" death penalty bill in 2005.[113]

Moreover, formal legislative enactments or partial legislative movement (of the kinds described above) toward limitations on the scope of the death penalty, short of total abolition, might also count as evidence of an emerging consensus against capital punishment. So might legislative calls for studies or moratoria on various aspects of the death penalty. Such scaling back of the scope of the death penalty or other "reform" movements by legislatures may be less persuasive evidence of an emerging consensus than more wholesale abolitionist initiatives because limitations on scope, studies, and moratoria are often proposed or passed with an eye toward ameliorating—and thus preserving—capital punishment. Nonetheless, such actions do reflect a discomfort with current practices and might identify or call greater attention to problems (such as disparate racial impacts, inadequate defense representation, unreliable forensic practices, or questionable execution protocols) that the proposed "reforms" may fail to correct.

Similar refinements can be made to the second, "jury verdicts" leg of the Court's traditional analysis. In capital cases, the Court has traditionally looked not only to actual jury verdicts returned but also to the number of capital prosecutions actually brought and to the number of executions actually carried out. All three of these indicia (charges, sentences, and executions) are currently consistently falling, and a prolonged period of such decline may make up for a paucity of formal legislative abolition. Moreover, there is reason to believe that federal capital juries are becoming more reluctant to return death sentences, especially juries in traditionally abolitionist jurisdictions, [114] so much so that some federal judges in New York have deemed pursuing federal capital sentences there a waste of time and money.[115] It is also possible to offer a qualitative, as well as a quantitative, account of capital jury verdicts. When "slam dunk" capital trials result in life sentences, the collective head scratching that is reported in the local media is also evidence of changing times. In Harris County, Texas—the most active death penalty jurisdiction in the United States—a jury's recent rejection of a death sentence for an illegal immigrant with a prior criminal record who shot a police officer in the back stunned the local community, leading to a sub-headline reading: "Was it result of good lawyering or a change in political climate?"[116]

To be sure, "the numbers"—that is, the rates of capital charges, sentences, and executions—may themselves be further influenced by continuing constitutional refinement of the scope of capital punishment, short of total abolition. Although the constitutional invalidation of capital punishment for juvenile offenders has likely had little effect on overall charging, sentencing, or execution rates (given the small numbers of juveniles involved in capital processes beforehand), the invalidation of capital punishment for offenders with mental retardation has probably played a more substantial role in recent declines, given the degree of post-*Atkins* litigation that has ensued, challenging individual executions and generally driving up the cost (in both time and resources) of capital prosecutions. Should the Supreme Court (or a substantial number of state or lower federal courts) conclude that the *Atkins* methodology calls for the invalidation of capital punishment for those with severe mental illness (as distinct from mental retardation), the ensuing litigation and limitation of the scope of the death penalty would be even more substantial, given both the possible breadth of the category of "mental illness" and the high incidence of some sort of mental illness among potentially capital offenders.[117]

Beyond the Court's traditional consideration of "the numbers" (even in the expansive sense outlined here) lies the vast terrain opened up by the Court's more controversial and qualitative factors—expert opinion, religious opinion, world opinion, and general public opinion. On the "expert" front, the list of possibly relevant views include the American Bar Association (ABA) and individual state bar associations, the American Law Institute, sitting and former judges in the federal and state systems, acting and former capital prosecutors, acting and former capital defense lawyers, wardens of federal and state prisons, prison guards, and police officers. Signs of movement here are ubiquitous, ranging from the obvious—the ABA's call for a nationwide moratorium[118]—to more discrete data points, such as the constitutional invalidation of state death penalty schemes by particular state supreme courts,[119] or the reflections of long-time wardens who have overseen decades of executions.[120]

The convergence of the views of various religious communities against the death penalty is a well-known and long-standing constant (religious organizations have long been active players in abolitionist efforts).

Moreover, there may be continuing expressions of this opposition in the theological statements of religious leaders and through the filing of amicus briefs such as those referenced by the Court in *Atkins*. The convergence of the industrialized West against capital punishment is a much more recent phenomenon, and it frequently generates new expressions of world disapproval (led by Europe) of the death penalty practices of the United States and elsewhere. For example, at the end of 2007, the United Nations passed a resolution calling for a worldwide moratorium on capital punishment, over the opposition of the United States, China, and Iran, among others.[121] This event was commemorated in Italy by the illumination in gold light of the coliseum in Rome—as was the state of New Jersey's legislative abolition of the capital punishment the same month.[122] Future expressions of world disapproval may range from the largely symbolic to the more tangible, especially in the likelihood that U.S. allies in the global "war on terror" will refuse in growing numbers of cases to extradite suspects to the United States without assurances that capital punishment will not be imposed.[123]

Finally, it seems possible, though not inevitable, that general public opinion within the United States on the issue of capital punishment will continue to drift downward. First, concerns about wrongful convictions clearly played a role in recent falling rates of public support for capital punishment, as reported by public opinion polls.[124] These concerns have yet to be laid to rest and could be exacerbated if further exonerations from death row take place or if it is conclusively proven that an innocent person has been executed in the modern (post-*Furman*) era. Moreover, the enormous recent increase in the authorization and usage of LWOP (life without parole) as a punishment for murder is also likely to decrease support for capital punishment (and decrease capital verdicts from juries). Polling data from many individual states and nationwide indicate substantial decreases in support for capital punishment when LWOP is offered as an alternative.[125] Given the *Atkins* Court's positive reference to public opinion polling data, it seems likely that abolitionist activists and litigators will continue to promote polling with the LWOP alternative question.

The extensive menu sketched above suggests the breadth of potential sources of support for a claim that a new national consensus is emerging, or will emerge in the foreseeable future, against the practice of capital punishment. There is, of course, no guarantee that such a claim will ever be accepted by any court, much less the Supreme Court. But it seems virtually certain that the claim will be made and will take its place among other wholesale constitutional challenges to capital punishment in the modern era. Indeed, we think that the Court's recent decisions suggest that a claim based on "emerging consensus" under the Court's new Eighth Amendment methodology has more hope of success as a wholesale challenge than the others that have been pursued in recent years (such as the *Furman* claim of arbitrariness, the *McCleskey* claim of racial discrimination, the claim that the system is too error-prone, or the claim that the length of time spent on death row awaiting execution is too lengthy).[126]

Is this new possibility a development to be celebrated? From a retentionist perspective, surely not. But even from an abolitionist perspective, there are reasons to be wary of these new, albeit faint, prospects for judicial nationwide abolition. First and foremost is the now-familiar fear of popular backlash prompted by overreaching "judicial activism." The Supreme Court's famous interventions in the arenas of civil rights and abortion legalization generated furious and sustained backlash from entrenched opposition, leading many to question later whether a wholly nonjudicial avenue to promoting these changes would have been preferable, even to those who most supported the changes. But one needn't turn to analogies to see the relevance of concerns about potential backlash in the context of capital punishment. The post-*Furman* experience of furious popular and legislative backlash provides ample reason to be cautious about judicial fiat in this highly charged area. At a time when there had been no executions for almost a decade and when popular support for capital punishment seemed even lower than it is today, a full 35 states redrafted capital statutes in the first few years in the immediate aftermath of the *Furman* Court's decision. In the absence of Supreme Court involvement, would support for capital punishment have galvanized so quickly and decisively?

It is possible, of course, that the answer to the question is "yes"—capital punishment is actually only a small part of the nation's sharply punitive swing since the late 1960s, an era that has seen a tidal swell of mass incarceration as a result of vastly more punitive penal policies across the board, in response to several decades (1960s through 1980s) of rising violent crime rates and a nationwide commitment to a "war on drugs." The revitalization of capital punishment in this period might well have been inevitable, even in the absence of the Court's intervention (which surely had a short-term galvanizing effect). But today, in an era of falling crime rates and falling interest in the pursuit of capital cases, might it be better to wait and hope that capital punishment will become increasingly marginalized as an outlier practice in a few jurisdictions rather than attempt to stamp it out altogether, thus inviting mobilization around this potently symbolic issue?

There are some good reasons for answering this question in the affirmative. Actual executions in the United States are already exceedingly geographically "lumpy"—that is, highly concentrated in a small number of states (and even within those states, concentrated in a small number of counties). So a substantial degree of marginalization or containment of the actual practice of capital punishment is already occurring. The imposition of capital sentences is somewhat less concentrated than executions, with many states (California being the prime example) producing a large number of death sentences but only a negligible number of executions.[127] If states like California never actually ramp up their execution rates but, rather, continue to use the death penalty largely symbolically, it is possible that such states, over time, may morph into wholly abolitionist states (as New York and New Jersey did, in different ways, over the past few years). And even if such states never muster the political will to abolish capital punishment formally, they may still continue to moderate its use so as to generate a state of de facto abolition. In such a scenario, nationwide abolition may never occur, but the practice of capital punishment may become more exotic—more like rare flora and fauna (or, more pejoratively, like rare diseases) that flourish only in isolated locales under particular circumstances.

Moreover, constitutional litigation runs a more serious risk of spectacular failure than does a slower process of marginalization. If constitutional challenges are brought and *rejected*, especially by the Supreme Court, the challenged capital punishment practices are insulated by constitutional imprimatur against reform and resistance that might otherwise slow or stop them in jurisdictions most skeptical of capital punishment (future New Yorks and New Jerseys potentially poised on the cusp of de facto or formal abolition). The country's recent experience of constitutional litigation that went all the way to the Supreme Court surrounding execution protocols is a cautionary case in point.

Before the Court's grant of certiorari and the nationwide moratorium on executions that resulted, the lethal injection issue presented something like a Rorschach test for state and federal actors across the country, particularly lower courts considering stays of execution and governors considering the issuance of death warrants. In some jurisdictions, the relevant institutional actors were troubled by the prospect of the infliction of excessive or unnecessary pain during lethal injections, and in these states, executions slowed significantly or came to a halt.[128] In other states, notably Texas, the lethal injection issue was rejected quickly and decisively, and executions continued at the regular pace (until the Supreme Court intervened). The lethal injection issue thus allowed "symbolic states" like California and even some "executing states" (like Florida, which had an embarrassing history of "botched" executions) to conduct few or no executions, further marginalizing the practice of capital punishment to a small handful of states. In the year 2007, before the moratorium imposed by the Supreme Court after its grant of certiorari, Texas conducted more than half of the country's executions, up from its 35 percent or so share during the preceding decade. Without the intervention of the Supreme Court, this process of marginalization would likely have continued for several years, as different jurisdictions spent varying amounts of time analyzing and litigating alternatives to the challenged lethal injection protocols.

The Supreme Court's intervention, however, seemed to galvanize supporters of the death penalty, as political actors spoke out disparagingly about the Court's intervention and sought to avoid the moratorium created by its liberal granting of stays of execution in the wake of its grant of certiorari.[129] The resulting Supreme Court decision upholding the challenged Kentucky protocol, though it did not definitively block all future lethal injection challenges, appears to have removed a significant roadblock to executions. The Court's decision makes it more difficult for local actors to restrict capital practices in the name of caution about concerns regarding lethal injection protocols. The overarching lesson of the lethal injection litigation may be that the absence of Supreme Court review of global death penalty challenges at this point in time might facilitate local limitations on the practice, as there is clearly a risk that *failed* constitutional challenges in the high Court paradoxically may move the country further from restriction and restraint than no constitutional challenges at all.

Alternatively, reliance on local resistance and restraint to produce a slow process of desuetude (perhaps punctuated by occasional formal abolition) creates no backstop to prevent revitalization of capital punishment in times of rising public fear of crime and rising homicide rates (similar to the role that the European Union plays today in Europe). As many abolitionist states within the United States (and countries within Europe) are aware, a popular surge to reinstate capital punishment is always just one gruesome crime away. For example, Massachusetts, though solidly abolitionist at present, was brought within a single vote of reinstatement of the death penalty in 1997 in the wake of the horrible rape/murder of a 10-year-old boy.[130] Constitutional abolition, in contrast to marginalization, can create just such a backstop in the federal courts, though at the cost of generating potential political backlash in the states.

Perhaps both extremes can be avoided by continuing with vigor on the present relatively new path—one of continuing *substantive* regulation of capital processes.[131] If *Atkins* and *Simmons* are followed by further constitutionally imposed substantive limitations (such as on the imposition of capital punishment on those with mental illness), the practice of capital punishment may simply become too constricted and too costly to survive in any robust way—much the way a tree that is hollowed out can no longer survive. States or localities may conclude that the game is simply not worth the candle—that the likelihood of generating and defending death sentences in the cases that call for them the most is too difficult or costly.

For the time being, all three paths toward some form of abolition—marginalization, wholesale constitutional abolition, and constitutional "hollowing out"—are substantially congruent. In these early days of faint possibility, each step toward one of the three outcomes might also be seen as a step toward the two others. At some point in the future, however, the paths will diverge—either because all three are rejected in a revitalization of capital punishment like that of the mid-1970s or because one or two of the possibilities are decisively rejected. Our goal here is to try to illuminate the road ahead, so that the moments of decision are recognized and self-consciously weighed by the legal actors involved rather than recognized only after they have passed.

NOTES

1. *Atkins v. Virginia*, 536 U.S. 304, 316 n.21 (2002).
2. *Roper v. Simmons*, 543 U.S. 551, 575–78 (2005).
3. Ibid., at 577.
4. *Gregg v. Georgia*, 428 U.S. 153 (1976).
5. *Furman v. Georgia*, 408 U.S. 238 (1972).
6. "E.U. Rebuffs Poland on Death Penalty," *International Herald Tribune*, Aug. 2, 2006, available at http://www.iht.com/articles/2006/08/02/news/death.php.

7. "Huckabee Attack Ad Runs Anyway," *Newsweek*, Jan. 3, 2008, available at http://www.newsweek.com/id/83514/output/print.

8. Adrian Walker and Doris Sue Wong, "No Death Penalty by One Vote," *Boston Globe*, Nov. 7, 1997, available at http://www.nodp.org/ma/stacks/globe_110797.html.

9. *Atkins*, at 304; *Roper*, at 551.

10. *Atkins*, at 315 ("It is not so much the number of these States that is significant, but the consistency of the direction of change."); *Roper*, at 565–66 (same).

11. See, e.g., *Atkins*, at 316 n.21 (recognizing public opinion poll data and "organizations with germane expertise" as reflecting "a much broader social and professional consensus"); ibid., at 316 and n.20 (noting the sentencing practices of several states).

12. See, e.g., *Kansas v. Marsh*, 126 S. Ct. 2516, 2544–46 (2006) (Souter, J., dissenting); *Ring v. Arizona*, 536 U.S. 584, 616–17 (2002) (Breyer, J., concurring); *Atkins v. Virginia*, at 320 n.25 (Stevens, J., writing for the majority).

13. See, e.g., *Knight v. Florida*, 528 U.S. 990, 993–99 (1999) (Breyer, J., dissenting from denial of certiorari); *Lackey v. Texas*, 514 U.S. 1045 (Stevens, J., respecting the denial of certiorari); *Elledge v. Florida*, 525 U.S. 944 (1998) (Breyer, J., dissenting from denial of certiorari).

14. *Powell v. Alabama*, 287 U.S 45 (1932).

15. *Moore v. Dempsey*, 261 U.S. 86 (1923).

16. *Robinson v. California*, 370 U.S. 660 (1962).

17. See, e.g., *Rudolph v. Alabama*, 375 U.S. 889 (1963) (Goldberg, Douglas, and Brennan, JJ., dissenting from denial of certiorari).

18. Ibid.

19. Michael Meltsner, *Cruel and Unusual: The Supreme Court and Capital Punishment* (New York: Random House, 1973), 75.

20. Ibid., 107.

21. Alexander M. Bickel, *The Least Dangerous Branch* (New York: Bobbs-Merrill, 1962), 242.

22. Marvin E. Wolfgang and Marc Riedel, "Rape, Racial Discrimination, and the Death Penalty," in *Capital Punishment in the United States*, pp. 99–121, ed. Hugo Adam Bedau and Chester M. Pierce (New York: AMS Press, 1976). See also *Maxwell v. Bishop*, 398 F.2d 138, 141–43 (6th Cir. 1968) (describing the results of the Wolfgang study).

23. *Witherspoon v. Illinois*, 391 U.S. 510 (1968).

24. *Maxwell v. Bishop*, 398 U.S. 262 (1969).

25. *Rudolph*, at 889.

26. Hans Ziesel, "Race Bias in the Administration of the Death Penalty: The Florida Experience," *Harvard Law Review* 95 (1981): 458 (quoting *Brief for the United States as Amicus Curiae* app. A at 5A, *Gregg v. Georgia*, 428 U.S. 153 (1976)).

27. *Boykin v. Alabama*, 395 U.S. 238 (1969).

28. *McGautha v. California*, 402 U.S. 183 (1971).

29. *Furman,* at 238 (and companion cases *Branch v. Texas* and *Jackson v. Georgia*).

30. Bickel, *Least Dangerous Branch,* 240–43.

31. *Brown v. Board of Education of Topeka*, 347 U.S. 483 (1954).

32. *Furman,* at 238.

33. Ibid., at 240 (Douglas, J., concurring); ibid., at 257 (Brennan, J., concurring); ibid., at 306 (Stewart, J., concurring); ibid., at 310 (White, J., concurring); ibid., at 314 (Marshall, J., concurring).

34. Meltsner, *Cruel and Unusual,* 66.

35. *Furman,* at 257 (Brennan, J., concurring); ibid., at 314 (Marshall, J., concurring).

36. Ibid., at 310 (White, J., concurring).

37. *Woodson v. North Carolina*, 428 U.S. 280 (1976); *Roberts v. Louisiana*, 428 U.S. 325 (1976).

38. *Gregg v. Georgia*, at 153.

39. *Coker v. Georgia*, 433 U.S. 584 (1977).

40. Ibid., at 592.

41. Ibid., at 601 (Powell, J., concurring in part); ibid., at 604 (Burger, C.J., and Rehnquist, J., dissenting).

42. *Rummel v. Estelle*, 445 U.S. 263 (1980).

43. *Hutto v. Davis*, 454 U.S. 370 (1982).

44. *Solem v. Helm*, 463 U.S. 277 (1983).

45. *Harmelin v. Michigan*, 501 U.S. 957, 1005 (1991).

46. *Enmund v. Florida*, 458 U.S. 782 (1982).

47. *Tison v. Arizona*, 481 U.S. 137 (1986).

48. *Stanford v. Kentucky*, 492 U.S. 361 (1989).

49. Ibid.,. at 30–71.

50. Ibid., at 370 n.2.

51. Ibid., at 369 n.1 (emphasis added).

52. Ibid., at 377.

53. Ibid., at 378.

54. *Penry v. Lyaugh*, 492 U.S. 302, 339 (1989).

55. Ibid., at 334.

56. *McCleskey v. Kemp*, 481 U.S. 279 (1987).

57. Ibid., at 285–87 (describing design and findings of the Baldus study).

58. Ibid., at 291–300.

59. Ibid., at 314–15 ("McCleskey's claim, taken to its logical conclusion, throws into serious question the principles that underlie our entire criminal justice system").

60. Ibid., at 312 ("Apparent disparities in sentencing are an inevitable part of our criminal justice sytem").

61. Ibid., at 313 n.37.

62. Pub. L. No. 104-132, 110 Stat. 1214 (1996) (codified as amended in scattered sections of 28 U.S.C.) ("Antiterrorism and Effective Death Penalty Act" (AEDPA)).

63. *Callins v. Collins*, 510 U.S. 1141, 1145 (1994) (Blackmun, J., dissenting from denial of certiorari).

64. Bickel, *Least Dangerous Branch*, 242.

65. Carol S. Steiker and Jordan M. Steiker, "The Seduction of Innocence: The Attraction and Limitations of the Focus on Innocence in Capital Punishment Law and Advocacy," *Journal of Criminal Law and Criminology* 95 (Winter 2005): 594.

66. Ibid., at 607.

67. Ibid., at 594–95.

68. Carol S. Steiker and Jordan M. Steiker, "A Tale of Two Nations: Implementation of the Death Penalty in 'Executing' versus 'Symbolic' States in the United States," *Texas Law Review* 84 (June 2006): 1869.

69. *Atkins*, at 304.

70. Ibid., at 314–16.

71. Ibid., at 315 n.16.

72. Ibid., at 316.

73. Ibid., at 315.

74. Ibid., at 315 n.18.

75. Ibid., at n.21.

76. Ibid.

77. Ibid., at 322.

78. Ibid., at 343–45.

79. *Coker*, at 584; *Enmund*, at 782.

80. *Atkins*, at 347.

81. Ibid., at 353.

82. *Ring*, at 584.

83. *Apprendi v. New Jersey*, 530 U.S. 466 (2000).

84. *Ring*, at 613–19.

85. Ibid., at 614–15.

86. Ibid., at 616.

87. Ibid., at 618.

88. Ibid., at 616–18.

89. Ibid., at 618.

90. *Roper v. Simmons*, 543 U.S. 551 (2005).

91. Ibid., at 563.

92. Ibid., at 570.

93. Ibid., at 573.

94. Ibid., at 578.

95. Ibid., at 564–65.

96. *Kansas v. Marsh*, 548 U.S. 163 (2006).

97. Ibid.

98. Ibid., at 2544–46 (Souter, J., dissenting).

99. Ibid., at 2544.

100. Ibid., at 2544–45.

101. Ibid., at 2528.

102. Ibid., at 2545.

103. Ibid., at 2535–39 (Scalia, J., concurring).

104. Ibid., at 2535–36 (noting that exonerations demonstrate "not the failure of the system but its success").

105. Ibid., at 2532.

106. *Baze v. Rees*, 128 S. Ct. 1520, 1551 (2008) (Stevens, concurring in judgment).

107. Ibid., at 1552.

108. Ibid., at 1546.

109. *Atkins*, at 315.

110. "New Hampshire Veto Saves Death Penalty," *New York Times*, May 20, 2000, available at http://partners.nytimes.com/library/national/052000nh-death-penalty.html.

111. Michael Powell, "In N.Y., Lawmakers Vote Not to Reinstate Capital Punishment," *Washington Post*, Apr. 13, 2005, available at http://www.washingtonpost.com/wp-dyn/articles/A47871-2005Apr12.html.

112. John Wagner, "Repeal of Md. Death Penalty Still Seems Out of Reach," *Washington Post*, Dec. 26, 2007, available at http://www.washingtonpost.com/wpyn/content/article/2007/12/25/AR2007122501004_pf.html.

113. Steve LeBlanc, "Death Penalty Bill Facing Stiff Opposition on Beacon Hill," *Boston Globe*, Oct. 23, 2007, available at http://www.boston.com/news/local/massachusetts/articles/2007/10/23/death_penalty_bill_facing_stiff_opposition_on_beacon_hill/.

114. Adam Liptak, "Federal Juries Rejecting More Death Penalties," *New York Times*, June 15, 2003, available at http://www.sfgate.com/cgibin/article.cgi?file=/chronicle/archive/2003/06/15/MN202748.DTL&type=printable.

115. Joseph Goldstein, "Judges Revolt over Death Penalty," *New York Sun*, Mar. 8, 2008, available at http://www2.nysun.com/new-york/judges-revolt-over-death-penalty/.

116. Mike Tolson, "Quintero Sentence Baffling to Many," *Houston Chronicle*, May 21, 2008, available at http://www.chron.com/disp/story.mpl/metropolitan/5793606.html.

117. Christopher Slobogin, "What *Atkins* Could Mean for People with Mental Illness," *New Mexico Law Review* 33 (2003): 293–314.

118. ABA Death Penalty Moratorium Implementation Project, available at http://www.abanet.org/moratorium/faq.html.

119. *State v. Marsh*, 278 Kan. 520 (2004), overruled by *Kansas v. Marsh*, 126 S. Ct. 2516 (2006); *People v. LaValle*, 3 N.Y.3d 88, 817 N.E.2d 341, 783 N.Y.S.2d 485 (2004).

120. *At the Death House Door* is a recent documentary chronicling Texas Warden Carroll Pickett's concerns about the possible execution of an innocent man. See http://www.ifc.com/atthedeathhousedoor.

121. "UN Votes for Death Penalty Freeze," *BBC News*, Dec. 18, 2007, available at http://news.bbc.co.uk/2/hi/in_depth/7151031.stm.

122. Associated Press, "Rome to Light Coliseum When New Jersey Bans Death Penalty," *New Jersey Real-Time News*, Dec. 14, 2007, available at http://www.nj.com/news/index.ssf/2007/12/rome_to_light_up_colosseum_in.html.

123. Daniel Givelber, "Innocence Abroad: The Extradition Cases and the Future of Capital Litigation," *Oregon Law Review* 81 (2002): 161–82.

124. Samuel R. Gross and Phoebe C. Ellsworth, "Second Thoughts: Americans' Views on the Death Penalty at the Turn of the Century," in *Beyond Repair? America's Death Penalty* (Stephen P. Garvey, ed.), 7–57. Durham, N.C.: Duke University Press, 2003.

125. See, e.g., Jennifer McMenamin, "In Maryland, Most Want Option of Execution," *Baltimore Sun,* June 2, 2008 (majority ceases to favor death penalty when LWOP offered as option); Frank Newport, "Sixty-Nine Percent of Americans Support Death Penalty," Oct. 12, 2007, available at http://www.gallup.com/poll/101863/Sixtynine-Percent-Americans-Support-Death-Penalty.aspx (support for death penalty typically fall to the 47–54 percent range when LWOP is offered as an option).

126. Carol S. Steiker and Jordan M. Steiker, "Abolition in Our Time," *Ohio State Journal of Criminal Law* 1 (2003): 323–43.

127. Steiker and Steiker, "Tale of Two Nations."

128. Peter Whoriskey and Sonia Geis, "Lethal Injection Is on Hold in Two States," *Washington Post*, Dec. 16, 2006, available at http://www.washingtonpost.com/wp-dyn/content/article/2006/12/15/AR2006121501499.html (describing reforms, moratoria, and delays in a variety of states long before the Supreme Court granted review).

129. Charles Lane, "Supreme Court Puzzles Some with Mixed Answers on Lethal Injection," *Washington Post*, Feb. 10, 2006, available at http://www.washingtonpost.com/wp-dyn/content/article/2006/02/09/AR2006020901954_pf.html (quoting Joshua Marquis, a prosecutor and vice president of the National District Attorneys Association, who urged executions to continue during the Supreme Court's consideration of the lethal injection case, describing the constitutional challenge as "sort of a legal 'Hail Mary' pass").

130. LeBlanc, "Death Penalty Bill Facing Stiff Opposition."

131. Most recently, in *Kennedy v. Louisiana*, 128 S. Ct. 2641 (2008), the Court rejected states' efforts to revive the death penalty for the nonhomicidal offense of child rape. The court's expansive decision prohibits the imposition of capital punishment for any ordinary crimes not resulting in death.

Rocked but Still Rolling

The Enduring Institution of Capital Punishment in Historical and Comparative Perspective

Michael McCann and David T. Johnson

The death penalty in the U.S. is a wreck, but it's our wreck—a collage of American attitudes, virtues, and values.

—David Von Drehle, 2008[1]

With all cylinders working as in Texas [the death penalty] produces a lot of executions.

—Richard Dieter, 2007[2]

[T]o the extent *Baze* was supposed to be a sort of test drive for doing away with capital punishment altogether. . . . [I]t seems to have been driven off a cliff.

—Dahlia Lithwick, 2008[3]

Complexities of "Abolition"

The abolition of capital punishment is a much discussed but complicated concept, and the standards for measuring where the United States is on the road to abolition are far from obvious. For one thing, a de facto halt in executions could (and often does) occur without a de jure prohibition of the death penalty. As of the end of 2007, some 33 nation-states had gone at least 10 years without a judicial execution, and many others had so greatly

FIGURE 5.1

Execution rate in the United States, 1640–1999

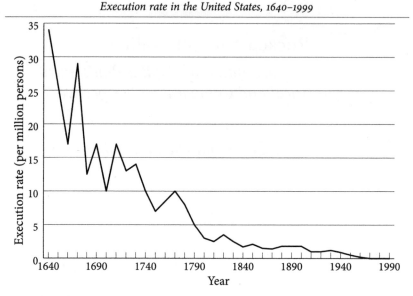

From Payne 2004, p. 130.

narrowed the category of crimes eligible for capital punishment and so limited prosecution of those crimes that they were essentially abolitionist in practice.[4] Yet halts in execution do not always mean that abolition is near. In Asia, for example, Brunei Darussalam, the Maldives, and Papua New Guinea have not conducted any executions for more than half a century but still have not legally eliminated the institution of capital punishment, while in the United States the retentionist states of Kansas and New Hampshire have gone more than 10 years without executing anyone.

The bifurcation between "abolitionist" and "retentionist" also obscures huge differences between nations and large changes within nations over time. This, too, is relevant for assessing where the United States is on the road to abolition. As figure 5.1 illustrates, executions per capita in the United States dropped dramatically between 1640 and 1990, from roughly 35 executions per million persons to nearly 0.[5]

In comparative perspective, the total volume of state killing[6] in the United States over the past 350 years is about one recent year's total for the People's Republic of China, making us wonder what is missed by placing these two countries in the same retentionist category. By some historical and comparative standards, the United States appears to be far along the road to abolition.

But the issues are even more complex. Leaders in China and Russia have conceded that capital punishment should eventually be abolished even if their countries are not yet "ready" to do so. Similar concessions about formal de jure abolition are rarely heard among elected leaders in the United States, where normative retentionists seem to far outnumber abolitionists—or at least the former are more vocal and better positioned to block the agendas of the latter. Clearly, changes in death penalty policy are often impermanent. Among American states, for example, there have been almost as many reversals from abolitionist to retentionist as there have been sustained abolitions.[7] Reversals have followed abolition elsewhere in the world as well—as in Nepal and the Philippines—albeit usually with few executions following reinstatement.

Our Skeptical Standpoint

In this chapter, we focus on the prospects for complete, sustained, de jure abolition in the United States, and some of the complexities identified here will surface at various points along the way. We write in full awareness that many experts not only seek abolition in the United States but also expect it to be achieved sometime soon. Some authors in this volume approach the latter position. Our argument, by contrast, proceeds with skepticism at two levels. On the one hand, we are wary of prediction itself, for important changes in public policy often turn on unpredictable triggering events or the convergence of factors that are difficult to discern confidently in advance. Social scientists are simply not very good at predicting policy change.[8] On the other hand, while we reserve judgment about the distant future, we find many reasons to believe that capital punishment will be difficult to terminate in the present historical context. Progress has been made in reducing executions, and the United States might be moving slowly down the long road to de jure abolition, but the end is not presently in sight and the forces that have prevailed for the last quarter of the twentieth century seem unlikely to dissipate anytime soon. In short, the death penalty will probably remain in American law even as it continues to be hobbled and slowed in practice. In this essay, we explain why state executions will be difficult to abolish completely, though we do envision potential developments that could hasten an end we both hope for.

Analytical Framework.

The general framework of our analysis is comparative, historical, and institutionalist. This approach recognizes that cultural values and meanings matter. Deeply rooted ideological traditions linking the freedom of rights-bearing citizens, anxiety over the fragility of disciplinary institutions (family, church, school, work), and the utility of harsh punishment for securing order and banishing the undeserving figure prominently in this account. But we view the meanings of such norms as historically contingent, contested, and variable rather than singular, static, and determinative. Explaining variations in death penalty policy requires linking subtle divergences in public discourse, especially regarding the rights of citizens, to broader changes in historically contingent politics and distinctive institutional structures.[9]

We assess the contemporary "American condition"[10] relative to two other historical contexts that witnessed changes in death penalty policy: the abolition of the death penalty in post–World War II Europe, and the often-claimed (wrongly, we will argue) "near miss" moment of abolition during the late civil rights era of the 1960s and 1970s in the United States. These comparisons of political and institutional factors provide the key to explaining why the United States diverged from the European pattern and why it will remain exceptional in its commitment to capital punishment.

Rather than viewing these two historical contexts as separate developments, we connect them in a single narrative by treating the post-*Furman* period as a moment in postwar American political history that differs from the general postwar patterns in Europe. The emergence of the United States as a preeminent military and economic world power, the escalation of the cold war, and the rise of the Southern civil rights movement which drew energy from these international developments set in motion political dynamics that proved decidedly mixed for American capital punishment. These forces initially put the death penalty on the defensive but ultimately helped to reinvigorate its practice and symbolic significance amid the Southern-inspired, highly racialized backlash that grew into the nationwide "culture wars." At the same time, the unique institutional features of American politics that facilitated the politicization of punishment policy during this period also protected harsh justice from the kinds of centralized elite interventions that occurred in Europe.

One result of America's fragmented institutional politics has been a chaotic, uncoordinated, ad hoc tampering that in recent years has weakened and slowed the death penalty in practice. But these developments have not undercut—and, perhaps, have even fortified—the endurance of capital punishment as a symbolic institution. The death penalty in the United States is in many ways broken, slowed, and barely functioning, but most American citizens and leaders retain faith in it, and those who oppose it lack the institutional means to end it.

Comparing Historical Legacies

We begin by taking a long-term historical perspective toward American capital punishment.[11] As a number of scholars have shown, American practices of state execution were until recent years remarkably similar to those in Europe and other parts of the world.[12] From early modern times, capital punishment was used for many kinds of wrongdoings and wrongdoers, and it was justified by a wide variety of secular and religious logics.[13] Executions were prominent instruments of order from the late aristocratic era through the transition to a more bourgeois society, when conceptions of property were changing in diverse ways. Indeed, capitalist development proceeded in tandem with reliance on capital punishment. A free republic wary of government requires individual rights-bearing citizens who are self-governing to help accumulate wealth and to exchange and use it in orderly ways. The very qualification for citizenship was the demonstration of self-discipline by individuals in everyday civil practice— the capacity to tame passions, to discipline one's body, to govern oneself in pursuit of material security and comfort, and to work hard and delay gratification. These qualities of citizenship were essential for a society organized around individual rights. As Tocqueville posed it, the grand question for democratic societies was how to organize and sustain the institutional mechanisms for instilling such disciplined self-governance into the masses (of white male citizens) amid the dynamic, disintegrative forces of an exchange-based, commodified society.

Traditionally, families, religion, and work provided the primary sources of socialization and normalizing discipline, but elaborate educational institutions, civic groups, unions, and associations of all sorts eventually developed to expand the disciplinary, norm-enforcing webs of social organization. These modes of social control required support from systems of criminal justice that backed up disciplinary sacrifice with threats of punishment for those undeserving individuals who failed to follow the norms and codes of law. The harshness of punishment varied by offense, but theft of property in addition to acts of violence commonly justified execution. British and other European colonists transplanted these interrelated institutions of property, social discipline, and criminal punishment—including capital punishment—to the new world of America, where they grew in diverse but strikingly parallel ways even after independence.[14]

On both sides of the Atlantic, capital punishment was subjected to a sustained process of scrutiny, reform, and restraint starting in the late-seventeenth century. The range of capital offenses and eligible offenders was narrowed, technologies of death were shed of their more barbaric trappings, critics of capital punishment multiplied, public opinion became more divided and complex, death penalty procedures were formalized and reformed, and the number of those sentenced to death and of those executed steadily declined during the nineteenth and twentieth centuries. Abolitionist voices became more prominent, too, spurred by Cesare Beccaria's influential *Essay on Crimes and Punishments*, published in 1764. As Franklin Zimring has summarized, "By late in the eighteenth century, a variety of reform proposals directed at reducing death sentences had been introduced in the United States and Europe," and half a century later a number of American states, most in the Midwest, led campaigns for abolition.[15] In 1867, Portugal became the first western European nation to abolish the penalty for ordinary crimes; by century's end, three nations had formally abolished and two others had stopped executing. Executions in both the United States and Europe declined throughout the nineteenth century, dropping to almost none in the two decades after World War II. In this way, judicial killing became an increasingly "exceptional punishment."[16] More broadly, David Garland is quite right to note that the histories of capital punishment in the United States and Europe were remarkably parallel until the 1970s.[17] Only then did the dramatic divergence occur. While Europe almost completed its abolitionist transformation by that decade—the last execution in western Europe occurred in France in 1977—executions in the United States escalated and the death penalty took on much greater symbolic significance in public and political life.

The divergence between the United States and Europe raises two key questions for this essay. First, what political and institutional factors account for the different death penalty trajectories? In our view, the political factors were mostly specific to the contemporary context, while the institutional features reflect great differences in the organization and administration of criminal policy and of politics more generally that stretch far back in time. Second and more centrally, what does this analysis suggest about the future of capital punishment in the United States and Europe?

Abolition in Postwar Europe

We begin with the European experience, drawing heavily on Franklin Zimring's insightful account. The key point is that European nations emerged from World War II humbled and ravaged, wary of the potential for murderous elite political demagoguery, and committed to constitutional and legal reforms that would make fascist rule difficult to repeat and world war less likely.[18] State execution almost became synonymous with totalitarianism. The Soviet Union executed more persons each year in the 1930s than all the nonfascist states of western Europe would over the entire twentieth century,[19] and Nazi Germany added millions more casualties to the execution toll. After defeat, the formerly fascist nations of Europe led the way to abolition, with Italy abolishing in 1944 and West Germany in 1949. By 1950, Austria, the Netherlands, and Belgium would cease resorting to capital punishment. The key U.S. allies in victory during the war, France and England, retained de jure capital punishment but abandoned it in practice over the following decades.

The specter of the bloody totalitarian past and of postwar foreign occupation generated strong pressures to abolish at this historical juncture, even if they were not openly acknowledged. Indeed, abolition efforts were decidedly bureaucratic, formal, legalistic, and parochial, led largely by coalitions of elites acting somewhat independently, typically defying public opinion that still favored capital punishment by margins of 2 or 3 to 1—though the intensity of such support was probably not great.[20] The fact that authority over criminal justice matters was centralized at the national parliamentary level and that elections emphasized national over local issues contributed in important if underappreciated ways to the capacity for elite-driven change. And commissioned studies, elite debates, and specific policy proposals for abolition developed in largely insular, nation-by-nation fashion, with each country looking to its own tradition for support and guidance. Whatever political tensions and divisions existed in the European nations during this postwar period, elite consensus about the need to limit state power along with centralizing institutional features insulated abolitionism from partisan politicization in individual polities. In these ways, capital punishment was dismantled methodically and, for the most part, quietly amid the much larger effort to rebuild Europe along more stable, democratic, and market-oriented lines.

Commitments to citizen rights surely played a role in motivating and justifying the initial wave of abolition during the era of demilitarization and constitutional change in postwar Europe, but discourses of rights reflected the diversity of parochial national traditions and owed little to any transnational authority or universal principles. Once institutionalized, however, abolition took on new meanings as the European-led human rights movement gained momentum during the 1980s. The "human rights" frame became salient only after all the critical battles in the local death penalty wars were done.[21] There have been many key moments in this process of transition, including the reversal of the exemption for state death penalties by Protocol No. 6 of the 1983 European Convention on Human Rights.

The institutionalization of a new human rights regime had at least two important consequences for capital punishment. First, a transnational discourse recognizing the rights of all persons and grounded in respect for the right to life itself began to subsume the variable traditions of national and local discourse in Europe. Second, new transnational authorities were authorized to define and enforce specific rights throughout Europe. Thus, abolition of the death penalty in Europe led to an elaborate new repertoire of moral and legal justifications for eliminating the ultimate punishment in other countries, as well as administrative mechanisms for achieving that end. At the same time, a vibrant social movement of abolitionist "missionaries" emerged in Europe to excoriate the immoral retentionist policies of the United States. We now turn to an analysis of that divergent legacy.

Dramatic Divergence: Postwar Politics in the United States

America's postwar death penalty policy and practice initially appeared to converge toward the abolitionist pattern of Europe, but by the late 1980s the United States was again sentencing large numbers of persons to death and executing more often than it had in a quarter century. The resurrection of capital punishment was widely supported by elites and the general public. In this section, we outline the main contours of the historically specific *political* developments that reversed America's abolitionist trend in the late twentieth century; in the next section, we consider some of the enduring *institutional* features that facilitated this politics and that seem likely to sustain retention for some time to come.

Triumphant America, Divided Americans

The United States emerged from World War II not simply triumphant but as the preeminent economic, political, and military power in the world. Despite a past of imperial expansion that cost countless lives of Native Americans, violent subjugation of African Americans in the still-segregated South, support for corporate thuggery against workers, and the recent internment of 100,000 Japanese Americans, domestic political elites could justifiably distance themselves from the murderous fascism and imperial militarism of totalitarian European states defeated in World War II. Even more than in Britain and France, leaders in the United States found little reason to increase legal limits on state power or to refrain from exercising violence against persons who wantonly broke the law.

In this context, a new conflict arose: the clash with communism that was perceived to be spreading rapidly around the world. The primary effect of this clash was to increase American anxiety about a new, more pervasive, and potentially more dangerous European adversary, one armed with nuclear weapons whose devastating effects America had demonstrated in the bombings of Japan. American leaders found justification for transforming this international crisis into a routinized steady-state protocol. As the military was equipped with an unprecedented capacity to impose violence, American disciplinary institutions—higher education, civic associations, churches, civil defense networks, and the Hollywood TV and movie industries—geared up to make America tough, vigilant, and unified for the struggle. Regular breakouts of hot conflict—from the Korean War to the long conflict in Vietnam—maintained pressures to prepare to use force against foreign and domestic adversaries alike.

In this anxious environment, concern about excessive state violence was remote, thus weakening the push for abolition of capital punishment that was experienced in Europe. For example, the execution of Julius and Ethel Rosenberg in 1953 was controversial, but approval for the execution of "subversives" was high among elites and the general public alike. Opinion polls reveal a jump in support for capital punishment, from 61 percent in 1936 to 70 percent in the year the Rosenbergs were electrocuted.[22] Associate Justice William O. Douglas even faced impeachment charges in 1952 after granting a stay of execution to this famous and notorious couple.

The campaign against the communist threat unified American elites in the 1950s, thereby generating strong pressures for conformity and elite rule around agendas that were notably different from those in Europe. But American politics also divided along other lines. The most important rupture emerged from growing challenges to the racist legacy of Jim Crow segregation, especially in the South. As a host of studies has documented, many black soldiers who fought in World War II returned home to find their rights denied, poor job prospects, segregated public facilities, widespread police violence, and lynchings.[23] Some black veterans spoke openly about the hypocrisy of the principles for which they had risked and sacrificed much, and many black leaders found in the changing world context resources to amplify these and related claims. Most important, the continuing racial hierarchy and violence in the South constituted a major embarrassment that dramatically undermined the efforts of the American government to win the "hearts and minds" of people around the world, especially those struggling to "decolonize" in Asia, Africa, and Latin America. Some black leaders appealed directly to nations around the world and to the new institutional authority of the United Nations to condemn American apartheid. In 1947, the NAACP, with W. E. B. DuBois as principal author, petitioned the United Nations, denouncing racism in the United States as "not only indefensible but barbaric." "It is not Russia that threatens the U.S. so much as Mississippi," said DuBois; "not Stalin and Molotov but Bilbo and Rankin; internal injustice done to one's brothers is far more dangerous than the aggression of strangers from abroad."[24] Black leaders also embraced the language of "international human rights" to mobilize world support for challenging the narrower, less-egalitarian, and more-hypocritical traditions of rights practice in the United States.[25]

Beginning in the Truman administration, these struggles on the international stage pressured U.S. officials and social leaders to formulate strategies for dismantling the most symbolically salient features of segregation in the South.[26] Since support for the Democratic Party was already slipping in the traditional stronghold of the white South, elected officials were too vulnerable to lead the charge, and hence a strategy was designed to reshape the Supreme Court with moderate justices, led by California Republican Earl Warren, who would use constitutional review to overturn the legal basis of segregation established in *Plessy*. At the same time, the NAACP and other groups supplemented the already well established litigation campaign with grassroots activism that grew into what we now know as the Southern civil rights movement.

Civil Rights Legacy: Moratorium, Backlash, and Death Reinstated

More than any other factor, the legacy of civil rights activism during the cold war shaped the future of capital punishment in the United States in contradictory ways. On the one hand, the civil rights movement paved the way and provided momentum for the famous halt in executions from 1967 to 1977. Activist lawyers built on the legal successes they were achieving through the courts in other spheres and escalated legal challenges against capital punishment. Their campaign was led by the NAACP Legal Defense Fund and the ACLU, and their strategy was legalistic and litigation centered, although educational and lobbying efforts were pursued as well.[27] The ultimate goal for most activists was abolition, grounded in claims about how execution conflicts with "evolving standards of decency" and therefore represents "unnecessarily cruel punishment." Repeatedly warned about the likelihood of massive resistance on and beyond the Supreme Court, the activists chose to attack capital punishment indirectly, by focusing on procedural inadequacies and racial discrimination at the sentencing phase of trials. The key strategy was to create a nationwide logjam of appeals by death-sentenced prisoners. As a result, the number of inmates awaiting execution rose significantly, and an unofficial moratorium on executions started in 1967.

The lawyer-led coalition managed to land a number of cases contesting procedural issues before the Supreme Court, but achievements were mixed and limited until the surprising *Furman* ruling of 1972. While only two Justices (William Brennan and Thurgood Marshall) went as far as to hold that capital punishment violated the Constitution, three others (William O. Douglas, Potter Stewart, and Byron White) joined them to invalidate state death penalty practices on procedural grounds, focusing on the lack of standards to guide discretion in the determination of capital sentencing. Four Justices—Warren Burger, William Rehnquist, Harry Blackmun, and Lewis Powell—refused to find constitutional violations in existing procedures or practices. The rest of the story is well known. After many states revised their sentencing guidelines and related procedures, seven Justices on the Court ruled in 1976 that the constitutional requirements of due process and equal protection were satisfied by the new legal regimes. The doors to the death chambers were thrust open, and the machinery of death soon began grinding again. Equally important, this period laid a narrow legal track for channeling challenges into procedural and technical grooves—what Blackmun later called "tinkering with the machinery of death"—and away from disputing the core practice itself.[28] These grooves still shape and contain the main currents of abolitionist challenges in the United States today.

During the moratorium years that preceded the 1976 holding in *Gregg*, many officials and activists recognized there was little support for total abolition on or beyond the Court. Some elites, including Justices Earl Warren and Hugo Black, even worried that a ruling that abolished capital punishment on constitutional grounds would undermine the Court's already shaky legitimacy and perhaps produce a major backlash.[29] In this regard, there is little reason to consider the moratorium period as a "near miss" for abolition. Indeed, a forceful backlash against civil rights advances and inclusionary goals was under way well before the *Furman* and *Gregg* decisions.

The backlash began in the South, where opponents of desegregation advanced legal arguments about judicial overreaching and disregard of federalism, as well as moral arguments about the breakdown of social values and discipline that would result from too much change.[30] More particularly, Southern leaders started to stress the dangers of civil rights activism, communist subversion, and increasing street crime as interrelated pathologies that undermined civic values and social order. These appeals rang true for many Americans in the South and elsewhere, as civil rights protests increased, white youth defiantly listened to commercial R&B when not singing "The Times They Are a Changing," and cold war anxieties mounted. The alarmist rhetoric spread into national politics, too, most notably in the voice of Barry Goldwater,[31] and then, amid escalating protests that joined civil rights concerns to antiwar chants, by Richard Nixon in 1968. When Nixon made restoration of "Law and Order" a central campaign theme, he struck a resonant chord with the "silent majority" about the closely linked dangers then threatening civil society.[32] As Garry Wills put it in his brilliant *Nixon Agonistes*, "Law and order was not *merely* a code phrase for racism. It was the last clause left from our old moral creed . . . the ideal of self-government, of the self-disciplined, self-made man," the bearer of rights. This ethos, Wills emphasizes, made people "see chaos come again when the young, or the blacks"—or communist sympathizers—"refuse to honor self-restraint."[33] By 1970, nearly four out of five Americans believed that "law and order had broken down" and that the cause was "Negroes who start riots" and "communists," along with burgeoning crime in the streets.[34]

This turbulent period marked the start of increased federal involvement in criminal justice policy and of the ratcheting up of punitive penal policies. The campaign began as a largely symbolic electoral appeal, but policy changes with material impacts began to multiply in the late 1970s.[35] These appeals drew on the continued anxieties linking cold war threats of violent war to racialized fears about street violence and political protest among the "underclass." Ronald Reagan, another long-time cold warrior, pushed the transformation along by putting a smiling paternal face on the punitive campaign for law and order, as well as on welfare rollbacks. But leadership on law and order issues was hardly limited to partisan Republicans. Congressional Democrats quickly followed suit in an effort to demonstrate how tough they could be on street criminals and foreign enemies, adding new punitive crime-fighting policies with each election.[36]

Tough talk and a demonstrated record of tough action on crime became a necessity for electoral competitiveness at all levels. In 1988, the ravaging of presidential candidate Michael Dukakis, who defended prisoner furlough policies and refused to endorse the execution of his wife's hypothetical rapist and killer, underscored the imperative to be seen as "tough." Thereafter, Democrat Bill Clinton won the presidency in part by out-toughing his opponents, as did his successor George W. Bush. That both of these presidents hailed from Southern states—following Jimmy Carter and sunbelt-based Ronald Reagan—is indicative of a larger trend. The promise of the civil rights era was to bring the Jim Crow South into legal conformity with the rest of the nation, and this vision surely represented an advance for social justice. But the civil rights movement also catalyzed forces of racially fueled reaction that grew from its Southern roots into a process that transformed the nation in increasingly conservative, hierarchical, and racially exclusionary directions.

The human costs of this changing politics are well known: incarceration rates quadrupled in 20 years; draconian mandatory minimums were enacted, especially for drug offenses; huge percentages of African American men and other minority males were subjected to incarceration or surveillance;[37] and public investments in prisons and policing skyrocketed as expenditures for education, welfare, job training, and other forms of social support were cut. This dramatic transformation in public policy began in an era of increased street crime (including homicide), social unrest, and international conflict with world rivals. But the punitive turn quickly lost touch with real material risks, taking on a momentum of its own in the 1980s. The War on Crime, the War on Drugs, and other dimensions of the responsibilizing "culture wars" only intensified as the cold war and civil unrest faded away.

The main forces driving these changes are subject to much debate, especially regarding how much causal importance should be credited to the initiative of politicians; to issue entrepreneurs like police, prosecutors, and prison contractors; to interest group and social movement advocates; and to "authentic" anxieties in the general public.[38] The role of evangelical and fundamentalist Protestantism, which is far less prominent in Europe, deserves attention, too.[39]

But the key point for this essay is how the larger context of punitive penality fueled the resurgence of capital punishment in America since the late 1970s. Richard Nixon strongly supported capital punishment, as has every successful presidential candidate since.[40] The demise of Michael Dukakis in 1988 clearly illustrates the converse: that insufficient enthusiasm for capital punishment can be a political deathblow. Bill Clinton paid considerable attention to this new reality. While campaigning for president, he returned to Arkansas to see that Ricky Ray Rector, a brain-damaged man with an IQ around 70, would be executed for killing a police officer and civilian. As president, Clinton signed an omnibus crime bill in 1994 that expanded the federal death penalty to some 60 different offenses, as well as the Antiterrorism and Effective Death Penalty Act of 1996. George W. Bush ran as the "death penalty governor." During his six years as governor of Texas, he presided over 152 executions, more than any other governor in the recent history of the United States, and he also signed a bill limiting death penalty appeals in state courts. Bush boasted that those sentenced to death under his watch were surely guilty and had been granted due process, even though studies showed that legal counsel in Texas were often inadequate and that procedural practices in capital trials were frequently deficient.

All in all, the context of the renewed political momentum for capital punishment is clear: electoral politics at the federal and state levels was joined by consistent Court rulings inviting procedural challenges but insulating the core practice of capital punishment from challenge, all justified by reference to public opinion support by margins of 70 percent or more. The divisive, racially charged, punitive politics that transformed U.S. politics created a highly supportive environment for the death penalty, both materially and symbolically, that diverged dramatically from the political context in most of western Europe. At the same time, continuous tinkering with the machinery of judicial killing may well have made the policy more palatable to elites and the public alike. [41] Extended opportunities for postsentencing review initially provided comfort that a full and fair process would be granted to each person sentenced to death row. And, increasingly, the mass media and dramatic fiction reveled in sensationalizing murder trials, amplifying the focus on victims and their families, as well as rituals of "responsibilization," while actual executions continued largely out of sight in the middle of the night with few observers and little news attention. Equally important is that electrocution, the gas chamber, and hanging were replaced by sanitized, ostensibly more humane processes of "killing softly" through lethal injection. The result was to portray executions as decent acts, not unlike "putting to sleep" a rabid or dangerous dog. One often-overlooked feature of these innovations is that they developed at the end of the twentieth century, after the completion of western Europe's abolitionist transformation but squarely amid the resurgence of judicial killing in the United States.

Contemporary Context: Permanent War

The preceding account of historical developments since the late 1970s is crucial to imagining the future of capital punishment in the United States. We see little reason to expect major changes in the larger political context. After all, the Clinton era consolidated neoliberal policy discourse, including assent to the domestic "wars" on crime, drugs, and the underclass, in ways that almost no contemporary politician of any standing in either party has seriously contested. And we already noted that President Bush exceeded his predecessors as an advocate of harsh justice. His public standing plummeted largely due to the debacle in Iraq, but there was little shift in electoral discourse on the domestic issue of penal policy, including capital punishment, or on militaristic force as a key commitment abroad.

Many factors will sustain these dynamics into the future, but the political features of the "war on terror" are probably most important.[42] As we see it, the "war on terror" has fueled the anxious obsessions with advancing security through hyperpunitive means that was associated with the cold war, but the former has little of the progressive silver lining of the latter. The similarities are not difficult to identify: a rhetoric constructing a dichotomous conflict between a virtuous We and a villainous Them; the high symbolic stakes for the future of "the free world";[43] the increased militarization of political and civic discourse, as well as domestic policing and security practices; the compromising and trampling of civil liberties at home and abroad; a fixation on willful violence as a problem and a solution; pressure for citizens to prove loyalty and defer to elites; and a relaxation of commitments to legal constraints and principles in order to meet the exigencies of "war."[44]

But the differences in context between the present "war on terror" and the cold war are less well appreciated. Among the most important contrasts is that the cold war was at heart an ideological struggle, whereas the U.S.–led "war on terror" recognizes no ideas or vision worthy of challenge. On this view, terrorism occurs not in the name of a rival worldview that threatens our freedom but, rather (as American leaders have constructed it), in the name of a curious mix of religious rage and primitive barbarism. Moreover, whereas the cold war was almost entirely waged in terms of a competition between secular values, the "war on terror" has been propelled by unmistakably religious rhetoric and fervor, especially the righteous fury that figures so prominently in the Old Testament.[45] In this sense, the present war is anything but "cold."

These factors have undercut sensitivity to cultural difference and magnified racial antagonism in the United States; in addition, they have reduced the pressure of two ideological forces highlighted by the struggles against communism. First, however empty and misleading it was, communism's egalitarian, inclusionary ideology pressured Americans to act as if those values mattered in our own society, and the emergence of a vision of a Great Society in the hottest moments of the cold war is one indication of that influence. In the contemporary context, by contrast, discourse about social justice, equality, and rights-based inclusion has yielded almost completely to the dichotomy of "freedom and security" versus "terror."[46] Likewise, whereas the cold war context sharpened U.S. sensitivity to the moral and institutional authority of human rights, the "war on terror" has led U.S. leaders to ignore or distance themselves more from such influences than at any time since the mid-1950s. Hence, cold war pressures linked domestic violations of civil rights and liberties to world concerns, but the international obsession with U.S. torture, rendition, and the like has diverted attention away from similar forms of violent state action that take place every day on American streets, in police stations, and in prisons. In short, the "war on terror" has produced almost none of the ideological pressure that supported internal struggles for civil rights and justice in the United States and Europe during the cold war.

Moreover, the cold war domestic struggles initially built on the foundations of the egalitarian New Deal transformation. The present "war on terror," by contrast, has developed in a domestic context grounded in re-action against the New Deal social welfare ethos and is committed, in-stead, to stigmatizing punitive discourse, policies, and practices. Far from providing ideological or political incentives to question racially charged punitiveness, the "war on terror" has built on and compounded such ten-dencies in our nation. We have no way of knowing how these pressures might play out in the future; they may diminish, but they are unlikely to recede quickly for the material and political sources of the tensions are rooted in enduring relationships around the world. Indeed, our leaders regularly remind us that this war is permanent and that there is no end in sight. When one adds the neoliberalizing pressures of globalization, the anxiously self-righteous punitiveness fed by the "war on terror," and the inertia of steady-state crisis that has dominated America in recent years, there is little reason to suppose that pressures to continue capital pun-ishment will subside anytime soon. Optimistic abolitionists counter that well-grounded challenges to capital punishment have increased during this period, but what impresses us is how little influence these sophisti-cated assaults have had on elite and public support for retaining the ulti-mate sanction. As Marie Gottschalk concludes in her insightful study of the politics of mass incarceration, "The institution of capital punishment in the United States has been stubbornly impervious to rational or scien-tific arguments that have been its undoing elsewhere."[47] For this reason, too, a "completion" of the abolitionist trend like those evidenced in Eu-rope is unlikely to occur anytime soon in the United States.

Institutional Promotion and Preservation of the Punitive Turn

Many factors contributed to the divergent political developments in Eu-rope and the United States, but we have called special attention to the ways in which enduring institutional differences have mattered. We high-light, in particular, the fact that criminal justice policy making tends to be centralized in national parliamentary institutions throughout Europe, while authority over policing, corrections, and punishment of crime—in-cluding the death penalty—is largely decentralized to the state and local levels in the United States. This federal structure has insulated the Ameri-can South from national pressure and centralized control. Decentraliza-tion has also facilitated the selective diffusion of reactionary punitive policies long identified with the South throughout other regions of the country, the lower Midwest and the Southwest especially, thus producing a variegated pattern of executing states, symbolic retentionist states that do not execute, and abolitionist states.[48]

At the same time, provisions for the election of national representatives and local sheriffs, attorneys general, and prosecutors, as well as mayors and other local executives responsible for appointing law enforcement leaders, opened the way for the politicized ratcheting up of punishment policy.[49] Stuart Scheingold has shown how the decentralized locus of criminal authority actually liberates national politicians to take the lead in developing the symbolic rhetoric of "law and order" politics for which they are obligated to deliver little in practice.[50] By contrast, many commentators emphasize that European nations are "less democratic," thus freeing elites to defy public opinion in ways that are not possible in the United States.[51] We find that general claim problematic, because harsh punishment has been driven in significant part by political elites,[52] though we do agree that the dynamics of U.S. institutions are distinctive in important ways. Finally, the role of appellate courts in policing the constitutionality of crime policy and practice has shaped American capital punishment in unique ways, chiefly by framing death penalty issues in ways that have preserved the institution of state killing.[53]

These institutional features not only encouraged growth of the punitive penal complex, they will sustain the politics of law and order, including capital punishment, for a long time to come. It is in this historical and institutional light that we examine three potential paths to abolition: Congress, the Supreme Court, and diffusion between individual states.

Congress

Congress has clearly helped escalate law and order politics, both symbolically and materially.[54] Indeed, the dramatic expansion of federal power in crime-control policy, fortified by national security concerns at various points, is one of the key features of the political history of the United States during the last half of the twentieth century. But even if some push toward reversing the punitive turn developed, Congress could abolish capital punishment in only two ways. It could eliminate the federal death penalty, which, in turn, might provide momentum for abolition at the state level. But the federal death penalty seems even less vulnerable to challenge than state penalties are because it is rarely applied in practice and because when it is used, it is usually for high-profile offenders—terrorists in particular (such as Timothy McVeigh)—which is the type of criminal for which the death penalty is least controversial. Congress could also pass a constitutional amendment to abolish the death penalty, but this requires a supermajority of two-thirds in both houses and ratification by three-quarters of the states—thresholds that would be extremely difficult to meet, primarily because of the strong support that exists for capital punishment in at least 13 of the 50 states.

Supreme Court

We have already seen that constitutional litigation was a key strategy in the 1960s, mobilizing the authority of judicial review that was important to the civil rights legacy and producing what many consider a "near miss" for death penalty abolition. But, again, we find that judgment misleading: only two abolitionists sat on the Court, new Nixon appointees led a large majority in support of capital punishment, and only a bare majority was willing to suspend the practice while procedural adjustments proceeded— and even then only for a short while. Far from stopping just short of abolition, the Court has consistently and almost unqualifiedly supported the death penalty as law, moral symbol, and practice. The Supreme Court not only upholds de jure judicial killing as consistent with the Eighth Amendment but also deflects direct challenges by channeling claims in procedural and technical directions. Many of the procedural adjustments have reinforced the institution. Among the most important of these have been restrictions on postsentencing appeals and dismissals of aggregate statistical evidence that demonstrates racial bias in capital sentencing. The Court has insulated capital punishment from such claims and delivered notice that the entire criminal justice system is immune to similar challenges. As Powell wrote in *McCleskey*:

> McCleskey's claim, taken to its logical conclusion, throws into serious question the principles that underlie our entire criminal justice system. The Eighth Amendment is not limited in application to capital punishment, but applies to all penalties. Thus, if we accepted McCleskey's claim that racial bias has impermissibly tainted the capital sentencing decision, we could soon be faced with similar claims as to other types of penalty.[55]

This passage is important for many reasons. Most centrally, it asserts that death is not a unique or different state mechanism that requires special legal limitations; it is, rather, an integral part of the hierarchical, exclusionary system of control in the modern neoliberal state.[56]

Individual justices have become prominent and frequently quoted advocates of capital punishment. The most important may be Antonin Scalia, who has defended executions as crucial for public order, as consistent with the Bible, as appropriate to avenge the death of victims and the pain of their loved ones, and as far more humane than the grisly murders committed by those condemned to death.[57] Against procedural and technical challenges, he intones, executions need not be painless or perfect in order to be constitutional. Scalia has also expressed scorn for European criticism of U.S. policy and law. By contrast, the few vocal opponents among the Justices—Blackmun in particular—only turned abolitionist in or near their retirement from the Bench, after ruling in support of capital punishment for many years. The present Court knows no vocal abolitionist, though Justice Stevens has turned critical after supporting death for decades, dating back to the 1970s. That five Catholics sit on the Court seems to matter little; a group of young, articulate, conservative males are likely to prevail for a long time to come. In short, the Roberts Court is a long way from the Warren Court, whose liberalism is routinely overestimated and did not extend to the abolition of capital punishment. For these reasons, we "see the posture of the current Supreme Court as a massive and virtually insurmountable obstacle" to abolition in the next few decades.[58]

We also are influenced by the considerable historical research showing that the Supreme Court rarely takes bold actions to challenge or change prevailing policies, intervening only when strong policy coalitions support its action.[59] Such extrajudicial forces supported both the *Brown v. Board of Education of Topeka* (1954) decision that overruled legal segregation and the Court's willingness to entertain procedural but not substantive challenges to capital punishment in the 1970s. A strong shift toward presidential and congressional support for abolition or a large increase in the number of abolitionist states would likely have to take place before the Court would impose substantive constitutional prohibitions.

The most recent ruling of the Court seems to confirm this reading. In *Baze v. Rees* (2008), the Court endorsed lethal injection—the same protocol used in all but one of the 38 death penalty states—by a 7–2 margin. It is true that Stevens added intrigue by protesting that execution is a "patently excessive and cruel and unusual punishment violative of the Eighth Amendment," but this cry of protest was overridden by his curious deference to precedent and concurrence with the majority ruling. The two dissenters, Souter and Ginsburg, argued blandly that the case should be remanded so that the Kentucky Supreme Court could reassess local protocol according to best practices in other states, while Scalia, Thomas, Alito, and Roberts debated how best to discourage further legal challenges. Dahlia Lithwick, senior editor at *Slate*, summarized the implication in terms that well fit the theme of this volume: "[T]o the extent *Baze* was supposed to be a sort of test drive for doing away with capital punishment altogether . . . it seems to have been driven off a cliff."[60]

We acknowledge that judicial "tinkering" with the processes of sentencing and the technologies of execution should not be treated as insignificant. Recent rulings that exclude juveniles and the mentally retarded from death sentences[61] and that emphasize the imperative of individualized decision-making are rightly welcomed by opponents of judicial killing. Similarly, the practice of admitting DNA tests has prevented wrongful executions. Although DNA evidence has often been used to confirm guilt and to legitimate harsh sentences imposed on the guilty, the innocence movement surely has softened elite and popular support for capital punishment.[62] Challenges to lethal injection and other technologies of death have further hobbled the machinery of death. Thus, our point is not that procedural tailoring by the Supreme Court and by legislatures is inconsequential; rather, we agree with Hugo Adam Bedau:

> Each of these reforms has entrenched ever deeper what remains of the death penalty, which makes what remains of it more resistant to complete repeal. Reform . . . does this by making those who are sentenced to death under its authority seem more deserving of such a penalty. Every step toward greater fairness in death penalty sentencing makes it that much harder to dismantle what's left.[63]

The Court's procedural rulings have also had the ironic, even tragic, effect of "normalizing" harsh punishments throughout the criminal justice system.[64] We have no crystal ball, but it is hard to imagine all that would have to happen for a major departure from support for the death penalty by the nation's highest courts. But this is not to say never. Some observers note that it took 60 years before *Plessy* was reversed by *Brown*; the latter took a long time, but it did eventually happen. Perhaps we will witness the abolition of capital punishment by the Supreme Court 60 or so years after *Gregg*. But we will not hold our breaths.

Diffusion among States

If the federal institutions of the Supreme Court and Congress are unlikely routes to abolition, what are the prospects for the diffusion of abolition among individual states? Ideas and policies sometimes spread "just like viruses do,"[65] and in many contexts "nothing spurs adoption of new ideas like other actors doing the same."[66] Might the United States be near a "tipping point" that could lead to national abolition within a decade or two?

Although there are some reasons for optimism, we believe the majority of states remain "a long, long way from giving up" capital punishment.[67] Consider the good news first. At the time of this writing (April 2008), 14 states have abolished the death penalty, and legislatures in several others—Maryland, Montana, Nebraska, New Mexico, and South Dakota— "appear to be within one or a few key votes of following suit." While the death penalty remains on the books but unused for decades in at least four other states, another five states "have each executed only one person during the last 40 years."[68] More broadly, there has been a "remarkable increase" in the number of abolitionist jurisdictions worldwide, from 29 percent of all countries in 1988 to 52 percent in 2007.[69] In fact, more countries abolished capital punishment in the 20 years after 1980 than in the preceding 200.[70] If American states were to ride this wave, capital punishment could disappear quickly.[71]

But that is a big "if." For one thing, the forces that have promoted abolition elsewhere in the world seem to have little traction in the United States.[72] For example, there has been little political leadership on death penalty issues in the United States, and without a history of totalitarianism to reject, there is also no incentive for American leaders or publics to distance themselves from the execution excesses of previous regimes, as happened in many nations that have abolished it.[73] Indeed, the perils of actively opposing capital punishment can be seen in the electoral misfortunes of former New York Governor Mario Cuomo, whose 1994 reelection loss to a political newcomer was at least partly the result of his annual vetoes of death penalty bills that New York's state legislature had passed.[74] Similarly, former Illinois Governor George Ryan's reservations about capital punishment improved neither his political fortunes nor his standard of living (he is now mopping floors in a federal prison). Further south, Virginia Governor Mark Warner's courageous decision to permit a new test of DNA from Roger Keith Coleman did not exactly create clear incentives for leaders in other Southern states to adopt unorthodox death penalty positions.[75]

Narrowing the frame of analysis to domestic considerations generates additional doubts about the prospects for state-to-state diffusion. In the years between *Furman* (1972) and the emergence of the innocence movement in the 1990s, America's own anti-death penalty movement was ineffective for three main reasons: it had little money, it framed death penalty issues in ways that held little appeal for most citizens and that inhibited more directly political opposition to the institution, and it consisted primarily of "eastern-based national organizations with weak state affiliates and few local ones."[76] Since the innocence movement started to accelerate in the early 1990s, state-based "Innocence Projects" have proliferated at the local level and anti-death penalty frames have become significantly more "pragmatic," as some analysts argued they must.[77] Yet America's anti-death penalty movement continues to be centered in national organizations such as Amnesty International USA, the ACLU, the NAACP Legal Defense and Educational Fund, the National Coalition to Abolish the Death Penalty, and the American Bar Association. Whatever the substantive merits of their positions—and we believe they are considerable—it must be recognized that the anti-death penalty views of these organizations are frequently greeted with indifference and scorn in death penalty strongholds such as Texas, Virginia, and Oklahoma. We see little reason to suppose those domestic missionaries will receive a more enthusiastic reception anytime soon.

Another reason for pessimism about the possibility of diffusion comes from the history of states that have already abolished the death penalty. There is not a large literature on the history of abolition in individual American states, but what there is suggests a few salient truths. The most comprehensive study indicates that elite views (of political and religious elites especially), the media, and population diversity have often played pivotal roles in death penalty debates at the state level. In particular, newspaper coverage of racial problems in capital punishment and either a high or low proportion of racial minorities in the population tend to correlate with abolition in individual states.[78] But of all Americans, evangelical Christians hold some of the strongest pro-death penalty views, and they and their organizations are especially influential in that part of the country—the South—where death sentences and executions are most frequent.[79] Similarly, most Southern states have minority populations that fall between the high and low abolition-prone poles, and their medium share of the population appears to be one reason why they pose a "racial threat" to state governments and publics—a threat that helps explain both the legal status of capital punishment in various American states and the distribution of death sentences and executions across the country.[80]

The real obstacles to abolition in America are old, durable, and Southern. The institution of slavery caused death penalty events to take very different trajectories in the North and South, so that by the time of the civil war there was already "a wide gulf between the northern and southern states in their use of capital punishment."[81] That gulf has since widened. Between 1950 and 1964, some 60 percent of all American executions were conducted in the South; during the last two decades of the twentieth century, the Southern share rose to 81 percent. And given a death sentence, the risk of execution in states such as Ohio, Pennsylvania, and California is only about 1/50th the risk in southern states such as Texas, Virginia, and Oklahoma.[82] In 2007, the most recent year for which figures are available, the United States conducted "only" 42 executions, 26 of them (62 percent) in Texas.[83] No other state executed more than three people. Some analysts believe that "the day is not far off when essentially all executions in the United States will take place in Texas,"[84] but we think that is an unlikely prospect. The day has already arrived, however, when executions in the United States are overwhelmingly a Southern thing. Greater diversification of executions across the United States could increase the vulnerability of death penalty systems to outside scrutiny by generating more attention to the issue in states where it was not previously salient,[85] but executions are actually becoming more heavily concentrated in the South, not more diversified elsewhere. What is more, there has been a notable trend in the South over recent years to *increase* the range of offenses that are eligible for capital punishment.[86] It is not surprising, then, that, immediately after the Supreme Court's recent ruling in *Baze*, "execution dockets are quickly filling up."[87] Less than three weeks after the ruling, 14 execution dates had been set, all except one in Southern states.[88]

Finally, some abolitionists believe that the current financial crisis will cause some states, including California and Georgia, to deal with the high public costs of capital punishment by eliminating the institution.[89] Recent evidence suggests that this might happen to some degree. In February 2009, the *New York Times* reported that lawmakers in at least eight states— Colorado, Kansas, Nebraska, New Hampshire, Maryland, Montana, New Mexico, and Washington—have seriously discussed abolishing the death penalty in order to cut costs amid huge budget deficits.[90] However, all of these are low execution states, and none is in the South. By contrast, the next day's headline in the *Dallas Morning News* reported that "high costs figure into the death penalty debate, but Texas holds firm."[91] It appears cost concerns are most salient where executions are infrequent, especially outside the South, and even then, fiscal imperatives have not yet led to many abolitions (though cost was one concern among many in the New Jersey abolition of 2007). To date, the main response of most states to fiscal pressures has been to release prisoners sentenced for the least violent crimes and to leave funding in place for dealing with the worst, and (in Louisiana and elsewhere) to cut back on the number of death sentences that prosecutors pursue.[92] This is consistent with one study comparing state policies on capital punishment which found that, "in themselves, economic factors do little to explain death penalty abolition in the United States."[93]

If "the beginning of the end" of American capital punishment has already started, as some analysts contend,[94] the actual end remains beyond our ability to see. The fact is, only one American state has abolished the death penalty since the Supreme Court reinstated it in 1976 (New Jersey, in December 2007). Several other states may now be teetering on the edge, but none is sufficiently Southern to suppose that abolition in them could spark change in those parts of the country that have long given American capital punishment its distinctively Dixie quality.

Imagining Change

Skepticism is not certainty. We think the prospects for formal abolition in the United States during our lifetimes are not good,[95] but we also can imagine circumstances in which the pace of change could accelerate. In this section, we explore some possibilities for change, including the potential for a reversal on the American "road to abolition" and the chance of one or more European jurisdictions restarting their own death penalty engines.

In some respects, there has been remarkable progress toward the desired destination of de jure abolition in the United States. In Amnesty International's terms, the United States remains in the same "retentionist" death penalty category as it always has been, even though its death penalty policy and practice are vastly different from what prevailed in Pilgrim society or even in the period before World War II: this occurs in the crimes punished with death, in execution methods and rituals, in arguments for and against state killing, in the centrality of religious justifications and ceremonies, in the way Americans experience and understand the death penalty, and in countless other ways.

There have been major changes in more recent years, too. Nationwide, the number of death sentences has dropped by almost two-thirds, and the volume of executions by nearly three-fifths since their post-*Furman* peaks in the late 1990s. Some numbers are down in Texas, too, with only 14 death sentences in 2006 compared with 40 a decade before. At present, fewer than 3 percent of the nation's death-row prisoners are executed in any given year, and in states such as California, execution is the third leading cause of death for death-row inmates (after suicide and natural causes). Concerns about lethal injection prompted 12 states to temporarily ban executions before the U.S. Supreme Court decided late in 2007 to stop executions everywhere until it ultimately decided (in *Baze v. Rees*) that Kentucky's lethal injection procedure does not pose an unconstitutional risk of pain to the condemned.[96] And we already noted that the nation's highest court recently declared that it is unconstitutionally "cruel and unusual" to impose capital punishment on the mentally retarded or on persons who committed their crimes while juveniles. In these ways, we are in "an amazing moment of national reconsideration that would have been unimaginable a decade ago."[97]

So we shall try to imagine another unimaginable outcome: the disappearance of the death penalty throughout the United States before the year 2030. What could cause that to happen? More precisely, what sorts of forces have the capacity to break through the gridlock of cultural ambivalence, institutional inheritance, and American angst over "the contradictions of capital punishment" and lead the country to the end of "the road to abolition" and the demise of a "thoroughly screwed-up system" of capital punishment that pleases almost no one?[98]

We see two possibilities. The first is some dramatic triggering event, such as a clear case of wrongful execution involving a sympathetic offender who gets put to death despite strong protests of actual innocence that are vindicated after the fact. This issue is raised by the film *The Life of David Gale*, and something like it was one proximate cause of the formal abolitions in the United Kingdom and Australia.[99] In South Korea, too, the president who moved Asia's abolitionist vanguard far along the road to abolition (Kim Dae Jung) was himself wrongly sentenced to death in the early 1980s, and his own personal experience with capital punishment—and the personal experiences of other Korean leaders and abolitionists—helps explain why that country has rapidly changed from being a vigorous executing state to being "abolitionist de facto."[100] Another step toward abolition in Korea could come from a 2007 court decision that posthumously acquitted eight innocent men who were executed in 1975.[101] As these and other national experiences suggest,[102] high-profile miscarriages of justice could provoke rapid and significant change in the United States as well, where "the issue of innocence, more than any other factor, has changed the climate surrounding state killing"[103] and prompted "a reconsideration of the legitimacy of capital punishment."[104]

The second stimulus for abolition could be international. Led by Europe, some nations of the world are using extradition policy and treaty obligations to pressure the United States to end capital punishment. So far, American political leaders have remained deaf to such cries, but the toll of domestic challenges about procedure and foreign challenges about substance has grown. If the United States finds itself vulnerable in some foreign policy venture and in need of allies in this age of terrorism, we can imagine an American leader making significant death penalty concessions. If, for example, Osama bin Laden is arrested for planning to blow up the Eiffel Tower in Paris or the Coliseum in Rome, the Ministry of Justice in either of those nations might refuse to extradite him to the United States for trial on charges of killing 3,000 people on that blue September morning unless American officials agree not to seek the death penalty.[105] A concession like that in a case involving an offender who is widely regarded as the very "worst of the worst" could undermine commitments to capital punishment in other cases and places, though that is not what happened in the Washington State case of the "Green River Killer," Gary Ridgeway, one of the most prolific serial murderers in American history (he admitted killing 48 women and may have killed many more) who plea bargained his way to a noncapital sentence in 2003. Alternatively, if America's "war on terror" takes a turn from the very bad to the considerably worse, the United States could find itself desperate for support from Europe in order to solve a pressing problem in (say) Iran or North Korea. If European leaders do something they have not done before—link their own cooperation to American compliance with the continent's death penalty orthodoxy—then America's executioners could be retired in relatively short order.

The confluence of domestic concern over a high-profile miscarriage of justice and an international imperative that gets linked to capital punishment might be an especially powerful combination,[106] but the conjuncture of two triggering events is a lot less likely than the occurrence of only one or the other. In any event, these seem to us unlikely possibilities. Since

1973, Americans have watched 126 persons walk away from death rows in 26 states because of evidence of their innocence (Florida and Illinois have the most releases, with 22 and 18, respectively). While this innocence movement has had several salutary consequences, including the commutation of 167 capital sentences in Illinois in 2003, formal abolition has not been one of them. Even in New Jersey, the only state that has abolished the death penalty since the *Gregg* decision of 1976, the commission that recommended abolition and the State Assembly and governor who passed the legislation were motivated by a collection of concerns much wider than the possibility of miscarriage.[107] More fundamentally, public opinion about crime and punishment "may be much more fixed and inflexible" than abolitionist analysts would like,[108] and public opinion about capital punishment may be considerably more central to the issue of its retention and considerably more resistant to change through rational argument than was the case in Europe.[109] Among other things, racial prejudice tends to be a strong and stable value, white support for capital punishment has a strong basis in racial prejudice, and white support is therefore "relatively intractable to intentional efforts by informational campaigns to change it."[110] Similarly, the transnational scenarios raised in the preceding paragraph are possible to imagine, but the persistent American insensitivity to European claims and frames seems to us a much likelier feature of America's death penalty future than would be significant death penalty concessions made during a foreign policy crisis. Indeed, it is unclear how the executive branch of government could dictate death penalty policy to Texas or Oklahoma even if the international stakes were nuclear.

So we end this attempt to imagine change with the same notes of caution and skepticism that introduced this essay. It is possible to visualize future events that could trigger the early demise of America's death penalty, and it is certainly easier to imagine that possibility than it is to see how America's prison complex could reduce its enormous scale by, say, one-half in the next 20 or 30 years. But it is still hard to imagine. For us, anyway, imagining an early funeral for American capital punishment is no easier to do than imagining scenarios in which the death penalty accelerates again, as it did after the decision in *Gregg*. This is also what happened in Japan after the gas attacks in the Tokyo subways in 1995. In the only other developed democracy that still uses capital punishment on a regular basis, records were set in 2007 for the number of death sentences (46), the number on death row (106), and the number of executions (9),[111] and these capital indicators could well go higher in the years to come. In the

United States, a terrorist attack at the Houston Astrodome or the Orlando Disney World could unleash enthusiasm for executions that has not been seen for decades. Although unlikely, an aggressively anti-death penalty decision by the U.S. Supreme Court—a second *Furman* decision—could also stimulate another death penalty backlash in some states.

The other pessimistic possibility to consider is whether terrorism or some other triggering event in Europe could cause the executioner's resurrection on the continent. Writers in this volume assume that the puzzle to explain is the pace of death penalty change, not its direction. The premise deserves scrutiny because the chance of a European comeback may not be negligible. In some parts of central and eastern Europe, leaders and citizens "pine for the capital punishment that they had to give up to join the European club."[112] On the eve of the millennium, public support for the death penalty in eastern Europe was 60 percent, compared with 60 percent against in western Europe, and in recent years politicians in the east have started to recognize and appeal to that sentiment. The guardians of European abolition tend to dismiss talk of a resurrection as little more than political gamesmanship, and they threaten to impose sanctions (or even expulsion from the European Union) on any death penalty deviants that might emerge. But if a terrorist attack strikes Budapest or Warsaw, where leaders have spoken openly and often about restoring capital punishment, the subject could shift from whether to have the death penalty to how to conduct executions. To venture a guess, we believe the chance of a terrorist-related execution in Europe before 2030 is at least as large as the chance of abolition in Texas by the same date.

Final Thoughts

So where is the United States on the road to abolition? In this essay, we argue that we are both close and far. Except for the fact of retention, the death penalty in America today is little like what it was in previous centuries and decades. At the same time, in some parts of the country capital punishment is still moving along "with all cylinders working."[113] In short, we believe American capital punishment has been rocked but still is rolling along, and in the preceding pages we have tried to demonstrate that there are good reasons to believe it will continue rolling—if neither smoothly nor fast—for some years to come.[114] Ironically, many of the repairs that have helped "tame" and "civilize" capital punishment—introducing degrees of murder, ending public executions, giving capital juries sentencing discretion, humanizing methods of execution, and federalizing appellate review—may well have had the effect of fortifying what remains of the ultimate penalty, making what survives even "more resistant to complete repeal."[115]

More broadly, the death penalty in the United States today is supported and sustained by many of the same institutional, historical, and cultural features that produce "harsh justice" in American penality more generally.[116] Abolition may depend on weakening the larger complex of penality and Americans' attachment to severe punishment as a preferred means of solving problems and expressing values. It is possible to imagine scenarios in which the death penalty and harsh justice could be decoupled, but if abolition is separated from reform of the larger penal complex, the advance will be limited and perhaps even Pyrrhic.

In recent years, America's anti-death penalty movement has made progress not seen for decades, and the increase of life without parole (LWOP) alternatives to capital punishment has played a prominent role in that push. But the availability of LWOP has had little effect on the number of executions, while causing significant increases in sentence lengths for offenders who never would have been sentenced to death under the preexisting system. In this regard, the increasing number of those who die on death row while awaiting execution parallels the increasing number of those who die while serving life terms. Since research shows that LWOP statutes are "neither a necessary nor a particularly useful step toward eliminating the death penalty," abolitionists "have a responsibility to consider carefully the effects of such laws on non-capital defendants before they engineer or encourage their passage."[117] But "careful consideration" of that kind is rarely seen. Abolition of capital punishment is an important good, but it is not the only good. This reminder would be facile were it not so frequently forgotten.

Another troubling possibility is that successful abolition could make other punishments harsher. Abolition was one precursor of America's massive prison expansion after the U.S. Supreme Court effectively eliminated the death penalty in 1972. In some contexts, the presence of capital punishment deflects attention from the harshness of punishments for noncapital crimes, thereby "normalizing" severe noncapital sanctions,[118] but the absence of capital punishment could also perform similar legitimating functions. The *Furman* Court's rejection of the death penalty gave rise to a major punitive pushback in the form of LWOP statutes, and the Supreme Court's decision on abolition for juveniles in the *Roper* case of

2005 had a similar effect in Texas.[119] As of 2005, almost 10 percent of the nation's prisoners—about 132,000 persons—were serving life sentences, and 28 percent of them (37,000) had no chance of parole.[120] Fully 10,000 American lifers in 48 states committed their crimes before they were old enough to vote, serve on a jury, or gamble in a casino, and more than one-fifth of them have no chance for parole.[121] This volume of life and life without parole punishment represents a reliance on severe sanctions that is unmatched in the world.[122] Indeed, the American life imprisonment rate—44 life sentences per 100,000 population—is higher than the *overall* incarceration rate was in Japan until the year 2000. It is by no means obvious that America's noncapital harshness will decrease merely because more states abolish the ultimate punishment. In this regard, it is notable that one impulse for abolition comes from "death in prison" proponents, who would make LWOP even more severe than it already is as a replacement for execution: "People so sentenced would still be sent to death row, a special prison unit where there would be no recreation time, no rehabilitation programs, no socializing, no life-extending medical treatment."[123]

Conversely, it is possible that retaining the death penalty in principle could provide politicians with the cover they need to reduce the severity of other sanctions and to begin dismantling some features of the carceral state, especially in the environment of fiscal crisis that now prevails in many states. In the end, this might be the best that realists can hope for in the anxious, stratified, neoliberal American present: few executions, some reduction in the incarceration of lower-level offenders, and retention of capital punishment as a symbol that assures the many people who believe harsh punishment is necessary in order to secure the freedoms of the deserving members of the moral community.[124]

NOTES

1. David Von Drehle, "Death Penalty Walking," *Time*, Jan. 3, 2008. Available at http://www.time.com/time/magazine/article/0,9171,1699855,00.html.

2. Richard Dieter, executive director of the Death Penalty Information Center, quoted in Ed Stoddard, "Religion, Culture behind Texas Execution Tally," *Reuters*, Aug. 12, 2007.

3. Dahlia Lithwick, "The Capital Gang: The Supreme Court Jump Starts the Machinery of Death," April 19, 2008. Available at http://www.slate.com/id/2189284/ (last accessed April 20, 2008).

4. Roger Hood and Carolyn Hoyle, *The Death Penalty: A Worldwide Perspective* (New York: Oxford University Press, 2008), p. 410.

5. James Payne, *A History of Force* (Sandpoint, Id.: Lytton, 2004).

6. We use the term "state killing" much as other abolitionists do, but we do so warily. Many states conduct extrajudicial executions (a category that includes police shootings, "disappearances," counterinsurgency efforts, and war), and the relationship between levels of extrajudicial and judical killing is a neglected topic of inquiry. For research suggesting there is little correlation between the two but there may be "common causation," see David T. Johnson and Franklin E. Zimring, *The Next Frontier: National Development, Political Change, and the Death Penalty in Asia* (New York: Oxford University Press, 2009).

7. Hugo Adam Bedau, "An Abolitionist's Survey of the Death Penalty in America Today," p. 24, in Hugo A. Bedau and Paul G. Cassell, eds., *Debating the Death Penalty* (Oxford: Oxford University Press, 2004).

8. For example, Nassim Nicholas Taleb, *The Black Swan: The Impact of the Highly Improbable* (New York: Random House, 2007); and Philip E. Tetlock, *Expert Political Judgment: How Good Is It? How Can We Know?* (Princeton, N.J.: Princeton University Press, 2005).

9. David Garland, "Capital Punishment and American Culture," *Punishment and Society* 7 (2005), p. 347.

10. Austin Sarat, *When the State Kills: Capital Punishment and the American Condition* (Princeton, N.J.: Princeton University Press, 2001).

11. Marie Gottschalk, *The Prison and the Gallows: The Politics of Mass Incarceration in America* (New York: Cambridge University Press, 2007), p. 41.

12. Franklin Zimring and Gordon Hawkins, *Capital Punishment and the American Agenda* (Cambridge: Cambridge University Press, 1986); Garland, "Capital Punishment"; Payne, *History of Force*.

13. Richard J. Evans, *Rituals of Retribution* (Oxford: Oxford University Press, 1996); Stuart Banner, *The Death Penalty: An American History* (Cambridge: Harvard University Press, 2002).

14. For more, see Peter Fitzpatrick, chap. 10 in this volume. In our view, the degree to which the United States has followed a different trajectory from Europe in reliance on the mechanisms of discipline and punishment is critical to understanding the history outlined here.

15. Franklin E. Zimring, *The Contradictions of American Capital Punishment* (Oxford: Oxford University Press, 2004), p. 17. See also Zimring and Hawkins, *Capital Punishment*, and Garland, "Capital Punishment."

16. Zimring, *Contradictions*, p. 18.

17. Garland, "Capital Punishment."

18. For a compelling documentation of this transformation, which grew out of aversion to war and state violence more generally, see the powerful book by James J. Sheehan, *Where Have All the Soldiers Gone? The Transformation of*

Modern Europe (New York: Houghton Mifflin, 2007). The linkage between capital punishment and other forms of state violence, especially war, is implied in our analysis, but systematic study of the subject is rare. For an exception, see Robin Wagner-Pacifici, chap. 9 in this volume.

19. Zimring, *Contradictions*, p. 18.

20. Ibid., p. 23.

21. Ibid., p. 27.

22. William A. Schabas, "Public Opinon and the Death Penalty," p. 317, in *Capital Punishment: Strategies for Abolition*, ed. Peter Hodgkinson and William A. Schabas (Cambridge: Cambridge University Press, 2004).

23. Mary L. Dudziak, *Cold War, Civil Rights: Race and the Image of American Democracy* (Princeton, N.J.: Princeton University Press, 2000); Azza Salama Layton, *International Politics and Civil Rights Policies in the United States, 1941–1960* (Cambridge: Cambridge University Press, 2000); Philip A. Klinkner, with Rogers M. Smith, *The Unsteady March: The Rise and Decline of Racial Equality in America* (Chicago: University of Chicago Press, 1999); Thomas Borstelman, *The Cold War and the Color Line* (Cambridge: Harvard University Press, 2001). In addition, the novels by Walter Moseley about life for the returning soldier Ezekial "Easy" Rawlins capture this aspect of black experience.

24. Quoted in Dudziak, *Cold War*, p. 87. John Rankin was a U.S. Representative from Mississippi who called civil rights activists "commies."

25. Carol Anderson, *Eyes Off the Prize: The United Nations and the African American Struggle for Human Rights* (Cambridge: Cambridge University Press, 2003).

26. Many national leaders recognized the issue, including Congressman Jacob Javits of New York, who repeatedly made this point in pressing for civil rights reforms: "With Communist China as a propaganda base, segregation and discrimination on grounds of race, creed or color in the U.S. can be used to win tens of millions to the Communist cause." The problem of discrimination was "a question of great relevance to the foreign policy of the U.S." Quoted in Duziak, *Cold War*, p. 87.

27. Herbert Haines, *Against Capital Punishment: The Anti-Death Penalty Movement in America, 1972–1974* (New York: Oxford University Press, 1996), pp. 23–54.

28. Ibid., p. 44.

29. Ibid.

30. Naomi Murakawa, "The Origins of the Carceral Crisis: Racial Order as 'Law and Order' in Postwar American Politics," unpublished ms., 2006.

31. Katherine Beckett, *Making Crime Pay: Law and Order in Contemporary American Politics* (New York: Oxford University Press, 1997).

32. Stuart Scheingold, *The Politics of Law and Order: Street Crime and Public Policy* (New York: Longman, 1984).

33. Garry Wills, *Nixon Agonistes: The Crisis of the Self-Made Man* (New York: Houghton-Mifflin, 1969), p. 533.

34. Quoted in Beckett, *Making Crime Pay*, p. 31.

35. Scheingold, *Politics of Law and Order*.

36. For more, see Naomi Murakawa's path-breaking empirical study, "Elected to Punish: Congress, Race, and the Rise of the American Criminal Justice State" (Ph.D. diss., Yale University, 2004).

37. By 1997, over 50 percent of the American prison population was black or Hispanic, which was twice the percentage of 1930. Bruce Western, *Punishment and Inequality in America* (New York: Russell Sage, 2006).

38. For example, Scheingold, *Politics of Law and Order*; Beckett, *Making Crime Pay*; and Jonathan Simon, *Governing through Crime* (New York: Oxford University Press, 2008). The most complex and subtle analysis of these processes is David Garland, *The Culture of Control* (Chicago: University of Chicago Press, 2001). See also Gottschalk, *Prison and the Gallows*.

39. Michael Tonry, "Crime and Human Rights: How Political Paranoia, Protestant Fundamentalism, and Constitutional Obsolescence Combined to Devastate Black America—The American Society of Criminology 2007 Presidential Address," *Criminology* 46 (2008), p. 1. The considerable overlap between the "Bible belt" and the "death belt" has received much scholarly attention. See, for example, Carol S. Steiker, "Capital Punishment and American Exceptionalism," *Oregon Law Review* 81 (2002), p. 124; and Carol S. Steiker and Jordan M. Steiker, "A Tale of Two Nations: Implementation of the Death Penalty in 'Executing' versus 'Symbolic' States in the United States," *Texas Law Review* 84 (2006), p. 1869.

40. Jimmy Carter supported capital punishment while governor of Georgia. He signed legislation to authorize the death penalty for murder, rape, and other offenses, as well as to implement trial procedures invited by *Furman* and approved in *Gregg*. Carter later became an opponent of capital punishment, but his previous role as a supporter was crucial to his bid for the presidency.

41. The best book connecting the matters discussed in this paragraph is Austin Sarat, *When the State Kills: Capital Punishment and the American Condition* (Princeton, N.J.: Princeton University Press, 2002).

42. For related insights, see Pacifici-Wagner, chap. 9 in this volume.

43. This dimension is well captured in Benjamin Barber's *Jihad vs. McWorld* (New York: Ballantine, 1996).

44. On the relationship between a nation's international involvement in war and internal punitiveness, see the chapter "Violent Acts and Violent Times: The Effect of Wars on Postwar Homicide Rates," in Dane Archer and Rosemary Gartner, *Violence and Crime in Cross-National Perspective* (New Haven, Conn.: Yale University Press, 1984), pp. 63–97.

45. Domestic discourse did pit righteous Judeo-Christian America against the godless Soviets and Chinese, but this was muted by the need to appeal to allies

around the world where our religious traditions were less prevalent. One result was an emphasis on secular civic visions, including faith in rule of law and scientific progress.

46. Carol Steiker has observed that the focus on terrorism may actually reduce concern about "everyday" murder: obsession with 9/11 terrorists may overshadow fear of routine violence at the 7/11 (conference on "The Road to Abolition," Harvard University, 15 February 2008). Even if this is true, it may reduce demand for executions without leading to termination of the death penalty itself.

47. Gottschalk, *Prison and the Gallows*, p. 233.

48. Steiker and Steiker, "Tale of Two Nations."

49. Stuart Scheingold, *The Politics of Street Crime* (Philadelphia: Temple University Press, 1992).

50. Scheingold, *Law and Order*.

51. James Q. Wilson, *Thinking about Crime* (New York: Basic Books, 1975); Banner, *Death Penalty*.

52. Beckett, *Making Crime Pay*; Gottschalk, *Prison and the Gallows*; Simon, *Governing through Crime*.

53. Gottschalk, *Prison and the Gallows*, p. 198.

54. For more, see Naomi Murakawa's study of congressional dynamics in the "law and order" surge from the 1970s through the 1990s, "Elected to Punish."

55. *McCleskey v. Kemp*, 481 U.S. 279 (1987).

56. This argument is also made by Timothy Kaufman-Osborne in "A Critique of Contemporary Death Penalty Abolitionism," *Punishment and Society* 8, no. 3 (2006), pp. 365–83. In several ways, Kaufman-Osborne's more philosophical argument parallels and complements the analysis in this chapter.

57. *Callins v. Collins*, 114 S.Ct. 1127 (1994). See also Antonin Scalia, "God's Justice and Ours," *First Things: A Journal of Religion and Public Life* (2002), pp. 17–21 (arguing that the constitutionality of capital punishment is clear and its morality is grounded in the conviction that government derives its authority from divine sources).

58. Bedau, "Abolitionist's Survey," p. 30.

59. Mark Graber, "The Non-Majoritarian Difficulty: Legislative Deference to the Judiciary," *Studies in American Political Development* 7 (1993), pp. 35–36; George I. Lovell, *Legislative Deferrals: Statutory Ambiguity, Judicial Power, and American Democracy* (New York: Cambridge University Press, 2003); Paul Frymer, *Black and Blue: African Americans, the Labor Movement, and the Decline of the Democratic Party* (Princeton, N.J.: Princeton University Press, 2008).

60. Lithwick, "Capital Gang."

61. *Roper v. Simmons* (03-633) (2005) and *Atkins v. Virginia, 536 U.S. 304 (2002),* respectively.

62. Frank R. Baumgartner, Suzanna L. Deboef, and Amber E. Boydstun, *The Decline of the Death Penalty and the Discovery of Innocence* (New York: Cambridge University Press, 2008).

63. Bedau, "Abolitionist's Survey," pp. 24–25.

64. Carol Steiker and Jordan Steiker, "The Shadow of Death: The Effect of Capital Punishment on American Criminal Law and Policy," *Judicature*, March/April (2006), p. 250.

65. Malcolm Gladwell, *The Tipping Point: How Little Things Can Make a Big Difference* (New York: Little, Brown, 2000), p. 7.

66. Lawrence W. Sherman, "Evidence-Based Crime Prevention: A Global View from the U.S. to Japan," *Hanzai Shakaigaku Kenkyu* 29 (2004), pp. 82–93, at 91. See also Joel Best, ed., *How Claims Spread: Cross-National Diffusion of Social Problems* (New York: Aldine De Gruyter, 2001).

67. Von Drehle, "Death Penalty Walking," 2008.

68. Ibid. The states with zero executions are New Hampshire, New Jersey, New York, and South Dakota, and the states with one execution are Connecticut, Colorado, Idaho, Wyoming, and New Mexico. David Von Drehle, "New Jersey: A Death Penalty Trend?" *Time*, Dec. 17, 2007. See also http://www.deathpenaltyinfo.org, under "state execution rates."

69. Roger Hood, "Capital Punishment: A Global Perspective," *Punishment and Society* 3, no. 3 (2001), pp. 331–54, at 331. See also Johnson and Zimring, *Next Frontier*. If one counts the number of countries in all three abolitionist categories—complete abolitionist, abolitionist for ordinary offenses only, and abolitionist de facto (no executions for at least 10 years)—then the percentage of abolitionist countries in the world has increased from 44 percent in 1988 to 69 percent in 2007. Hood, *Death Penalty*, p. 334, and Amnesty International reports for 2007.

70. Zimring, *Contradictions*, p. 35.

71. The global effects of the anti-death penalty movement are also evident in the distribution of votes on the December 2007 U.N. resolution calling for a worldwide moratorium on executions with a view to abolishing capital punishment. After several similar efforts failed in the 1990s, the vote this time in the 192-member body was 104 nations in favor (54 percent) with 54 opposed (28 percent), 29 abstentions (15 percent), and 5 absences (3 percent). Overall, the ratio of "for" to "against" was almost 2 to 1, though support varied considerably by region. All the countries of Europe supported the resolution except Belarus, which abstained and which executed a serial killer by firing squad in the same month the U.N. acted (Kuban Abdymen, "Uzbek Abolition Draws Line under Past," Inter Press Service News Agency, Jan. 17, 2008). In North, South, and Central America, only four nations voted against the resolution: Belize, Guyana, Suriname, and the United States. The nations of Oceania also supported the resolution by an 8–2–1 margin. In the Middle East and the Caribbean, by contrast, only 3 of 26 nations supported it: Israel, Haiti, and the Dominican Republic. The votes in Africa (17–11–20–4) and Asia (7–15–4–0) were more mixed (email report from Hands Off Cain, Dec. 18, 2007).

72. Hood, "Capital Punishment," p. 337.

73. Bernard Harcourt, chap. 3 in this volume. See also Eva Puhar, "The Abolition of the Death Penalty in Central and Eastern Europe: A Survey of Abolition Processes in Former Communist Countries," paper prepared for the European Master's Degree in Human Rights and Democratisation, National University of Ireland, pp. 1–54.

74. John F. Galliher, Larry W. Koch, David Patrick Keys, and Teresa J. Guess, *America without the Death Penalty: States Leading the Way* (Boston: Northeastern University Press, 2002), p. 3.

75. Roger Coleman was the convicted rapist and murderer who, leading abolitionists passionately argued, had been wrongfully electrocuted in 1992 right up until the January morning in 2006 when a Q-tip's worth of semen finally convinced them that Coleman was indeed a killer. Glenn Frankel, "Burden of Proof," *Washington Post*, May 14, 2006, p. W08.

76. Herbert H. Haines, *Against Capital Punishment: The Anti-Death Penalty Movement in America, 1972–1994* (New York: Oxford University Press, 1996), p. 167.

77. Ibid., p. 168.

78. Galliher et al., *America without the Death Penalty*, p. 206.

79. The Pew Research Center for the People and the Press, "Religion and Politics: Contention and Consensus," July 14, 2003. See also G. Jeffrey MacDonald, "Religious Foes of Capital Punishment See New Momentum," *Religion News Service*, Jan. 7, 2008.

80. For more, see David Jacobs and Jason T. Carmichael, "The Political Sociology of the Death Penalty: A Pooled Time Series Analysis," *American Sociological Review* 67 (2002), pp. 109–31; David Jacobs and Jason T. Carmichael, "Ideology, Social Threat, and Death Sentences: Capital Sentencing across Time and Space," *Social Forces* 83 (2004), pp. 249–78; David Jacobs, Jason T. Carmichael, and Stephanie L. Kent, "Vigilantism, Current Racial Threat, and Death Sentences," *American Sociological Review* 70 (2005), pp. 656–77; and David Jacobs, Zhenchao Qian, Jason Carmichael, and Stephanie Kent, "Who Survives on Death Row? An Individual and Contextual Analysis," *American Sociological Review* 72 (2007): 610–32.

81. Banner, *Death Penalty*, p. 137.

82. Zimring, *Contradictions*, p. 189.

83. Johnson and Zimring, *Next Frontier*, pp. 20, 312. Between 1997 and 2005, the execution rate per million population in Texas was more than 100 times higher than in the Muslim-majority nation of Bangladesh. Ibid. Similarly, executions in the Islamic Republic of Pakistan surged to 82 in 2006, giving that country the third highest volume of executions in the world (after China and Iran), but Pakistan's per capita rate of 0.5 executions per million population was still less than half the execution rates in Texas and Virginia. Since the late 1990s, Southern states such as

Texas, Virginia, Missouri, Oklahoma, and South Carolina have ranked among the few jurisdictions in the world with per capita execution rates greater than 1.0 per million population. Hood and Hoyle, *Death Penalty*, p. 92. Their company in that category includes China, Singapore, Vietnam, Saudi Arabia, and Iran.

84. Adam Liptak. "Executions Decline Elsewhere, but Texas Holds Steady," *New York Times*, Dec. 26, 2007.

85. Zimring, *Contradictions*, p. 190.

86. Justices Scalia and Alito made much of this trend during oral argument regarding challenges to Louisiana's effort to extend the death penalty to nonhomicidal rapists. Lithwick, "Capital Gang."

87. Ralph Blumenthal, "After Hiatus, States Set Wave of Executions," *New York Times*, May 3, 2008. Available at http://www.nytimes.com/2008/05/03/us/03execute.html?th&emc=th.

88. Ibid. Texas unsurprisingly led the way with five scheduled execution dates, Virginia with four, Louisiana with two; one was scheduled each in Oklahoma, Georgia, and South Dakota, the only non-Southern state. Officials in each of these states have proclaimed that more scheduled executions will follow.

89. Michael Radelet, chap. 1 in this volume. See also Jeffrey Toobin, "Death in Georgia: The High Price of Trying to Save an Infamous Killer's Life," *New Yorker*, Feb. 8, 2008.

90. Ian Urbina, "Citing Cost, States Consider End to Death Penalty," *New York Times*, Feb. 25, 2009.

91. Feb. 26, 2009.

92. See Michelle Mill Hollon, "Economics of Execution," *Advocate*, Mar. 8, 2009. The Louisiana case also illustrates our assertion that even where cost concerns cause capital punishment cutbacks, they are unlikely to lead to formal abolition. In this Southern state (which has the highest incarceration rate in the United States but which has not carried out an execution since May 2002), local prosecutors "are limiting the number of executions they pursue because of the price tag and the length of appeals," yet elected officials—including Governor Bobby Jindal, Senate President Joel Chaisson, and House Speaker Jim Tucker—insist that the death penalty's "deterrent value is worth the cost, however high" (Hollon, "Economics of Execution"). Many prosecutors claim the costs are "staggering" and "unbelievable," and defense lawyers seem to agree. Jean Faria, the head of the Louisiana State Public Defender Board, says that $9 million of her $28 million budget—nearly one-third—is spent on capital cases (ibid.). In this state and elsewhere, one important cause of the high costs is post-conviction appeals and delays (Zimring, *Contradictions*, p.78). In 2007, the average time between sentencing and execution was 12.7 years, compared with a seven-year wait in 1990 and a 14.4-month wait for 1956–1960 (Hollon, "Economics of Execution"); Robert M. Bohm, "The Economic Costs of Capital Punishment: Past, Present, and Future," p. 574, in James R. Acker, Robert M. Bohm, and Charles

S. Lanier, eds., *America's Experiment with Capital Punishment* [Durham, N.C.: Carolina Academic Press, 2003]). The average wait on death row today is thus 10 times longer than it was 50 years ago. And significant delay seems here to stay. For one thing, the quick is often the enemy of the careful in death penalty decision making, but even in the post-Furman delay-plagued system, some 130 people from 26 states have been released from death row with evidence of their innocence (Death Penalty Information Center, at http://www.deathpenaltyinfo.org/innocence-and-death-penalty). For another, on March 9, 2009, the U.S. Supreme Court ruled that a Florida inmate's 32-year wait on death row did not constitute cruel and unusual punishment (*Thompson v. McNeil*, No. 08-7369; see also Adam Liptak, "Justices Rule on Legal Effects of Slow-Moving Cases," *New York Times*, Mar. 10, 2009). Like many rulings before it, this one enables the death penalty to keep rolling along, however slowly it might move.

93. Galliher, et al., *America without the Death Penalty*, p. 211.

94. Zimring, *Contradictions*, p. 179.

95. This pessimistic hunch depends not only on the future course of capital punishment but also on the quality of our genes, our luck, and our health care providers—and perhaps on providence, too.

96. Elizabeth Weil, "The Needle and the Damage Done," *New York Times Magazine*, Feb. 11, 2007, pp. 46–51.

97. Ibid., p. 48.

98. Zimring, *Contradictions*; Von Drehle, "Death Penalty Walking."

99. In the United Kingdom, concerns about the wrongful execution of Derek Bentley and the wrongful conviction of Timothy Evans helped produce "a healthy majority for abolishing the death penalty for murder in 1965 for a trial period of five years," a shift that was made permanent in 1969. Hood, *Death Penalty*, p. 26. In Australia, the last person executed (in 1967) was Ronald Ryan, who received a mandatory death sentence after his conviction for murder of a prison officer during an escape from a Melbourne prison. Defense lawyer Phillip Opas argued that Ryan was innocent, a position he has maintained to the present: "The controversy surrounding Ryan's hanging generated widespread revulsion at the use of the death penalty—and its politicization—and created the momentum for eventual abolition" (Asia Death Penalty Blog, Feb. 5, 2007, available at http://asiadeathpenalty.blogspot.com).

100. Johnson and Zimring, *Next Frontier*.

101. Byung-Sun Cho, "Is Abolition Close? Reflections on South Korea's Changing Capital Punishment Policy," *Punishment and Society* (forthcoming).

102. In Japan and China, miscarriages of justice in capital cases did not lead to abolition but did spark significant execution declines. For more, see David T. Johnson, "Where the State Kills in Secret: Capital Punishment in Japan," in *Punishment and Society* 8, no. 3 (2006), pp. 281–85 at 282; Johnson and Zimring, *Next Frontier*, chap. 7.

103. Austin Sarat, "Innocence, Error, and the 'New Abolitionism': A Commentrary," *Criminology and Public Policy* 4, no. 1 (2005), pp. 45–54 at 45.

104. James D. Unnever and Francis T. Cullen, "Executing the Innocent and Support for Capital Punishment: Implications for Public Policy," *Criminology and Public Policy* 4, no. 1 (2005), pp. 3–37 at 3.

105. Something like this resistance is what France gave the United States in the case of Zacarias Moussaoui, who was said to be "the twentieth hijacker" on September 11, though the United States ultimately did decide to seek death for this French national of Moroccan descent, despite France's refusal to provide information that could be used in a capital trial. For more, see Zimring, *Contradictions*, p. 42. In 2006, Moussaoui received a life sentence in the U.S. District Court for the Eastern District of Virginia.

106. Alan W. Clarke and Laurelyn Whitt, *The Bitter Fruit of American Justice: International and Domestic Resistance to the Death Penalty* (Boston: Northeastern University Press, 2007).

107. Editorial, "A Long Time Coming," *New York Times*, Dec. 15, 2007.

108. Lawrence D. Bobo and Devon Johnson, "A Taste for Punishment: Black and White Americans' Views on the Death Penalty and the War on Drugs," *Du Bois Review* 1 (2004), pp. 151–80 at 155.

109. Gottschalk, *Prison and the Gallows*, p. 233.

110. Steven E. Barkan and Steven F. Cohn, "On Reducing White Support for the Death Penalty: A Pessimistic Appraisal," *Criminology and Public Policy* 4, no. 1 (2005), pp. 39–44 at 42. Barkan and Cohn also argue that "[i]f white support during the 1990s dropped only 9.4 percent despite the publicity over wrongful convictions in capital cases and a sharp drop in homicide rate and still remained at almost 70 percent, we do not hold much hope that this opinion can be swayed through the public education campaigns [other] observers advocate" (p. 42). We do not hold much hope, either.

111. "46 Sentenced to Death in 2007, Most Since 1980," *Japan Times*, Jan. 14, 2008.

112. Craig S. Smith, "In Europe, It's East vs. West on the Death Penalty," *New York Times*, Nov. 19, 2006, Week in Review section, p. 4.

113. Dieter, quoted in Stoddard, "Religion, Culture."

114. Our use of the term "rocked" suggests two related meanings. First, the legitimacy of capital punishment as an institution has been rocked by repeated challenges, especially from abolitionist critics. Second, these assaults have rocked the machinery of death itself, destabilizing and slowing it down, as a crowd might rock a police car to take it out of commission. Yet judicially authorized killing in the United States is still rolling along, we argue, quite a ways away from some imagined abolitionist terminus.

115. Bedau, "Abolitionist's Survey," p. 25; Gottschalk, *Prison and the Gallows*.

116. James Q. Whitman, *Harsh Justice: Criminal Punishment and the Widening Divide between America and Europe* (New York: Oxford University Press, 2003). See also Gottschalk, *Prison and the Gallows*; Simon, *Governing through Crime*.

117. "A Matter of Life and Death: The Effect of Life-without-Parole Statutes on Capital Punishment," *Harvard Law Review* 119 (2008), pp. 1838–54 at 1854.

118. Carol Steiker and Jordan Steiker, "The Shadow of Death: The Effect of Capital Punishment on American Criminal Law and Policy," *Judicature* 89, no. 5 (2005), pp. 250–53 at 253.

119. "Matter of Life and Death," p. 1841.

120. Adam Liptak, "To More Inmates, Life Term Means Dying behind Bars," *New York Times*, Oct. 2, 2005.

121. As of 2007, a total of 73 American prisoners were serving life without parole for crimes they committed at age 13 or 14. Adam Liptak, "Lifers as Teenagers, Now Seeking Second Chance," *New York Times*, Oct. 17, 2007. See also Adam Liptak, "Jailed for Life after Crimes as Teenagers," *New York Times*, Oct. 3, 2005; Human Rights Watch, "The Rest of Their Lives: Life without Parole for Child Offenders in the United States," October 2005, at http://www.hrw.org/en/reports/2005/10/11/rest-their-lives; Marc Mauer, Ryan S. King, and Malcolm C. Young, "The Meaning of 'Life': Long Prison Sentences in Context," Sentencing Project, May 2004, at http://sentencengproject.org/Admin/Documents/publications/ins-meaning of life.pdf.

122. In December 2006, the United Nations introduced a resolution calling for the abolition of LWOP for children and young teenagers. The vote was 185 to 1, and the sole dissenter was the United States. Liptak, "Lifers as Teenagers." In practice, there is a big difference between the situation of prisoners in other countries who have remained in custody for the rest of their lives while retaining the opportunity to earn early release and the situation of many prisoners in the United States where "a life sentence can from the outset be for a full-life period with no possibility of review or parole." Roger Hood, "Developments on the Road to Abolition: A Worldwide Perspective," paper prepared for the workshop Global Survey on Death Penalty Reform, Beijing, August 25–26, 2007, pp. 1–23 at 17. The substitution of LWOP for capital punishment "simply raises many of the human rights issues that have been at the heart of the attack on the death penalty itself." Hood, "Developments," p. 23; see also Hood and Coyle, *Death Penalty*, chap. 11.

123. Steve Blow, "Time for Texas to Try Death Penalty without Executions." *Dallas Morning News*, Jan. 13, 2008. Available at http://www.dallasnews.com/sharedcontent/dws/dn/localnews/columnists/sblow/stories/012408dnmetblow.223b668.html.

124. Kaufman-Osborne, "Critique." This cultural logic reminds us of Davis Grubb's American literary gothic, *The Night of the Hunter*. The story, translated by James Agee's screenplay into a film featuring Robert Mitchum, focused on a suave, indulgent, and murderous country preacher (Harry Powell) whose trademark sermon illustrated the eternal struggle between love and hate, with the letters of each word tattooed on his writhing, clasped hands—*l-o-v-e* on one, and *h-a-t-e* on the other. Love wins out (barely) in the preacher's demonstrative sermons and also when matriarch Lillian Gish saves the children from his villainy. That Gish's love was backed up by her shotgun and culminated in condemning the preacher to the gallows captures well some of the complexities that still haunt America.

Part II

||||||||||||||||||||||||||||||||||||||||||||||||||||||||||

Debating Lethal Injection

For Execution Methods Challenges, the Road to Abolition Is Paved with Paradox

Deborah W. Denno

The death penalty's popularity has waned appreciably in recent years. Whether because of disturbing discoveries of innocence among death row inmates, the narrowing of the classes of individuals eligible for execution, racial disparities, botched executions, or other reasons, the courts and the public have shown more skepticism of the capital punishment process in the twenty-first century than they have since the early 1970s.[1] Riding high on the momentum of this snowballing development are challenges to lethal injection under the Eighth Amendment's Cruel and Unusual Punishments Clause.[2] According to one death penalty commentator, these challenges "have already held up more executions, and for a longer time than appeals involving such . . . issues as race, innocence, and mental competency."[3]

In this chapter, I contend that, despite the contributions that lethal injection challenges have made toward decreasing the number of executions, the oft-perceived link between execution methods litigation and the potential abolition of the death penalty is a double-edged sword. Because lethal injection challenges apply to nearly every death-row inmate in the country, their impact on the death penalty generally is more sweeping than more particularized efforts to protect a specific class of inmates, such as the mentally incompetent. Nonetheless, the presumed tie between successful lethal injection challenges and abolition can distract legislatures, courts, and prison personnel from examining the actual issue under consideration—the constitutionality of states' execution protocols. The result can be paradoxical and damaging to the goals of death penalty proponents and opponents alike. The very strategy that is supposed to enhance the acceptability of the death penalty—making executions humane—is now among those efforts most apt to dismantle it. Therefore, states cling to troublesome execution methods to blanket the death penalty's flaws, while litigation over the inhumanity of those execution methods furthers abolitionist goals through execution declines.

The perils of this paradox are evident in the U.S. Supreme Court's most recent execution methods case. On April 16, 2008, for the first time in at least six decades, the Supreme Court considered whether a state's method of execution violated the Eighth Amendment.[4] In *Baze v. Rees*, a 7–2 plurality ruling,[5] the Court upheld the constitutionality of Kentucky's method of executing inmates by lethal injection.[6] The Court determined that the defendants had failed to show that Kentucky's administration of the three-drug combination used by most death penalty states posed a "substantial" or "objectively intolerable" risk of "serious harm"[7] compared with "known and available alternatives."[8] The Court also observed that the petitioners' proposed alternative method of execution, consisting of a large dose of only the first of the three drugs, carried its own risks.[9] Yet many of the Justices' splintered rationales reflected deep concerns about avoiding future lethal injection litigation or insulating the death penalty itself—an interpretation seemingly buoyed by Justice John Paul Stevens's use of *Baze* as the vehicle to declare for the first time his view that the death penalty is unconstitutional.[10] In Stevens's eyes, *Baze* will satisfy neither of the Court's dual goals about the future of executions. "Instead of ending the controversy," he explained, *Baze* "will generate debate not only about the three-drug protocol . . . but also about the justification for the death penalty itself."[11]

The road leading to *Baze* is well traveled with lethal injection litigation; however, post-*Baze*, there appear to be many more litigation miles still to go. Ever since Oklahoma first adopted lethal injection in 1977, attorneys have challenged the method's constitutionality on a variety of grounds, ranging from the selection and qualifications of the execution team to the involvement of physicians in the execution process to the formula developed for the injections.[12] The typical formula, which Kentucky uses, consists of a serial sequence of three drugs: sodium thiopental, a common anesthetic for surgery that is intended to cause unconsciousness; pancuronium bromide, a total muscle relaxant that stops breathing by paralyzing the diaphragm and lungs; and potassium chloride, a toxin that induces cardiac arrest and permanently stops the inmate's heartbeat.[13]

A primary concern in *Baze* and lethal injection challenges generally rests with the second drug, pancuronium bromide. Without adequate anesthesia, pancuronium can cause an inmate excruciating pain and suffering because the inmate slowly suffocates from the drug's effects while paralyzed and unable to cry out. The agony is dramatically increased when executioners inject the third drug, potassium chloride, which creates an intense and unbearable burning. There is agreement that if the sodium thiopental is ineffective, it would be reprehensible to inject the second and third drugs into a conscious person. A key issue in litigation is whether prison officials and executioners can determine if an inmate is aware and in torment because the pancuronium is such a powerful mask of emotions.[14] Starting in 2006, this litigation so successfully prompted death penalty moratoria and execution stalemates across the country that a Supreme Court case like *Baze* appeared inevitable.

The purported tie between abolitionism and execution method challenges now spotlights lethal injection, but that has not always been the case. This country has used a number of other execution methods (hanging, electrocution, and lethal gas) that have also been associated with abolitionist strategies, although perhaps not as directly. For example, botched electrocution executions were commonly used as a vehicle for supporting anti-death penalty stances. In the discussion that follows, however, I focus predominantly on lethal injection challenges, in light of their particularly strong and recent impact on the number of executions.

In the first section of this chapter, I explain briefly the history and context of the development of lethal injection, showing how the lethal injection formula was accepted quickly without medical or scientific scrutiny. Adoption of the method was primarily related to issues pertinent to the death penalty generally (such as cost and retribution) rather than simply lethal injection's humaneness. In the second section, I discuss lethal injection's perplexing persistence, emphasizing the speed and confidence with which lethal injection was adopted by states, despite evidence that the method was troublesome from the very start. Within the past decade, the method's problems were strikingly evident in three district court cases in California, Missouri, and Tennessee in which the courts ruled that lethal injection was unconstitutional. In the third section, I examine *Baze* and the varying rationales behind the Justices' disparate opinions, noting the Justices' concerns over endless lethal injection litigation and the existence of the death penalty itself. The paradoxical relationship between the inhumaneness of the execution method and the viability of the death penalty potentially impedes the Court from resolving the matter of lethal injection's constitutionality in an acceptable manner. The use of lethal injection

FIGURE 6.1

Methods of execution

| Hanging/ Firing Squad | Electrocution (1890) | Lethal Gas (1921) | Lethal Injection (1977) |

challenges as a tool to perpetuate—or dissolve—the death penalty may only result in tortuous execution methods, a goal sought neither by most opponents nor by most proponents. While *Baze* is a new case, it appears that it has already inspired ongoing litigation that will continue for quite some time. This litigation raises important questions, which demand careful consideration, but its effect on the road to abolition is uncertain.

Brief History of Execution Methods

This country's adoption of lethal injection follows more than a century of searching for humane methods of execution.[15] While hanging and the firing squad were the first primary methods, problems implementing both techniques spurred legislators and courts to investigate other, seemingly more acceptable, means of carrying out the death penalty. This examination began with electrocution (1890), then included lethal gas (1921), and, in an evolving pattern beginning over 30 years ago, moved nearly exclusively to lethal injection (figure 6.1).[16]

Lethal Injection's Troubling Start

Looking back throughout history, there is as little excuse for lethal injection's adoption as there is for its perpetuation. Lethal injection's deficiencies, although repeatedly documented over the decades, were simply ignored. As early as 1888, New York State considered using one form of lethal injection (cyanide injection) as a potential method of execution.[17] But a state commission rejected injection because of the medical profession's belief that the public would then begin to link the practice of medicine with death,[18] a concern that persists.[19]

In 1953, Great Britain's Royal Commission on Capital Punishment also dismissed a form of lethal injection, concluding, after a five-year study, that injection was no better than hanging, Great Britain's long-standing method.[20] The host of problems these medical experts detected with lethal injection still ring true today, ranging from the method's inapplicability to individuals with certain "physical abnormalities" making their veins virtually inaccessible, to the recognition that lethal injection requires medical skill because of the technique's complexity.[21]

In 1976, the United States started to examine the lethal injection issue after the Supreme Court reinstated the death penalty in *Gregg v. Georgia*[22] after a nine-year moratorium on executions.[23] Remarkably, during this time, none of the evidence gathered on lethal injection—either from the New York or the British commissions—was addressed in legislative discussions or debates. American lawmakers seemed oblivious to prior concerns.[24]

Such disregard for history and medical investigation was clearly evident in May 1977, when Oklahoma became the first state to adopt lethal injection.[25] Only one or two medical experts contributed to the method's hasty creation.[26] Indeed, at each step in the political process, concerns about the method's cost, aesthetics, legislative marketability, and, in particular, speed in bringing back the death penalty trumped any concern that the procedure ensure a humane execution.[27] Initially, the lack of medical testing was considered so pronounced that Oklahoma's lethal injection bill stalled before state senate approval.[28] But such scruples were not powerful enough to prevent the bill from going forward.

When the Oklahoma State Senate ultimately voted to make the change from electrocution to lethal injection, the two-hour floor debate went beyond the matter of humaneness. Additional issues included deterrence (with some senators saying that the electric chair was the better deterrent to murder) and retribution (with some senators arguing that lethal injection was "an easy way out").[29] Discussion about lethal injection's risks was limited, despite the concerns raised in other venues over the method's pain and complications. For example, during the debate, one senator warned that some drug-using inmates might be less affected by the injection and survive, rendering the inmate a "vegetable to take care of."[30] Of course, a comment like this laments the economic repercussions of such a result— the state's need to provide care for an inmate after a botched execution— not the Eighth Amendment issue of cruelty or the sheer inhumanity of causing such a horrifying and preventable mistake. But cost was a key topic among legislators, who noted that lethal injection would be far cheaper than renovating the state's electric chair or building a gas chamber.[31]

More evidence of Oklahoma's rush to implement lethal injection was to come. The bill that was eventually passed by the Oklahoma legislature dropped a key provision that would have required the state to continue using

FIGURE 6.2
States Adopting Lethal Injection by Year

1977	Oklahoma • Texas
1978	Idaho
1979	New Mexico
1981	Washington
1982	Massachusetts
1983	Arkansas • Illinois • Montana • Nevada • New Jersey • North Carolina • Utah
1984	Mississippi • Oregon • South Dakota • Wyoming,
1986	Delaware • New Hampshire
1988	Colorado •Missouri
1990	Louisiana • Pennsylvania
1992	Arizona • California
1993	Ohio
1994	Kansas • Maryland •Virginia
1995	Connecticut • Indiana • New York • South Carolina
1998	Kentucky • Tennessee
2000	Florida • Georgia
2001	Ohio*
2002	Alabama

* Ohio is unique in terms of changing from a choice state to a single method state.

the electric chair until death by drugs had been ruled legal by the U.S. Supreme Court.[32] This amendment's disappearance, along with other aspects of lethal injection's legislative and department of corrections history, indicates that originally Oklahoma's legislators may have doubted the method's humanity.[33]

Lethal Injection's Quick Rise

Uncertainty did not tarnish lethal injection's appeal. After Oklahoma adopted the method, state after state, including Kentucky, followed suit. From 1977 to 2002, some 38 states joined this movement, switching to lethal injection in a fast-moving cascade, indicating that shared forces and communications fueled legislative action (figure 6.2).

The 38-state figure alone is remarkable. What is extraordinary is that four states in addition to Oklahoma made the switch before lethal injection was ever used. (The first lethal injection execution took place in 1982.) Moreover, seven states changed in 1983 alone. Therefore, within a year of the country's first lethal injection execution, over one-third of all death penalty states had decided to execute employing the new method.[34] In addition, 12 states enacted lethal injection in the eight-year stretch between 1994, when Kansas, Maryland, and Virginia adopted the method, and 2002, when Alabama did (see figure 6.2).

FIGURE 6.3
Execution Methods by State

Single Method States (26)

Lethal Injection (25): Arizona • Arkansas • Colorado • Connecticut • Delaware • Georgia • Illinois • Indiana • Kansas • Kentucky • Louisiana • Maryland • Mississippi • Montana • Nevada • North Carolina• Ohio • Oklahoma • Oregon • Pennsylvania • South Dakota • Tennessee • Texas • Utah • Wyoming

In Limbo (1): Nebraska

Choice States (9)

Lethal Injection or Hanging (2): New Hampshire • Washington
Lethal Injection or Firing Squad (1): Idaho
Lethal Injection or Electrocution (4): Alabama • Florida • South Carolina • Virginia
Lethal Injection or Lethal Gas (2): California • Missouri

States Without the Death Penalty (15)

Alaska • Hawaii • Iowa • Maine • Massachusetts • Michigan • Minnesota • North Dakota • New Jersey • New Mexico • New York • Rhode Island • Vermont • West Virginia • Wisconsin
Also—District of Columbia

Currently, lethal injection is the leading method of execution in the United States, used by all but one of the 35 death penalty states, as well as by the federal government. Lethal injection is the sole method of execution in 25 states. In the nine states where inmates are given a choice between lethal injection and another method, most condemned people select lethal injection (figure 6.3).

A growing number of states, 15 in total, no longer have the death penalty, a figure that includes New Mexico and New Jersey, the two latest abolitionist states (see figure 6.3).[35] In addition, as of this writing, Nebraska is in limbo with respect to executions. On February 8, 2008, the Nebraska Supreme Court declared electrocution unconstitutional under the Nebraska Constitution,[36] a decision that has left a death penalty statute in place but no method to implement it.[37] The Nebraska stalemate illustrates that a state's decision to abolish its method of execution can lead to a moratorium on all of the state's executions, as well as legislative debates about whether the state should even have a death penalty. It is this seemingly causal association between the drive for "humane executions" and the consequence of "no executions" that links lethal injection challenges to abolitionist movements.

Indeed, statistics demonstrating lethal injection's dominance ignore the effect that lethal injection challenges can have on the death penalty generally. In 2006, for example, executions plunged to about one-half of their 1999 numbers. Numerous states—and the federal government—ceased executing entirely, many due, in whole or part, to lethal injection–related challenges. Likewise, in 2007, there were only 42 executions, a number that decreased to 37 in 2008, primarily because of the de facto moratorium resulting from *Baze*.[38]

Of course, there have also been counteractions. Several states considered legislation to expand the application of the death penalty. Louisiana attempted to enforce its statute providing the death penalty for the rape of a child. In response, the Supreme Court declared unequivocally that punishment by death for the rape of a child violates the proportionality between crime and punishment required by the Eighth Amendment.[39] Regardless of backlashes, undeniable evidence has shown the death penalty's slide, with lethal injection as a substantial contributing force.

Lethal Injection's Perplexing Perpetuation

Remarkably, over the years, states have not been deterred from switching to lethal injection with relative confidence and speed, despite the numerous documented accounts of botched lethal injection executions over the decades, including the first execution in 1982.[40] The protocols in those lethal injection states that reveal their chemical information are modeled after Oklahoma's original three-drug combination. Thus most states mirror the legal and scientific choices that Oklahoma officials made 30 years ago. As the U.S. Court of Appeals for the Ninth Circuit stated, "The history of the use of the three chemical protocol gives some force to [the] argument that . . . the precise protocol was never subjected to the rigors of scientific analysis."[41] Similarly, in 2005, the trial court in *Baze* concluded that "there is scant evidence that ensuing States' adoption of lethal injection was supported by any additional medical or scientific studies . . . Rather, the various States simply fell in line relying solely on Oklahoma's protocol."[42]

The criteria set out in many of the protocols are far too vague to allow adequate assessment even if there were a demand for further investigation. When the protocols do offer details, such as the amount and type of chemicals that executioners inject, they often reveal striking errors and a shocking level of ignorance about the procedure. States likely withhold crucial details because, almost invariably, when states reveal their lethal injection procedures, they demonstrate their ignorance and incompetence about what the method entails. The result is a continuous effort by states to maintain secrecy about all aspects of the execution.[43] But this effort raises the question of why states retain a method of execution that appears to be so faulty. Again, the answer pertains to the broader desire to keep the death penalty generally.

How States Resist Changing Execution Methods

Legislatures and courts sometimes engage in statutory and judicial behavior that belies their purported humanity. Throughout history, a number of legislatures have been motivated to change a method of execution not for reasons of beneficence but because the perpetuation of the death penalty itself became jeopardized due to that state's particular method. In 1888, for example, the New York legislature sought a more humane method of execution than hanging because the public's perception of hanging's barbarity spurred movements toward a total abolition of capital punishment.[44] Thereafter, most death penalty states eventually adopted electrocution, which offered a far less visible and therefore less-scrutinized procedure.[45] Some electrocution states slowly began to switch to lethal gas when problems with electrocution became more public.[46] Likewise, states' decisions to change to lethal injection after *Gregg* also appear to have been based on efforts to make the death penalty more palatable to the public after the punishment's long hiatus.[47]

The concern for ensuring the continuation of the death penalty is perhaps most clearly illustrated by the provisions in state statutes that set forth fallback methods in case lethal injection is deemed unconstitutional.[48] In Oklahoma, for example, if lethal injection is rendered unconstitutional, the death sentence "shall be carried out by electrocution."[49] If both lethal injection and electrocution are rendered unconstitutional, the death sentence "shall be carried out by firing squad."[50] Presumably, the three execution methods are ordered in terms of their relative humaneness: lethal injection is considered more humane than electrocution, and electrocution is viewed as more humane than firing squad. The legislative record, however, provides no evidence supporting that kind of hierarchy. Indeed, quite the contrary, the state's interest is not with seeking the method that avoids inflicting unnecessary pain but, rather, the constancy of the death penalty process itself. Unfortunately, this constitutional substitute strategy disregards the fact that the fallback method (in Oklahoma's case, electrocution) is what prompted the turn to lethal injection originally.[51] The Oklahoma statutory paradox is contradictory, but it precludes the kind of execution hiatus that Nebraska is experiencing by not having such a fallback. That was Oklahoma's goal.

States also appear to change methods to stay one step ahead of constitutional challenges to a particular method of execution. This approach buffers the death penalty itself from scrutiny, or, again, from any possible death penalty hiatus that might occur if a method is rendered unconstitutional. For example, when California Governor Pete Wilson signed a bill into law that allowed California's death-row inmates a choice between lethal gas and lethal injection, he emphasized that "he hoped the new law would stop last-minute appeals" of the constitutionality of lethal gas.[52] The Florida legislature's decision to allow prisoners a choice between electrocution and lethal injection came quickly on the heels of the Supreme Court's grant of certiorari to review the constitutionality of electrocution.[53] Likewise, in *Baze*, members of the plurality suggested that their opinion would diminish the need for future lethal injection challenges.[54]

These efforts allow the death penalty to proceed, but they stifle accountability. By switching from one method of execution to another when constitutional challenges arise, legislatures, courts, and prison personnel need never acknowledge that what they were doing was wrong. The evidence speaks for itself: states' concerns over the halting of a particular execution method and the potential turn to abolition have justified the retention of an execution method that is far from adequate.

Surge in Lethal Injection Challenges

How did lethal injection litigation start to leap these state hurdles? A series of developments help explain why lethal injection challenges have achieved a level of significance in current death penalty efforts that would have been unattainable earlier.[55] One key is that the Eighth Amendment's Cruel and Unusual Punishments Clause was not even applicable to the states until 1962;[56] therefore, execution method challenges were generally limited to state constitutional provisions, which hindered the construction of a sturdy Eighth Amendment precedent that would provide guidelines for challenges to come.[57] In addition, the Antiterrorism and Effective Death Penalty Act of 1996 (AEDPA)[58] put constraints on the filing of habeas petitions, as well as limits on the issues that could be raised.[59]

Given this restricted context, lethal injection challenges were relatively ineffectual. That situation began to change, however, with the introduction of DNA testing. Starting in the late 1990s, a seeming explosion of exonerations of innocent death-row inmates prompted the perception that the states were making serious errors in carrying out the death penalty.

As a result, around the turn of the century, death sentences, executions, and public support of the death penalty began to decline while the level of scrutiny of individual cases increased. This focus had ripple effects. With time, the accumulating numbers of highly publicized electrocution and lethal gas botches prompted states to turn even more exclusively to lethal injection, hiding behind the method's medical veneer of humaneness and peace.[60]

Procedural approaches to death penalty cases have also changed; in particular, attorneys have used civil rights actions under section 1983 of the Civil Rights Act[61] to avoid AEDPA's restrictions.[62] Recognizing that inmates were challenging lethal injection and not the death penalty itself, in 2004, the Supreme Court unanimously upheld a section 1983 lethal injection claim,[63] a decision the Court validated further two years later in another context.[64] The accompanying increase in section 1983 challenges resulted in vastly different reactions. Some federal courts recognized the challenges as legitimate civil rights suits, while other federal courts allowed suits to be filed but refused to grant stays or hearings.[65]

Role of Medical Professionals

Another critical development aiding lethal injection challenges has been the increasing role of medical professionals in the lethal injection process, whether as experts testifying in court, as academics publishing articles, or as actual participants in the execution chamber. Facets of all three of these medical roles converged in 2006 with *Morales v. Hickman*,[66] a groundbreaking Northern District of California decision in which Judge Jeremy Fogel helped resolve some of the lethal injection dilemmas with an educated, hands-on approach crucial to evaluating the state's execution process.[67]

Fogel rendered a ruling in *Morales* that was unlike any earlier decision. His conclusion was based on a variety of data, including evidence suggesting that six lethally injected inmates in California may have been conscious and tormented by the three-drug regimen, potentially constituting cruel and unusual punishment under the Eighth Amendment.[68] To conduct the lethal injection execution of Michael Morales, Fogel required California to choose one of two options: provide qualified medical personnel who would either ensure that Morales was unconscious during the procedure or alter the department of corrections's protocol so that only sodium thiopental would be given rather than the standard sequence of three different drugs.[69]

Strikingly, the state chose to have medical experts present at Morales's execution—a decision that garnered controversy at the time.[70] Additional controversy was generated when the two anesthesiologists slated to participate resigned mere hours before Morales's scheduled execution time.[71] The anesthesiologists considered it to be a violation of their ethical duties to accept the requirement of the U.S. Court of Appeals for the Ninth Circuit that they personally intervene to provide medical assistance if Morales appeared conscious or in great pain.[72] This predicament prompted Fogel to organize an unusually long and thorough evidentiary hearing— one that would result in a December 15, 2006, memorandum order stating that "unless California made substantial revisions to its protocol, [Fogel] would declare it unconstitutional."[73] On May 15, 2007, California filed a detailed response.[74] The litigation is currently on hold while California revises its death penalty protocol.[75]

Lessons Learned from Lethal Injection Challenges

In this context, Fogel's observations regarding *Morales* offer insight on many issues, including the extent to which lethal injection challenges are conflated with challenges against the death penalty generally. In a recent article reflecting on *Morales*, Fogel highlighted five particularly important aspects of his experiences in dealing with the case.[76] First, Fogel described the evolution of his views on lethal injection. Initially, he was skeptical about lethal injection's risks and thought that the challenges might be frivolous tools of delay; in the end, he was convinced of the method's hazards and, as a result, required changes to the protocol and ultimately enjoined Morales's execution when the state failed to comply.[77]

Next, Fogel recognized the different cultural understandings dividing the various actors who are involved in implementing the death penalty.[78] This divide has been emphasized in lethal injection litigation because an Eighth Amendment analysis of execution methods requires an examination of the behaviors of the different institutional decision makers. Even though a legislature may consider a particular method to be the most humane under ideal circumstances, prison officials may, in practice, continually misapply the method. If a pattern of misapplication exists, the court should find the method unconstitutional.[79] In Fogel's view, this interrelationship was further complicated because "the legal system and corrections bureaucracy are different cultures in which the same words and events often have different implications and consequences."[80] This revelation prompted a key take-home message for judges: "While our obligation to be meticulous in our legal analysis and legally coherent in our orders and decisions remains the same, we also have to consider the dynamics of the institution in which our orders and decisions will be implemented."[81] A driving force behind Fogel's unusual involvement in *Morales* was his desire to understand how the corrections's bureaucracy may respond to problems with lethal injection.

Fogel's third observation pertained to the media—yet another institution critical to the criminal justice system because media coverage informs the public about the why and what of lethal injection challenges.[82] In Fogel's eyes, media coverage changed over time as journalists became more educated about the issues. At least initially, many news articles broadly, and inaccurately, pitched the topic as "whether lethal injection in the abstract is cruel and unusual punishment" or "whether it is constitutional for a condemned inmate to suffer *any* pain at all"; only a small number addressed the actual issue in *Morales*, which was whether California's protocol operated in the manner intended when it was enacted.[83] After Morales's execution was postponed, however, the news media became substantially more accurate about how narrow the issues really were.[84]

The public's conflation of the death penalty generally with the California lethal injection protocol specifically was the focus of Fogel's fourth observation.[85] During the public debate about California's lethal injection cases, particularly *Morales*, the focus was on the death penalty itself rather than the particularized concerns pertaining to lethal injection. Because a lethal injection challenge can postpone an inmate's execution, it prompts deeper reflections about the meaning and purpose of punishment more generally.[86] In Fogel's eyes, judges must balance awareness of the non-lawyer public's reactions to the handling of lethal injection cases with a need to abide by the legal process.[87]

Fogel's fifth and last revelation was the extent to which judges are usually personally separated from the consequences of their decisions.[88] For Fogel, this barrier dissolved in February 2006 when he became enmeshed "in the most intense discussions and hearings imaginable" concerning how Michael Morales would be executed.[89]

Indeed, *Morales* would reveal yet another execution method paradox: the people most knowledgeable about the process of lethal injection—doctors, particularly anesthesiologists—are often reluctant to share their insights and skills. This dilemma, highlighted when the chosen anesthesiologists refused to personally participate in Morales's execution, moved

Morales into the spotlight and led Fogel to assume unprecedented involvement in an area that had been controlled primarily by legislatures and department of corrections personnel.

Morales cast a shadow over executions across the nation. By the time Fogel issued his December 2006 second decision in *Morales*, determining that California's lethal injection protocol "as implemented" violated the Eighth Amendment,[90] District Court Judge Fernando J. Gaitan, Jr., had already reached a similar conclusion about Missouri's protocol in *Taylor v. Crawford*.[91] Litigation in *Taylor* showed numerous problems with Missouri's execution procedures, including the doctor who assisted at the executions. Not only did the state lack a written protocol, but testimony also revealed that the doctor's dyslexia hindered his ability to mix drugs properly and that he adjusted dosages without oversight.[92] Although the doctor's identity was concealed during the litigation, the *Saint Louis Post-Dispatch* was able to find him. That discovery exposed disturbing details; despite the doctor's supervision of 54 executions over the course of a decade, he had a record of more than 20 malpractice suits, revocation of privileges at two hospitals, and a public reprimand from the Board of Healing Arts.[93]

The combined impact of the holdings in *Morales* and *Taylor* was a powerful legal force. Indeed, less than a year after those decisions, in *Harbison v. Little*, a Tennessee federal district court would similarly find its state's revised protocol unconstitutional.[94] The growing number of section 1983 challenges and the varying statewide responses resulted in a sufficient number of circuit splits for the Supreme Court to grant certiorari to review the issue.[95] The Court chose *Baze*, a Kentucky case, to decide the future direction of lethal injection challenges.

The Supreme Court Speaks: Baze v. Rees *in Perspective*

In the eyes of one commentator, "Kentucky seemed an unlikely state [for the Court] to select for such a review."[96] The state had conducted only one lethal injection execution and offered a limited record on which to base a lethal injection challenge. The suit that petitioners brought also had not been scrutinized by the federal hearings being carried out in similar kinds of cases. Rather, Kentucky's hearings took place only in state court and concerned only Kentucky's procedures and short execution history.[97] Other states had far better evidentiary and execution data.[98] Initially, death penalty opponents believed that by selecting *Baze* the Justices indicated their openness to hearing the problems with the three-drug protocol. But some of the Justices' negative reactions during oral arguments raised a competing interpretation: "that the votes to hear the case had come from justices who regarded the challenge as insubstantial and wanted to dispose of it before many more state and federal courts could be tied up with similar cases."[99]

Regardless, the Court's selection of *Baze* had immediate effects. Apart from a highly controversial execution carried out in Texas on September 25, 2007, the same day the Court granted certiorari in *Baze*, no additional executions were conducted until May 6, 2008.[100] While the Court did not declare a general moratorium on executions during this seven-month period, a de facto moratorium evolved when the Court granted stays of execution for individual cases that came before it.[101] Historically, such a lengthy hiatus is rare. After *Baze* was decided, those stays ended when the Justices denied the underlying appeals. But given the narrowness of *Baze*, "[t]he Supreme Court's decision will only partially affect this [lethal injection] debate."[102] Executions may have begun again, but so has lethal injection litigation.

Indeed, there are limits to the *Baze* Court's analysis that suggest that the decision is by no means a definitive response to the issue of lethal injection's constitutionality.[103] *Baze* is so splintered that none of its seven opinions comprises more than three votes.[104] The Justices also offer a wide range of explanations and qualifications in their reasoning.[105] In addition, the decision is confined to Kentucky and its particular protocol. While the Court asserts that its holding pertains to state protocols that are "substantially similar" to Kentucky's, the Court provides no guidance as to the parameters of such a comparison.[106] Rather, the Court refers to the "substantially similar" standard in just one sentence without citing case law or providing further elaboration on what the standard means. In fact, the "substantially similar" standard has generally been used in the area of intellectual property and far less commonly in other subject areas, such as evidence and criminal law.[107] The standard's vagueness and lack of context is particularly problematic in *Baze* because the details of lethal injection protocols are so critical to determining what procedures are comparable to those of Kentucky. The obscurity is compounded by Kentucky's sparse execution history. In essence, voices on both sides of the death penalty debate have emphasized that *Baze* left doors open for future lethal injection challenges.[108]

The *Baze* Court's Arguments

Although *Baze* set an Eighth Amendment standard for evaluating the unconstitutional risk that a condemned person would suffer severe pain, the opinion offers few global generalizations. Six of the seven Justices in the majority wrote separate opinions, and they each raised a number of concerns.[109] The potential overlap of lethal injection challenges and the controversy over the dealth penalty itself was a prominent theme. Indeed, at the very start, the *Baze* Court echoes the trial court's recognition that "[t]here are no methods of legal execution that are satisfactory to those who oppose the death penalty on moral, religious, or societal grounds."[110] With that caveat in place, the Court determined that "petitioners have not carried their burden of showing that the risk of pain from maladministration of a concededly humane lethal injection protocol, and the failure to adopt untried and untested alternatives, constitute cruel and unusual punishment."[111]

According to Chief Justice John G. Roberts, Jr., author of the Court's opinion, a successful Eighth Amendment challenge must determine both that a state's method "creates a demonstrated risk of severe pain"[112] and that there exist alternative methods of execution that are "feasible, readily implemented, and in fact [could] significantly reduce a substantial risk of severe pain."[113] Furthermore, "a slightly or marginally safer alternative" would not be enough.[114] The petitioners' proposed alternative—that of injecting only the first drug, sodium thiopental, along with "trained personnel" to monitor the drug's effectiveness—"would embroil the courts in ongoing scientific controversies beyond their expertise, and would substantially intrude on the role of state legislatures in implementing their execution procedures."[115] As Roberts explained, "Simply because an execution method may result in pain, either by accident or as an inescapable consequence of death, does not establish the sort of 'objectively intolerable risk of harm' that qualifies as cruel and unusual."[116] The risks the petitioners cited with regard to Kentucky's protocol were not "so substantial or imminent as to amount to an Eighth Amendment violation."[117] Justice Stephen G. Breyer reached a somewhat parallel conclusion based on the scientific evidence before him. While he found some basis for "legitimate concern,"[118] neither the "record" nor "the readily available literature" that he had reviewed provided him with "sufficient grounds to believe that Kentucky's method of lethal injection creates a significant risk of unnecessary suffering."[119]

In contrast, Justice Ruth Bader Ginsburg's dissenting opinion, which Justice David H. Souter joined, emphasized that a number of other states have instituted far more adequate procedures to ensure that an inmate is anesthetized before execution (for example, Alabama, California, Florida, Indiana, and Missouri):[120] "[I]f readily available measures can materially increase the likelihood that the protocol will cause no pain, a State fails to adhere to contemporary standards of decency if it declines to employ those measures."[121]

Pointing to *Morales*, Justice Samuel A. Alito, Jr., in his concurring opinion, stressed that lethal injection protocols requiring the participation of doctors and nurses "cannot be regarded as 'feasible' or 'readily' available" because of ethical prohibitions on most medical professionals participating in executions.[122] For Alito it was important that "[t]he issue presented in this case—the constitutionality of the *method* of execution—should be kept separate from the controversial issue of the death penalty itself."[123] Therefore Alito was concerned that "misinterpretation" of Roberts's standard could "produce a *de facto* ban on capital punishment," as well as "litigation gridlock."[124]

Justice John Paul Stevens shared Alito's belief that *Baze* might generate "endless"[125] litigation. When the Court granted certiorari to hear *Baze*, he "assumed that [the] decision would bring the debate about lethal injection as a method of execution to a close," but "[i]t now seems clear it will not."[126] The constitutional acceptability of the three-drug protocol as implemented by other states "remains open, and may well be answered differently in a future case on the basis of a more complete record."[127] Sensing no resolution to the matter, Stevens asserted that he is "now convinced" that *Baze* "will generate debate not only about the constitutionality of the three-drug protocol . . . but also about the justification for the death penalty itself."[128] Indeed, for the first time, Stevens unexpectedly voiced his own opposition to the death penalty generally.[129]

Stevens stated that he concurred in the decision upholding the constitutionality of Kentucky's protocol because he felt so obligated under the Court's precedents.[130] At the same time, like Justices before him, he had gradually changed his mind about the death penalty. During his first year on the Court, he coauthored the plurality's decision in *Gregg* to reestablish the death penalty.[131] Over time, however, he observed the problems with the way capital punishment is actually implemented and the paradoxical result, for example, that "more recent cases have endorsed procedures that provide less protections to capital defendants than to ordinary offenders."[132] In his eyes, capital punishment is the "product of habit and inattention rather than any acceptable deliberative process that weighs the costs and risks of administering that penalty against its identifiable benefits;"[133] therefore, it "represents 'the pointless and needless extinction of life with only marginal contributions to any discernible social or public purposes.'"[134]

Justice Antonin Scalia's separate opinion strongly counters the anti-death penalty views of Justice Stevens, at times nearly point by point.[135] And his opinion introduces its own sense of paradox. According to Scalia, it was Stevens's past struggles with the punishment that have created the very dilemmas that Stevens laments: "Those costs, those burdens, and that lack of finality are in large measure the creation of Justice Stevens and other Justices opposed to the death penalty."[136] To Stevens's claim that he relied on his "*own experience* in reaching the conclusion that the imposition of the death penalty' is unconstitutional," Scalia responds: "Purer expression cannot be found of the principle of rule by judicial fiat."[137] And Scalia makes clear that views about the death penalty generally have no place in a decision about execution methods: "I take no position on the desirability of the death penalty, except to say that its value is eminently debatable and the subject of deeply, indeed passionately, held views— which means, to me, that it is preeminently not a matter to be resolved here."[138] At the same time, he does spend quite some time discussing it.

Justice Clarence Thomas comes from a somewhat different angle. *Baze* was "an easy case"[139] because Kentucky's protocol was not "deliberately designed to inflict pain," which Thomas believes to be the standard for an Eighth Amendment violation.[140] Yet he is suspicious of the underlying purpose of lethal injection challenges. Thomas provides two reasons for his stance: "[I]t is obvious that, for some who oppose capital punishment on policy grounds, the only acceptable end point . . . is for this Court . . . to strike down the death penalty as cruel and unusual in all circumstances." However, "the next best option for those seeking to abolish the death penalty is to embroil the States in never-ending litigation concerning the adequacy of their execution procedures."[141] Given the weaknesses and vagueness of the Court's decision, Thomas also presents sound rationales for why he believes that *Baze* "is sure to engender more litigation." Thomas notes key phrases that the plurality opinion never fully explicates—the meaning of "substantial" or "significant" or "feasible," to name just a few.[142] Perhaps even more telling is Thomas's assertion that the Court's proposed standards "suffer from other flaws, not the least of which is that they cast substantial doubt on every method of execution other than lethal injection." It could be argued that the other four existing methods "involve risks of pain that could be eliminated by switching to lethal injection"[143]—a pointed contention that the principal opinion never addresses. If the other four methods were rendered unconstitutional in light of lethal injection's superiority, the debate over execution methods would be viewed as even more threatening.

The *Baze* plurality has laid the foundation for more lethal injection litigation. Stevens and Thomas got it right when they noted that the plurality's standard offers limited guidance for lower courts, which must rule on future fact-specific claims. Faced with the details of a lethal injection challenge, a number of the Justices in *Baze* drew simplistic conclusions based on limited medical information concerning the administration of lethal injection drugs. A primary example is the reliance by Roberts, Alito, and Breyer on an outdated book chapter discussing early euthanasia guidelines followed in the Netherlands.[144] Since that chapter was published, the Royal Dutch Society for the Advancement of Pharmacy has published two additional editions of the guidelines, the latest of which was released in 2007, a year before *Baze*.[145] Moreover, all the Dutch Society's editions and updates demonstrate the extent to which euthanasia procedures in the Netherlands differ from lethal injection practices in the United States. Roberts, Alito, and Breyer are correct in asserting that the Dutch guidelines recommend the use of a paralytic agent such as pancuronium to follow thiopental.[146] However, the parallels between the Netherlands and Kentucky (as well as other states) end there. For example, as Stevens stressed, "physicians with training in anesthesiology are involved in assisted suicide [in the Netherlands, but] physicians have no similar role in American executions."[147] Even with physician participation, however, problems have been reported causing some Dutch patients to experience substantial discomfort.[148]

In light of the range of perspectives, Justice Ginsburg's recommendation to remand makes sense, particularly for a state like Kentucky which has limited evidence available. According to Ginsburg, the Court should "vacate and remand" the Kentucky Supreme Court's decision with the instruction that the state court determine whether the omitted safeguards create "an untoward, readily avoidable risk of inflicting severe and unnecessary pain."[149] While, of course, the *Baze* Court did not remand, other courts have started to address some of the issues that Justice Ginsburg and her colleagues raised.

Post-*Baze* Developments

The full impact of *Baze* is difficult to determine at this point in time. Yet one conclusion is clear: concerns about the future of the death penalty permeate the Justices' opinions. *Baze* and the key cases preceding it have also demonstrated the range of problems that lethal injection has engendered. Increased coverage of lethal injection research and litigation in medical journals and the controversy over physician involvement in actual executions have brought the lethal injection debate out of hiding. In addition, a number of different news sources have reported in great detail over the past few years the difficulties and inconsistencies with lethal injection, including widely publicized botches. The accumulation of this kind of evidence can shake the public's confidence, not only about particular execution methods but also about the death penalty itself.[150]

As of this writing, one of the most striking post-*Baze* developments throws doubt on how definitive the Court's decision was. On June 10, less than two months after *Baze* was decided, an Ohio state court judge ruled in *State v. Rivera* that Ohio could no longer employ the standard three lethal injection drugs (used in Kentucky) for executing inmates because the drug combination violated Ohio's own lethal injection statute and therefore violated due process.[151] In making this determination, the court heard testimony from two of the key medical experts who also testified for the defense and the state, respectively, in *Baze*.[152] Yet the *Rivera* court reached different conclusions from *Baze*, holding specifically that "the use of two drugs in the lethal injection protocol (pancuronium bromide and potassium chloride) creates an unnecessary and arbitrary risk that the condemned will experience an agonizing and painful death."[153] The *Rivera* court accepted that "[i]f pancuronium bromide and potassium chloride are eliminated from the lethal injection protocol, a sufficient dosage of sodium thiopental will cause death rapidly and without the possibility [of] causing pain to the condemned."[154]

By way of affirming these dangers, the *Rivera* court listed as a finding of fact nearly every criticism made of the three-drug combination, ranging from the difficulties in assessing the condemned person's depth of anesthesia before administering the second and third drugs, to the heightened risk because physicians refuse to participate in the process, to the number of mistakes made in the delivery of anesthesia even in a clinical setting.[155] The *Rivera* court also recognized "[c]ircumstantial evidence . . . that some condemned prisoners have suffered a painful death, due to a flawed lethal injection."[156] This recognition prompted the court to hold that the state's lethal injection protocol should use only "a lethal injection of a single, anesthetic drug."[157]

One reason for the seeming divergence of *Rivera*'s holding from that of *Baze* is Ohio's lethal injection statute. That statute requires "a lethal injection of a drug or combination of drugs of sufficient dosage to quickly and painlessly cause death."[158] The *Rivera* court emphasized that the statute's purpose "is to provide the condemned person with an execution which is 'quick' and 'painless'; and the legislature's use of the word, 'shall,' when qualifying the state's duty to provide a quick and painless death signifies that the duty is mandatory."[159] Because "the duty of the state to the individual is mandatory, a property interest is created in the benefit"; the statute confers on the condemned person a property interest in a painless death.[160] For the state to then execute the condemned person in a manner that carries an "unnecessary risk of pain, and, as well, any unnecessary expectation by the condemned person that his execution may be agonizing, or excruciatingly painful"[161] violates the Due Process Clause of the Fifth and Fourteenth Amendments.[162] As a result, the *Rivera* court ordered that "the words, 'or combination of drugs,' be severed" from the Ohio statute in light of the court's ruling that only one anesthetic drug be employed.[163] In contrast, "the Kentucky lethal injection statute has no mandate that an execution be painless." Therefore, an interpretation of Kentucky's statute "is not applicable" in *Rivera* because "the [U.S.] Constitution does not demand the avoidance of all risk of pain in carrying out its executions." Ohio's statute, though, "demands the avoidance of any unnecessary risk of pain."[164]

Rivera is the first case in which a court ordered a state to employ only a single anesthetic drug. While other judges and appointed commissions have criticized the three-drug combination, the *Rivera* court went a substantial step further.[165] The *Baze* Court emphasized the uniqueness of this very situation by noting that the petitioners' proposed alternative protocol (the use of a single barbiturate) was "one that . . . has not been adopted by any State and has never been tried."[166] At least momentarily, that claim in *Baze* is no longer accurate in light of *Rivera*.

How much effect *Rivera* will have on other states is unknown because the case may be appealed. Regardless, states typically look at what other states are doing when it comes to making decisions about execution methods. By breaking away from the three-drug formula pact, *Rivera* starts to weaken the safety in numbers that states have embraced in determining that the shared lethal injection formula provides a humane death.

Like *Morales, Taylor,* and *Harbison, Rivera* also cuts through much of the paradox that even the Supreme Court in *Baze* was unable to avoid. For example, with the single-barbiturate injection, *Rivera* provides a potential solution to the absence of a medical professional in the execution chamber because a one-drug formula is so much easier to use. This result was aided by the *Rivera* court's focus on the constitutional viability of the execution method itself, and not the larger topic of the death penalty generally. After all, medical professionals have recommended abolition as a solution for avoiding the potential hazard of physician involvement in executions.[167] Without the distraction of having to grapple with a decision's effects on the death penalty more broadly, the *Rivera* court was better able to address the problem at hand and select a more viable type of lethal injection.

Conclusion

In this chapter, I suggest that lethal injection challenges be dissociated from the larger abolitionist picture. To be sure, execution methods challenges inspire strong negative feelings on both sides of the death penalty debate. Some death penalty proponents fear that execution methods challenges may be the last straw in the accumulating bundle of evidence pointing to the need to abolish the death penalty. Some death penalty opponents believe, however, that enhancing the humaneness of an execution method may make executions far more acceptable scientifically and politically than ever before.[168]

The fears of proponents and opponents alike have yet to be realized. No state is near achieving a perfect death by execution, quite the contrary. And even though this country appears to be moving further down the road to abolition, the political and paradoxical ramifications involved in such a venture erect barriers for lethal injection challenges. For those legislatures, courts, and prison personnel attempting to predict the future of execution methods, however, too much emphasis on the road to abolition may not benefit either side in the death penalty debate. The better course is to steer clear of such obstacles and focus on the purpose of the ride: providing a humane and civilized execution the way the Eighth Amendment originally intended.

NOTES

I am most grateful to the following individuals for their contributions to this chapter: Pieter Admiraal, Gerrit Kimsma, Daniel Rinaldi, Julie Salwen, Jeroen van Kwawegen, Robin Wagner-Pacifici, and the participants at Harvard Law School's "The Road to Abolition" workshop. I also thank members of Fordham Law School's library staff for exceptional research assistance: Juan Fernandez, Karin Johnsrud, Todd Melnick, and Alison Shea. Fordham Law School provided generous research support.

1. See, for example, Richard C. Dieter, *A Crisis of Confidence: Americans' Doubts about the Death Penalty* (Washington, D.C.: Death Penalty Information Center, 2007); Michael L. Radelet, "More Trends toward Moratoria on Executions," *Connecticut Law Review* 33 (2001): 845–60; Helen Shin, "Is the Death of the Death Penalty Near? The Impact of *Atkins* and *Roper* on the Future of Capital Punishment for Mentally Ill Defendants," *Fordham Law Review* 76 (2007): 465–516; Ronald J. Tabak, "Finality without Fairness: Why We Are Moving towards Moratoria on Executions, and the Potential Abolition of Capital Punishment," *Connecticut Law Review* 33 (2001): 733–63; Stuart Taylor, Jr., "Opening Argument: The Death Penalty—Slowly Fading?" *National Journal*, Nov. 17, 2007, 15. See also Death Penalty Information Center, *The Death Penalty in 2007: Year End Report* (Dec. 2007), available at http://www.deathpenaltyinfo.org/2007/YearEnd.pdf (accessed Feb. 3, 2008). Compare Carol S. Steiker and Jordan M. Steiker, "Sober Second Thoughts: Reflections on Two Decades of Constitutional Regulation of Capital Punishment," *Harvard Law Review* 109 (1995): 355–438.

2. The Eighth Amendment provides that "[e]xcessive bail shall not be required, nor excessive fines imposed, nor cruel and unusual punishments inflicted." U.S. Const. amend. VIII.

3. Richard C. Dieter, "Methods of Execution and Their Effect on the Use of the Death Penalty in the United States," *Fordham Urban Law Journal* 35 (2008): 789. For discussions of race and the death penalty, see Charles J. Ogletree, Jr., and Austin Sarat, eds., *From Lynch Mobs to the Killing State: Race and the Death Penalty in America* (New York: New York University Press, 2006); Stephanie Hindson, Hillary Potter, and Michael L. Radelet, "Race, Gender, Region and Death Sentencing in Colorado, 1980–1999," *University of Colorado Law Review* 77 (2006): 549–94; Glenn L. Pierce and Michael L. Radelet, "Race, Region, and Death Sentencing in Illinois, 1988–1997," *Oregon Law Review* 81 (2002): 39–96; Charles J. Ogletree, Jr., "Black Man's Burden: Race and the Death Penalty in America," *Oregon Law Review* 81 (2002): 15–38. For a discussion of innocence and the death penalty, see Carol S. Steiker and Jordan M. Steiker, "The Seduction of Innocence: The Attraction and Limitations of the Focus on Innocence in Capital Punishment Law and Advocacy," *Journal of Criminal Law and Criminology* 95 (2005): 587–624. For a discussion of mental competency and the death penalty,

see Carol Steiker and Jordan Steiker, "Defending Categorical Exemptions to the Death Penalty: Reflections on the ABA's Resolutions Concerning the Execution of Juveniles and Persons with Mental Retardation," *Law and Contemporary Problems* 61 (1998): 89–104. For a discussion of juveniles and the death penalty, see Jay D. Aronson, "Brain Imaging, Culpability and the Juvenile Death Penalty," *Psychology, Public Policy, and Law* 13 (2007): 115–42. For discussions of gender and the death penalty, see Timothy V. Kaufman-Osborn, "Gender and the Death Penalty," *Signs: Journal of Women in Culture and Society* 24 (1999): 1097–1102; and Timothy V. Kaufman-Osborn, "Reviving the Late Liberal State: On Capital Punishment in an Age of Gender Confusion," *Signs: Journal of Women in Culture and Society* 24 (1999): 1119–29. For a discussion of religion and the death penalty, see Michael L. Radelet, "The Role of Organized Religions in Changing Death Penalty Debates," *William and Mary Bill of Rights Journal* 9 (2000): 201–14.

4. This six-decade demarcation was proffered by the Court. *Baze v. Rees*, 128 S. Ct. 1520, 1530–31 (2008) (plurality opinion) (discussing the Eighth Amendment precedent of *Wilkerson v. Utah*, 99 U.S. 130 (1878); *In re Kemmler*, 136 U.S. 436 (1890); and *Louisiana ex rel Francis v. Resweber*, 329 U.S. 459 (1947)). There is room for disagreement, however, on when the Court last reviewed the constitutionality of an execution method.

5. Chief Justice Roberts announced the judgment of the Court and delivered an opinion in which Justices Kennedy and Alito joined (*Baze*, 1525–38); Justice Alito filed a concurring opinion (ibid., 1538–42); Justice Stevens filed an opinion concurring in the judgment (ibid., 1542–52); Justice Scalia filed an opinion concurring in the judgment, which Justice Thomas joined (ibid., 1552–56); Justice Thomas filed an opinion concurring in the judgment, which Justice Scalia joined (ibid., 1556–63); Justice Breyer filed an opinion concurring in the judgment (ibid., 1563–67); and Justice Ginsburg filed a dissenting opinion in which Justice Souter joined (ibid., 1567–72).

6. Ibid., 1526.

7. Ibid., 1531 (internal quotation marks omitted).

8. Ibid., 1537.

9. Ibid., 1534–38.

10. Ibid., 1551–52 (Stevens, J., concurring).

11. Ibid., 1542–43.

12. See generally Deborah W. Denno, "The Lethal Injection Debate: Law and Science," *Fordham Urban Law Journal* 35 (2008): 701–998; Deborah W. Denno, "The Lethal Injection Quandary: How Medicine Has Dismantled the Death Penalty," *Fordham Law Review* 76 (2007): 49–128.

13. Denno, "Lethal Injection Debate," 702.

14. Ibid.

15. Austin Sarat, in *When the State Kills: Capital Punishment and the American Condition* (Princeton, N.J.: Princeton University Press, 2001), 84, refers to the

"unending search for technologies that in their capacity to kill with a pretense of humanity allow those who kill both to end life and, at the same time, to believe themselves to be guardians of a moral order that, in part, bases its claims to superiority in its condemnation of killing."

16. For discussions of legislative changes in execution methods over time, see Denno, "Lethal Injection Quandary," 59–75; Deborah W. Denno, "When Legislatures Delegate Death: The Troubling Paradox behind State Uses of Electrocution and Lethal Injection and What It Says about Us," *Ohio State Law Journal* 63 (2002): 82–85, 90–92, 130–31, 188–206; Deborah W. Denno, "Getting to Death: Are Executions Constitutional?" *Iowa Law Review* 82 (1997): 363–75; Deborah W. Denno, "Is Electrocution an Unconstitutional Method of Execution? The Engineering of Death over the Century," *William and Mary Law Review* 35 (1994): 559–77. For a discussion of the electric chair from a historical perspective, see Jürgen Martschukat, "'The Art of Killing by Electricity': The Sublime and the Electric Chair," *Journal of American History* 89 (2002): 900–21.

17. Commission to Investigate and Report the Most Humane and Practical Method of Carrying into Effect the Sentence of Death in Capital Cases, *Report of the Commission to Investigate and Report the Most Humane and Practical Method of Carrying into Effect the Sentence of Death in Capital Cases* (Albany: Argus, 1888), 85.

18. Denno, "Is Electrocution an Unconstitutional Method of Execution?" 572–73.

19. Denno, "Lethal Injection Quandary," 80.

20. Royal Commission on Capital Punishment, *Royal Commission on Capital Punishment, 1949–1953, Report* (London: Her Majesty's Stationery Office, 1953), 258–61.

21. Ibid., 258.

22. *Gregg v. Georgia*, 428 U.S. 153, 207 (1976) (plurality opinion).

23. *Baze v. Rees*, 128 S. Ct. 1520, 1526 (2008) (plurality opinion).

24. Denno, "Lethal Injection Quandary," 65.

25. Denno, "Getting to Death," 375.

26. Denno, "Lethal Injection Quandary," 65–75.

27. Ibid.

28. John Greiner, "Drug Execution Plan Suffers Senate Setback," *Daily Oklahoman*, Feb. 16, 1977, 16.

29. Denno, "Lethal Injection Quandary," 70 (internal quotation marks omitted). For a critique of the argument that demonstrated deterrence would render the death penalty morally necessary, see Carol S. Steiker, "No, Capital Punishment Is Not Morally Required: Deterrence, Deontology, and the Death Penalty," *Stanford Law Review* 58 (2005): 751–89.

30. Denno, "Lethal Injection Quandary," 71 (internal quotation marks omitted).

31. Ibid.

32. Compare Okla. Stat. Ann. tit. 22, Section 1014 (West 2008) with An Act Relating to Criminal Procedure; Amending 22 O.S. 1971, Section 1014; and Specifying the Manner of Inflicting Punishment of Death, S. 10, 36th Leg., 1st Sess. (as passed by Oklahoma House of Representatives, Apr. 20, 1977). See also John Greiner, "Senate OKs Drug Plan, Execution Bill Gains," *Daily Oklahoman*, May 4, 1977, 1; and Mike Hammer, "Drug Death Bill Passes," *Daily Oklahoman*, Apr. 21, 1977, 65.

33. Denno, "Lethal Injection Quandary," 65–75.

34. As of the end of 1983, a total of 38 states had the death penalty. U.S. Department of Justice, Bureau of Justice Statistics, *Capital Punishment 1983* (Washington, D.C.: U.S. Government Printing Office, 1983), 6–7.

35. New Mexico, which had previously used lethal injection as its sole method of carrying out death sentences, abolished the death penalty on March 18, 2009; New Jersey abolished the death penalty in 2007. "Death Penalty Is Repealed in New Mexico," *New York Times*, Mar. 19, 2009, A16.

36. *State v. Mata*, 745 N.W.2d 229, 279 (Neb. 2008).

37. As of this writing, there are two bills pending in the Nebraska Legislature relating to the death penalty: Legislative Bill 36, which is intended to change the method of execution to lethal injection (Leg. 36, 101st Leg., 1st Sess. (Neb. 2009)), and Legislative Bill 306, which is intended to abolish the death penalty and impose a maximum sentence of life imprisonment without possibility of parole (Leg. 306, 101st Leg., 1st Sess. (Neb. 2009)). On January 29, 2009, a hearing for both bills was held before the Nebraska Legislature's Judiciary Committee, which included testimony from a range of individuals on both sides of the debate (*Hearing on Leg. 36 and Leg. 306 before the Judiciary Committee*, 101st Leg., 1st Sess. (Neb. 2009)). It is unclear whether the Judiciary Committee will consider other changes. Paul Hammel, "Death Penalty Qualifications May Change," *Omaha World-Herald*, Mar. 4, 2009, 2B.

38. Death Penalty Information Center, "Searchable Execution Database," available at http://deathpenaltyinfo.org/executions (accessed Mar. 3, 2009).

39. *Kennedy v. Louisiana*, 128 S. Ct. 2641, 2645–46, 2664–65 (2008). The other states with similar provisions to Louisiana are Georgia, Montana, Oklahoma, South Carolina, and Texas.

40. Denno, "Lethal Injection Quandary," 79. For a study concerning the frequency of botched executions, see Marian J. Borg and Michael L. Radelet, "On Botched Executions," in *Capital Punishment: Strategies for Abolition*, eds. Peter Hodgkinson and William A. Schabas (New York: Cambridge University Press, 2004), 143–68.

41. *Beardslee v. Woodford*, 395 F.3d 1064, 1074 n.11 (9th Cir. 2005) (per curium).

42. *Baze v. Rees*, No. 04-CI-01094, 2005 WL 5797977 (Ky. Cir. Ct., Div. I, July 8, 2005), *aff'd*, 217 S.W.3d 207 (Ky. 2006), *aff'd*, 128 S. Ct. 1520 (2008). Moreover, the argument has been made that when states attempt to further study lethal

injection through experimentation with varying procedures and protocols, they are performing illegal and unethical research on prisoners. Seema Shah, "How Lethal Injection Reform Constitutes Impermissible Research on Prisoners," *American Criminal Law Review* 45 (2008): 1101–47.

43. Denno, "Lethal Injection Quandary," 91–101; Denno, "When Legislatures Delegate Death," 116–26.

44. Denno, "Is Electrocution an Unconstitutional Method of Execution?" 562–76; Craig Brandon, *The Electric Chair: An Unnatural American History* (Jefferson, N.C.: McFarland, 1999), 32–38.

45. Denno, "Getting to Death," 364–65; Denno, "Is Electrocution an Unconstitutional Method of Execution?" 676–77.

46. Denno, "Getting to Death," 364–66.

47. Ibid., 373-74; Denno, "Lethal Injection Quandary," 65, 118.

48. Denno, "Getting to Death," 378–79, table 8.

49. Okla. Stat. Ann. tit. 22, sec. 1014 (West 2008).

50. Ibid.

51. Denno, "Lethal Injection Quandary," 62–63.

52. "California Inmates Get Choice in Executions," *New York Times*, Aug. 30, 1992, A28.

53. *Bryan v. Moore*, 528 U.S. 1133 (2000), *dismissing cert. granted by* 528 U.S. 960 (1999).

54. *Baze v. Rees*, 128 S. Ct. 1520, 1537 (2008).

55. Dieter, "Methods of Execution," 792–95.

56. Ibid., 793 (citing *Robinson v. California*, 370 U.S. 660, 675 (1962)).

57. Denno, "Getting to Death," 333–39.

58. Antiterrorism and Effective Death Penalty Act of 1996, Pub. L. No. 104-132, 110 Stat. 1214.

59. Dieter, "Methods of Execution," 795.

60. Ibid., 795–99.

61. 42 U.S.C. sec. 1983 (2009).

62. Dieter, "Methods of Execution," 800.

63. Ibid., 801 (citing *Nelson v. Campbell*, 541 U.S. 637, 645 (2004)); Denno, "Lethal Injection Quandary," 103–4.

64. Dieter, "Methods of Execution," 801–2 (citing *Hill v. McDonough*, 547 U.S. 573, 584 (2006)); Denno, "Lethal Injection Quandary," 104–6.

65. Dieter, "Methods of Execution," 802.

66. *Morales v. Hickman*, 415 F. Supp. 2d 1037 (N.D. Cal. 2006), *aff'd*, 438 F.3d 926 (9th Cir. 2006), *cert. denied*, 546 U.S. 1163 (2006).

67. For an account of Judge Fogel's personal experiences in lethal injection litigation generally and *Morales* specifically, see Jeremy Fogel, "In the Eye of the Storm: A Judge's Experience in Lethal-Injection Litigation," *Fordham Urban Law Journal* 35 (2008): 735–61.

68. *Morales v. Hickman*, 415 F. Supp. 2d, at 1044–46.

69. Ibid., 1047–48.

70. *Morales v. Tilton*, 465 F. Supp. 2d 972, 976 (N.D. Cal. 2006).

71. Ibid.

72. Ibid. Some state legislatures have begun taking steps toward statutorily protecting medical professionals who participate in executions. Nadia N. Sawicki, "Doctors, Discipline, and the Death Penalty: Professional Implications of Safe Harbor Statutes," *Yale Law and Policy Review* 27 (forthcoming 2009); available at http://papers.ssrn.com/abstract=1096545, 4.

73. Fogel, "Eye of the Storm," 743 (citing *Morales v. Tilton*,, 465 F. Supp. 2d, at 974).

74. Ibid., 743 n.51.

75. Howard Mintz, "Execution Method at Square One Again," *San Jose Mercury News*, Jan. 7, 2009, 1B.

76. Fogel, "Eye of the Storm," 735.

77. Ibid., 736–44.

78. Ibid., 744–49.

79. Denno, "When Legislatures Delegate Death," 67, 75–76.

80. Fogel, "Eye of the Storm," 748.

81. Ibid., 749.

82. Ibid., 749–53. For a general account of media influences on the death penalty, see Sarat, *When the State Kills*, 185–246.

83. Fogel, "Eye of the Storm," 750.

84. Ibid., 751, 753.

85. Ibid., 753–57.

86. Ibid., 757.

87. Ibid.

88. Ibid., 757–60.

89. Ibid., 759.

90. *Morales v. Tilton*, 465 F. Supp. 2d, 972, 978, 981 (N.D. Cal. 2006).

91. *Taylor v. Crawford*, No. 05-4173-CV-C-FJG, 2006 WL 1779035, at *8 (W.D. Mo. June 26, 2006) (determining that Missouri's current method of administering lethal injections "subjects condemned inmates to an unacceptable risk that they will be subject to unconstitutional pain and suffering"), *rev'd*, 487 F.3d 1072, 1085 (8th Cir. 2007) (reversing district court's holding that the state's revised protocol violated the Eighth Amendment), *cert. denied*, 128 S. Ct. 2047 (2008).

92. *Taylor* 2006 WL 1779035, at *4–7.

93. Ellyde Roko, "Executioner Identities: Toward Recognizing a Right to Know Who Is Hiding beneath the Hood," *Fordham Law Review* 75 (2007): 2791–92; Jeremy Kohler, "Behind the Mask of the Execution Doctor: Revelations about Dr. Alan Doerhoff Follow Judge's Halt of Lethal Injections," *St. Louis Post-Dispatch*, July 30, 2006, A1.

94. *Harbison v. Little*, 511 F. Supp. 2d 872, 903 (M.D. Tenn. 2007) ("[T]he court finds that the plaintiff's pending execution under Tennessee's new lethal injection protocol violates the Eighth Amendment. . . . The new protocol presents a substantial risk of unnecessary pain").

95. Dieter, "Methods of Execution," 802–3.

96. Ibid., 803. For a discussion of how judicial concern about the nature of lethal injection remedies limited the consideration of the right to a humane execution in *Baze*, see Eric Berger, "Lethal Injection and the Problem of Constitutional Remedies," *Yale Law and Policy Review* 27 (forthcoming 2009); available at http://papers.ssrn.com/sol3/papers.cfm?abstract_id=1311909.

97. Dieter, "Methods of Execution," 803–4.

98. Adam Liptak, "Moratorium May Be Over, but Hardly the Challenges," *New York Times*, Apr. 17, 2008, A26.

99. Linda Greenhouse, "Justices Chilly to Bid to Alter Death Penalty," *New York Times*, Jan. 8, 2008, A1.

100. Shaila Dewan, "Releases from Death Row Raise Doubts over Quality of Defense," *New York Times*, May 7, 2008, A1. See also Dieter, "Methods of Execution," 804 (discussing the execution of Michael Richard—the final execution performed in 2007).

101. Linda Greenhouse, "Justices Uphold Lethal Injection in Kentucky Case," *New York Times*, Apr. 17, 2008, A1.

102. Dieter, "Methods of Execution," 806.

103. Liptak, "Moratorium May Be Over" (citing commentators' responses to *Baze*).

104. For a list of the opinions filed in *Baze*, see note 5 of this chapter.

105. Greenhouse, "Justices Uphold Lethal Injection."

106. *Baze v. Rees*, 128 S. Ct. 1520, 1537 (2008) (plurality opinion) ("A State with a lethal injection protocol substantially similar to the protocol we uphold today would not create a risk that meets this standard."). But see ibid., 1562 (Thomas, J., concurring) ("At what point does a risk become substantial?").

107. There appears to be only one case where a court used the phrase "substantially similar" in the lethal injection context, and that court also did not elaborate. *Abdur'Rahman v. Bredesen*, 181 S.W.3d 292, 310 (Tenn. 2005).

108. *Baze*, 128 S. Ct. at 1542 (Stevens, J., concurring) ("When we granted certiorari in this case, I assumed that our decision would bring the debate about lethal injection as a method of execution to a close. It now seems clear that it will not."); ibid., 1562 (Thomas, J., concurring) ("[F]ar from putting an end to abusive litigation in this area . . . today's decision is sure to engender more litigation."). See also Liptak, "Moratorium May Be Over" (discussing commentators' views that litigation would continue).

109. Justice Kennedy was the only Justice in the majority who did not write separately.

110. *Baze*, 128 S. Ct. at 1542 (plurality opinion).

111. Ibid.

112. Ibid., 1537.

113. Ibid., 1532.

114. Ibid., 1531.

115. Ibid.

116. Ibid.

117. Ibid., 1534.

118. Ibid., 1567 (Breyer, J., concurring).

119. Ibid., 1566.

120. Ibid., 1570–71 (Ginsburg, J., dissenting).

121. Ibid., 1569.

122. Ibid., 1540 (Alito, J., concurring).

123. Ibid., 1542.

124. Ibid.

125. Ibid.

126. Ibid., 1542 (Stevens, J., concurring).

127. Ibid.

128. Ibid., 1542–43.

129. Ibid., 1546–51.

130. Ibid., 1552.

131. *Gregg v. Georgia*, 428 U.S. 153, 158 (1976).

132. *Baze*, 128 S. Ct. at 1550 (Stevens, J., concurring).

133. Ibid., 1546.

134. Ibid., 1551.

135. Ibid., 1552–56 (Scalia, J., concurring).

136. Ibid., 1555.

137. Ibid.

138. Ibid., 1555–56.

139. Ibid., 1563 (Thomas, J., concurring).

140. Ibid., 1556.

141. Ibid., 1562.

142. Ibid.

143. Ibid., 1561.

144. Ibid., 1535 (plurality opinion); ibid., 1541 (Alito, J., concurring); ibid., 1566 (Breyer, J., concurring). All three of these opinions reference Gerrit K. Kimsma, "Euthanasia and Euthanizing Drugs in the Netherlands," in *Drug Use in Assisted Suicide and Euthanasia*, eds. Margaret P. Battin and Arthur G. Lipman (New York: Pharmaceutical Products Press, 1996), 193–210. Kimsma's chapter relies most heavily on Royal Dutch Society for the Advancement of Pharmacy, *Administration and Compounding of Euthanasic Agents* (1994), the 1994 edition of the guidelines, which was translated into English.

145. Koninklijke Nederlandse Maatschappij ter bevordering der Pharmacie, *Standaard Euthanatica: Toepassing en Bereiding* (2007).

146. Ibid., 11–12. Pieter Admiraal devised the first euthanasia guidelines for physicians in the Netherlands for the Advisory Commission for the Legislation of Admissible Euthanasia based on procedures he had recommended in a book chapter published in 1977. P. V. Admiraal, *Verantwoorde Euthanasie: Handleiding voor Artsen*, Prepared for the Nederlandse Vereniging voor Vrijwillige Euthanasie, Adviescommissie inzake Wetgeving Toelaatbare Euthanasie, 3, 5. *Verantwoorde Euthanasie* has been translated into English: P. V. Admiraal, *Justifiable Euthanasia: A Manual for the Medical Profession*, Prepared for the Netherlands Society for Voluntary Euthanasia, Advisory Commission for the Legislation of Admissible Euthanasia. The referenced book chapter is P. V. Admiraal, "Euthanasie in het Ziekenhuis," in *Euthanasie*, ed. P. Muntendam (Leiden: Stafleu's Wetenschappelijke Uitgeversmaatschappij B.V., 1977), 188–208. In those guidelines, Admiraal recommended the administration of sodium thiopental followed by a curare-type agent such as pancuronium, a combination he believed hastened a "peaceful death" (Admiraal, *Justifiable Euthanasia*, 6–8).

147. *Baze*, 128 S. Ct. at 1546 n.9 (Stevens, J., concurring).

148. Johanna H. Groenewoud, Agnes van der Heide, Bregje D. Onwuteaka-Philipsen, Dick L. Willems, Paul J. van der Maas, and Gerrit van der Wal, "Clinical Problems with the Performance of Euthanasia and Physician-Assisted Suicide in the Netherlands," *New England Journal of Medicine* 342 (2000): 551–56. See also Pieter Admiraal, e-mail message to author, July 18, 2008.

149. *Baze*, 128 S. Ct. at 1567 (Ginsburg, J., dissenting).

150. Dieter, "Methods of Execution," 815–16.

151. *State v. Rivera*, No. 04CR065940, slip op. at 1, 9 (Ohio Ct. Com. Pl., Lorain County, June 10, 2008).

152. Ibid., 1. The two doctors were Mark Heath for the defense and Mark Dershwitz for the government. Susi Vassallo, "Thiopental in Lethal Injection," *Forham Urban Law Journal* 35 (2008): 958–59.

153. *Rivera*, No. 04CR065940, slip op. at 6.

154. Ibid., 4.

155. Ibid., 3–4.

156. Ibid., 4.

157. Ibid., 9.

158. Ohio Rev. Code Ann. sec. 2949.22(A) (West 2008).

159. *Rivera*, No. 04CR065940, slip op. at 5.

160. Ibid., 5.

161. Ibid., 7.

162. Ibid., 8.

163. Ibid., 9.

164. Ibid., 7.

165. Adam Liptak and Adam B. Ellick, "Judge Orders Ohio to Alter Its Method of Execution," *New York Times*, June 11, 2008, A16.

166. *Baze v. Rees*, 128 S. Ct. 1520, 1526 (2008) (plurality opinion).

167. Atul Gawande, "When Law and Ethics Collide: Why Physicians Participate in Executions," *New England Journal of Medicine* 354 (2006): 1229.

168. Timothy Kaufman-Osborn suggests another possibility: if lethal injection causes executions to become nonevents, they may become pointless, unable both to fulfill their role of revenge and to serve to demonstrate the state's power thereby "rejuvenat[ing] the claims of a classical conception of sovereignty." Timothy V. Kaufman-Osborn, *From Noose to Needle: Capital Punishment and the Late Liberal State* (Ann Arbor: University of Michigan Press, 2002), 214.

Perfect Execution
Abolitionism and the Paradox of Lethal Injection

Timothy V. Kaufman-Osborn

The U.S. Supreme Court's ruling in *Baze v. Rees*, which affirmed the constitutionality of Kentucky's lethal injection protocol, represented a setback, if not an outright defeat, for foes of the death penalty in the United States. Most obviously, the plurality opinion rejected the petitioners' proposed standard, which contended that the Eighth Amendment prohibits execution methods that pose an "unnecessary risk of pain" in light of available alternatives.[1] Instead, Chief Justice John Roberts declared that, in order to constitute cruel and unusual punishment, a protocol must create "a demonstrated risk of severe pain," and there must exist "feasible" and "readily available" alternatives whose use will "significantly reduce a substantial" measure of such harm.[2] While this more stringent standard does not preclude challenges to the procedures employed by other states, it renders their success less likely, especially given Roberts's express declaration that any protocol that is "substantially similar"[3] to that employed in Kentucky will pass constitutional muster.

In addition, for many members of the public, headlines such as "Justices Uphold Lethal Injection Procedure"[4] are likely to alleviate if not eliminate worries that may have arisen in recent years about the alleged humanity of what is now effectively the sole method of execution employed in the United States. Moreover, the effort to challenge Kentucky's protocol required an enormous expenditure of time, labor, and money on the part of various segments of the abolitionist community; and, with the benefit of hindsight, those scarce resources might have been more profitably deployed to contest other problematic aspects of the death penalty. Last, and perhaps most important, with the lifting of the national stay that was effectively imposed when the Court first agreed to hear *Baze*, several states quickly announced that they would move to resume and, if unstopped by the courts, accelerate the pace of executions.[5]

Members of the anti-death penalty community responded to the ruling in *Baze* by putting on a brave face,[6] and they were not entirely without reason in doing so. Sotto voce, many no doubt breathed a sigh of relief on learning that the opinions of Justices Clarence Thomas and Antonin Scalia, which would have generated a standard finding a protocol unconstitutional only if it was deliberately designed to inflict gratuitous pain, had not prevailed. More positively, given the fractured character of the six opinions written in favor of the 7–2 ruling, in which only two other justices signed on to Roberts's plurality opinion, it would appear that the Court remains of several minds on the exact standard to be employed in assessing the constitutionality of lethal injection protocols. No doubt, future suits will seek to exploit this apparent absence of consensus, especially given the thinness of the available record in Kentucky, where only one execution by lethal injection had been conducted before *Baze*.[7] In addition, although advanced in a concurring opinion, some solace was no doubt derived from Justice John Paul Stevens's announcement of his full-fledged conversion to the abolitionist cause, at least in part because one of the principal justifications for the death penalty, retribution, is undermined by a method of execution that seems to inflict little if any pain on the condemned.

Given the untidiness of the nearly 100 pages of *Baze*, perhaps all that one can conclude with confidence is that Justice Thomas was correct in predicting that the Court's ruling will encourage those opposed to capital punishment in their efforts "to embroil the States in never-ending litigation concerning the adequacy of their execution procedures."[8] Although Thomas disparages such efforts, attorneys representing those on death row would be negligent if they were to fail to do what they can to delay the killing of their clients, and, when that proves no longer possible, seek to ensure that their executions are conducted as humanely as possible. Acknowledgment of this professional obligation, though, should not foreclose critical inquiry into the strategic wisdom, as well as the larger political import of attacking the death penalty via challenges to the protocols that regulate the administration of lethal injections.[9] Indeed, from this vantage point, however paradoxical it may sound, it is arguable that the least desirable outcome in *Baze* would have been not a majority opinion authored by Thomas or Scalia but a victory for the petitioners. There are good reasons, that is, to worry that judicial mandates requiring states to tinker with the machinery of lethal injection, to paraphrase Justice Harry Blackmun,[10] may have the unintended effect of entrenching the death penalty in the United States by encouraging states to perfect the techniques that appear to cause death absent an act of taking life. While Justice Stevens may be correct to suggest that such perfection undermines the retributive rationale that sustains support for the death penalty today, it is equally true that the success of these same efforts may attenuate the conviction that the death penalty, because qualitatively different from all other forms of punishment, demands extraordinary justification.

The Impossible Dream

Recent debates over lethal injection are haunted by the dream of a perfect execution. This ideal has never been expressly affirmed as a constitutional imperative; indeed, it has been explicitly repudiated by justices, like Scalia and Thomas, who insist that the Eighth Amendment is satisfied as long as tortuous methods of inflicting death are disallowed.[11] The very fact that Thomas finds it necessary to deny that the Constitution requires what he labels an "anesthetized death" testifies to the presence of this dream, however ill-formed, in the penumbra of the contemporary debate over execution methods.

In this section, I provide an abbreviated account of the history and content of this dream. That involves, first, a cursory review of various states' transformation of their execution methods, beginning in the mid to late nineteenth century and continuing throughout much of the twentieth; and, second, an equally cursory look at the concurrent but very spare articulation of Eighth Amendment doctrine by the U.S. Supreme Court regarding the methods of execution that were adopted as part of this experimentation. In the next section of this essay, I move on to discuss the alleged failure of lethal injection to meet the imperatives of the ideal of the perfect execution, as that question was debated in the briefs submitted in *Baze*.

In his account of New York State's shift from hanging to electrocution as its method of execution in the late nineteenth century, Michael Madow contends that the infliction of death sentences in much of the United States, but especially in the Northeast, was transformed in three interconnected ways, which he labels "privatization," "rationalization," and "medicalization":

First, capital punishment was relocated from public spaces to prison inte-
riors, and the number of permitted witnesses was sharply restricted [priva-
tization]. Next, executions were progressively stripped of their ritualistic
and religious aspects, and converted into hurried technical routines [ratio-
nalization]. Lastly, as Americans developed a keen dread of physical pain,
medical professionals teamed up with electrical engineers to devise a purportedly "painless" method of administering the death penalty: electrocution [medicalization]. By the end of the century, capital punishment in New
York had already become "death work." The condemned man, previously
the central actor in a public theater of justice, had now become simply the
object of medico-bureaucratic techniques—his body read closely for signs
of pain, but his voice muffled and barely audible.[12]

First, in the early nineteenth century, executions were typically conducted in places of open assembly, often drawing thousands of spectators
and sometimes taking on the appearance of rowdy carnivals.[13] By the close
of the century, Madow explains, in most but not all states, executions
were privatized in the sense that they were moved from outdoor spaces to
the interior of walled and well-guarded prisons to which only a few were
permitted access. This removal did not entirely purge executions of their
character as performances, but it did entail a significant transformation
in the composition of its audiences. Whereas before, in principle, no one
from any social class was excluded from the crowd, witnesses to death
sentences inflicted within penitentiaries became increasingly homoge-
neous in composition, drawn chiefly from the ranks of government offi-
cialdom, the press, and, often, the medical profession. Unlike the less-pre-
dictable and more-impassioned participants in executions that took the
form of public spectacles, as a rule, the witnesses to privatized executions,
especially those attending in the name of professional obligation, could be
counted on to respond to state killings with appropriate affective restraint
and with the refined sensibilities suitable to an age of self-proclaimed
progress. This shift in audience composition, Annulla Linders points out,
entailed a correlative adjustment in the "evaluation criteria to be applied
to the execution, now derived from science rather than passion. . . . The
professionalized audience might tolerate the ghastliness of death itself, but
not incompetence and mismanagement." By the mid-nineteenth century,
"brutality had become a liability and visible pain a sign of failure."[14]

Second, in the early nineteenth century, the typical execution
took shape as what Madow calls a "richly ceremonial civico-religious

spectacle."[15] Designed at least in part to affirm the authority of church and political figures, these events included considerable moral and religious discourse about, for example, the power of God to redeem the sinful and the slippery slope that carried men and women from small vices to vile crimes. By the end of the century, however, the infliction of death sentences had been rationalized in the sense that they were "almost entirely de-ritualized and secularized—emptied of visible moral purpose, shorn of imagery and symbolism, stripped of passion and emotional content."[16] As the goal of retribution came to supplant that of redemption, executions came to be construed as technical tasks governed by the instrumental norms appropriate to such matters. As such, increasingly, they came to be conducted in accordance with elaborately articulated protocols, including precise timetables, careful specification of the equipment to be employed, and detailed plans outlining the division of labor among those whose specialized assignments were to be exactly coordinated in order to ensure efficient completion of the matter at hand. As with its performative dimension, this transformation did not entirely purge executions of ritual, as indicated, for example, by retention of the customary granting of a "last meal" and the opportunity to utter "final words"; but it did mean that such elements increasingly appeared as relics folded awkwardly, even anachronistically, into operating procedures governed by the very different logic of managerial expertise.

Third, and intertwined with the first two transformations, in the early nineteenth century, Madow argues, executions were chiefly construed as punishments that served larger purposes of political, moral, and religious edification. For this reason, a member of the clergy was indispensable to the proceedings, and his principal concern was the soul of the condemned. Leaving aside denominational peculiarities, as a rule, bodily pain was understood as a sign of the punishment endured by an irremediably diseased soul, trapped in the carnal envelope that is the body, and deserved in virtue of the primal sin of Adam and Eve. By the end of the century, however, the conduct of executions came to be informed by major shifts in the practice of professional medicine. Prompted in part by the isolation of morphine, the invention of the hypodermic syringe, and, above all, the discovery of inhalation anesthesia, physicians began to entertain the ideal of alleviating, if not eliminating, most bodily pain. As such, suffering came to be considered a contingent as opposed to an inexorable feature of the human condition, so that, to an ever-greater extent, the central question asked of an execution was not whether the condemned had confessed before expiration but whether he or she had experienced pain and, if so, why and for how long. In sum, in time, more-encompassing theological understandings of suffering gave way to the secular construction of pain as a nociceptive event produced in the peripheral and central nervous system by noxious stimuli and most adequately explicated via the causal categories of modern medical science.

While it would misrepresent the jagged character of historical change to claim that execution by lethal injection was somehow the necessary teleological terminus of the transformations identified by Madow, adoption of this method is certainly a development that is intelligible in terms of its trajectory. Leaving no mark on the body's surface, doing its work behind a wall of flesh that is as opaque as those surrounding a penitentiary, the lethal needle consummates the privatization of capital punishment, as the violence necessary to kill, once visually available to all who chose to attend, is now hidden even from the eyes of the carefully selected witnesses to an execution. Drawing its legitimacy from modernity's most respected form of authority, that of science, lethal injection perfects the rationalization of the death penalty, as the clergy and its sacraments are displaced by civil servants trained in the secular proficiencies of penological expertise. Finally, by promising a quick and painless death, one that does not occasion any visible suffering, lethal injection perfects the medicalization of capital punishment, as the accomplishment of death via the injection of chemicals associated with the conduct of surgery supplants the cruder technologies definitive of the firing squad, the gallows, the gas chamber, and the electric chair.

Given that these reformations in the conduct of inflicting death sentences occurred when they did, it is perhaps not coincidental that the U.S. Supreme Court made its initial forays into execution methods in the last quarter of the nineteenth century; nor, given this history, is it surprising that as it did so, the Court became increasingly preoccupied with the question of the intensity and duration of pain suffered by the condemned. The earliest case, *Wilkerson v. Utah*, decided in 1879, involved a challenge to a sentence to death by firing squad imposed by a territorial court. The Court ruled that this method of execution was not cruel and unusual, chiefly because it was not among the forms of punishment deemed intolerable by the Constitution's framers, especially in light of the 1689 English Bill of Rights, which furnishes the basic template for the Eighth Amendment. However, after noting the "difficulty" that "would attend the effort to define with exactness the extent of the [Eighth Amendment]," the Court did allow for the possibility of a modest expansion beyond the confines of this strict historicist reading when it affirmed that "punishments of torture," including public disemboweling, beheading, drawing and quartering, and burning alive, "and all others in the same line of unnecessary cruelty, are forbidden."[17]

The second execution methods case decided by the U.S. Supreme Court, *In re Kemmler*, involved an 1890 challenge to a New York statute changing its method of inflicting the death penalty from hanging to electrocution. Although not decided under the Eighth Amendment, which had not yet been deemed applicable to the states, *Kemmler* did include dicta that have often been cited by contemporary courts in their efforts to clarify the meaning of the prohibition against cruel and unusual punishment in the context of capital punishment. Echoing the decision in *Wilkerson*, the Court stated that punishments such as "burning at the stake, crucifixion, breaking on the wheel, or the like" are "manifestly cruel and unusual."[18] However, in explaining its conclusion about what constitutes cruelty, the Court began to shift, albeit subtly, away from *Wilkerson's* reliance on a doctrine of original intent, which privileges questions of pain's deliberate infliction, as well as the body's visible mutilation, and toward an assessment of the condemned's subjective experience of death's infliction: "Punishments are cruel when they involve torture or a lingering death; but the punishment of death is not cruel within the meaning of that word as used in the Constitution. It implies there something inhuman and barbarous—something more than the mere extinguishment of life."[19] Concerned among other things with the duration of killing, the Court hinted that, in principle, infliction of the penalty of death should be confined to the austere cancellation of life, its "mere extinguishment," and, by implication, that any suffering not strictly necessary to the accomplishment of that end is at least potentially constitutionally suspect.

The shift intimated by *Kemmler* was amplified in *Louisiana ex rel. Francis v. Resweber* (1947), when the Court considered its third and final pre-*Baze* methods challenge, brought in this instance by an inmate who had been placed in an electric chair, but, apparently because of a mechanical problem, was not killed. In considering whether the state of Louisiana could engage in a second attempt to execute Francis, the plurality opinion began by insisting, absent reference to deliberate intent, that "the traditional humanity of modern Anglo-American law forbids the infliction of unnecessary pain in the execution of the death sentence."[20] However, providing fodder for the position advanced by Scalia and Thomas in *Baze*, the Court immediately went on to state that in the instant case there "is no purpose to inflict unnecessary pain nor any unnecessary pain involved in the proposed execution,"[21] and, on that basis, it authorized Louisiana to try again.

One consequence of *Resweber* was to set the stage for later courts, including that which decided *Baze*, to dismiss the constitutional import of executions that can be subsumed beneath the category of the "accidental" on the ground that, by definition, such events are outside the domain of what can be foreseen and hence prevented.[22] At the same time, however, *Resweber*'s prohibition of "unnecessary pain" effectively invited the question of whether legislatures, in order to avoid the charge of cruelty, have a constitutional obligation to adopt whatever method of execution is at that time calculated to inflict the least amount of pain possible, and, as petitioners in *Baze* argued, whether administrative officers to whom legislatures delegate the particulars of carrying out executions have an obligation to do the same.

Justice Ginsburg is probably the most intellectually honest member of the Court when, in *Baze*, she acknowledges that "no clear standard for determining the constitutionality of a method of execution" emerges from these three cases and that "the age of the opinions limits their utility as an aid to resolution of the present controversy."[23] While Ginsburg is correct to suggest that these decisions offer no unambiguous rule, it would be a mistake to conclude that they or their differences, however erratic, are irrelevant to contemporary constitutional disputation about execution methods. Their cumulative relevance, I would suggest, is best appreciated when they are read retrospectively in relation to the Court's insistence that the meaning of the cruel and unusual punishment clause is neither static nor bound by specific historical practices.

First articulated in 1910, in a case dealing with a sentence of 15 years of incarceration and hard labor for the crime of falsifying a public document, the Court held that the Eighth Amendment "is not fastened to the obsolete but may acquire meaning as public opinion becomes enlightened by a humane justice."[24] This principle was extended in a 1958 case holding that denationalization as a punishment for desertion during wartime violates the Eighth Amendment: "The Amendment must draw its meaning from the evolving standards of decency that mark the progress of a maturing society."[25] That this reading of the cruel and unusual punishment clause applies to assessment of the constitutionality of capital punishment was made clear in *Gregg v. Georgia*. There, in authorizing the states to resume the death penalty following the hiatus imposed in 1972 by *Furman*, the Court affirmed that this clause must be "interpreted in a flexible and dynamic manner" and, consequently, that "an assessment of contemporary values concerning the infliction of a challenged sanction is relevant to the application of the Eighth Amendment."[26]

The terrain on which the battle over lethal injection has recently been fought is well understood by reading *Wilkerson*, *Kemmler*, and *Resweber* in light of the progressive narrative affirmed in *Gregg* and in relation to the story told by Madow about the reform of execution practices since the late-nineteenth century. More specifically, if *Wilkerson* is read as a prohibition of the forms of public mutilation that defined the conduct of many early modern European executions, if violence visibly inflicted on the body runs the risk of being branded a form of torture and so a reversion to barbarism, lethal injection negates this allegation because, in principle, its administration entails little more than a pinprick. If *Kemmler* stands at least in part for the proposition that death must not be "lingering," lethal injection appears to fit the bill well because the infliction of death is relatively quick and, more important, because the precise moment of death is concealed from witnesses by the fact that its achievement is indistinguishable from the unconsciousness induced by anesthesia. If *Resweber* signifies that capital punishment, in order to be deemed legitimate, must involve as little pain as is necessary to bring about death, and never any pain that is "gratuitously" or "wantonly" inflicted, this condition would appear to be well satisfied by a method that claims to ward off all conscious suffering. Finally, if *Weems* and *Trop*, as applied to capital punishment in *Gregg*, express a commitment to ever-greater realization of the claims of humanitarianism, lethal injection would appear to offer proof of the death penalty's progressive subjection to the norms of civilization, which, in being respected, assures us of the distance we have traveled from forms of savagery animated by a rough desire for private vengeance.

When the trajectory intimated by these cases is located within a broader historical context that animates and reinforces the curve of this path, it becomes apparent why, today, death penalty proponents and opponents alike, as well as the courts, are haunted by the ideal of a death sentence whose infliction is so imperceptible that it effectively elides the act of killing. Key elements of that ideal are intimated in Justice Harold Burton's dissent in *Resweber*, which made explicit the desideratum implicit in *Kemmler*'s reference to the "mere extinguishment of life": "The all-important consideration is that the execution shall be so instantaneous and substantially painless that the punishment shall be reduced, as nearly as possible, to no more than that of death itself."[27] Pressured by the forward thrust inherent in the phrase "evolving standards of decency," the dynamics of rationalization, medicalization, and privatization project an ideal that cannot help but trouble both sides of the death penalty debate, precisely because it can never quite be realized. It can never be perfectly realized, that is, as long as those condemned to die remain beings whose recalcitrant bodies resist extermination and so require violence, no matter how well sterilized or concealed, in order to kill them.

As such, this ideal assumes the character of a phantasm, which, although formally unacknowledged, is not for that reason absent from the contemporary debate about the death penalty.[28] A hint regarding this phantasm's ultimate but impossible end was unwittingly provided by a spokesperson for the Florida Department of Corrections who, shortly after that state completed its first two executions by lethal injection, explained that the point is to render such killings "as uneventful as possible."[29] To fully satisfy the normative expectations engendered by our collective squeamishness about deliberate killing as a form of criminal punishment, ideally, an execution will assume the form of something akin to a non-event: an occurrence that never quite happens. It is the seductive allure of this aspiration that explains why efforts to reform the protocols governing the conduct of lethal injections are likely to continue after *Baze*. But, at the same time, and as indicated in the next section, it is the inability to guarantee reliable achievement of a death that appears to involve no killing that explains why to date states have refused to alter the specific chemicals employed in lethal injections, even though this has proven the most controversial and legally vulnerable ingredient of such protocols.

The Haunting of Baze v. Rees

As heirs to the political and legal history outlined in the preceding section, both parties to *Baze v. Rees* are haunted by the dream of a perfect execution. Albeit for different reasons, both find it necessary to avow (as well as to disavow) its imperatives, which entails that the arguments advanced in their respective briefs to the Supreme Court are often disingenuous, albeit in different ways. In this section, to show how these competing imperatives operate, I deploy Madow's overlapping categories of rationalization, medicalization, and privatization to interpret those briefs as a prelude to the essay's final section, where I ask about possible implications of the Supreme Court's ruling in *Baze* for the future of the death penalty in the United States.

On Rationalization

Although unacknowledged, both parties to *Baze* share considerable ground. The lay of that land can be indicated by recalling Madow's appropriation of Max Weber's concept of "rationalization." The concept of rationalization signals the transformation of a given domain of practice—in this case, the execution of death sentences—in accordance with the standards of instrumental rationality. Instrumental rationality has a normative dimension insofar as, above all else, it prizes technical efficiency in the accomplishment of any given end, and that, in turn, entails placing a premium on the values of reliability, predictability, calculability, and comprehensibility, where the criteria of intelligibility are those furnished by the causal logic of modern science. Or, to put this point in reverse, from the vantage point of instrumental rationality, what is most disvalued are practices, which, in whole or in part, remain unreliable, unpredictable, incalculable, and so opaque to the epistemic categories of modern science.

The transformation of execution practices in accordance with the imperatives of instrumental rationality is what Madow alludes to when he states that, by the end of the nineteenth century, the infliction of death sentences, especially in the Northeast, had been largely stripped of their ritualistic, theoethical, and affective content. A measure of our departure from that era can be indicated by imagining the response that would be evoked if either brief were to appeal to the notion of sin in explaining the deeds of Ralph Baze and Thomas Bowling or to the eternal damnation awaiting those who commit deeds of their ilk. Nor would we find it persuasive if either side were to appeal to the authority of immemorial tradition in articulating its position on the constitutionality of Kentucky's protocol. For both parties, adoption of the criteria appropriate to instrumental rationality is mandated by transformation of execution into a task that is not a form of political theater conducted in order to demonstrate the consequences of disobedience to spectators assembled in a public square, nor a form of religious drama aimed at revealing the divine wrath wrought on those who dare defy God's law, but a matter, to quote Madow again, of technological expertise aimed at "'getting the man dead' as quickly, smoothly, efficiently, and impersonally as possible."[30]

To point out this common terrain is not to say that differences of legal opinion disappear in consequence. But it is to say that these disputes take place almost entirely on the narrow band of turf designated by the term "rationalization," which, in turn, considerably restricts the sorts of arguments that will be deemed intelligible and plausible. To see the point, consider the centrality of the question of risk in the *Baze* briefs. This question was not a part of the political or legal calculus when, as in early modern Europe (think of the opening pages of Foucault's *Discipline and Punish*), executions assumed the form of spectacular ceremonials through which an injured sovereign reaffirmed the absolutism of state authority by deliberately reducing an offender to the status of a mere body in pain. However, when the permissibility of intentionally inflicted torture has been rejected, and when even the suffering unintentionally inflicted by any given execution method has become a source of collective anxiety, the question of pain's risk becomes pivotal. The language of "risk," in sum, designates those elements of the practice of inflicting death sentences that have yet to be subordinated to the imperatives of instrumental rationality, thereby thwarting realization of the ideal of a perfect execution.[31]

In *Baze*, petitioners and respondents alike agree that one of the key questions in this case is how much risk is permissible, which is legally parsed in terms of the distinction between "substantial" and "significant."[32] Respondents contend that, if adopted, petitioners' less-demanding standard, which would find unconstitutional any risk of pain that is "unnecessary" in light of "reasonably available alternatives," will impose an intolerable burden on the state.[33] On their account, this standard does so because "once an alleged improvement to the protocol has been identified or becomes available, any potential risks arising out of a state's failure to immediately adopt the alleged improvement are deemed 'foreseeable' and thus, in petitioners' view, avoidable, without regard to the magnitude of the risk."[34] In other words, albeit not in these terms, respondents recognize that the brief submitted by petitioners tacitly summons the progressive logic of rationalization in order to hold out the prospect of an execution practice that perfectly fulfills the norms of instrumental rationality, and, in doing so, eliminates all possible risk.[35] Yet, in order to immunize their proposed standard against the claim that it effectively mandates abolition of what the Constitution has been held to permit, petitioners cannot openly confess that they seek the universal and unqualified elimination of risk, and so, as respondents insist, they must acknowledge the constitutional acceptability of some measure of risk. But because respondents, too, are in the grip of the normative expectations generated by the ideal of rationalization, they must, in turn, insist that the current protocol, especially as voluntarily modified by the state in order to provide still greater safeguards, "poses no substantial risk of unnecessary pain or suffering" and so "ensure[s] a quick, humane, pain-free death."[36]

As a strictly legal matter, the differences between the arguments advanced in the two briefs and the competing legal standards they advance are neither insignificant nor unsubstantial. My point, though, is that the centrality of the question of risk to this case is indicative of its construction in the terms dictated by the logic of rationalization. Both parties, at least in principle, are beguiled by the prospect of a legal order in which all events are perfectly controllable and so predictable. Neither can nor will contend that creation of this order is constitutionally mandated. But nor is neither likely to acknowledge, as did the physicians who served on the Governor's Commission on Administration of Lethal Injection in Florida, that "the *inherent* risks and therefore the potential unreliability of lethal injection *cannot* be fully mitigated."[37] Petitioners will not do so because this would sully the ideal they project in order to render their challenge rhetorically persuasive, and respondents will not do so because this would come close to conceding the impossibility of devising an execution protocol that satisfies contemporary standards of decency. "Risk," in sum, is the signifier that must be affirmed in order to acknowledge the limits of rationalization but, at the same time, denied in order to assuage the uneasiness generated by any apparent failure to satisfy the ideal projected by the appeal to rationalization.

On Medicalization

The points of controversy in the *Baze* briefs highlighted by the category of "medicalization" are largely situated on the turf defined by rationalization and the ideal it insinuates (although, for reasons I indicate below, correspondence between the imperatives of rationalization and of medicalization is not complete). If the language of risk is the way in which the parties to this case frame the residue left behind by imperfect rationalization, the terminologies of suffering and incompetence are the ways they frame the residue left behind by imperfect medicalization. Although these categories overlap, for the most part, I fold my account of the parties' discussion of suffering, specifically in the form of physical pain, into my discussion of "privatization." Here I focus on the briefs' consideration of the competence of the personnel involved in executions in performing the technical tasks required of them.

How this issue is framed turns on a prior question that lurks in the briefs, as well as in the oral argument before the Supreme Court, but is never conclusively resolved: What exactly is a lethal injection? Is it a medical procedure, in which case, as one physician has recommended, the person undergoing this procedure should be designated a "patient?"[38] Or is it a form of criminal punishment, in which case the person undergoing this procedure should be designated as the "condemned"? Or as Mark Heath, an anesthesiologist who often testifies at lethal injection hearings, has recently suggested, is it a procedure that can be logically segmented into several different steps, some of which are medical because they serve "therapeutic" ends, while others are punitive insofar as their purpose is to kill, in which case it would appear that the person undergoing this procedure is, at successive moments, the "patient" and then the "condemned?"[39] Furthermore, how are the chemicals employed in a lethal injection to be categorized? Is the American Society of Anesthesiologists correct to insist, as it does in the amicus brief it submitted in conjunction with *Baze*, that although these same drugs are commonly used in conjunction with surgery they are not to be identified with those employed in medical practice?[40] If that is so, does it follow that these chemicals are best regarded as instrumentalities of state killing, something akin to the noose, the bullet, and the cyanide pellet? Or, can they, too, be subdivided into those that are therapeutic and those that are punitive? But how can that be if each, administered in a dose that far exceeds the amount typically employed in surgery, is itself (probably) lethal?

With good reason, making the most of the opportunities offered by these ambiguities, petitioners do what they can to frame lethal injection as a medical procedure. This is perhaps most apparent in their contention that the virtually universal adoption of lethal injection by death penalty states, as well as "contemporary standards of decency," articulate a consensus in favor of "anesthetized death"[41] (which, recall, is precisely the characterization that Justice Thomas insists is not constitutionally mandated). To the extent that petitioners can render this representation persuasive, it would appear to follow that executions can and should measure up to the standards of surgical practice. Specifically, on this construction, those participating in the conduct of executions should demonstrate the same forms of expert proficiency that are routinely expected of certified anesthesiologists; the reliability of drugs and the equipment employed to dispense them in the death chamber should equal those employed in the surgical theater; and the protocols that govern the relationship between executioners and their technologies should be as exacting as those that govern the best practices of medicine.

However, and although the logic of their argument clearly presses them in this direction, petitioners cannot openly insist on the participation of certified physicians in executions (although they come close to doing just that when they cite California rulings requiring "a qualified individual" or an "anesthesia professional"[42]). They cannot do so because they know that this requirement would run afoul of an advisory of the American Medical Association, which declares that a physician, "as a member of a profession dedicated to preserving life when there is hope of doing so, should not be a participant in a state execution."[43] And they cannot do so because this would establish a condition that the Department of Corrections cannot meet, given Kentucky's death penalty statute, which, unlike those of most other states, expressly prohibits the participation of physicians in executions "except to certify the cause of death provided the condemned is declared dead by another person."[44] Were petitioners to argue on behalf of a requirement of physician involvement, they would open themselves to the charge that they thereby violate the conditions of their own suit, which, as a complaint filed under 42 U.S.C. § 1983,[45] is limited to the proposal of protocol reforms that are not merely desirable but also feasible. In sum, petitioners must do everything possible to imply the indispensability of certified medical professionals while, at the same time, denying that they seek to do just that.

To forestall the import of the medical model, respondents contend that petitioners are in error when they seek to "transform the execution chamber into a surgical suite, complete with anesthesiologist and monitoring equipment."[46] The obvious implication is that execution by lethal injection is not a medical procedure, for it is aimed neither at enhancing health nor at preserving life. It is not clear, though, that respondents can afford to affirm, as does the amicus brief filed on their behalf by the Criminal Justice Legal Foundation, that "standards of medical practice for surgery have no direct relevance to punishment."[47] Nor can they afford to endorse the call, advanced by at least one physician, to replace current procedures and personnel with those "that are clearly representative of the legal system and clearly distinguished from representing medical care."[48] To make either of these claims is to invite the response that executions conducted absent observance of the best practices of medicine risk gratuitous pain, thereby contravening what the Eighth Amendment requires. In short, respondents must do everything possible to deny that lethal injections are required to meet the standards of established medical practice while, at the same time, intimating that the present protocol already ensures just that.

The issue posed by the question of physician involvement in lethal injections is indicative of a broader tension in the relationship between the imperatives of rationalization and those of medicalization. Especially since the late nineteenth century, the conduct of medicine has been substantially transformed in accordance with the imperatives of instrumental rationality. For example, as indicated in the preceding discussion, pain is now understood in terms of the causal logic of modern science (as opposed to God's punishment for sin); the practice of medicine is organized as a profession that upholds norms of expert proficiency; and the conduct of medicine is ever more tied to a secular imperative of progress that expects, even demands, increasing technical mastery in eliminating the forms of distress that fall within its purview. Reconstruction of the practice of medicine by the desiderata of rationalization is complicated, however, by the fact that the formal norms of efficiency, certainty, and reliability are constrained by the substantive commitment of this profession to the Hippocratic oath and, particularly, its injunction to do no harm. Granted, the precise import of this norm has become vexed in recent years as doctors have grappled with the issue of physician-assisted suicide on the part of the terminally ill; and, granted, the willingness of physicians to abide by the AMA's advisory is qualified at best (as evidenced by a recent study indicating that a surprisingly large percentage of physicians (41 percent) are willing to participate in lethal injections in ways that extend beyond the certification of death).[49] That said, were the formal imperatives of rationalization entirely exhaustive of the claims of medical rationality, leaving aside whatever personal reservations they might have, in principle, physicians could unproblematically lend their expertise to the accomplishment of death as efficiently as possible in light of the profession's present knowledge and technical capacity.

The conundrum posed for both sides by the disjunction between the claims of formal and substantive rationality is well illustrated by an editorial published in the *New England Journal of Medicine* shortly before the ruling in *Baze* was announced. That editorial stated that, "without the involvement of physicians and medical professionals with special training in the use of anesthetic drugs, it is unlikely that lethal injection will ever meet a constitutional standard of decency." However, it then immediately proceeded to insist that "physicians and other health care providers should not be involved in capital punishment, even in an advisory capacity. A profession dedicated to healing the sick has no place in the process of execution."[50] For petitioners, this editorial bolsters their claim that lethal injection protocols must be reformed to meet the standards of medical practice, but it also indicates why those best equipped to do so cannot be expected to participate in formulating or administering these reforms. For respondents, this editorial bolsters their claim that lethal injection protocols cannot be expected to conform fully to the standards of medical practice, but it also indicates why executions are likely to continue to go awry as long as those involved in executions do not have appropriate forms of professional training and expertise.

The controversy over whether medical standards should be imported into the death chamber is yet another illustration of the ambiguity noted by Simon Cole and Jay Aronson when, in this volume, they argue that the appeal to various modalities of scientific rationality in the debate over capital punishment has proven to be a two-edged sword. On the one hand, the fact that lethal injections bear significant resemblance to medical procedures confuses the punitive with the therapeutic, thereby helping to legitimate executions in the eyes of the public, including those who serve as witnesses. On the other hand, this very resemblance engenders an ideal that invites legal challenges when lethal injections fail to conform to medical imperatives, and, in doing so, recalls the punitive and, more particularly, the retributive purpose of executions. It is precisely this tension that leads Justice Stevens in his concurring opinion in *Baze* to conclude that "state-sanctioned killing" becomes increasingly "anachronistic" when we require that the inmate be protected "from enduring any punishment that is comparable to the suffering inflicted on his victim."[51] Whether this divergence will "generate debate . . . about the justification for the death penalty itself,"[52] as Stevens predicts, or merely encourage additional increments of formal rationalization that ultimately turn attention away from this substantive question is the issue I take up in this essay's closing section.

On Privatization

What troubles the logic of rationalization and the image of perfection it projects is the specter expressed via the terminology of risk. What troubles the logic of medicalization and the image of perfection it projects is the specter expressed via the terminology of incompetence. The forms of privatization that are unique to lethal injection answer the anxieties occasioned by these twin specters. Privatization, that is, responds to the elements of executions that continue to elude the combined imperatives of rationalization and medicalization, however imperfect their union may be.

Recall that the move from hanging to electrocution as the dominant method of execution, beginning in the late nineteenth century, was accompanied by a shift in the locus of executions from public places to the interior of penitentiaries, and this, in turn, was accompanied by a change in execution audiences from a randomly constituted crowd to a pool of carefully selected witnesses consisting, for the most part, of those with professional credentials. Against this backdrop, the contemporary presence of spectators lacking any claim to certified expertise (e.g., relatives of the condemned, as well as of the victim) may be read as a vestige of an era when the condemned's head was hooded (and sometimes that of the executioner), but all else was visibly available to the members of a heterogeneous public. The contemporary impetus to privatize executions can be understood in terms of, on the one hand, the relationship between the problem posed by such spectators and, on the other hand, the allure of an ideal that always beckons but whose realization cannot be consistently or fully guaranteed.

Perhaps the foremost element of concern in *Baze* is the form of suffering that is cognizable as physical pain. Indeed, in *Baze*, the question of pain often appears to crowd out all others, which is not surprising, given the late-nineteenth-century shift of Supreme Court attention away from *Wilkerson*'s concern with the kinds of bodily mutilation gathered together beneath the rubric of "torture" and toward its preoccupation, first anticipated in *Kemmler*, with the subjective experience of the condemned during an execution. Formally, although petitioners do not and cannot seek a guarantee that executions will be painless, they are more than eager to invoke *Kemmler*'s phantasm of an execution that involves nothing but the "mere extinguishment of life." How they present this phantasm as a constitutional challenge to their opponents is indicated by noting the logical leaps involved in moving from the first to the last of the following three sentences from their brief: "Advancements in science have made it possible to carry out a death sentence *in a nearly painless manner*. And the States that impose death sentences have, with near unanimity, adopted lethal injection in order *to make executions painless* to the condemned person. . . . Thus, there is today an undeniable 'national consensus' that executions *must be essentially painless*."[53]

The second sentence takes the predictive claim registered in the first and transforms it into a claim about legislative intent, while the third transforms the claim about intent into a vital precondition of establishing a constitutional requirement. The presuppositions that permit these leaps to be made are those tacitly present in Justice Lewis Powell's declaration in *Furman* that "no court would approve any method of implementation of the death sentence found to involve unnecessary cruelty in light of presently available alternatives."[54] Arguably, in light of the progressive narrative implied by the logic of rationalization, this declaration mandates that courts, and perhaps legislatures as well, engage in an ongoing search for more "humane" alternatives, where "humanity" is measured chiefly by the amount of pain a particular method inflicts and where the logical terminus of this search is discovery of one that ensures its total absence.

Respondents, of course, must formally reject this claim, as they do. However, because they, too, are gripped by the vision of a perfect death, one that evinces no evidence of suffering, they find themselves pressed to contradict, or, at the very least, to render effectively irrelevant, the argument they made earlier about the constitutional acceptability of the risk that some measure of pain will be suffered during an execution. A clear medical consensus, they argue, indicates that administration of the chemicals specified in the Kentucky protocol will "eliminate any of the pain that petitioners frequently discuss in their argument" and "ensure an immediate and certain death."[55] In sum, at least in principle, both parties appear to share the ideal of eliminating all pain, or, more carefully, the risk of any pain, during the infliction of death sentences. Given this shared substantive end, it is perhaps all the more surprising that the most bitter issue of disagreement between the two parties is on the face of it a question of formal rationalization—specifically, a question of what technical modifications to the chemical mix employed by Kentucky, if any, are best suited to achieve the end of a pain-free death.

Why this question proves so divisive can be understood by situating it within the context of the quest to privatize executions. As a preface to doing that, a brief pharmacological digression is necessary. In the 29 states for which this information is available, lethal injections employ the same (or virtually the same) three chemicals, and, in all probability, this same "cocktail" is employed in the states that do not divulge this information. The first is sodium thiopental, which, although once routinely employed during the induction phase of anesthesia before surgery, has now for the most part been replaced by propofol. In a surgical setting, a dose of 3 to

5 milligrams per kilogram of body weight is typically employed, whereas the Kentucky protocol specifies administration of a dose of 3 grams. The second is pancuronium bromide, a curare-derived agent that paralyzes all muscles by blocking the action of acetylcholine at the motor endplate of the neuromuscular junction but has no effect on awareness, cognition, or sensation. In a surgical setting, a standard dose is 0.2 milligrams per kilogram of body weight, whereas the Kentucky protocol calls for 50 milligrams. The final chemical, potassium chloride, is an electrolyte that is commonly prescribed by physicians in response to hypokalemia (insufficient potassium in the blood). The usual intravenous dose is 10 to 20 milliequivalents per hour, whereas the Kentucky protocol calls for 240 milliequivalents, which is intended to disrupt the electrical signaling of the heart and so cause cardiac arrest.

Because of its role in securing the unconsciousness that is indispensable to the achievement of a painless death, the intravenous injection of the initial drug, sodium thiopental, requires particular attention in order to ensure, among other things, that the catheter is properly set and so does not migrate, that the vein is not perforated in the process, that the tubing does not leak, that the intended amount is successfully injected into the bloodstream (as opposed to, say, subcutaneously), and so forth. These and other possible misadventures are likely to transpire with some regularity, petitioners argue, given that executions by lethal injection are typically conducted by paramedics, emergency medical technicians, or prison staff who have little if any formal medical training. Should any of these mishaps occur, the condemned may never become completely unconscious or may regain partial or total consciousness at some point prior to or coincident with injection of pancuronium bromide and/or potassium chloride; and, should that occur, because pancuronium bromide is a paralytic, the condemned will prove unable to give voice to the respiratory arrest induced by this second chemical and the intense burning sensations, massive muscle cramping, and the violent heart attack that follow injection of potassium chloride. In short, and in a unique twist on executions botched by other means, under these circumstances, the condemned will prove powerless to articulate his or her agonies, whether by crying out, grimacing, writhing, or offering any of the other signs we conventionally regard as expressions of acute physical distress. For this same reason, witnesses to an execution will prove oblivious to the reality of the pain suffered by an inmate who is both mute and immobile but neither insentient nor unaware.

The experience of suffering is thereby utterly privatized, as the philosopher's nightmare of radical solipsism is perfectly realized in practice.

As they must, petitioners argue that, in light of currently available alternatives, they are in a position to contend that the Kentucky protocol poses an unnecessary risk of pain, especially the sort of agony indicated by this ghoulish scenario. In part, they indicate how such risk might be reduced by recommending that the equipment employed be improved, that the training of personnel be enhanced, and that the death chamber be modified to ensure better monitoring of the condemned throughout an execution. Even more central to their argument, however, is their recommendation that pancuronium bromide and potassium chloride be removed from the execution protocol and that a barbiturate be exclusively employed to cause death. Assuming it is competently administered, they insist, exclusive reliance on an anesthetic agent will, by definition, eliminate the possibility of pain. Removal of potassium chloride, moreover, will eliminate the possibility that the condemned will experience the pain associated with severe cardiac arrest. And, finally, in addition to eliminating the danger of conscious suffering that is masked by paralysis, removal of pancuronium bromide will enable prison officials to know when intervention is necessary in order to correct a lethal injection that has gone awry, thereby enabling a more complete realization of the ideal that both parties invoke when it serves their purposes to do so.

Not surprisingly, given that their task is to defend the state, respondents reject the proposal to shift to a single chemical on the ground that the current protocol satisfies the requirements of the Eighth Amendment and that the proposed alternative is speculative insofar as the record "is devoid of proof that any alternative drugs identified by petitioners pose substantially less risk than the drugs currently used."[56] Doing so, the Kentucky Department of Corrections echoes its counterparts in Florida, California, and Tennessee, all of which have recently rejected or failed to act on recommendations advanced by either court or commission to shift to a one-drug or, should potassium chloride or its equivalent be retained, a two-drug protocol.[57] While this decision may at first seem puzzling, given what seem to be the obvious gains of such a reform, defense of the current chemical mix, and retention of pancuronium bromide in particular, becomes comprehensible when understood as a response to the felt need to render invisible and in that sense privatize those elements of an execution that serve to recall the inconvenient fact that infliction of a death sentence still requires an act of taking life.

The state of Kentucky, according to petitioners, "presented no legitimate rationale for using pancuronium."[58] By this, presumably, they mean to contend that any given ingredient of a lethal injection can be justified legally only if it can be shown to contribute to accomplishment of a death that conforms to constitutional imperatives. Pancuronium bromide, they argue, does not meet this test. Its sole and impermissible purpose is to prevent "muscular movements in the condemned, involuntary or otherwise, that may result from the subsequent injection of [p]otassium," movements that might be read by witnesses unversed in medical science as indicators of conscious suffering.[59] But that, on petitioners' account, contributes not to the achievement of a humane death but to protection of the state from the (possibly) mistaken interpretations of witnesses who, on seeing these convulsions, twitches, or spasms, may conclude that an execution has been accompanied by pain. On that basis, in turn, they may then conclude that the state is inept, when measured against the ideal projected by its rationalization, or that it is barbaric, when measured against the ideal projected by capital punishment's medicalization.

Respondents cannot grant this argument, or, more carefully, they cannot acknowledge it when it is framed in these terms. Accordingly, they contend that pancuronium bromide can be justified as a means to the end of inflicting a death sentence because it contributes to the cessation of respiration (although their admission that this is a "secondary function"[60] concedes that some other purpose is primary). In much the same vein, they argue that the administration of a paralytic, by reducing the risk of involuntary muscle contractions, minimizes the likelihood of movements that "could disrupt an execution by interfering with an IV"[61] (although this seems less than compelling, given that one of the purposes of strapping an inmate to a gurney is precisely to prevent such movement).

The dubiousness of these arguments was placed in relief when, during oral argument before the U.S. Supreme Court, counsel for respondents granted that, within the context of a lethal injection, pancuronium bromide "serves no therapeutic purpose."[62] This concession seems to imply that this drug cannot be understood in terms of the logic of medicalization, and that implication, in turn, may go far toward admitting the truth of petitioners' contention that its purpose is unrelated to, if not at odds with, the achievement of a humane execution. To neutralize this threat, respondents cite *Gregg* to the effect that the Eighth Amendment forbids punishments "that are not in accord with 'the dignity of man'" and then argue that the use of pancuronium bromide facilitates the dignity of death imposed by lethal injection. In the terminology of the argument in this essay, this may be read as an attempt to subordinate the claims of formal rationalization to a substantive end, or, more specifically, to derive a justification for a technical means, in this case, pancuronium bromide, by demonstrating its contribution to a value, in this case, dignity, that is of intrinsic worth.

But how exactly does pancuronium do so? When the Court advanced this proposition in *Gregg* in 1976, it stated that respect for the value of "dignity" prohibits punishment that is "excessive," which, in turn, involves consideration, first, of whether it involves "the unnecessary and wanton infliction of pain" and, second, whether it is "grossly out of proportion to the severity of the crime."[63] In their *Baze* brief, however, respondents appropriate a claim about what it means to respect the dignity of the condemned and transmute it into a constitutional validation of the vulnerable sensibilities of spectators: "Petitioners argue that involuntary muscle contractions have no bearing on the dignity of condemned, since the administration of thiopental renders the inmate impervious to pain. However, petitioners' argument ignores the impact on family members and other witnesses who view the involuntary contractions."[64] Echoing this claim in *Baze*, Justice Roberts claims that the state has "an interest in preserving the dignity of the procedure," which one might take to refer to, or at least to encompass, the respect owed to the condemned, were it not for the fact that Roberts immediately thereafter specifies that this interest arises when "convulsions or seizures could be misperceived as signs of consciousness or distress."[65]

Here, in a troubling extension of the victim impact appeals that are now so central to the sentencing phase of capital trials, the uneducated witnesses to an execution are represented as its potential casualties; the condemned is relegated to the role of a silenced body whose inertness must be guaranteed to ensure that these innocents are not psychologically harmed; and the state appears as the guardian of proper decorum, which, of course, is not incidental to its perceived legitimacy. As Justice Stevens states in his concurring opinion, even if one accepts this construction of "dignity," this is "a woefully inadequate justification" since whatever minimal interest the state has here is "vastly outweighed by the risk that the inmate is actually experiencing excruciating pain that no one can detect."[66]

Somewhat feebly, petitioners respond to the argument from dignity by suggesting that, were potassium chloride and pancuronium bromide to be removed from the mix, witnesses might be given rudimentary training in what, during the 2005 evidentiary hearings in *Baze*, was given the neologistic but apt title of "necrokinetics."[67] That is, amateur spectators might be taught not to "mistake unconscious movements for evidence of pain . . . by informing them about the nature of the movements they might see."[68] Such movements, they might be told, are merely agonal reflexes (e.g., the accumulation of respiratory secretions in the throat that sometimes give rise to what is colloquially known as the "death rattle," or the involuntary respirations caused by cerebral ischemia), and, as such, should not be read as signs of conscious suffering. Respondents, though, have good reason to find naive an Enlightenment appeal to the efficacy of such education, especially in a nation that loves the idea of punishment (witness the forms of "harsh justice" analyzed by Michael McCann and David Johnson in this volume), but grows fastidious when confronted with graphic evidence that threatens to unsettle self-congratulatory narratives about our collective aversion to cruelty.

If petitioners are correct in their reading of the work accomplished by pancuronium bromide, then its employment may be figured as something akin to a modernized analogue of the hood that was customarily placed over the condemned's head during executions by lethal gas, firing squad, electrocution, and the noose. This cloaking device, though, is far more insidious because it is itself unseen. As Mark Heath explains: "Because pancuronium bromide is an invisible chemical veil and not a physical veil like a blanket or hood that is easily identifiable, the use of pancuronium bromide in lethal injection creates a double veil. It disguises the fact that there is a disguise over the process." [69] What we find here, in other words, is an effort to "save the appearances," even if the net effect is to increase the likelihood that executions will violate established constitutional standards of decency by causing pain akin to that experienced during torture. Ironically, though, to the extent that this pharmaceutical veil does its job well, only the dead will ever be in a position to testify to the truth of what is likely to be dismissed as so much unverified and, indeed, unverifiable, speculation.

In a declaration completed in conjunction with a recent section 1983 challenge to California's death penalty protocol, Heath provided expert testimony in support of petitioners' argument that "use of the drug pancuronium bromide serves no rational or legitimate purpose."[70] From a medical perspective, this claim is almost certainly correct. From a political perspective, however, this claim is almost certainly wrong. "It's not about the prisoner," explained another anesthesiologist, Mark Derschwitz, who often testifies on behalf of states whose lethal injection protocols are under challenge: "It's about public policy. It's about the audience and prison personnel who have to carry out the execution."[71] In part, what is going on here is a simple matter of duplicity. That, I take it, is what a judge in Tennessee meant to get at when she stated that the use of pancuronium bromide "taps into every citizen's fear that the government manipulates the setting and gilds the lily."[72]

But an account confined to these terms fails to capture the element of hypocritical self-deception that is at work as well. Responding to a question about how much she knew about sodium thiopental, presumably in order to learn whether she understood that an inmate may regain consciousness prior to administration of the other two chemicals, a registered nurse with primary responsibility for mixing the chemicals employed in California's lethal injections stated: "I don't study. I just do the job. I don't want to know about it."[73] By applying what Heath has called a "cosmetic" to the act of killing,[74] thereby ensuring that executions will conform to appropriate aesthetic standards, the mix of chemicals authorized by the Supreme Court in *Baze* renders it quite unnecessary for this nurse, or anyone else for that matter, to step beyond this condition of willed ignorance.

The Better as the Enemy of the Best

In the post-*Gregg* era, with little hope of securing outright abolition, opponents of the death penalty have sought to increase the effective cost of administering the machinery of capital punishment and to reduce the frequency with which death sentences are imposed or inflicted, principally, although not exclusively, by appealing to the courts. Among others, efforts to chip away at the death penalty have included narrowing the sorts of crimes that are death eligible, eliminating certain categories of persons from the scope of the death penalty, and using DNA evidence to secure the release of those erroneously convicted and sentenced to die. Adoption of strategies aimed at circumscribing rather than eradicating the death penalty is certainly understandable, given the impact of the Antiterrorism and Effective Death Penalty Act of 1996, which considerably restricted the scope of habeas appeals in capital cases; the current political climate, which renders it hazardous for most officeholders to oppose the death penalty, even if it is rarely executed and so of primarily symbolic import; and the current composition of the U.S. Supreme Court, which is unlikely any time soon to conclude that the states have now demonstrated their inability to meet *Furman*'s requirement that the death penalty be administered in a way that precludes its arbitrary and capricious application.

At the same time, and while perhaps not a "manifest failure,"[75] these strategies have proven of ambiguous political import. As several students of the death penalty have argued, to the extent that these incremental victories have succeeded in creating the perception that fair processes govern administration of capital punishment, that this punishment is indeed limited to the worst of the worst, that those who cannot be ascribed full legal culpability are exempt from this punishment, and that the innocent will in time be exonerated, such strategies may well have the unintended effect of rationalizing and so legitimating the death penalty, thereby rendering it more resistant to de jure or de facto abolition.[76]

Much the same argument may be made of recent lethal injection challenges. Here, too, the abolitionist community has turned to the courts in order to undermine the death penalty; and here, too, this litigation has taken the form not of a frontal assault, which again is understandable, given the many precedents affirming the constitutionality of this method of execution, but, instead, of additional efforts to refine its administration via section 1983 challenges to state execution protocols. The upshot of these suits, culminating in *Baze*, provides an opportune moment to raise questions about the long-term wisdom of pursuing abolitionist ends via methods challenges. Specifically, we should ask whether progressive refinement of the death sentence's infliction may serve to legitimize capital punishment, thereby rendering it more immune to challenge; and, contrary to Justice Stevens, we may want to ask whether executions conducted in accordance with more-refined protocols, precisely because they fail to satisfy the retributive desires that currently sustain public support for capital punishment, may encourage the adoption and extension of other forms of harsh justice, such as life imprisonment without parole, in related domains of the carceral order.

Although the Supreme Court in *Baze* affirmed the constitutionality of the current Kentucky protocol on the basis of a legal standard that renders it more difficult to challenge those of other states, as the improbable duo of Justices Thomas and Stevens predicted, there is every reason to expect that additional suits will be forthcoming, whether because of the wiggle room inherent in the new standard; because of the lack of a clear majority on the Court in favor of this standard; because of the insufficiency of the record in Kentucky; and because of the unacknowledged but very real pressure exerted on states by the combined forces of rationalization, medicalization, and privatization, as well as the ideal they collectively project. Because no fundamentally new execution technology appears in the offing, states that elect to alter their protocols either in anticipation of or in response to such suits will find it necessary to tinker with the particulars of lethal injection, including improved training for executioners, refinement of the equipment employed, and, perhaps most urgently, adoption of various ways of ensuring that the condemned is and remains unconscious throughout an execution. From the vantage point of abolitionism, as with judicially mandated alterations in the conduct of capital trials, whether in the guilt or sentencing phase, such reforms represent so many two-edged swords. On the one hand, they may reduce the risk of botched executions and so unnecessary suffering on the part of the condemned; to the extent that they do so, although perhaps not a cause for celebration, they are to be welcomed. On the other hand, and at the same time, such reforms may bring us one step closer to fulfilling the imperatives of the perfect execution; to the extent that they enable executions that more fully approximate the ideal of a non-event, they may impede achievement of the ultimate goal of abolitionism.

This argument, as well as the strategic conundrum posed by *Baze* for death penalty opponents, can be illustrated by returning to the claim that in one way the most problematic outcome in this case might have been a victory for petitioners—particularly, the Court's adoption of a standard that would have effectively required or encouraged states to adopt the principal protocol reform they proposed. The switch to a single-drug method of execution, although perhaps less likely at present than reforms of less-controversial elements of state protocols, is not foreclosed by the ruling in *Baze*. Indeed, Justice Roberts appeared to leave open the possibility that this question may be readjudicated at some later date when, neither endorsing nor denying the objections raised by the state, he noted that, at present, "the comparative efficacy of a one-drug method of execution is not so well established that Kentucky's failure to adopt it constitutes a violation of the Eighth Amendment."[77] Should this alternative become sufficiently "well established" at some point in the future, or should one or more states accept Justice Stevens's contention that those "wishing to decrease the risk that future litigation will delay executions or invalidate their protocols would do well to reconsider their continued use of pancuronium bromide,"[78] what might follow for the cause of abolitionism? What, specifically, might follow from adoption of an execution protocol, which, especially if combined with other technical refinements, relied exclusively on a single anesthetic, whether sodium thiopental, propofal, or perhaps, following the lead of veterinarians, sodium pentobarbital?

A hint is provided by Mark Heath, who, while testifying *against* the state of California in its most prominent section 1983 challenge, was asked whether it would be feasible to proceed with an execution using only sodium thiopental:

> Removal from the execution protocol of the unnecessary and potentially painful drugs pancuronium and potassium would greatly reduce the possibility that the execution would be cruel and inhumane. The administration of sufficient thiopental will, as the CDCR [California's Department of Corrections and Rehabilitation] and its expert have stated, with certainty cause death, because in the doses planned by the CDCR thiopental will ablate all respiratory activity. Thiopental itself cannot cause pain if it is properly injected into the venous system, and instead will act as a powerful anesthetic to render the prisoner deeply unconscious. . . . The use of thiopental as the sole agent in the lethal injection procedure would represent an enormous and easily-taken step toward minimizing the risk of an excruciatingly painful execution.[79]

To paraphrase Heath in the terms employed in this essay, adoption of this reform would secure a more complete rationalization of executions, in the sense of risk reduction, by decreasing the number of chemicals employed and so minimizing the complications posed thereby, including their possible administration out of order, as well as their possible precipitation in intravenous catheters. In addition, this reform would secure a more complete medicalization of executions, in the sense of pain elimination, by removing the use of chemicals that can cause pain or mask its occurrence. Finally, by eliminating potassium chloride and the convulsions it may occasion, it would go some considerable distance toward eliminating the need to secure the form of privatization presently accomplished via pancuronium bromide.

Even if accompanied by improvements in training, equipment, and monitoring, however, adoption of a single-drug protocol is likely to generate new dilemmas that could undercut other desiderata implicit in the ideal execution. For example, although medical consensus on this question is not perfect, it appears likely that reliance on a single barbiturate would protract the period of time before death can be pronounced, especially should the effects of this drug include electromechanical dissociation, a condition in which there is no pulse perceptible by means of a stethoscope, but the heart continues to emit electrical impulses measurable by an electrocardiogram (whose employment, incidentally, is required by the Kentucky protocol). As counsel for respondents maintained during oral argument,[80] the result of reliance on a single-drug formula might be to delay the official declaration of death by as long as half an hour; that, in turn, might compromise what Justice Roberts labeled the "states' legitimate interest in providing for a quick, certain death,"[81] as well as *Kemmler's* Eighth Amendment concerns about a "lingering death." Additionally, for the reasons indicated by Jürgen Martschukat in this volume, any departures from the ideal of instantaneity that is projected by the norm of life's "mere extinguishment" may occasion discomfort on the part of executioners and, possibly, raise new concerns about the humanity of executions on the part of untrained spectators. Finally, even in the absence of potassium chloride, given that vital organs actively resist their extinguishment, even when the body is fully unconscious, there is no guarantee that all movements that might be interpreted as evidence of bodily pain will be obviated (although their likelihood may be reduced, if only because the number of causal mechanisms of death will be decreased from three to one).

In light of these complications, given present pharmacological knowledge, it may prove impossible to satisfy simultaneously all of the various criteria inherent in the ideal of a perfect execution—that is, one that is certain, painless, immediate, and untroubling to witnesses, amateur as well as professional. If that is so, then this ideal may remain a phantasm that continues to haunt parties to future challenges because, given the current state of medical science, it harbors contradictory imperatives, each of which presses equally insistent demands. And if that is so, then awkward choices about which criteria are most pressing may have to be made by both parties to this debate, although my special concern here is with the choices to be made by death penalty opponents.

For example, if no state elects to move in this direction without prompting, attorneys for those on death row may elect to continue to press for protocol reforms, such as the shift to a one-drug method, that reduce the risk of suffering but, in doing so, sacrifice some measure of speed. While this choice is defensible and perhaps even required in light of professional and ethical norms, it is shortsighted to move to it without considering its possible cost to the overall goal of abolitionism. That cost can be indicated by citing a prediction advanced in petitioners' reply brief in *Baze*: "To the extent that States adopt a barbiturate-only approach, . . . it is difficult to envision future Eighth Amendment challenges because administration problems would not result in the infliction of pain."[82]

If this prediction is correct, it is so because the perfection of lethal injection will go a long way toward closing the semantic gap, which, under present protocols, enables one to ask whether any given execution involved the infliction of unnecessary (but masked) pain and so possibly violated the Eighth Amendment. Granted, the cunning of pancuronium bromide is that it renders invisible any pain that *may* be endured; but the term "may" also leaves open the possibility of wondering whether pain *might* have been suffered, and it is that possibility that would be largely foreclosed via adoption of an execution method that relies exclusively on a single anesthetic. The space for such questioning will then be confined to the temporal gap left open by the fact that executions are not now and are unlikely to become instantaneous. The existence of that gap is not irrelevant in promoting the cause of abolitionism, but, as a way of animating public or legislative opposition to the death penalty, it carries far less weight than do claims about eliminable, and so gratuitous, pain.

A cynic might claim that the present pursuit of reforms to execution protocols involves little more than "a bit of tinkering intended to salve the national conscience regarding the infliction of pain."[83] While this is no doubt true in part, such fine-tuning is potentially far more consequential than any of the earlier qualitative shifts from one method to another (e.g., from hanging to electrocution or lethal gas), all of which left open the possibility of advancing plausible claims about the experience of pain on the basis of its sensible signs, whether that be moaning, writhing, choking, or whatever. If, on the one hand, pancuronium bromide is retained while other protocol refinements are adopted in order to ensure the achievement and maintenance of unconsciousness, epistemologically speaking, the effect will be to render us less prone to the forms of uncertainty that give rise to speculation about the possible experience of pain.[84] If, on the other hand, this paralytic is eliminated in favor of a single anesthetic, and should this reform be combined with technical rationalization of the procedures employed to administer this drug and monitor its effects, epistemologically speaking, the effect will be to make it more difficult to recognize that what takes place in an execution is not a non-event but an act of killing. Either way, the situation now confronting abolitionists is paradoxical, if not tragic, for there is no path that is not substantially compromised. Abolitionists can abandon challenges to current lethal injection protocols, recognizing that to do so entails accepting the real risk—indeed, the likelihood—of gratuitous suffering on the part of the executed. Alternatively, they can press on with these challenges, recognizing that any victory entails complicity in the state's effort to accomplish the sort of anesthetized death that fosters collective amnesia about the violence of capital punishment.

NOTES

1. Brief of Petitioners, *Baze v. Rees*, 128 S. Ct. 1520 (2008) (No. 07-5439), at 38, available at http://www.law.berkeley.edu/clinics/dpclinic/LethalInjection/LI/briefs. html.

2. *Baze v. Rees*, 128 S. Ct. 1520, 1537, 1532 (2008) (plurality).

3. Ibid., at 1537.

4. Robert Barnes, "Justices Uphold Lethal Injection Procedure," *Washington Post*, Apr. 17, 2008, A1.

5. Ralph Blumenthal, "After Hiatus, Setting a Wave of Executions," *New York Times*, May 3, 2008, A1.

6. For example, Jordan Steiker, a contributor to this volume, was quoted as follows in Adam Liptak, "Moratorium May Be Over, but Hardly the Challenges," *New York Times*, Apr. 17, 2008, A26: "We will end up largely where we were before *Baze*. . . . It has set us on a course in which there will be continuing challenges, efforts to document botched executions and efforts to continue to explore alternative protocols."

7. For example, *Baze v. Rees*, at 1542 (Stevens, J., concurring): The question of "whether a similar three-drug protocol may be used in other States remains open, and may well be answered differently in a future case on the basis of a more complete record."

8. Ibid., at 1562 (Thomas, J., concurring).

9. In Timothy V. Kaufman-Osborn, "A Critique of Contemporary Death Penalty Abolitionism," *Punishment and Society* 8 (July 2006): 365–83, I indicate my more general concerns about the ways in which contemporary abolitionist claims are commonly framed and, more specifically, the ways in which they may inadvertently reinforce the practices they mean to condemn. The essay in this volume may be read as an application of that argument to lethal injection challenges.

10. *Callins v. Collins*, 510 U.S. 1141, 1145 (1994) (Blackmun, J., dissenting from denial of cert.): "From this day forward, I no longer shall tinker with the machinery of death."

11. For example, *Baze v. Rees*, at 1561–62 (Thomas, J., concurring): "But the notion that the Eighth Amendment permits only one mode of execution, or that it requires an anesthetized death, cannot be squared with the history of the Constitution."

12. Michael Madow, "Forbidden Spectacle: Executions, the Public and the Press in Nineteenth Century New York," *Buffalo Law Review* 43 (1995): 465.

13. For accounts of such spectacles, see Louis Masur, *Rites of Execution* (New York: Oxford University Press, 1989), 25–49, and Stuart Banner, *The Death Penalty* (Cambridge: Harvard University Press, 2002), 24–52.

14. Annulla Linders, "The Execution Spectacle and State Legitimacy: The Changing Nature of the American Execution Audience, 1833–1937," *Law and Society Review* 36, no. 3 (2002): 629–30.

15. Madow, "Forbidden Spectacle," 479.

16. Ibid., 482.

17. *Wilkerson v. Utah*, 99 U.S. 130, 135–36 (1879).

18. *In re Kemmler*, 136 U.S. 436, 446 (1890).

19. Ibid., 447.

20. *Louisiana ex rel. Francis v. Resweber*, 329 U.S. 459, 463 (1947).

21. Ibid., 463–64.

22. *Baze v. Rees*, at 1531 (plurality): "[A]n isolated mishap alone does not give rise to an Eighth Amendment violation, precisely because such an event, while regrettable, does not suggest cruelty."

23. Ibid., at 1568 (Ginsburg, J., dissenting). Although *Resweber* was the last case to focus explicitly on a method of execution before *Baze*, several subsequent opinions have included dicta on methods of execution. See, for example, *Furman v. Georgia*, 408 U.S. 238, 430 (1972) (Powell, J., dissenting) ("No court would approve any method of implementation of the death sentence found to involve unnecessary cruelty in light of presently available alternatives."); and *Coker v. Georgia*, 433 U.S. 584, 592 (1977) (plurality) (stating that a punishment is unconstitutional if it "makes no measurable contribution to acceptable goals of punishment and hence is nothing more than the purposeless and needless imposition of pain and suffering"). Several Justices have also issued dissents from denials of certiorari in method challenges. See *Campbell v. Wood*, 511 U.S. 1119, 1119 (1994) (Blackmun, J., dissenting from denial of certiorari) (hanging); *Glass v. Louisiana*, 471 U.S. 1080, 1080 (1985) (Brennan, J., dissenting from denial of certiorari) (electrocution); and *Gray v. Lucas*, 463 U.S. 1237, 1240 (1983) (Marshall, J., dissenting from denial of certiorari) (gas chamber).

24. *Weems v. United States*, 217 U.S. 349, 377 (1910).

25. *Trop v. Dulles*, 356 U.S. 86, 101 (1958).

26. *Gregg v. Georgia*, 428 U.S. 153, 173 (1976).

27. *Resweber*, at 474.

28. Indeed, and although the point cannot be elaborated in this context, I would argue that it is this method's apparent realization of a death that involves no violence that goes a long way toward explaining why it proved immune to successful court challenge for a quarter century or so. Correlatively, it is growing evidence of this method's failure to fulfill the terms of this ideal that explains

why such challenges, culminating in *Baze*, were able to secure some measure of traction in lower courts over the course of the past half decade or so.

29. C. J. Drake, quoted in "Lethal Injections More Secretive Than by Chair," *Sarasota Herald-Tribune*, Mar. 3, 2000, ZB.

30. Madow, "Forbidden Spectacle," 482.

31. For a different but related manifestation of the felt need to rationalize the death penalty, consider the report submitted in 2004 by the Massachusetts Governor's Council on Capital Punishment. That document, which is reproduced as "Report of the Governor's Council on Capital Punishment," *Indiana Law Journal* 80 (2005): 1–27, offers a set of 10 proposals, which, "if adopted in their entirety, can allow creation of a fair capital punishment statute for Massachusetts that is as narrowly tailored, and as infallible, as humanly possible" (2). The proposals include the requirement that "conclusive scientific evidence" be produced "as a prerequisite to the imposition of the death penalty" and that the jury "find that there is 'no doubt' about the defendant's guilt of capital murder" (19–20). Both of these proposals may be read as efforts to perfect the rationalization of capital punishment by effectively reducing to nil the risk that an innocent person might be sentenced to die.

32. For example, Brief of Respondents, *Baze v. Rees*, at 18, and Reply Brief of Petitioners, *Baze v. Rees*, at 23, both available at http://www.law.berkeley.edu/clinics/dpclinic/LethalInjection/LI/briefs.html.

33. Reply Brief of Petitioners, at 2.

34. Brief of Respondents, at 18.

35. Indeed, on occasion, petitioners appear to argue that the end of risk management will be fully secure only when it is guaranteed and accomplished without exception, thereby collapsing any meaningful distinction between risk and accident. For example, Brief of Petitioners, at 35: "The foreseeable infliction of unnecessary pain on *some* condemned inmates cannot be any more tolerable under the Eighth Amendment than the infliction of unnecessary pain on *all* condemned inmates. . . . Therefore, the Eighth Amendment obligates the government to carry out executions in a manner that avoids creating an unnecessary risk of pain with respect to individual inmates."

36. Brief of Respondents, at 12–13, 36–37.

37. "The Physicians' Statement," Appendix A, *Final Report with Findings and Recommendations*, Governor's Commission on Administration of Lethal Injection, Tallahassee, Florida, March 1, 2007, available at http://www.law.berkeley.edu/clinics/dpclinic/LethalInjection/LI/documents/commission/fl/lethalinjection-finalreport.pdf; emphasis added.

38. David Waisel, "Physician Participation in Capital Punishment," *Mayo Clinic Proceedings* 82 (2007): 1079: "I conceptualize physician participation in capital punishment as an altruistic practice of medicine. The future *patient* should request physician participation, and the physician should be licensed to practice medicine in that state."

39. Mark Heath, "Revisiting Physician Involvement in Capital Punishment: Medical and Nonmedical Aspects of Lethal Injection," *Mayo Clinic Proceedings* 83 (2008): 113–23.

40. Brief of the American Society of Anesthesiologists, *Baze v. Rees*, at 4, available at http://www.law.berkeley.edu/clinics/dpclinic/LethalInjection/LI/briefs.html.

41. Brief of Petitioners, at 39.

42. For the requirement of a "qualified individual," see *Morales v. Hickman*, 415 F. Supp. 2d 1037, 1047 (Cal. N.D, 2006). For the requirement of an "anesthesia professional," see *Morales v. Hickman*, 438 F.3d 926, 931 (9th Cir. 2006).

43. Council on Ethical and Judicial Affairs, "Physician Participation in Capital Punishment," *Journal of the American Medical Association* 270 (1993): 365–68. That this advisory is not entirely toothless is indicated by the recent filing of an ultimately unsuccessful suit aimed at forcing the state medical board to take disciplinary action against doctors who elected to participate in executions. See *Zitrin v. Georgia Composite State Bd. of Med. Examiners*, 288 Ga. App. 295; 653 S.E.2d 758 (2007).

44. Kentucky Revised Statute § 431.220(3): "No physician shall be involved in the conduct of an execution except to certify the cause of death provided the condemned is declared dead by another person."

45. In *Nelson v. Campbell*, 541 U.S. 637 (2004), the Court ruled that the administration of a cut-down procedure—that is, an incision employed to secure access to a vein as a preface to a lethal injection—could be raised as a complaint under 42 U.S.C. § 1983, which creates a cause of action against state officials for the violation of "any rights, privileges, or immunities secured by the Constitutions and laws [of the United States],"rather than as a habeas petition, which can only be employed to contest the legality of an inmate's conviction or sentence. In *Hill v. McDonough*, 126 S. Ct. 2096 (2006), the scope of that ruling was expanded when the Court held that challenges to lethal injection protocols, including the chemicals specified by those protocols, could be similarly raised. Given the strict rules governing the filing of successive habeas claims, as set forth in the Antiterrorism and Effective Death Penalty Act (1996), the cumulative effect of these two decisions was to make it considerably easier for inmates sentenced to death by lethal injection to seek injunctive relief in order to correct a constitutional violation. However, in doing so, those sentenced to die cannot employ a methods challenge to contest the death penalty itself.

46. Brief of Respondents, at 49.

47. Brief of Criminal Justice Legal Foundation, *Baze v. Rees*, at 10, available at http://www.law.berkeley.edu/clinics/dpclinic/LethalInjection/LI/briefs.html.

48. William Lanier, "Physician Involvement in Capital Punishment: Simplifying a Complex Calculus," *Mayo Clinic Proceedings* 82 (September 2007): 1046.

49. Neil J. Farber, Brian M. Aboff, Joan Weiner, Elizabeth Davis, Gil Boyer, and Peter Ubel, "Physicians' Willingness to Participate in the Process of Lethal Injection for Capital Punishment," *Annals of Internal Medicine* 135 (November 2001): 884–88.

50. Gregory Curfman, Stephen Morrissey, and Jeffrey Drazen, "Physicians and Execution," *New England Journal of Medicine* 358 (2008): 403–4.

51. *Baze v. Rees*, at 1548 (Stevens, J., concurring).

52. Ibid., at 1543.

53. Brief of Petitioners, at 31, 39; emphasis added.

54. *Furman v. Georgia*, at 430 (Powell, J., dissenting).

55. Brief of Respondents, at 9–10.

56. Brief of Respondents, at 44.

57. For the recommendation to explore the possibility of eliminating pancuronium bromide from the Florida protocol, see *Final Report with Findings and Recommendations*, Governor's Commission on Administration of Lethal Injection, Tallahassee, Florida, March 1, 2007, available at http://www.flgov. com/pdfs/20070301-lethalinjection.pdf. The Commission urged "that the Governor have the Florida Department of Corrections on an ongoing basis explore other more recently developed chemicals for use in a lethal injection execution with specific consideration and evaluation of the need of a paralytic drug like pancuronium bromide in an effort to make the lethal injection procedure less problematic" (p. 13). The revised lethal injection protocol, which became effective on May 9, 2007, gives no indication that this recommendation was given consideration and retains pancuronium bromide, without explanation, as one of the three chemicals to be administered (http://www.deathpenaltyinfo.org/FlorLethInject.pdf). For the judicial recommendation to remove potassium chloride and pancuronium bromide from the California protocol, see *Morales v. Tilton*, 465 F. Supp. 2d 972, 983 (N.D. Cal. 2006): "Removal of [pancuronium bromide and potassium chloride] from the lethal-injection protocol, with the execution accomplished solely by an anesthetic, such as sodium pentobarbital, would eliminate any constitutional concerns, subject only to the implementation of adequate, verifiable procedures to ensure that the inmate actually receives a fatal dose of the anesthetic." For the rejection of that recommendation, see State of California, *Lethal Injection Protocol Review*, May 15, 2007, at 19, available at http://www.cdcr. ca.gov/Communications/docs/ReportToCourt.pdf: "A one-chemical protocol was considered. Five grams of sodium thiopental would be expected to cause death. The use of only one chemical, sodium thiopental, has the advantages of being simpler to administer and virtually eliminates the potential for pain. However, the use of only one chemical has disadvantages. Since no other jurisdiction currently uses only one chemical, the protocol remains untested. The use of only a barbiturate would likely result in involuntary muscle movement, with unpredictable consequences. Finally, the execution would take an extended period of time." For an

account of the recommendation to shift to a single chemical protocol in Tennessee, as well as the ultimate rejection of that recommendation by the commissioner of the Department of Corrections because he did not want "Tennessee to be at the forefront of making the change from the three-drug protocol to the one-drug protocol," and because he thought adoption of a one-drug protocol could lead to "political ramifications," see *Harbison v. Little*, 511 F. Supp. 2d. 872 (2007), at 874–81.

58. Brief of Petitioners, at 51.

59. Ibid., at 52.

60. Brief of Respondents, at 50.

61. Ibid., at 51.

62. Transcript of oral argument, *Baze v. Rees*, at 43, available at http://www.supremecourtus.gov/oral_arguments/argument_transcripts/07-5439.pdf.

63. *Gregg v. Georgia*, at 173.

64. Brief of Respondents, at 51.

65. *Baze v. Rees*, at 1544 (plurality).

66. Ibid. (Stevens, J., concurring).

67. Transcript of evidentiary hearings, *Baze and Bowling v. Rees et al.*, Civil Action No. 04-CI-01094, Franklin Circuit Court, Commonwealth of Kentucky (May 2, 2005), at 1063.

68. Brief of Petitioners, at 53.

69. Quoted in Complaint for Declaratory Judgment and Injunctive Relief, *Baze v. Rees*, CJ-KY-0002-0005, Franklin Circuit Court, Commonwealth of Kentucky (August 2004), at 21.

70. Declaration of Dr. Mark Heath, *Morales v. Woodford*, Case No. 06-219, U.S. District Court, Northern District of California (June 12, 2006), at 21.

71. Quoted in Maura Nolan and Henry Weinstein, "Concerns about Pain Put Lethal Injection on Trial," *Los Angeles Times*, Apr. 24, 2006, A1.

72. Judge Ellen Hobbes Lyle, quoted in Adam Liptak, "Critics Say Execution Drug Hides Suffering," *New York Times*, Oct. 7, 2003, A1.

73. Quoted in Maura Dolan and Henry Weinstein, "Doctor: Sedation May Fail in Executions," *Los Angeles Times*, Sept. 28, 2006, B1.

74. Mark Heath, "The Medicalization of Execution: Lethal Injection in the United States," in R. B. Greifinger, ed., *Public Health behind Bars* (New York: Springer, 2007), 93.

75. Wayne Logan, "Casting New Light on an Old Subject: Death Penalty Abolitionism for a New Millennium," *Michigan Law Review* 100 (May 2002): 1344.

76. For arguments to this effect, see Carol S. Steiker and Jordan M. Steiker, "Should Abolitionists Support Legislative 'Reform" of the Death Penalty," *Ohio State Law Journal* 63 (2002): 413–32; and Carol S. Steiker and Jordan M. Steiker, "The Seduction of Innocence: The Attraction and Limitations of the Focus on Innocence in Capital Punishment Law and Advocacy," *Journal of Criminal Law and Criminology* 95 (2005): 587–624.

77. *Baze v. Rees*, at 1535 (plurality).

78. Ibid., at 1546 (Stevens, J., concurring). It is not entirely apparent, incidentally, on what basis states might predicate a specifically scientific justification for altering the mix of chemicals prescribed by current lethal injection protocols. As Seema Shah notes in "How Lethal Injection Reform Constitutes Impermissible Research on Prisoners," *American Criminal Law Review* 45, no. 3 (2008), if the systematic collection of data aimed at determining the ideal mix of chemicals qualifies as research, it may conflict with state regulations and policies or the norms of professional ethics that govern the conduct of experimentation on prisoners.

79. Declaration of Heath, *Morales v. Woodford*, at 2, 4.

80. Transcript of oral argument, at 37. In their brief, by way of contrast, petitioners argue that "a three-gram dose of thiopental would cause death within three minutes to fifteen minutes" (at 54, n.16).

81. *Baze v. Rees*, at 1535 (plurality).

82. Reply Brief of Petitioners, at 26.

83. Mark Essig, "This Is Going to Hurt," *New York Times*, Nov. 4, 2007, sec. 4, p. 15.

84. For a more detailed argument about the epistemological difficulties posed by any effort to ground legal arguments in claims about the reality of pain, see Timothy V. Kaufman-Osborn, "Silencing the Voice of Pain," *From Noose to Needle: Capital Punishment and the Late Liberal State* (Ann Arbor: University Michigan Press, 2002).

8

|||||||||||||||||||||||||||||||||||||||||||||||||||||||||||

"No Improvement over Electrocution or Even a Bullet"

Lethal Injection and the Meaning of Speed and Reliability in the Modern Execution Process

Jürgen Martschukat

"The debate over capital punishment has reached a tipping point," the editors of *Lancet* characterized the current situation in the February 2007 issue of their magazine, which is top ranked among medical publications.[1] For years, wrongful convictions and a steadily growing number of exonerations from death row had raised concerns about capital punishment, before confusing revelations about lethal injection had taken the death penalty system in the United States closer to the brink of collapse. In the late 1970s, after the *Gregg* decision by the Supreme Court and the return of capital punishment to the United States, it had been the syringe and the needle that had made executions appear tolerable, in the first place, by turning them into the ultimate representation of reliable, precise, and painless death in an environment more like a hospital operating room than a prison death chamber. Yet, lately, lethal injection has been severely criticized as unreliable, imprecise, and therefore painful and inadequate, and it has undergone a disapproving examination similar to other execution methods in modern history. The latest debate has subjected lethal injection to the criticism that it is not humane at all, a criticism that is likely to live on even though the Supreme Court announced the constitutionality of Kentucky's lethal injection procedure in the *Baze v. Rees* decision on April 16, 2008.[2]

In this chapter, I turn to this debate about humane executions and specifically focus on the notion of speed and well-managed timing as their guarantors. In the first section, I address the latest critique of lethal injection, while in the second section, I contextualize this critique historically, by relating it to two landmarks in the history of modern executions: the guillotine and the electric chair, before I return in the third and final section to lethal injection and its introduction as a method of execution. The discursive and rhetorical similarities regarding the guillotine, the electric chair, and lethal injection are striking, and they form a revealing pattern. Yet, the differences are also important to consider if the object is to understand how close to the tipping point America really is with regard to the death penalty. Providing today's debate with historic depth will sharpen our understanding of the implications of arguments on speed, timing, pain, and humaneness with regard to specific execution styles and of capital punishment in general. Only by historicizing lethal injection, and at the same time by perceiving historic arguments in the light of today's debate, will we be able to diagnose where the United States currently is on the road to abolition.

Lethal Injection under Attack

On April 24, 2007, *PLoS (Public Library of Science) Medicine*, edited by Harvard Medical School, published an article substantially questioning lethal injection as a tolerable execution method. The authors sought "to evaluate the three-drug protocol [of lethal injection] for its efficacy in producing a rapid death with minimal likelihood of pain and suffering."[3] A major point in their criticism was that, taking the latest research into account, "the regimen as currently administered does not work as efficiently as intended. Some prisoners take many minutes to die, and others may become very distressed." Obviously, the authors' focal point of concern and complaint was specifically the speed—or, more precise, nonspeed—of the dying process because it affects the efficiency, reliability, and tolerableness of the execution process: inmates being "potentially aware" of living through their unbearably slow dying process seem to make "the conventional view of lethal injection as an invariably peaceful and painless death . . . questionable."[4]

The *PLoS* critique reinforced an argument that has been raised increasingly in recent years. For instance, in 2005, an article in the renowned British *Lancet* had claimed, "Methods of lethal injection anaesthesia are flawed and some inmates might experience awareness and suffering during execution."[5] In this case, "some" meant 43 percent of a fairly large sample of data (referring to 49 executed inmates) in various states. Instead of dying quickly and under anesthesia, those executed did probably live through extreme suffering during slow executions, experiencing intense and burning pain and "suffocation." Specifically, the reference to "suffocation" conjures the association of (badly performed) hangings at the gallows and harks back to premodern societies or authoritarian rule in cultures considered barbaric. From that point of view, today's lethal injection is even worse than premodern executions at the gallows because the potential suffocating agony of a convict is perfidiously masked and remains invisible due to the use of a paralytic medication. The paralytic agent pancuronium bromide (Pavulon) "gives a false sense of peacefulness" because the agony of death cannot be communicated by the dying person, as David Lubarsky, anesthesiologist at the University of Miami and one of the main authors of the *Lancet* article, was quoted by the *New York Times*.[6]

Even though this criticism refers to recent and specific trends in the history of the death penalty, it is emblematic of a major delusion of modern cultures. Anthropologist and historian Norbert Elias has pointed to a desire of modern cultures to hide unpleasant things resembling death, suffering, and physical decay. We still enjoy eating meat, Elias stresses in his study on the "Civilizing Process," but we do not want to be reminded of the fact that our dish is related to killing living creatures. The disemboweling of the prey and the carving of a roast have become embarrassing procedures, and they have been laid into the hands of experts and taken behind the curtains of the public social life.[7] As Timothy Kaufman-Osborn stresses in a different chapter of this book, in lethal injection and with Pavulon, human flesh and skin are turned into a veil, hiding the injuries and suffering of the condemned.

On top of that, recent studies in medicine and criminal justice have critically pointed to the fact that the now-embarrassing procedure of executing a human being has not even been delegated to real experts.[8] It is not only that execution guidelines in American death penalty states are less precise than those for animal euthanasia. Precision and professionalism are lacking in the monitoring of the dying procedure, the personnel (mostly medical technicians or corpsmen without training in anesthesia[9]) are unqualified for conducting medical tasks with the required routine and precision, and there hardly exists any basic or clinical research for the execution procedure to rely on. For instance, an evidence-based correlation between the administered amount of the "ultra-fast acting barbiturate" and the body weight of the inmate does not exist—even though it is well known that body composition, in addition to several other factors such as health status, anxiety, premedication, and history of drug abuse, influence the patient's response to thiopental. The result of this haphazard application, then, means that immediate lethal effects of the barbiturate and the other drugs employed in the execution are not guaranteed at all. To the contrary, recent studies stress, among other things, that several inmates in California did not die "within a minute of drug administration," as state expert witnesses had testified, but "continued to breathe for up to 9 min after thiopental was injected."[10] Data from Arizona, Georgia, North Carolina, and South Carolina even suggest that this is the case in the majority of executions.[11] After all, whether the executed dies with or without pain and suffering, whether he or she dies of suffocation or not, seems to be a question of timing and the efficiency of the barbiturate.[12]

Certainly, this medically centered criticism of the execution style is tied to a larger and more general discussion of the American death penalty system that has been going on for almost a decade. Critics of flawed legal procedures or of racist structures and perceptions still at work in the death penalty system have paved the way for the intense repercussions of the lethal injection debate in the American public and legal system. Even though the 2005 *Lancet* article also received skeptical response in the scientific community, questioning the validity of the study,[13] it nevertheless provided the basis for the argument of California death candidate Michael Morales's lawyers in February 2006 that the upcoming execution of their client would mean a violation of the "cruel and unusual punishment" clause of the constitution. In May 2006, the U.S. District Court of Northern California agreed with the lawyers' concerns, and the case led to a moratorium in California.

Several other states had similar cases pending, and in June of the same year, Florida death-row inmate Clarence Hill was granted leave to appeal because lethal injection was unreliable as a painless mode of execution. In December 2006, Florida suspended all executions after the execution of Angel Diaz had taken twice as long as usual, and Diaz was described by witnesses of his execution as "grimacing, blinking, licking his lips, blowing and appearing to mouth words" for up to 24 minutes after the first injection.[14]

One of the major concerns was that an unskilled use of medical technology prolonged the inmate's period of consciousness during the execution and thus created the possibility of his being aware of going through his own dying process. In September 2007, these concerns finally reached the U.S. Supreme Court, which agreed to consider the constitutionality of lethal injections as practiced in the State of Kentucky. The case was argued on January 7, 2008, and even though the judges finally confirmed the constitutionality of Kentucky's protocol on April 16, 2008, and executions have resumed, the complexity of the fractured decision opened the door for more conflicts on lethal injection and for further litigation.[15]

At the same time that the medical critique found its way into the criminal law discourse and the courts, it began resonating in the American public and the national press. As mentioned, the medical and scientific doubts fell on fruitful ground, because intense debates about wrongful convictions, exonerations, DNA testing, and declining execution numbers had made the American public more ambivalent than in the 1990s and had shaken the confidence of the public in the death penalty. The articles in *Lancet* and *PLoS* were immediately cited in the public debate. One of the major public concerns is that the inmate's prolonged period of consciousness due to the unplanned and unbearable slowness of his dying process makes the death candidate go through "severe pain as he slowly dies," as journalist Ron Word has put it.[16]

Historicizing the Critique: The Guillotine

In historic terms, the urge of authorities and the community to provide a condemned lawbreaker with a quick and painless execution, the desire to change "from deliberate barbarity to attempted civility,"[17] is a relatively recent phenomenon. In most countries, multiple execution styles existed until the eighteenth century, reflecting the severity of the crime and the guilt of the wrongdoer. Some of them were explicitly meant to create pain as part of a slow dying procedure, in anticipation and in preceding fulfillment of the agonies of hell.[18] In the eighteenth century, the concept of divine rule was supplanted by the idea of a contract between human beings furnished with inalienable rights, and the relation of life, death, and pain began to change substantially. In 1748, in his pathbreaking study *The Spirit of Laws*, French author Baron de Montesquieu declared that, in an egalitarian, humane, and progressive society, life itself was the highest asset. Therefore, the infliction of pain in the taking of a life was not only unnecessary but also a breach of the ethics and the principles of this society and its government. "In moderate states," wrote Montesquieu in the

English edition of 1794, people "are more afraid of losing their lives than apprehensive of the pain of dying; those punishments therefore that deprive them simply of life are sufficient."[19]

Taking into account, first, that Montesquieu's writings were embedded in a powerful discourse on state formation, authority, and punishment and, second, that the late-eighteenth century is considered the "age of the machine," which, third, went hand in hand with a general acceleration of everyday life and an increasing micromanagement of human affairs down to the detail, the guillotine epitomized the transitions of the age. In general, enlightened thinkers and writers advocated for the use of speed and machinery for the benefit of mankind.[20]

The guillotine was embedded into this configuration, and it gave a response to the contemporaries' demands to distinguish their culture from those of preenlightened times by demonstrating the willingness and ability to punish, and even to kill, without pain. At the same time, the mechanization of executions was a reaction to increasingly pressing difficulties with manual beheadings. Botched beheadings had been a phenomenon for centuries, and early modern chronicles tell numerous stories about executioners who needed two or three strokes with the sword or the axe to cut a convict's head off. Yet, eighteenth-century authorities considered themselves and their culture as progressive and enlightened, so that they perceived incidents of this kind as more and more disturbing, and they feverishly strove to prevent too weak, too old, too compassionate, or badly trained executioners from spoiling the performance of law and authority. First, a miss by the executioner meant a loss of authoritarian control over the execution procedure and gave room for unforeseen meanings and reactions by the audience to take shape.[21] Second, writers and politicians stressed with increasing insistence that botched executions would dishonor an enlightened society. For instance, in 1770, an account of a failed decapitation emphasized that "it is the duty of humanity to keep the moment of fear and agony for the convicted wrongdoer as short as possible."[22] In subsequent years, a rising number of commentators stressed that speed was a major indicator of success in executions, because speed promised a painless death. Yet, "the sudden perishing of physical life" through beheading would easily tilt into an "ugly slaughter" through the incompetence of executioners who tortured both the convict and the crowd at an execution.[23]

When during the French Revolution the physicians Joseph Ignace Guillotin and Antoine Louis recommended to the National Assembly the use of a decapitation machine instead of manual beheadings, they both stressed the rapidity and painlessness of mechanized executions as their major asset; according to Guillotin's famous statement, a machine brought death "within a single moment without making you feel even the slightest pain."[24] In September 1791, the revolutionary "code pénal" stressed that the execution of a death penalty should be no more than the mere termination of life.[25]

To contemporary observers, the rapidity of dying under the guillotine was breathtaking. Countless commentators emphasized that the blade penetrated the neck "as fast as lightning" and that the head was cut off within a fraction of a second. Yet, what was praised as the highest achievement of civilization was at the same time highly confusing.[26] Since the mid-1790s, an intense and vivid debate about the viability of a detached head aroused the temper of numerous physicians and politicians. If, after the decapitation, the head was still alive, how much pain did it feel? And, even worse than that: Was there anything crueler than exposing a human creature to the experience of living through his or her own dying process?[27] Under these circumstances, the beheading machine was not the messenger of enlightened acting and humanitarian culture any longer, but "un genre de mort horrible," as emphasized by the physician Samuel Thomas von Soemmering, one of the driving forces behind this debate.[28]

Physicians continued to observe closely if and how severed heads physically expressed signs of sensation and brain activity. Some doctors even conducted experiments with heads of the executed right on or below the scaffold. Their findings were astoundingly similar to Angel Diaz's or other dying men's physical utterances during lethal injection. They registered grimacing, blinking, and even efforts to mouth words. Dr. Johann Wendt from Wroclaw described his experiments with the head of Martin von Troer on the morning of February 25, 1803, as follows: "When I irritated his afterbrain, he convulsively closed his eye, clenched his teeth, and the muscles of his cheeks vellicatingly approached the lower eyelid. I put my finger into the mouth of the unhappy, and his teeth bit my finger noticeably."[29]

The debate about mechanical decapitation and the living heads of the executed simmered down after the end of the Napoleonic wars when the guillotine spread over Europe, but the doubts continued to blaze on and off into the twentieth century. An uncertainty regarding the painlessness and humaneness of beheadings remained. Some experts suggested improving the process of beheading itself, even though this would not solve the problem of a head evolving consciousness of its own separation from the trunk. Other experts suggested inventing even more elaborate execution devices—for instance, machines "that would scrunch the head of the executed in a single moment so that a possibility of a continued consciousness is not conceivable."[30] The idea was to destroy the brain as the center of sentiment instantly so that the experience of any pain would be impossible. Yet, physicians had doubts regarding the functioning and the aesthetic tolerableness of such a machine and its performance. This was also true for the suggestion to devise a mechanism that would chop the body into several pieces and try to interrupt the blood supply to the brain immediately.[31]

Historicizing the Critique: The Electric Chair

In the mid-1880s, the state of New York decided to find a new execution style as a substitute for the gallows, which was considered inhumane, barbarous, and inappropriate in modern times. An expert commission was charged with finding a new instrument of execution, and the commission turned in its final report to the guillotine as first option. Yet, even though the experts claimed that the guillotine probably brought an "instantaneous and painless" death and therefore seemed to fulfill the first and most-significant criterion for the new execution style, the commissioners deemed the "profuse effusion of blood" an "injury to humane feelings" and the association of the "terreur" of the French Revolution "totally repugnant to American ideas."[32]

The urge to mechanize executions was embedded into a second "American Genesis" since the 1870s, when torrents of technological transition and enthusiasm had begun to capture America's imagination.[33] Specifically, electricity and its widespread use stood for the transformation of American society, and the speed of daily life rose to a level of intensity that had been unexperienced and unexpected until this moment in history. In these decades, the concept of modernity as closely tied to speed and precisely managed—"taylorized"—processes in each and every segment of human existence was fundamentally bolstered.[34]

Taking the dynamics of mechanized modernity into account, the urge of late-nineteenth-century Americans, specifically in the northeastern part of the country, "to improve" their capital punishment system is not surprising. The then-existing execution style of hanging at the gallows seemed inefficient, protracted, and barbarous. Just like in late-eighteenth- and early-nineteenth-century Europe and the early days of modern statehood and governing, the rapidity of the dying process was still understood as the preeminent condition of nontorturing executions: that is, executions that did not exceed the mere deprivation of life. In the 1870s, journalists began to register to the second how long hangings at the gallows took to end the convicts' life, and some of these journalists even suggested conducting executions with "an electric shock, or . . . some deadly anaesthetic."[35]

Requests for "instantaneous and painless" executions instead of a protracted, painful, and indecent dying at the gallows were now voiced everywhere. Yet, even more than that, not only were executions expected to be "painless and prompt" but also a modern criminal justice system should resort to "a neat and non-disfiguring homicidal method," as, for instance, an editorial in the New York Herald demanded in August 1884.[36]

A century earlier and on the other side of the Atlantic Ocean, the invention of the guillotine had presented a solution to a problem that had been embedded into contingent modes of perception and thinking. Similarly, the electric chair offered a historically specific reaction to what was perceived as a crisis of the death penalty system in the United States around 1900, a situation that had evolved as a crisis within a culture in the midst of a wave of technological innovation and enthusiasm and, at the same time, closely tied to the traditions of enlightened thinking. Taking the revelations of discourse theory into account, it is the diagnosis of a crisis that gives birth to its existence in the first place and thereby shapes the cultural urge to search for its solution, a solution that is part of the predominant cultural configuration and perceived as improvement of the critical situation.

Thus, when late-nineteenth-century Americans diagnosed a crisis in the capital punishment system due to mismanagement, bad timing, and the length (and therefore cruelty) of the dying process at the gallows, an almost self-evident solution was to employ electricity instead. The invention of the electric chair inaugurated "the modern era of capital punishment," to borrow a phrase by Hugo Adam Bedau.[37]

In May 1890, the Supreme Court approved executions by electricity as both constitutionally legal and culturally appropriate. The judges paraphrased Montesquieu's dictum from 1748 (probably without being aware of it) by stressing that modern executions must not be "more than the mere extinguishment of life," and that electricity would "certainly . . .

produce [an] instantaneous, and therefore painless, death."[38] After all, physicians had amply stressed that, due to the high speed of electricity, the experience of pain on the electric chair was biologically and technically impossible. Electricity would travel through the nerves and to the brain 10,000 times faster than nerve transmission worked so that "the brain is paralyzed; is indeed dead before the nerves can communicate any sense of shock."[39] This meant that a "person would not suffer pain a fraction of a second," as contemporary experts on electricity and the human body stressed.[40]

To be sure, an electric machine appeared as the culturally appropriate mechanism to terminate a human existence that was based on the concept of a machine-like body—a "human motor," to borrow historian Anson Rabinbach's words.[41] Death by electricity, brought by pushing a button or shifting a gear, "is literally quicker than thought," stressed Elbridge Gerry, one of the inventors of electrocution, and Alfred Southwick, another commission member, fantasized about having the electric chair's first guinea pig, William Kemmler, "talking when the current is turned on, for then the attendants could have an opportunity to see how quickly death would follow an electrical shock."[42]

Even botched executions could not substantially shatter the trust in the humane killing power of electricity. The belief that the medical and technical conditions of dying on the electric chair guaranteed a quick, painless, reliable, and therefore culturally appropriate death of a machine-like body was recited like a mantra. Even if the convict moaned and grimaced, and his facial muscles were stretched to the point of disfigurement, experts interpreted them as involuntary physical movements initiated by "pain that was not felt."[43]

Historicizing the Critique: Lethal Injection

In the late 1880s, by fantasizing about the death penalty as "euthanasia by electricity," parts of the press alluded to recently developed anesthetic skills of the medical profession.[44] Nevertheless, the New York death penalty commission did not consider injections of poison as a promising execution style, because they anticipated the collective opposition of medical doctors.[45] The commission's hesitant position was supported by the fact that, up to that point, an anesthetic death as alternative to the gallows had been suggested by only few of their contemporaries.[46]

Using chloroform to alleviate the agonies of executions had been discussed now and then since the late 1840s, beginning immediately after medical operations under chloroform had been successfully conducted. In the *American Whig Review* of 1848, G. W. Peck elaborated extensively on the urge to execute quickly and painlessly by presenting it as the fruit of a collective improvement in manners and as a major hallmark of modernity and civilization. Peck stressed that in modern and enlightened times, the execution of atrocious lawbreakers should be made as easy as possible, and one of the biggest hardships to be alleviated was the mental torture experienced by the condemned at the gallows between the beginning of the drop and the breaking of the neck. In that short moment, they would experience themselves as being between life and death. To Peck, the anesthetization of the condemned seemed to offer the best of all solutions, because it switched off "the time that his soul is in abeyance, neither dead nor alive, . . . the agonizing instant of certain apprehension." Anesthetization would significantly modify the relation between speed, consciousness, and an easy death by rendering the convict unconscious.[47]

This modification was also expressed by J. B. Thornton, Jr., a medical doctor from Scarborough, Maine, who suggested that the anesthetization of death candidates during execution would provide doctors with ample time to conduct medical experiments on their bodies before the anesthetic dose would be increased to a level that led to the death of the condemned lawbreaker.[48]

About a century later, in January 1977, the United States resumed executions after a nationwide moratorium of almost 10 years, and Gary Gilmore was shot by a firing squad in Utah. Reformers and commentators predicted that Gilmore's death would reopen the floodgates of capital punishment in the United States immediately.[49] The assumption proved wrong, and instead of spreading floodlike over America, until the early to mid 1980s, the number of executions increased gradually. Certainly, one reason for the slow return of executions was the legal and procedural modifications demanded by the Supreme Court in the *Gregg* decision. Another reason was that, by and large, then-existing execution techniques were no longer fully compatible with contemporary cultural demands. After all, even though the transformation of medicine into one of the culturally most influential fields of knowledge had been going on for centuries,[50] and even though the fight against pain had been a major topic of the enlightened and humanitarian reform movements since the late eighteenth century,[51] the medicalization of human existence gained even more momentum in the second half of the twentieth century. Crucial factors were a further strengthened belief in the final conquest over pain in the 1960s and 1970s, as well as an increasing hospitalization for the treatment of painful suffering and for the dying process.[52] In his study *The Culture of Pain*, David B. Morris stresses that late-twentieth-century Americans were the first generation on earth who considered a painless life and death an almost constitutionally given right.[53]

Within this context, conducting executions in a hospital-like atmosphere resembling a medical operation seemed to be an appropriate solution to the problem of how to conduct executions. Even though Great Britain's Royal Commission on Capital Punishment had extensively debated lethal injection as an execution method in the early 1950s, and even though the controversial American pathologist Jack Kevorkian had sporadically suggested to submit death convicts to thiopental-induced anesthesia and to medical experiments before ultimate death, up to that point the gurney and the needle had never been seriously considered as an execution method in the American medical and legal discourse.[54]

In the 1970s, among the first government officials to imagine lethal injection for execution was Ronald Reagan. Reagan's widely published, well-known, and often-cited 1973 comment was matchless in its simplicity, but at the same time it had prophetic qualities. California's then-governor boasted that he had figured out what the contemporary problem with capital punishment was, because as a former horse breeder he knew exactly how hard it was to eliminate an injured horse by shooting it. Yet, calling the veterinarian to put the horse to sleep with "a simple shot or tranquilizer" made this hard task much easier. Reagan's comment is telling in many respects, but it is most noteworthy that the major desire Reagan expressed in his statement was not to spare the dying person pain but to shape circumstances in order to facilitate the ease of the executioner and civil society to kill a fellow creature quickly and without further ado. Thus, the decisive feature was obviously to make the execution appear smooth and painless, or, as Scott Christianson wrote in the *Criminal Law Bulletin* in 1979, lethal injection is praised for rendering "death painless for victim and witnesses alike."[55]

The urge to safeguard an aesthetically acceptable execution that provided a "painless" death for the witnesses as well was also driven by debates about televising the first execution in Texas after the decision in *Gregg*. Television reporter Tony Garrett was fighting in court against the Texas Department of Corrections for permission to film the first state-devised killing since 1964. Garrett's claim was finally rejected by the U.S. Court of Appeals for the Fifth Circuit, but, nevertheless, televised executions were not unlikely for quite a while, and this also seemed to make a more aesthetic method and sanitary appearance advisable.[56]

Ronald Reagan's statement was often referred to in the late 1970s and early 1980s, when the introduction and employment of lethal injection was a major topic in the discussion among both experts and the public.[57] The debate still centered around the speed of dying as one of its most significant topics, but the meaning of speed and the implications of well-timed procedural micromanagement obviously changed in the age of anesthetic executions. To be sure, up to that point in history, guaranteeing an instantaneous death in executions was meant to achieve the following goals. First, the executed should not have enough time to feel and realize that he was going through his own dying process (or, even worse than that, as in the case of the guillotine, have sufficient time to acquire knowledge of his or her own death). Second, speed should help minimize the physical pain of dying. Third, a fast execution should maximize the state's control over the procedure and minimize the probability of unwanted interpretations of the execution, for instance by the public.

The sedation and paralysis of the execution object signified the modified implications of time and speed. When Oklahoma's chief medical examiner Dr. A. Jay Chapman, who was in charge of devising the state's new execution procedure in 1977, stressed that "the whole concept of execution is that it's carried out rapidly," he neither meant split seconds nor allegorically described the exact moment of death as necessarily coming "as fast as lightening."[58] Taking a drugged person with utmost high speed from the realm of the living to the realm of the dead is simply needless. The diminished meaning of high-speed precision in the execution process reflects modifications that dominant body concepts have been undergoing since the 1970s. Following the anthropologist Emily Martin, in recent decades the conceptualization of bodies as machine-like has diminished in significance, and the irregularity and unpredictability of corporeal processes and reactions has moved to the foreground. With the farewell of modernity and the spread of more postmodern perceptions of human life and organization, the predominant body concept of the preceding centuries has undergone a transition from the "human motor" to a more fluid and flexibly functioning entity.[59]

Considering this, the anesthezation and inactivation of the condemned might be perceived as mirroring the understanding that no procedure involving human bodies is predictable down to the very last detail. Time and again, this type of understanding had subconsciously pervaded observations in the discourses of criminal justice and medicine in the preceding centuries—for instance, in texts on the living heads of the decapitated or in the urge to develop machines that totally smashed the head of the condemned in a fraction of a second—with the intention to guarantee the humaneness of the execution.

Yet, even though the relevance of high speed and exact timing diminished under these circumstances, still only a fast, untroubled, and smooth overall execution performance was deemed appropriate for a late-twentieth-century society. Even though anesthesia was now considered the best means to minimize pain and safeguard control over the performance, rapid efficiency seemed still necessary to signify decency. Because a large overdose of a single drug would take up to 45 minutes or even longer to cause death, Oklahoma's chief medical examiner, Dr. Chapman, proposed to add a second, and later a third, substance, with the intention to accelerate the execution process by stopping the heartbeat within minutes. When Oklahoma was the first state to introduce a lethal injection law in May 1977, immediately followed by Texas, its execution statute proudly stressed the eminent quality of the administered barbiturate as "ultrashort-acting."[60]

Between the passing of the Oklahoma and Texas laws in May 1977 and the first execution by lethal injection in Texas in December 1982, the evolving debate among experts and the public still took up speed and the tolerability of executions as one of its major issues. Consenting statements regarding the new Oklahoma execution law highlighted that the drug cocktail would lead to death within less than five minutes,[61] some even estimated that unconsciousness would ensue within 15 seconds, death within 30 seconds.[62] Several reports on Charles Brooks's execution emphasized that it had lasted no longer than seven minutes.[63] Yet, some statements also stressed that Brooks had not simply and peacefully drifted off in a state of trance but, to the contrary, had shown signs of arousal and pain.[64] On top of that, an obviously medically inexperienced prison employee, who had volunteered to handle the needle, had difficulties in finding Charles Brooks's veins, and the blood splattering on the sheet indicated barbarity and a highly unprofessional handling of the execution.[65]

In the early 1980s, some contemporaries meant to attack capital punishment as such by voicing doubts regarding the rapidity and the procedural precision of lethal injections. By arguing that "death by lethal injection could be slower and more agonizing than electrocution," opponents to the death penalty tried to impede its return. However, at the same time, they subconsciously affirmed the notion that, in general, a reliable and quick procedure would provide a good death and thus legitimize capital punishment.[66]

Similar to prior execution styles, killing by lethal injection required specifically qualified execution personnel, as well as a well-organized and successful system. When the first lethal injection execution of Charles Brooks was botched, contemporary critics' fears had proven true. Legal and medical experts had cautioned against problematic ethical entanglements and the pseudotherapeutic design of state-induced killing, as well as against upcoming practical problems with lethal injection ending up in botched and painful executions.[67] Specifically, the fundamental academic critique of lethal injection by William J. Curren and Ward Casscells, deploring the "corruption and exploitation of the healing profession's role in society," was of eminent political influence because it inspired the American Medical Association (AMA) to pass a resolution against the active participation of physicians in executions. Medical doctors, and specifically the AMA, stressed the incompatibility of the Hippocratic Oath and medical ethics with the duties in executions.[68]

The experts' doubts, warnings, and apprehensions resonated in the American public, and these resonances sound astoundingly familiar to the observer of today's debates and concerns. Since 1982, medically untrained and unprofessional personnel have been unable to comply with the requirements of a procedure mimicking the intravenous induction of an anesthetic agent before a medical operation. Faced by human beings with scarred veins due to long drug careers, executioners have repeatedly failed in their endeavors, or they have miscalculated the dosage of the anesthetic agent needed to numb overweight inmates—mistakes that had been predicted by medical experts even before the first execution by lethal injection, which meant, according to Ward Casscells of the Harvard Medical School, "no improvement over electrocution or even a bullett."[69] In October 1981, an article in the *Washington Post* repeated their warnings by alluding to the incalculable reactions of human bodies on physical interventions (specifically done by nonexperts) and warned that "no one knows what will happen if the sedative wears off before the curare does its work, if the dosages are not correct, if the technician misses the vein."[70] Irregularities of this kind, wrote an editorial in the *Los Angeles*

Times, would disarrange the procedure, spoil the timing, and render lethal injection dysfunctional in the age of medicalized dying. At the same time, utterances of this kind reiterated the belief in the impeccability of the expert: "Properly done, it [lethal injection] would render the person unconscious before stopping all heart and lung action. Improperly done, it could cause an agonizing death. . . . An unskilled or poorly trained technician administering the intravenous needle could cause suffering."[71]

The skeptical voices of the late 1970s and early 1980s anticipated today's arguments against lethal injection raised by physicians, reform groups, the public, and the press. Most of the critical voices from the early 1980s were articulated in comments on a legal procedure initiated by two inmates of the Oklahoma and Texas death rows and their lawyers. Larry Chaney's and Doyle Skillern's central argument was that the drugs to be used for lethal injection according to the Oklahoma protocol had never been approved for this specific purpose by the Food and Drug Administration (FDA) and they "could result in agonizingly slow and painful deaths that are far more barbaric than those caused by the more traditional means of execution." FDA testing and approval is required for a wide array of drugs, including those used in animal euthanasia.[72]

The appeals court of the District of Columbia decided that the evidence brought forth by the plaintiffs in the FDA case supported their claim "that execution by lethal injection poses a serious risk of cruel, protracted death,"[73] but political decision makers continued to praise lethal injection in public as safeguarding a "calm" and even "pleasant" death[74] and as being able "to accomplish the job faster, cheaper and with less distasteful pain and suffering" than all the previously used execution methods.[75] On March 20, 1985, the U.S. Supreme Court finally ruled that the FDA was under no obligation to test the drugs used for lethal injection.[76] Instead of its almost prophetic proportions seen from today's perspective, the appeals court's 1983 warning that "even a slight error in dosage or administration can leave a prisoner conscious but paralyzed while dying, a sentient witness of his or her own slow, lingering asphyxiation," had no consequences in the end.[77] The clothing of "a potentially objectionable policy in the morally neutral trappings of medical science," as Herbert Haines has commented on the decision in a 1989 article, and the culturally persuasive power of an execution style mimicking a therapeutic intervention in a hospital room, and by that providing a maximum of control over a sedated inmate, were too convincing arguments in favor of lethal injection.[78]

Conclusion

Since the eighteenth century, concepts of humanity, civilization, and prog-ress have preoccupied societies, their leading thinkers, and political deci-sion makers. As opposed to premodern times, in this changing cultural context, conducting an execution was no longer meant to be a demon-stration of authority, violence, and suffering but a performance of human-ity and rationality by a well-organized state and society. For roughly two centuries, this transition has demanded executions of utmost speed and efficiency because speed promised a painless death, almost unfelt by the dying convict, with minimal discomfort for the witnesses and almost un-noticed by the public. Changing cultural configurations have gone hand in hand with a modification of execution methods, whereas the underly-ing discursive strategy has remained very much the same: modern and enlightened execution styles were meant to achieve (at least the impres-sion of) an instantaneous and painless death, and they were supposed to minimize and hide the visible cruelty of killing in executions.

Yet, the achievement of painlessness through speed proved to be a phantasm—something desired and sought after but never achieved be-yond any serious doubt. The introduction of lethal injection showed at least a subconscious awareness that painlessness through speed was unat-tainable. The anesthetization of the condemned meant that bringing death in a "fraction of a second" or "as fast as lightning" was no longer necessary to ensure the painlessness of dying. Nevertheless, first, contemporaries highlighted that the employed barbiturate was "ultrafast-acting," and, sec-ond, they hastened the procedure by employing two more drugs that—among other things—stop the heartbeat sooner. Of all things, this desire to speed up execution procedures by using a combination of three drugs is the predominant cause for botched lethal injections. Thus, the relationship of speed and painlessness has been turned upside down: the desire to safe-guard a fast execution procedure makes pain and suffering more likely.[79]

In general, the historicization of execution styles and their reforms—from manual decapitation and hanging at the gallows to the guillotine, the electric chair, and lethal injection—shows that the problems with execu-tions and the strategies for their solution have hardly changed since the late eighteenth century. The critical comments heard in today's debate sound astoundingly familiar to the historically informed observer. A close-up on lethal injection shows how today's criticism is hardly different from that of the capital punishment discourse in the late 1970s and early 1980s.

For over two centuries, continuous efforts "to improve" execution methods have never led to a painless and gentle death penalty. Nevertheless, some voices of the current critical debate seem to suggest once again that a perfection of executions and a closer convergence to painless dying is possible. Suggested solutions are either to convince physicians to contribute with their knowledge and expertise "to 'fix' the 'broken' system" of capital punishment,[80] or, as suggested in comments from the late 1970s to the recent Supreme Court case of *Baze v. Rees* in 2008, to use a "single dose of barbiturate, which does not require the participation of a medically trained professional."[81] Obviously, as a writer in *New Scientist* emphasized after the State of California had postponed the execution of Michael Morales, many comments seem to suggest that "the issue is not whether it [the death penalty] should be applied, but how,"[82] or, as the president of the American Society of Anesthesiologists pointed out, loud voices in the current debate on the death penalty ask particularly how carefully and professionally the death penalty is executed—and not whether the death penalty should exist at all.[83] These voices seem to suggest that the American debate over capital punishment is further away from the tipping point to abolition than reformers and death penalty critics want it to be.

Yet, as I have stressed before, history suggests that neither the integration of experts nor the modification of the execution method will solve the problem of executing painlessly in the long run. "Killing with kindness" is an oxymoron.[84] To the contrary, the half-life of culturally acceptable execution styles has been going down constantly. Whereas the guillotine was used in large parts of Europe for over a century, and in France for almost two centuries, and whereas the electric chair was used in the United States for about one century, the gas chamber slowly died off after 50 years, and lethal injection is facing substantial critique regarding its adequacy as execution technique after less than only 30 years. Nevertheless, if, as suggested by anthropologist Emily Martin, the concept of the human body is currently in a state of transition from a reliable engine with highly predictable reactions to a more fluid and unstable entity,[85] using barbiturates for execution seems a culturally compatible method that might keep America away from the road to abolition and the death penalty alive for another while. The phantasm of "gentle, humane, . . . pleasant" executions, "just like going in, laying down and going to sleep," is still alive and alluring, and its robustness seems to be confirmed by the recent Supreme Court decision.[86]

Staying on the road to abolition, first, requires taking the historical analysis seriously and discarding the centuries-old belief in unlimited human ingenuity and in the correlation of civilization, invention, progress, and the death penalty.[87] Second, staying on the road to abolition also requires that both public and political leaders accept assertions of a growing number of medical experts that the flaws of lethal injection are insurmountable.[88] However, taking historical analysis seriously also reminds us that problematizing the execution method often enough boosted the perception of a crisis situation that seemed to demand finding a solution. Thus, staying on the road to abolition, third, requires tackling lethal injection and the "pervasive lack of professionalism" in its application not as an isolated problem but as part of a broad and multifaceted critique of the death penalty and its flaws.[89] If past is prologue, historical experience might suggest that America will continue to grope for technical solutions as it has always done, and *Baze v. Rees* seems to confirm that it will do so in the near future. Only a confluence of multiple factors besides failure to perfect the execution method might create a critical mass of opposition. The debate about the imperfection of the method and the resulting pain and suffering of the condemned, on the one hand, and an ongoing discussion about other problematic issues of the capital punishment system, on the other hand, might mutually reinforce each other.

NOTES

The title of this chapter is from Ward Casscells, Harvard Medical School, in a telephone interview on Oct. 31, 1984, according to Michele Stolls, "*Heckler v. Chaney*: Judicial and Administrative Regulation of Capital Punishment by Lethal Injection," *American Journal of Law and Medicine* 11, no. 2 (1985): 251–77, at 260.

1. "Stop Killing People Who Kill People," *Lancet* 369 (2007): 343.

2. *Baze v. Rees*, available at http://laws.findlaw.com/us/000/07-5439.htm (accessed April 19, 2008).

3. Teresa A. Zimmers, Jonathan Sheldon, David A. Lubarsky, Francisco López-Munoz, Linda Waterman, Richard Weisman, and Leonidas G. Koniaris, "Lethal Injection for Execution: Chemical Asphyxiation?" *PLoS (Public Library of Science) Medicine* 4, no. 4 (2007): 646–53, at 647.

4. Ibid., 653.

5. Leonidas G. Koniaris and Teresa A. Zimmers, "Inadequate Anaesthesia in Lethal Injection for Execution," *Lancet* 365 (2005): 1412–14, at 1412.

6. Quoted in Denise Grady, "Doctors See Way to Cut Suffering in Executions," *New York Times* (June 23, 2006).

7. Norbert Elias, *Über den Prozeß der Zivilisation: Soziogenetische und psychogenetische Untersuchungen*, 2 vols. (Frankfurt: Suhrkamp, 1976), vol. 2: 162–63.

8. In addition to the cited studies by Zimmers et al., "Lethal Injection for Execution," and Koniaris and Zimmers, "Inadequate Anaesthesia," see, for instance, Deborah W. Denno, "When Legislatures Delegate Death: The Troubling Paradox of State Uses of Electrocution and Lethal Injection and What It Says about Us," *Ohio State Law Journal* 63 (2002): 63–261, and Atul Gawande, "When Law and Ethics Collide: Why Physicians Participate in Executions," *New England Journal of Medicine* 354, no. 12 (2006): 1221–29.

9. For example, Koniaris and Zimmers., "Inadequate Anaesthesia," 1412.

10. Zimmers et al., "Lethal Injection for Execution," 649.

11. Koniaris and Zimmers, "Inadequate Anaesthesia."

12. Florida inmate Angel Diaz, for instance, kept on moving his lips and his eyes for 24 minutes, and he was declared dead after 34 minutes. Exclusively relying on barbiturates for execution is rejected because the dying process might take up to 45 minutes and be accompanied by significant jerking of the inmate. Intramuscular injections, which would avoid the often-difficult process of finding a suitable vein, are also rejected because the effectuation of the drug would take much longer.

13. See the debate among Jonathan I. Groner, Mark J. S. Heath, Donald R. Stanski, Derrick J. Pounder, Robyn S. Weisman, Jeffrey N. Bernstein, and Richard S. Weisman on "Inadequate Anaesthesia in Lethal Injection for Execution," *Lancet* 366 (September 2005): 1073–74, with an "Author's Reply" by Teresa A. Zimmers, David A. Lubarsky, Jonathan P. Sheldon, and Leonidas G. Koniaris, pp. 1074–76.

14. Ron Word, "Florida, California Suspend Executions," *Washington Post* (Dec. 16, 2006), available at www.washingtonpost.com/wp-dyn/content/article/2006/12/15/AR2006121502108_z.html (accessed 6 Mar. 2009).

15. *Baze v. Rees* (2007), available at http://www.supremecourtus.gov/qp/07-05439qp.pdf for the hearing in January, and http://laws.findlaw.com/us/000/07-5439.htm for the decision (accessed April 19, 2008); Linda Greenhouse, "Justices to Enter the Debate over Lethal Injection," *New York Times* (Sept. 26, 2007); Linda Greenhouse, "Justices Uphold Lethal Injection in Kentucky Case," *New York Times* (Apr. 17, 2008); Adam Liptak, "Moratorium on Lethal Injection Is over, but Hardly the Challenges," *New York Times* (Apr. 17, 2008). No death penalty was executed in the United States from September 25, 2007, to the decision on April 16, 2008. Executions resumed on May 6, 2008.

16. Ron Word, "Lethal Injection under Microscope," *Washington Post* (Dec. 16, 2006). See also Michael Reilly, "Lethal Injection Drugs 'Unreliable,'" *New Scientist* (Apr. 24, 2007), available at http://www.newscientist.com/channel/opinion/death/dn11695-lethal-injection-drugs-unreliable.html.

17. Patrick Malone, "Death Row and the Medical Model," *Ohio State Law Journal* (1979): 5–6, at 5.

18. The classic, of course, is Michel Foucault, *Discipline and Punish: The Birth of the Prison* (New York: Vintage, 1977).

19. Charles-Louis de Secondat, Baron de la Brède et de Montesquieu, *The Spirit of Laws* (London: P. Dodesley and R. Owen, 1794), 88. See also Lynn Hunt, *Inventing Human Rights* (New York: Norton, 2007).

20. On the notion of time and the turn from the eighteenth to the nineteenth century, see the writings by Reinhart Koselleck—for instance, his collected essays, *Zeitschichten: Studien zur Historik* (Frankfurt: Suhrkamp, 2000). On the acceleration of life, see, for instance, Peter Borscheid, *Das Tempo-Virus: Eine Kulturgeschichte der Beschleunigung* (Frankfurt: Campus, 2004), 76–79. On the history of the guillotine, see Daniel Arasse, *The Guillotine and the Terror* (London: Allen Lane, and New York: Penguin, 1989), and Jürgen Martschukat, *Inszeniertes Töten: Eine Geschichte der Todesstrafe vom 17. bis zum 19. Jahrhundert* (Cologne: Böhlau, 2000), 113–48.

21. For example, Thomas W. Laqueur, "Crowds, Carnival and the State in English Executions, 1604-1868," in A. L. Beier, David Cannadine, and James M. Rosenheim (eds.), *The First Modern Society: Essays in English History in Honour of Lawrence Stone* (Cambridge: Cambridge University Press, 1989), 305–55. See also Martschukat, *Inszeniertes Töten*, 113–16.

22. Johann F. Eisenhart, *Erzählungen von besonderen Rechtshändeln*, 10 vols. (Halle/Helmstedt: Hemmerde, 1767–1779), vol. 4 (1770), 568.

23. Christoph Meiners, "Betrachtungen über die Hinrichtung mit dem Schwerdte," *Berlinische Monatsschrift* (May 1784): 408–22, at 418.

24. For Guillotin's talk, see "Gazette nationale ou le Moniteur universel 101" (Dec. 1, 1789), and a comment in 118 (Dec. 18, 1789), *Réimpression de l'ancien Moniteur*, vol. 2 (Paris, 1859): 280, 410. For Louis's talk, see "Moniteur universel 82" (Mar. 22, 1792), *Réimpression* 11 (Paris, 1862): 689; and Arasse, *Guillotine*, 20, 26–27, 216–18.

25. Article 2 requires that "la peine de mort consistera dans la simple privation de la vie," *Code Pénal du 25 septembre—6 octobre 1791, première partie*, available at http://ledroitcriminel.free.fr/la_legislation_criminelle/anciens_textes/code_%20penal_25_09_1791.htm.

26. I cannot discuss the whole specter of meanings that were attached to the guillotine, specifically during the "terreur." See besides Arasse the essay by Regina Janes, "Beheadings," *Representations* 35 (1991): 21–51.

27. Other moments of this debate have been presented in essays by Jürgen Martschukat, "Ein schneller Schnitt, ein sanfter Tod? Die Guillotine als Symbol der Aufklärung," in *Die Gewalt in der Kriminologie*, ed. Susanne Krasmann and Sebastian Scheerer (Weinheim: Juventa, 1997): 45–63; Kerstin Rehwinkel, "Kopflos, aber lebendig? Konkurrierende Körperkonzepte in der Debatte um

den Tod durch Enthauptung im ausgehenden 18. Jahrhundert," in *Körper mit Geschichte: Der menschliche Körper als Ort der Selbst- und Weltdeutung,* ed. Clemens Wischermann and Stefan Haas (Stuttgart: Steiner, 2000): 151–71; Roland Borgards, "Qualifizierter Tod: Zum Schmerz der Hinrichtung in der Rechtsprechung um 1800," in *Diskrete Gebote: Geschichten der Macht um 1800—Festschrift für Heinrich Bosse,* ed. Roland Borgards and Johannes Friedrich Lehmann (Würzburg: Königshausen and Neumann, 2002): 77–98.

28. Samuel Thomas von Soemmerring, "Lettre de M. Soemmering à M. Oelsner sur le supplice de la guillotine," *Moniteur universel* 48 (Nov. 9, 1795), reprinted in *Réimpression de l'ancien Moniteur* 26 (Paris, 1862): 378–79.

29. Johann Wendt, *Über Enthauptung im Allgemeinen, und über die Hinrichtung Troer's insbesondere: Ein Beytrag zur Physiologie und Psychologie* (Breslau: Author 1803), 27.

30. Ernst F. Klein, "Über die Hinrichtung der Verbrecher, mit Rücksicht auf den von Troerschen Fall," *Neues Archiv des Criminalrechts* 5 (1804): 1–19, at 14.

31. Carl F. Clossius, *Über die Enthauptung* (Tübingen: Heerbrandt, 1797), 27–28; Carl A. Eschenmayer, *Über die Enthauptung gegen die Sömmeringsche Meinung* (Tübingen: Heerbrandt, 1797), 39–41; Pierre Jean Georges Cabanis, "Bemerkungen über die Meinung des Herrn Sömmering, Oelsner, und des Bürgers Sue über die Enthauptung," in *Jean Joseph Sue, Physiologische Untersuchungen und Erfahrungen über die Vitalität; nebst dessen Abhandlung über den Schmerz nach der Enthauptung . . . .* (Nuremberg: Raspe, 1799) (Paris 1797): 117–35; Franz Paula von Gruithuisen, *Über die Existenz der Empfindung in den Köpfen und Rümpfen der Geköpften und von der Art sich darüber zu belehren* (Augsburg: Bolling, 1808), 34.

32. Elbridge T. Gerry, Matthew Hale, and Alfred P. Southwick, *Report of the Commission to Investigate and Report the Most Humane and Practical Method of Carrying into Effect the Sentence of Death in Capital Cases* (Albany, N.Y.: Troy, 1888), 49–50.

33. Thomas Hughes, *American Genesis: A Century of Invention and Technological Enthusiasm 1870–1970* (New York: Viking, 1989). On the cultural meaning of technology around 1900, see Cecilia Tichi, *Shifting Gears: Technology, Literature, Culture in Modernist America* (Chapel Hill: University of North Carolina Press, 1987).

34. Robert Levine, *Eine Landkarte der Zeit: Wie Kulturen mit Zeit umgehen* (Munich: Piper, 1998), 103–15; Peter Borscheid, *Das Tempo-Virus* (Frankfurt: Campus, 2004), 151–75. On the reformation of time and time-measurement in America around 1900, see Michael O'Malley, *Keeping Watch: A History of American Time* (Washington, D.C.: Smithsonian Institution Press, 1990), 145–90. On the electric craze, see Tim Armstrong, *Modernism, Technology, and the Body: A Cultural Study* (Cambridge: Cambridge University Press, 1998), and David E. Nye, *Electrifying America: Social Meanings of a New Technology* (Boston: MIT Press, 1990).

35. In general, see Jürgen Martschukat, "'The Art of Killing by Electricity': The Sublime and the Electric Chair," *Journal of American History* 89, no. 3 (2002): 900–921; Michael Madow, "Forbidden Spectacle: Executions, the Public and the Press in 19th-Century New York," *Buffalo Law Review* 43, no. 2 (1995): 461–562, at 529–530; Edmund Clarence Stedman, "The Gallows in America," *Putnam's Magazine* (Feb. 1869): 225–36, cited in Philip E. Mackey (ed.), *Voices against Death: American Opposition to Capital Punishment, 1787–1975* (New York: Franklin, 1976), 131–40, at 139.

36. Quoted in Craig Brandon, *The Electric Chair: An Unnatural American History* (Jefferson, N.C.: McFarland, 1999), 38–39.

37. Hugo A. Bedau, "Death Sentences in New Jersey 1907–1960," *Rutgers Law Review* 19 (1964): 1–54, at 1.

38. *In re Kemmler*, 136 U.S. 436 (1890), May 19, 1890, available at http://laws.findlaw.com/us/136/436.html (accessed April 27, 2001). On the constitutionality of the electric chair, see Deborah Denno, "Is Electrocution an Unconstitutional Method of Execution? The Engineering of Death over the Century," *William and Mary Law Review* 35, no. 2 (1994): 551–692.

39. Gerry et al., *Report of the Commission*, 75.

40. Alphonse Rockwell, Professor of Electrotherapy in New York, quoted in "Four Men Die by the Law: The Electric Current Does Its Deadly Work," *New York Times* (July 8, 1891): 2.

41. Anson Rabinbach, *The Human Motor: Energy, Fatigue, and the Origins of Modernity* (Berkeley: University of California Press, 1992).

42. Elbridge T. Gerry, "Capital Punishment by Electricity," *North American Review* (Sept. 1889): 321–25, at 324. Southwick quoted in "Kemmler Makes His Will," *New York Times* (Apr. 29, 1890): 8.

43. "Dead after Two Minutes," *New York Sun* (Feb. 9, 1892): 7, quoted in Madow, *Forbidden Spectacle*, 474.

44. "Capital Punishment," *New York Times* (Dec. 17, 1887): 4.

45. Gerry et al., *Report of the Commission*, 75.

46. Wooster Beach, "The Death Penalty: Proper Mode of Its Infliction," *Medical Record* 30 (1886): 89–90, and J. B. Thornton, Jr., "Some Further Remarks on the Death Penalty and Method of Infliction," *Medical Record* 30 (1886): 222–23.

47. G. W. Peck, "On the Use of Chloroform in Hanging," *American Whig Review* 8 (1848): 283–96, at 295.

48. Thornton, "Some Further Remarks," 222–23.

49. For example, "Predicted Flurry of Executions Has Not Followed Gilmore's; 398 on Death Rows," *Los Angeles Times* (July 25, 1977): C4; Jürgen Martschukat, "'With Grace and Dignity': Gary Gilmore, Todesstrafe und Männlichkeit in den USA der 1970er Jahre," *Amerikastudien/American Studies* 49, no. 3 (2004): 385–408.

50. Michel Foucault, *The Birth of the Clinic* (1963) (London: Routledge, 2003).

51. Martin S. Pernick, *A Calculus of Suffering: Pain, Professionalism, and Anesthesia in Nineteenth-Century America* (New York: Columbia University Press, 1985); Karen Halttunen, "Humanitarianism and the Pornography of Pain in Anglo-American Culture," *American Historical Review* 100, no. 2 (1995): 303–34.

52. Thomas Szasz, *The Medicalization of Everyday Life: Selected Essays* (Albany: SUNY Press, 2007), reprinting essays from 1973 to 2006 not exclusively but with a focus on psychiatry; see also H. B. Gibson, *Pain and Its Conquest* (London: Owen, 1982).

53. David B. Morris, *The Culture of Pain* (Berkeley: University of California Press, 1991), 71

54. On Great Britain's Royal Commission on Capital Punishment, see Deborah Denno, chap. 6 in this volume. On the suggestion to use lethal injection, see Jack Kevorkian, "Capital Punishment or Capital Gain," *Journal of Criminal Law, Criminology and Police Science* 50 (1959): 50–51, and Jack Kevorkian, "Medicine, Ethics, and Execution by Lethal Injection," *Medicine and Law* 4 (1985): 307–13, at 311.

55. Reagan was quoted in "They Shoot Horses, Don't They?" *Time* (Oct. 8, 1973); the Reagan quote is discussed by Dwight Conquergood, "Lethal Theatre: Performance, Punishment, and the Death Penalty," *Theatre Journal* 54 (2002): 339–67, at 364. See also Scott Christianson, "Execution by Lethal Injection," *Criminal Law Bulletin* 15, no. 1 (1979): 69–78, at 69.

56. George J. Annas, "Killing with Kindness: Why the FDA Need Not Certify Drugs Used for Execution Safe and Effective," *American Journal of Public Health* 75, no. 9 (1985): 1096–99, at 1096; Austin Sarat, *When the State Kills: Capital Punishment and the American Condition* (Princeton, N.J.: Princeton University Press, 2001), 195–203; James W. Marquart, Sheldon Ekland-Olson, and Jonathan R. Sorensen, *The Rope, the Chair, and the Needle: Capital Punishment in Texas, 1923–1990* (Austin: University of Texas Press, 1994), 132–33.

57. For example, "Execution by Injection: Is It Best?" *Los Angeles Times* (June 5, 1981): A9–10.

58. Deborah Denno, "The Lethal Injection Quandary: How Medicine Has Dismantled the Death Penalty," *Fordham Law Review* 76, no. 1 (2007): 49–128, at 65–70. Chapman in 2006 quoted in Denise Grady, "Doctors See Way to Cut Suffering in Executions," *New York Times* (June 23, 2006).

59. Emily Martin, *Flexible Bodies: Tracking Immunity in America from the Days of Polio to the Age of AIDS* (Boston: Beacon, 1994). See also Emily Martin, "Die neue Kultur der Gesundheit: Soziale Geschlechtsidentität und das Immunsystem in Amerika," in Philipp Sarasin and Jakob Tanner, eds., *Physiologie und industrielle Gesellschaft: Studien zur Verwissenschaftlichung des Körpers im 19. und 20. Jahrhundert* (Frankfurt: Suhrkamp, 1998), 508–25.

60. Oklahoma Statutes, Title §22-1014(A), "Manner of Inflicting Punishment of Death," available at http://www.lsb.state.ok.us/ (accessed Dec. 21, 2007). See also two memos quoted in Denno, "Lethal Injection Quandary," 74, n.150. On the introduction of lethal injection to Texas, see Marquart, Ekland-Olson, and Sorensen, *Rope, Chair, and Needle.*

61. For example, "Two States Adopt Execution by Drugs," *Los Angeles Times* (May 12, 1977): B6

62. Quoted in Christianson, "Execution by Lethal Injection," 75.

63. Robert Reinhold, "Technician Executes Murderer in Texas by Lethal Injection," *New York Times* (Dec. 7, 1982): A1, A19.

64. "Death, Purified," *New York Times* (Dec. 8, 1982): A30; Robert Reinhold, "Execution by Injection Stirs Fear and Sharpens Debate," *New York Times* (Dec. 8, 1982): A28.

65. "Texas Doctor Defends Role at Execution by Injection," *Washington Post* (Jan. 29, 1983): A11.

66. Mary Thornton, "Death by Injection. Convicted Killer in Oklahoma Faces Execution by an Untried Procedure," *Washington Post* (Oct. 6, 1981): A1, A12.

67. For the first example, see Lonnie R. Bristow, "Methical Ethics: Quo Vadis?" *Forum on Medicine* (June 1979): 417–18, and "Concerns Grow As States Adopt Lethal Injection," *American Journal of Nursing* 84, no. 1 (1984): 116–18. For the second example, see "On Lethal Injection and the Death Penalty," *Hastings Center Report* (Oct. 1982): 2–3; Thomas O. Finks, "Lethal Injection: An Uneasy Alliance of Law and Medicine," *Journal of Legal Medicine* 4 (1983): 382–403; Harold L. Hirsh, "Physicians as Executioners," *Legal Aspects of Medical Practice* (Mar. 1984): 1–4, at 8; and Herbert Haines, "'Primum Non Nocere': Chemical Execution and the Limits of Medical Social Control," *Social Problems* 36, no. 5 (Dec. 1989): 442–54.

68. William J. Curren and Ward Casscells, "The Ethics of Medical Participation in Capital Punishment by Intravenous Drug Injection," *New England Journal of Medicine* 302 (1980): 226–30. See also Barbara Bolson, "Strange Bedfellows: Death Penalty and Medicine," *Journal of the American Medical Association* 248, no. 5 (1982): 518–19, and Denno, "Lethal Injection Quandary," 77–91. See also the discussion of medical ethics and the death penalty by Jukka Varelius, "Execution by Lethal Injection, Euthanasia, Organ-Donation and the Proper Goals of Medicine," *Bioethics* 21, no. 3 (2007): 140–49.

69. Ward Casscells in a telephone interview on Oct. 31, 1984, quoted in Stolls, "*Heckler v. Chaney*," 260.

70. Thornton, "Death by Injection," A1, A12. See also Malone, "Death Row and the Medical Model," 6: "Dr. Hodes [an anesthesiologist from Tampa] warns that if the procedure is not carried out with great skill, the barbiturate could wear off and the prisoner could wake up only to realize that he was suffocating."

71. "Execution by Injection: Is It Best?" *Los Angeles Times* (June 5, 1981): A9–10.

72. "On Lethal Injections and the Death Penalty," *Hastings Center Report* 12, no. 5 (Oct. 1982): 2; Stolls, "*Heckler v. Chaney.*"

73. Judge J. Skelly Wright for the 2–1 majority, quoted in Linda Greenhouse, "F.D.A. Is Rebuffed on Drug Execution: Court Orders Agency to Study Evidence that Injections Cause Torturous Death," *New York Times* (Oct. 16, 1983): 26.

74. Quoted in "Calm, Pleasant Death," *New York Times* (Aug. 15, 1982): E20. Gov. Kean from New Jersey is quoted as having said, "If ever I've seen a calm, pleasant death it's an anesthetic death."

75. The latest development in New Jersey was discussed by Michael Norman, "Why Jersey Is Leaning to Executions by Injection," *New York Times* (May 18, 1983): B6. New Jersey obviously relied in its decision making process on articles by Christianson, "Execution by Lethal Injection," 69–78, and Martin R. Gardner, "Executions and Indignities: An Eighth Amendment Assessment of Methods of Inflicting Capital Punishment," *Ohio State Law Journal* 39 (1978): 96–130.

76. *Heckler v. Chaney*, 470 U.S. 821 (1985), available at http://supreme.justia.com/us/470/821/case.html (accessed April 19, 2008). See also Al Kamen, "FDA Can't Be Forced to Certify Lethal Drugs: High Court Decision Overturns 1983 Ruling," *Washington Post* (Mar. 21, 1985): A19.

77. Quoted in "Drugs Used in Executions Must Be Painless, Appeals Court Says," *Los Angeles Times* (Oct. 14, 1983): A1. This skepticism was widely mentioned, not only in the public press but also in professional magazines such as in the article by Patrick Malone, "Death Row and the Medical Model," at 6: "Dr. Hodes [anesthesiologist from Tampa] warns that if the procedure is not carried out with great skill, the barbiturate could wear off and the prisoner could wake up only to realize that he was suffocating."

78. Haines, "Primum Non Nocere," 451. See also Annas, "Killing with Kindness," and Conquergood, "Lethal Theatre," 360–65.

79. In 1978, the author of an article in the *Ohio State Law Journal* even described a reverse relation of speed and painlessness in lethal injections by emphasizing that practical problems "could be minimized by administering a nonlethal sedative, either oral or intramuscular, prior to beginning the process of lethal injection. Thus, the process of execution would extend over a longer period of time than it now does and for this reason would be less desirable than the mode outlined in the paradigm [the three-step-protocol—JM]; but the victim would feel only the pain of the sedative injection and not even that if he consented to oral sedation. There would be minimal violence, no mutilation, and little more indignity than attends an ordinary surgical operation." Gardner, "Executions and Indignities," 129.

80. Denno, "Lethal Injection Quandary," 122–23.

81. Hearings in *Baze v. Rees* on January 7, 2008, available at http://www.nodeathpenalty.eu/dokumente/07–5439.pdf, p. 6. Attorney Donald Verrilli, Jr., is also quoted by Linda Greenhouse, "Justices Weigh Issue for Death Row," *New York Times* (Jan. 8, 2008).

82. Rowan Hooper, "Insight: US in Dilemma over Death Row Injections," *New Scientist* 2541 (Mar. 4, 2006).

83. Orin F. Guidry, "Message from the President: Observations Regarding Lethal Injection," June 30, 2006, available at http://www.asahq.org/news/asanews063006.htm.

84. Annas, "Killing with Kindness."

85. Martin, *Flexible Bodies*.

86. Rev. Clyde Johnston, Protestant chaplain for the Texas Department of Corrections in June 1977, quoted in Christianson, "Execution by Lethal Injection," 69.

87. For example, Edward W. Byrn, "The Progress of Invention during the Past Fifty Years," *Scientific American* (July 25, 1896): 82–83. For a critique, see Austin Sarat, "Introduction: On Pain and Death as Facts of Legal Life," in *Pain, Death, and the Law*, ed. Austin Sarat (Ann Arbor: University of Michigan Press, 2001), 1–14, at 10. See also Austin Sarat, "Killing Me Softly: Capital Punishment and the Technologies for Taking Life," in *Pain, Death, and the Law*, ed. Sarat, 43–70, and Sarat, *When the State Kills*, 60–84.

88. Leonidas G. Koniaris, Jon P. Sheldon, and Teresa A. Zimmers, "Can Lethal Injection for Execution Really Be "Fixed?" *Lancet* 369 (2007): 352–53.

89. Judge Jeremy D. Fogel of the U.S. District Court for Northern California, quoted in Peter Whoriskey and Sonya Geis, "Lethal Injection Is on Hold in Two States," *Washington Post* (Dec. 16, 2006). In this sense, the intention of criticizing lethal injection cannot be "to encourage further research to 'improve' lethal injection protocols." Editors, "Lethal Injection Is Not Humane," *PLoS (Public Library of Science) Medicine* 4, no. 4 (2007): e171, available at doi:10.1371/journal.pmed.0040171.

Part III

Putting the Death Penalty in Context

Torture, War, and Capital Punishment
Linkages and Missed Connections

Robin Wagner-Pacifici

May 2008. The presidential primary campaigns are in full swing in the United States. Mortgage foreclosures, high gas prices, the war in Iraq, and health care dominate the campaign debates and policy pronouncements. Meanwhile, crucial decisions are made by current incumbents of the three branches of government and its administrative and military agencies about the constitutionality of forms of state execution, specifically lethal injections, and forms of "unlawful enemy combatant" interrogation, specifically waterboarding. The Supreme Court has recently released its decision on the lethal injection protocol challenge (*Baze v. Rees*); another death-row inmate (three in the past several months) in North Carolina is released because of prosecutorial withholding of evidence potentially favorable to the defendant, a new study is released finding racial disparities in capital sentencing, the Justice Department finally releases the previously classified March 2003 John Yoo memorandum on "Military Interrogation of Alien Unlawful Combatants Held outside the United States," seven alien enemy detainees at Guantanamo have been officially charged with war crimes and, with the prosecutor's decision to seek the death penalty, are set to be tried after many years of detention and after some of them had been subject to harsh interrogation methods (deemed by many to be torture). On the campaign trail, precious little is said about these consequential actions and decisions. Yet they raise critical issues about the self-understanding of the United States, the limits of state violence, the rule of law (including international law), and human rights—all topics a public might legitimately expect its candidates for office to engage. In their totality, they present a picture of where this country now stands on the road to abolition.

Confounding Cultural Formations of State Violence

On January 3, 2008, readers of the *New York Times* may have been particularly puzzled by two articles on the first page that touched on issues of state violence and its limits in the United States. One article, "U.S. Announces Criminal Inquiry into C.I.A. Tapes," announced that the Justice Department had launched a formal criminal investigation of the 2005 destruction of videotapes of Central Intelligence Agency (CIA) interrogations of suspected al-Qaeda operatives carried out in 2002. While obstruction of justice was the anticipated focus of any possible charges, the potent backstory involved the probable use of "waterboarding" on those suspected al-Qaeda operatives during the taped interrogation sessions. Waterboarding, an interrogation technique many have acknowledged to be torture, had become in 2007, and would continue to be into 2008, a symbolic fetish of the torture approach-avoidance public discourse on the "war on terror." Further down was another article about state violence. This one was titled "States Hesitate to Lead Change on Executions." The piece addressed the political and legal contexts surrounding the upcoming Supreme Court case, *Baze v. Rees*. The story reported that various states had decided not to follow recommendations about revising the lethal injection method of execution, recommendations that aimed to eliminate the possibility of excruciating physical pain during executions.[1]

Excruciating pain caused and carried out by agents of the state floated on the surfaces of both of these articles. And both articles suggested that certain limits in state violence have either been reached or breached—in both instances, leading to nothing short of torture. But the two front-page articles, and the worlds of law, politics, policy, war, and strategy in which they lived, remained hermetically insulated from one another.

A week later, on January 11, 2008, several articles appeared in the *New York Times'* first section that also touched on current issues of state violence in the world. One article, "General Clears Army Officer of Crime in Abu Ghraib Case," reported that the only U.S. officer to face a court-martial over the scandal at the Abu Ghraib prison in Iraq, Lt. Col. Steven Jordan, had been cleared of the crime of disobeying an order not to discuss the abuse investigation. Another article, "Administration Is Rebuffed in a Ruling on Deportation," reported on the decision of a federal judge in Pennsylvania to block the government's attempts to deport an Egyptian

Coptic Christian man, Sameh Khouzam, back to Egypt to face a murder conviction there (a conviction carried out in absentia). Khouzam had claimed that he had already been subject to torture in Egypt because of his refusal to convert to Islam and that he would likely face more torture on his return. The presiding federal judge, Judge Thomas I. Vanaski, based his decision on the likelihood that absent an "impartial and binding review" of assurances that the Egyptian government had given that Mr. Khouzam would not, in fact, be tortured on his deportation back to Egypt, "the procedures established to give protection under the Convention Against Torture 'would be a farce.'"[2]

Finally, on page A3, an article titled "Hanging and Amputation Find Favor in Iran Courts," described Iran's continuing use of torturous punishments for a variety of crimes, including the cutting off of hands and feet, and its continuing practice of capital punishment via hanging. In the middle of the article, the following passage appears:

> Iran has been an active user of the death penalty, usually hanging, and is one of several countries that opposed its abolition last month during a vote on the UN General Assembly resolution, joining in an unusual alliance with the United States. Officials argued that the abolition of the death penalty would be an infringement on Iran's sovereignty.[3]

How might an attentive and yet reasonably distractible reader make sense of the references to what might be viewed as torture of Iraqi prisoners of war by American soldiers at Abu Ghraib, the torture that possibly awaits a deportable Egyptian citizen back home (and the U.S. government's attempt to deport him), and the death penalty in Iran (and the torturous practices that accomplish and accompany it) that unites it with its sworn enemy, the fellow death penalty practitioner, the United States? The usual categories by which modern thoughtful agents understand their social and political worlds—domestic and foreign, ally and enemy, human rights and sovereign prerogatives—seem to collide, or converge, or contradict each other. The vexed appearances of the death penalty and of torture in these articles are analogous precisely in the manner in which they perform their contradictions.

In this chapter, I argue that debates in the United States about the death penalty and about torture ought to be connected, as they are both fundamentally about the prerogatives and limits of sovereignty and state violence. The active decision of the state to cause pain and to take lives must be tracked across diverse domains and through apparently distinct historical contingencies. Only in this way can the ideologies, existential assumptions, and habitual thinking about capital punishment in the United States be fully comprehended.

In this chapter, I raise and begin to answer two sets of questions about recent and current discourse about the death penalty and torture in the United States:

1. What are the dominant discursive frames for each of these public discussions or debates? Do the debates about the death penalty in the United States and the debates about torture in the United States resemble each other or differ from each other?
2. Do these discourses make contact with each other or live in separate discursive universes? Do they ever actually converge? Are they ever cross-referencing issues in larger discussions of "who we are as a nation" or "human rights"? Are they influencing each other in shaping policy, specifically policy that seeks to halt capital punishment and/ or torture?

It is the hope that these investigations will assist in developing a history of the present state of capital punishment. Investigating missed connections, poses, but does not resolve, questions about moral and political coherence and consistency in nation-states such as the United States. As such, it raises questions about the contradictions found in the moral and political principles and practices of the United States as a sovereign power.

One auxiliary question posed by the comparison and juxtaposition of the discourses of the death penalty and torture in this essay is that of the intellectual, political, and moral grounds for issue specificity. With all of the many issues already attendant on the death penalty debates, it may seem foolhardy and politically fraught to suggest an expansion upward or outward. As Leon Shaskolsky Sheleff provocatively writes:

> In terms of attitudes, it may be only the committed pacifist who can sustain the total logic of an absolute abolitionist stance. . . . Any deliberate taking of life is forbidden—whether voluntary individual decisions as to suicide or euthanasia, or whether imposed state decisions as to the death penalty and war; and for many they embrace also opposition to abortion or the needless killing of animals.[4]

The perils of such embracing logics are ubiquitous. Bob Woodward and Scott Armstrong report that the U.S. Supreme Court decided not to release a decision on *Roe v. Wade* in 1972 because of the near-simultaneous decision of the *Furman v. Georgia* death penalty case: "If the Court struck down the death penalty and at the same time allowed abortion . . . the public reaction would be awful. The Court would be portrayed as allowing convicted killers to live, and sentencing unborn babies to die."[5] Given these issue fault lines, it is necessary to develop theoretical and methodological justifications and strategies for analyzing the discursive connections that are forged among issues, as well as those that are not

Methodological Frames

For studies of legal, political, and military policy and practice, the importance of social and cultural discourses is unassailable. As Austin Sarat wrote in a collection of essays on the death penalty: "[I]n order to understand the death penalty, we need to know more about the 'cultural lives'—past and present—of the state's ultimate sanction. . . . By 'cultural lives' we mean capital punishment's embeddedness in discourses and symbolic practices in specific times and places."[6] Sociologists have been keenly interested in the "discursive surround" of social movements, policy debates, social and political crises, and civil sphere debates more generally.[7] The methodological decision to analyze a range of discourses across a range of social institutions and forces involves a turn to transcripts of newspaper articles, editorials, judicial and legislative hearings, and interviews as primary data.[8]

Models for assessing the dynamics of these discourses in interaction come from the sociology of social problems and of social movements. One in particular, the "public arenas model" developed by Steven Hilgartner and Charles Bosk, is suggestive for an analysis of collective definitions of social issues and for the way these definitions either do or do not link these issues.[9] Hilgartner and Bosk were interested in the interactions among problems: "First, social problems exist in relation to other social problems; and second, they are embedded within a complex institutionalized system of problem formulation and dissemination."[10] Three key insights of their public arenas model are relevant here. First, multiple ways exist for framing a given social condition or practice as a problem. Second, collective definitions of social problems are formed in particular public arenas (including the executive and legislative branches of government, the courts, organs of the mass media, political campaign organizations, social action groups, religious organizations, the research community, and professional societies). And third: "[T]he number of social problems is determined not by the number of harmful or dangerous situations and conditions facing society, but by the carrying capacities of public institutions."[11]

The concept of "carrying capacities" is powerful, if underdeveloped in Hilgartner and Bosk's public arenas model. Different institutions have different carrying capacities, not just because they have differential generic capacities but because they have differential "cultural resonance," a concept formulated by David Snow and Robert Benford to refer to the congruence between a society's values and specific institutional frames. Obviously, differential institutional power provides dominant discourses with a "resonance" advantage, and it would be naive to suggest that cultural resonance is an organic process of free discursive competition.[12]

Orders of Justice, Sovereignty, and Violence

Even as they are constrained by hegemonic institutions and power differentials, the mechanics of discursive competition relies on classification operations. Recent work by French social scientists Luc Boltanski and Laurent Thevenot have built on Pierre Bourdieu's focus on classification, the ways that society is constituted through "classifying operations and practical interventions." In *On Justification*, Boltanski and Thevenot introduce their theoretical program of deducing different extant "orders of justice," thereby developing "a theory of justice that would take into account the diversity of ways to specify the common good . . . [and] the sense of injustice that is aroused when different orders of justice are confused."[13] They discern these orders of justice from the discourses of classical political philosophy treatises and contemporary business manuals. Boltanski and Thevenot find that these two incongruous sets of texts align along six orders of justice, six higher-order common principles to which people resort in finalizing agreements or pursuing contentions: inspiration, the domestic world, fame, the civic world, the market, and industry. In other words, in real-life situations of negotiation and contention, one or another of these forms of justification for action will inevitably dominate—revolutionaries may call on *inspiration* to take to the barricades, employers may refer to *market* forces to deny raises to their employees, politicians may appeal to *industrial* efficiency in setting monetary policy.

Sometimes, in situations of clear collective definition, the invocation of a specific world is unproblematic. But in many cases, there is a level of contingency, even in apparently clearly defined situations. It is this usually suppressed contingency, and the intermittent eruptions of new justifications within them, that I highlight in this analysis of contemporary debates and decisions about the death penalty and about torture. I am interested in the ways that modes of justification are conditioned by the distinct public arenas that Bosk and Hilgartner claim "carry" particular social problems. Ultimately, both the confusion of orders of justice (in Boltanski and Thevenot's terms) and conflicts across public domains stymie contemporary debates about state violence.

While Boltanski and Thevenot's model excludes violence, the authors nevertheless acknowledge its reality: "Some situations of discord may well turn out to be temporarily suspended between justification and violence."[14] The analytical investigations in this chapter live in that place of suspension. The claim is that the unsettled and oscillating forms of justification in the debates about the death penalty and torture precisely reflect the inability to definitively move these situations beyond this suspension, an inability to even articulate justifications of certain forms of state violence. An extreme version of this takes the form of declarations that substitute for justification—for example, the purposefully unreasoning assertion of sovereign "necessity."[15] Further examples of situational suspension between justification and violence include the paradoxical attempts to ensure that the actions of torture and execution professionals are perceived as "dignified." The practical consequence of this suspension between justification and violence is that of uneven and inchoate civilizational development.

One example of such suspension comes from a recent interview with Michael McConnell, the Bush administration National Intelligence director, who was asked to pass judgment on the interrogation practice of waterboarding by the interviewer, Lawrence Wright:

I asked if he considered [waterboarding] torture. McConnell refused to answer directly, but said, "My own definition of torture is something that would cause excruciating pain. . . . Referring to his teen-age days as a lifeguard, he said, "I know one thing. I'm a water-safety instructor, but I cannot swim without covering my nose. I don't know if it's some deviated septum or mucus membrane, but water just rushes in." For him, he said, "waterboarding would be excruciating. If I had water draining into my nose, oh God, I just can't imagine how painful! Whether that's torture by anybody else's definition, for me it would be torture."[16]

In Boltanski and Thevonot's framework, waterboarding-as-torture could only be justified, and its practitioners considered to be worthy, if an appeal were made to a common principle. One can imagine various justifications being mounted, including civic justifications often framed as the "ticking time bomb" scenario. But McConnell's definitional diffidence reveals the powerful preliminary work of classification in such justification tests. His answer also reveals the hidden, expansive nature of the civic world taken to its logical extreme. McConnell is able only to say that waterboarding would be torture were *he* to experience it. And this is so because he, as a specifically sentient individual, with a deviated septum, feels pain in a particular way when water is pouring into his nose. But the acknowledgment and highlighting of his own individual experience produces questions about the experiences of *any* victim of waterboarding. It raises, in other words, the question of their similarly individual humanity. The specter of an action that would be classified as torture, and thus outside the bounds of civilized behavior, only when used on certain individuals or groups, but not on designated others, suggests xenophobia.[17]

Making distinctions among classes of people and their basic human capacities to feel pain evokes questions of state sovereignty and exceptionalism. It is, as Max Weber described it, indeed the very essence of the state to designate a monopolized area of legitimate violence. And, while those inside that area are subject to state violence, its actual deployment is normally suppressed, as monopolization has tended toward de facto domestic pacification.[18] When it is deployed, either against those who understand themselves to be the state's subjects or against those who do not, state violence is always politicized, whatever form it may take. The pressure toward legitimation of that violence forces its codification in law, but such codification is always either ex post facto or existentially insufficient. As Paul Kahn writes: "Sovereignty, in our political experience, shows itself in the violence that precedes law and is never exhausted by law. Wherever the existence of the state is at issue—in the moment of creation or of defense—*sovereign violence exceeds the capacities of law.*"[19] Nevertheless, as Peter Fitzpatrick notes in his accompanying essay in this volume, sovereignty lives an unendingly conditional existence. Thus, for example, debates over the mechanisms of state violence inevitably scrutinize the *conditions* bearing on the *unconditional* power of sovereignty.[20]

Of course, the particular forms that state violence takes do matter. Scholars across a wide array of disciplines have carefully distinguished killing and maiming in war from torture and from capital punishment.[21] The specific categorical designation provided for any violent act of the state recognizes a particular world comprised of particular kinds of beings, and any context that positions itself as overarching lays claim to all sorts of beings in its ambit. The overarching context of *this* historical present is the "war on terror," and it must be brought into any analysis of state violence, including analyses of the current state of the death penalty and torture. The hold of the designation of the current national situation as the "war on terror" also effects extant ideas about national sovereignty and, in the case of the United States, national exceptionalism. Contemporary debates about the actions of the military (e.g., the prison guards at Abu Ghraib and Guantanamo and the military commissions established by the Military Commissions Act of 2006), the intelligence agencies (e.g., the CIA interrogators in Afghanistan and elsewhere), the executive branch, and the civilian courts have direct bearing on the purview of capital punishment and torture.

Hegemonic Context: Global "War on Terror"

Kim Lane Scheppele, in a powerful analysis of what she terms, "The International State of Emergency," calls attention to broad legal changes that have taken place since September 11, 2001, changes that ricochet back and forth between international institutions and national domestic institutions. She writes:

> In the anti-terrorism campaign, the new international public law seems primarily to provide the conditions for undermining domestic constitutional law, particularly its concern for balanced and checked constitutional powers, for human rights and due process. . . . Under new transnational legal pressures, states around the world have moved toward using emergency powers domestically to fight terrorism internationally.[22]

Scheppele argues that these legal changes have not been sufficiently noticed by lawyers, neither those focusing on international law nor those focusing on domestic constitutional law, because they have occurred "in the interstices between the two legal specialties." With the U.S. PATRIOT Act setting a foundational legal-change agenda, the movement then has been from U.S. domestic legislation, to other nation's domestic legislation, to U.N. Security Council legislation, back to domestic law, leading ultimately to "increased abilities of national executives to use the cover of international law to undermine domestic constitutions at home."[23] Scheppele, using data from the International Commission of Jurists, describes the actual nature of the "emergency" changes: (1) power is centralized, with strong executives favored; (2) military methods are substituted for ordinary policing; (3) procedures are displaced; (4) the legal status of speech is changed; (5) transparency is reversed, with an increase in government secrecy; (6) anticipatory violence is used.[24]

If the "war on terror" is indeed a relevant and consequential context for debates and decisions about the death penalty and torture now, it is important to clarify how war differs generically from these other forms of violence. And, further, it is important to identify how this particular "war" engages torture and capital punishment differently than the more "ideal typical" war does.[25]

First, when looked at from the perspective of law, wars can be legal or illegal in several ways. As Chris Jochnick and Roger Normand acknowledge in their critical history of the laws of war:

> International jurisprudence makes a distinction between laws governing the resort to force (*jus ad bellum*) and laws regulating wartime conduct (*jus in bello*). *Jus in bello* is further divided into the Geneva laws (the "humanitarian laws"), which protect specific classes of war victims (such as prisoners of war), and the Hague laws (the "laws of war"), which regulate the overall means and methods of combat.[26]

While it is generally accepted that the U.N. Charter has superseded the idea of separate *jus ad bellum* laws, Jochnick and Normand note an important historical precedent. They argue that, in spite of the codes of legality governing war, such laws have consistently favored "military necessity" over humanitarian values. And "necessity" as a self-authorizing justification for action in the context of war does indeed surface in contemporary executive memoranda on torture.

When trying to get a handle on the hegemonic "war on terror," it is useful to grasp war's essence, even when the war is a-temporal (e.g., undeclared and with no clear endpoint) and de-territorialized. Elaine Scarry has asserted that there are two interior facts about war's ideal-typical formulation that are essential to its description: "First, it is a form of violence; it is a member of a class of occurrences whose activity is 'injuring.' Second, it is a member of a class of occurrences that are contests."[27] Paul Kahn takes exception to the "contest" vocabulary because of its implicit idea of empirical symmetry between consenting subjects.[28] Nevertheless, Kahn does appear to agree with the sense of Scarry's distinction between war and torture when he proposes focusing on the quality of risk: "Torture is a form of risk-less warfare, which is always ethically problematic."[29] Relative degrees of contestation or risk to the physical, psychological, and moral personhood of the participants may be one way of parsing the different modes of state violence. War is a contest with risks to combatants that are perhaps minimally controllable. Torture is a contest with very minimal, if any, control on the part of the victim. And the death penalty, when carried out, is no contest at all.[30]

Beyond such ideal typical categorical distinctions, beyond the ethical problems of these practices, there are also questions of law. Wars are not just contests whose activity is injuring; they are violent contests that engage with law. If the assertion is correct that the relevant context for capturing the present moment of sovereign violence is the "war on terror," we need to probe more deeply into what kind of a war this is. Is it a legal war? Is it a war subject to laws? If so, what laws? How, exactly, does this war affect domestic law? Does it do so in ways that influence other forms of sovereign violence, such as capital punishment?

Certainly, these questions were on the minds of some of the Supreme Court Justices hearing arguments in the June 2006 *Hamdan v. Rumsfeld* case. Bothered particularly by the military tribunals established by the Bush administration, and by the absence of rights of those designated "enemy combatants," Justice Stephen Breyer, for example, anticipated a scenario of arbitrary, lawless executive action, an argument that had been put forward by the case's petitioner. In a 5–3 decision, the Supreme Court ruled that the military tribunals were illegal, violating both the Uniform Code of Military Justice and four Geneva Conventions (violating Article 3 of the Third Geneva Convention, in particular). It also ruled that congressional authorization was required to lawfully establish military commissions.

Thus, the Supreme Court settled, if only provisionally (Congress passed a law to authorize just such military commissions to try "unlawful enemy combatants" later that year), questions about the nature of the "war on terror" and about legitimate forms of sovereign violence while prosecuting this war. Both torture and the death penalty were directly drawn into this ambit. Hamdan's lawyer, Neil Katyal, was questioned by Justice Anthony Kennedy about the December 2005 Detainee Treatment Act and whether they actually authorized a military commission. Katyal's response drew attention to the "most grave" powers of government:

> Approval by inference has never been sufficient when it comes to authorizing military jurisdiction, in the most awesome powers of the Government, to dispense life imprisonment and death. That is, I think, a clearer statement would be required in this unique setting, because we aren't talking about, after all, minor things. We're talking about the most grave powers of our Government, the power to dispense life imprisonment and death. And I certainly don't think Congress, on the basis of a few hours of debate, intended to ratify this entire apparatus. [31]

The appearances of the death penalty and torture in this exceptional war are thus confounding on many levels as government, military, and civilian agents orient now toward the national context, now toward the international context, now toward a military context, now toward a civilian context, and so on. In this way, orders of justification continuously fluctuate. The net effect of this "war everywhere," as Rosa Brooks Ehrenreich calls it, is the persistent opportunism of normally unjustified action.[32] And a justification that claims to trump all others is that of American exceptionalism.

Sovereign Exceptionalism

The United States has been identified, and has self-identified, as exceptional in many ways. With reference to the death penalty, scholars such as Carol Steiker have analyzed America's wayward position vis-à-vis Europe and much abolitionist world opinion and practice.[33] Recent forays into and prevarications on torture, from the Bush administration Justice Department and from the CIA, point to another troubling discourse of exceptionalism. This exceptionalist stance is easy to understand because it is reasonable that, as long as the United States remains hegemonic militarily and economically, it will do what it wants, regardless of international tendencies and pressures. However, it is not apparent why it would take the positions it has taken on these various forms of state violence.

Some scholars have argued that a clue to the U.S.'s regressive tendencies vis-à-vis international human rights law lies in the unabating foundational idea of popular sovereignty in the United States. Paul Kahn has written: "A global order of law would break the connection between popular sovereignty and the rule of law. One way of understanding American exceptionalism—ironic as it sounds—is to say that America remains bound to the age of revolution. It is a deeply conservative, revolutionary state."[34] The hegemony of revolutionary origins is an interesting frame for understanding U.S. actions and policies. Yet American exceptionalism might be best understood as a stance conglomerating multiple modes of justification, refusing to choose among them. Any situation that presents itself can be managed by appealing, serially, to one or another justification. In other words, the United States acts in a particular way because it is "inspired" (the revolutionary founding), or because it is "industrial" (most expert in satisfying needs), or because it is "civic" (spreading democracy), and so on. Among other effects, this protean exceptionalism stymies opposition.

Thus America claims exceptional status because it is the sole exemplar and guarantor of freedom, democracy, and liberty. It is exceptional because it is the sole superpower in this unipolar world. It is exceptional in its sovereign exceptionalism (this exception is one claimed by all sovereign nations—it's just that they are not all successful in making this claim stick). In other words, American exceptionalism is what happens when a specific sovereign nation declares itself the metaexception, the exception above all the other exceptions. And this is where the deterritorialization and achronotopy of the current "war on terror" works in symbiosis with these claims.

American Responses to Evolving International Law Regarding the Death Penalty and Torture

The (im)moral standing of capital punishment itself has been highlighted by recent international initiatives, conventions, and law. These agreements have moved in the direction of total abolition (even in time of war or imminent war) as codified by the Second Optional Protocol of the International Covenant on Civil and Political Rights (ICCPR), Protocol No. 6 to the Convention for the Protection of Human Rights and Fundamental Freedoms, and Protocol No. 13 to the European Convention on Human

Rights. Nevertheless, through opposition and reservations on signed treaties, the United States has resisted taking the same explicitly morally framed path to abolition.

While current international law is unsettled on the permissibility of the death penalty for war crimes, an "international state of emergency" is a new species of undeclared war. When the permissibility for use of the death penalty follows from a definition of the situation as one of war, such extended and amorphous wars present unique opportunities. Greta Proctor contends that "any State could claim that it is currently 'wartime' considering the ongoing global war on terror. In fact, a State would not even need to go so far as to assert that it is engaged in war. It might simply cite the perpetual threat of international terrorism to fall under the 'impending war' exception."[35]

Nevertheless, many scholars argue that there is an evolving international repudiation of all capital punishment, war included. Even in extreme cases of genocide, international juridical bodies such as the International Criminal Tribunal for Rwanda are eliminating the death penalty. The "war on terror" though, prosecuted through the international law and domestic law cross-referencing ways that Scheppele has described, has generated no international tribunal. Rather, it is a given that the military tribunals established by the U.S. Military Commissions Act of 2006 can levy the penalty of death as a punishment. Indeed, as of May 2008, seven detainees were being brought to trial for capital offenses. As of February 2009, the Obama administation has suspended Guantanamo cases in order to review the status of the detainees and the process of closing the base.

The Military Commissions Act also prevaricates on torture and its relation to anticipated trials of identified "unlawful enemy combatants." In the section regarding admissibility of defendant statements obtained "by use of torture," such statements are deemed admissible if they were

> obtained before December 30, 2005 (the date of the enactment of the Detainee Treatment Act of 2005) in which the *degree of coercion* is disputed . . . only if the military judge finds that—1) the totality of the circumstances renders the statement reliable and possessing sufficient probative value; and 2) the interests of justice would best be served by admission of the statement into evidence.[36]

Only if the statement was obtained after that date must a judge consider the prohibition of "cruel, inhuman, or degrading treatment," as defined by the Detainee Treatment Act of 2005. Here the significance of the missed linkages between the death penalty and torture is at its most glaring: the military tribunal's permitting of testimony elicited from torture also permits that testimony to lead to a sentence of death, giving lie to the assertion by the United States (justifying its opposition to the U.N.-sponsored vote on a death penalty moratorium) that the death penalty "for the most serious crimes [must be] carried out pursuant to a final judgment rendered by a competent court and in accordance with appropriate safeguards and observance of due process."[37]

As regards evolving international law on torture, the United Nations Convention Against Torture and Other Cruel, Inhuman, and Degrading Treatment and Punishment defines torture in the following manner:

> Any act by which severe pain or suffering, whether physical or mental, is intentionally inflicted on a person for such purposes as obtaining from him or a third person information or a confession, punishing him for an act he or a third person committed or is suspected of having committed, or intimidating of coercing him or a third person, or for any reason based on discrimination of any kind, when such pain or suffering is inflicted by or at the instigation of or with the consent or acquiescence of a public official or other person acting in an official capacity. It does not include pain or suffering arising only from, inherent in or incidental to lawful sanctions.[38]

This definition connects severe pain or suffering with public officials, making torture necessarily an act associated with a political entity.

A breach in the wall of an apparently unequivocal stand against torture by the U.S. government appeared to follow from Justice Department memoranda written in 2002 and 2003, primarily by John Yoo, a legal scholar working at the time in the Office of Legal Counsel. Weighing in on the "standards of conduct under the Convention Against Torture and Other Cruel, Inhuman and Degrading Treatment or Punishment as implemented by Sections 2340–2340A of title 18 of the United States Code," the 2002 memo (known as the Bybee Memorandum) argued the following:

> Physical pain amounting to torture must be equivalent in intensity to the pain accompanying serious physical injury, such as organ failure, impairment of bodily function, or even death. For purely mental pain or suffering

to amount to torture under Section 2340, it must result in significant psychological harm of significant duration e.g., lasting for months or even years.[39]

This memo's redefinition of torture, eventually repudiated by the Bush administration, would echo in consequential ways. As Kim Lane Scheppele
writes:

> Even before the stunning repudiation of the earlier Bybee Memo, however,
> no one in a position of authority had argued that torture was of no mo-
> ment or that it should generally be allowed. Moreover . . . the enactment of
> a federal criminal law based on the Convention apparently sets up domestic
> criminal sanctions for torture committed abroad. Torture, then, always was
> and still is illegal; the *content* of the legal idea of torture, however, shifted
> dramatically after 9/11.[40]

Of course, the *context* in which torture is newly debated is that of the international state of emergency that Scheppele has described.[41]

This prolonged state of emergency has allowed for detailed recalibra-
tions of the rights and obligations of states toward particular enemies. For
example, the 2003 Memorandum, "Military Interrogation of Alien Unlawful Combatants Held outside the United States" (released to the public
in 2008), spends considerable time not just restricting its own definition
of torture (e.g., excluding all acts that do not result in "death, organ failure, or permanent impairment of a significant bodily function") but also
justifying sovereign exceptions to various international laws and conventions prohibiting torture in the context of dealing with "unlawful alien
combatants."[42]

Exceptionalist Discourse in Practice

Death Penalty

Current public discourse in the United States about the death penalty is
located in several "public arenas." In the *political* arena, New Jersey's legislature abolished the death penalty in that state, and it was signed into law
by Governor Jon S. Corzine on December 17, 2007. In the *judicial* arena,
the U.S. Supreme Court decided to hear the lethal injection case of *Baze v.
Rees* in early January 2008 and rendered an opinion in April of that year.

In the *academic* scholarship arena, several recent U.S.-based studies were published that argued an effectiveness of the death penalty in lowering crime. The *mass media* highlighted these findings in mid-November 2007. Finally, in the *military* arena of the "war on terror," discussions about the persistence of the death penalty in particular countries, including the United States, have touched on issues of treaties and extraditions.[43]

The discursive grounds justifying various positions on the death penalty emerge in the contexts of these events and issues.[44] These grounds include moral mandates, technical considerations, professional considerations, utilitarian claims, claims of sovereign privilege, and ethical considerations about degrees and types of appropriate punishment. Specific events and decisions may foreground one or another of these justifications, but it is also important to pay close attention to the hybridity of rationales in trying to get at the suspension between justification and state violence.

Torture

The majority of post-9/11 debates over torture revolve around some basic questions. What is torture? What is the relationship between torture and punishment? Does the United States engage in torture? Should the United States engage in torture? With so many national and international proscriptions on torture, one might believe the subject to be obvious and closed.[45] Nevertheless, the current situation is one in which a deeply troubling exegesis has moved onto center stage. I have identified several of the most recent sites of justification of torture for this essay, in order to focus on their discursive formations. In doing so, I am aware that the current discursive field of talk about torture is literally immense and persistent, with new stories emerging all the time.

Some key discursive sites and texts include the following: the Senate Committee on the Judiciary Hearings on Michael Mukasey's nomination for Attorney General of the United States (October 17–18, 2007); news articles about the current investigation of destroyed videotapes of CIA "extreme interrogation" of al-Qaeda suspects in 2002 and about accusations of torture at Abu Ghraib, Guantanamo, and other undisclosed locations outside U.S. territory; and an extensive interview with National Intelligence Director Michael McConnell.

Even as these emergent discourses recalibrate and recategorize the what, why, where, when, and who of torture, there are dominant strains of argumentation and concern that mirror those associated with the death penalty.

In other words, we find claims about moral mandates, technical considerations, professional considerations, effectiveness, and sovereign privilege. There is the concern with professional interrogators (in, e.g., the military and the CIA) and how their participation in "harsh" interrogations might damage their careers or, worse, make them legally liable. There is the argument about the effectiveness of torture (akin to the argument about the possible deterrent effect of capital punishment). There is a persistent preoccupation about what the practice of torture (or near-torture) says about the moral evolution of the United States. Finally, the specter of state-sponsored torture resurrects debates about past practices of torture in the United States, practices that were carried out on the border between legal institutions and explicit lawlessness, and, in the cases of lynching, highlighted persistent racial oppression. This last discourse connects with the intermittently attended-to death penalty issue of racial discrimination in capital cases.

Means and Ends: Technical Concerns

A dominant discourse about American death penalty practices has focused on questions about cruel and unusual punishment, highlighting the issue of means. The recent oral arguments in *Baze v. Rees* emphasize some of the preoccupations about the cruelty of lethal injections as currently administered. Donald Verrilli, the lawyer for the plaintiffs, presents the case that the current three-drug method of lethal injection used by, in this instance, Kentucky is cruel and excessively painful. He states:

> Kentucky's lethal injection procedures pose a danger of cruelly inhumane executions. If the first drug in the three-drug sequence, the anesthetic thiopental, is not effectively administered to the executed inmate, then the second drug, pancuronium, will induce a terrifying conscious paralysis and suffocation and the third drug, potassium chloride, will inflict an excruciating pain as it courses through the veins.[46]

Later, Verrilli responds to a question posed by Chief Justice John Roberts about possible future cases by explicitly raising the issue of torture: "[what] this Court's cases are talking about is the consciousness of lingering death and torture that that imposes."[47]

The explicit identification of torture and its link to the Eighth Amendment's prohibition of cruel and unusual punishment sets off a series of questions and answers about the nature of the pain experienced during execution. Justice Antonin Scalia is adamant in arguing that there is no constitutional requirement to choose a method that causes the least pain, and he attempts to identify a terrain for state violence that is almost agnostic on pain: "The concern [in the Eighth Amendment] was with torture, which is the intentional infliction of pain. Now, these States, the three-quarters of the States that have the death penalty, all except one of whom use this method of execution, they haven't set out to inflict pain."[48] This, in turn, leads to a rapid parsing of differences between "unnecessary" and "wanton" infliction of pain. The question of the state's power and right to inflict pain in carrying out the death penalty and in engaging in torture becomes one largely about how and how much.

We might choose to understand such discussions of the *means* as moments of sovereign violence, glimpsed for an instant in its guise as practical calculation and conservation of moral effort (Scalia caustically notes that they are not talking about surgery). Other current discourses of justification (for and against) appear more oriented to ends than means—deterrence and effectiveness are examples. And such ends-oriented discourses may seem more self-evidently potent or transcendent. But Max Weber demonstrated the power of means-oriented delineations of social and political forces when he pressed on the significance of violence as the signal means of the state.[49] When the means are violent, public consideration of means is critical. Exegeses of Carl von Clausewitz's famous formulation that war is the continuation of politics by other means usually focus on his yoking of politics and war together.[50] The "by other means" phrase does not necessarily call attention to itself in the same way.

But the "by other means" phrase resonates explicitly in a line of questioning in *Baze v. Rees* that points in an anxious direction of endless deferral. When attention is drawn to means of execution that carry risk (however substantial) of pain (however extreme), an asymptotic quest for the method with least risk of any pain exposes itself as the very undoing of sovereign state violence. Justice Samuel Alito articulates the real danger associated with such a goal in the following interchange with Gregory Garre, the deputy solicitor general:

Justice Alito: Is there any comparative element in the substantial risk standard, if it were clearly established, undisputed that there was an alternative method that was much less risky, would there be an 8th Amendment problem with the State or the Federal government nevertheless persisted in using a method that was inferior?

> Mr. Garre: We think that that could be part of the analysis—that you would look to other feasible available alternatives . . .
>
> Justice Scalia: If that's part of the analysis, this never ends . . . there will always be some claim that there is some new method that's been devised and once again executions are stayed throughout the country.[51]

A de facto moratorium on executions is the result of a potentially endless scrutinizing of means and reveals the power of means-oriented discourse to undo capital punishment.

The *Baze v. Rees* decision, ruling that Kentucky's three-drug lethal injection protocol does not constitute cruel and unusual punishment, was handed down in April 2008. Chief Justice Roberts, Justice Kennedy, and Justice Alito wrote one of the several concurring opinions in which *degrees of risk* of *degrees of pain* is exquisitely parsed along a compound (risk and pain) continuum from "some" to "wanton and unnecessary" (with everything from "least risk," to "quantum of risk," to "unnecessary risk," to "untoward risk" in between): "To constitute a cruel and unusual punishment, an execution must present a 'substantial' or 'objectively intolerable' risk of serious harm. A State's refusal to adopt proffered alternative procedures may violate the 8th Amendment only where alternative procedure is feasible, readily implemented, and in fact significantly reduces a substantial risk of severe pain."[52] Only Scalia, in his concurring opinion, goes as far as to suggest that some pain is not only inevitable but also necessary for the carrying out of capital punishment, "because a criminal penalty lacks a retributive purpose unless it inflicts pain commensurate with the pain that the criminal has caused."[53] But a considerable tension persists over the course of the seven separate opinions presented in this ruling over the nature, the degree, and the function of pain inflicted by the state when it puts someone to death.[54]

Such semantic parsing in death penalty decisions precisely mirrors that already demonstrated regarding the status of waterboarding (torture or not) and the redefinitions of torture by executive branch lawyers to exclude everything but death or permanent severe impairment. Technicalities prove to be potent touchstones.

Professional Expertise and Its Prerogatives

There are parallel discourses about the professional qualifications and behavior of those actually involved in executions and those carrying out "enhanced interrogation" practices (torture). Whether, and how, medical doctors and other medical professionals should participate in the administration of lethal injections is a subject of heated professional, legal, and ethical controversy. Revelations of forensic errors at the other (beginning) end of capital trials have also highlighted professional fallibility.[55] Questions about the qualifications and training of those involved in capital punishment surface in *Baze v. Rees* in ways that reflect modernity's preoccupations about professions, careers, training, bureaucracy, and experience.

These discourses ask: Who is doing the killing? What expertise or credentials do they bring to the job? And what does the actual performance of the job do to the individual's professional identity, what impact might it have on his or her career?

In *Baze v. Rees*, a series of questions and answers highlights the ambivalence around professional expertise when it comes to state killing. Asked about the identities of those prison employees who participate in Kentucky's executions by Justice David Souter, Roy T. Englert, arguing on behalf of the respondents asserts as follows:

> Mr. Englert: Kentucky uses what is probably literally the best qualified human being in the Commonwealth of Kentucky to place the IV line. It uses a phlebotomist who in her daily job works with the prison population. . . .
>
> Justice Souter: I take it this is obvious, but I wondered when I went through the brief. I assume this phlebotomist is not an MD?
>
> Mr. Englert: Correct. . . . The training is a certain amount of learning followed by on-the-job experience. This person places 30 needles a day in the prison population. . . .
>
> Justice Souter: So it's somebody like the *Red Cross worker* who puts in the needle when somebody donates blood.
>
> Mr. Englert: No, Your Honor. It's someone like the person who inserts an IV in a hospital. . . . And it's somewhat derisively referred to as *scut work* in the hospital setting.[56]

The trouble here in pinning down the professional identity of the phlebotomist reflects both a sociological dilemma of occupational status and a political dilemma of recognizing state violence. The phlebotomist who participates in executions suffers from the status anxiety of those not credentialed as doctors—they do the "scut work" in hospitals, work that doesn't rise to the metaphorical levels of heroism of doctors or ministrations of nurses. And because they are participating in executions, a comparison with the socially beneficent action of inserting a needle in the arm of someone donating blood to the Red Cross is inappropriate, unseemly. So while lauding this person's expertise as "the best qualified human being in the Commonweath of Kentucky," Englert denies her both professional status and moral standing.

This professional conundrum carries over into the Court's opinion. Characterized there as "qualified personnel having at least one year's professional experience," those individuals actually inserting the intravenous catheters in the condemned person's veins are eventually identified as a certified phlebotomist and an emergency medical technician.[57] However, Justice Alito's concurring opinion also notes that the national organizations of doctors, nurses, emergency medical technicians, and paramedics all have position statements against their members' participating in executions on ethical grounds, the reasonableness of which Alito acknowledges. But he then goes on to justify not changing Kentucky's protocol precisely because of the general unavailability of any medical practitioners whose expertise would be necessary to modify it. Here is the paradox of medical nonparticipation in a "medical" procedure. These professional dilemmas of executions are never merely technical or practical.

One might be surprised by the discourse of concern for the careers of intelligence and military interrogators involved in what may be determined to be torture. The worry is that association with torture will taint their professional standing (the argument is also made that compromising their identity could endanger them). Of all of the justifications involved in such acts, the identification of a "domestic" frame, which highlights the dependency of a public official on his superiors, may seem jarring and inappropriately banal at the same time. Yet in many ways, this persistent discourse mirrors that of the preoccupations about the technical skills and qualifications of those involved in executions. When, for example, the story of the destroyed CIA videotapes of detainee interrogations first broke in earnest in December 2007, an unnamed official was quoted as explaining a prime motive for the tapes' destruction: "Apart from concerns about physical safety in the event of a leak, the official said, there was concern for the careers of officers shown on the tapes. 'We don't want them to become political scapegoats,' he said."[58] This form of justification for avoiding a robust and definitive discussion of what does or does not constitute torture had already surfaced during the Mukasey confirmation hearings:

> Senator Durbin: I want to understand as to these interrogation techniques whether you believe that they would constitute torture and therefore could not be used against any detainee, military or otherwise, by the United States government.
>
> Mr. Mukasey: I don't think that I can responsibly talk about any technique here because . . . I'm sorry I can't discuss, and I think it would be irresponsible of me to discuss particular techniques with which I am not familiar when there are people who are using coercive techniques and who are being authorized to use coercive techniques. And for me to say something that is going to put their *careers or freedom at risk* simply because I want to be congenial, I don't think it would be responsible of me to do that.
>
> Senator Durbin: I—this is not a congeniality contest . . . on the issue of waterboarding, simulated drowning. The United States has long taken the position that this is a war crime.[59]

The sharp rebuke by Senator Durbin raises the stakes of the action of the interrogator and raises the level of the (un)justification. Participation in torture is a war crime. The sublime ambit of the war crime crashes into the mundane ambit of careers gone off the rails.

The professional anxiety of the interrogators of detainees in the "war on terror" also mirrors the hierarchy of professions (and their respective ethical mandates) called to participate in executions. There, medical doctors were generally insulated from participation in acts causing death, emergency medical technicians were intermittently utilized (though they, too, had an organizational proscription against such acts), and the lowly phlebotomist is left to insert the IV tube. In the realm of interrogations, trained military interrogators are protected from potential indictment or harassment through the destruction of videos of what has been construed as torture; some military prison guards at Abu Ghraib have been convicted of assault for similar acts; contractors accused of torture are being sued; and, according to lawyers in the ACLU (American Civil Liberties Union), a recently released Department of Defense document, the Church Report, reveals that psychologists and medical workers failed to report detainee abuse that they witnessed as late as 2004.[60]

Utilitarian Discourse: Deterrence and Effectiveness

Commenting on U.S. opposition to the U.N.'s nonbinding resolution supporting a moratorium on capital punishment, a *New York Times* editorial on December 20, 2007, noted:

> The United States, as usual, lined up on the other side, with Iran, China, Pakistan, Sudan and Iraq. Together this blood brotherhood accounts for more than 90 percent of the world's executions, according to Amnesty International. These countries' devotion to their sovereignty is rigid, as is their perverse faith in execution as a criminal deterrent and an instrument of civilized justice.[61]

Such assessments bring together questions of *morality* with those of *deterrence* and *sovereignty*, suggesting again the resistance to settling into one order of justification. Sometimes the moral evolution argument is so closely coupled with arguments about effectiveness that it is difficult to disentangle them or to understand which argument is foundational and which is supplemental. In his surprising concurring opinion in *Baze v. Rees*, Justice John Paul Stevens marked his own definitive turn away from capital punishment by both noting that "State-sanction killing is . . . becoming more and more anachronistic" and highlighting the chronic technical, political, and procedural problems with its functioning: "A penalty with such negligible returns to the State [is] patently excessive and cruel and unusual punishment violative of the Eighth Amendment."[62] Connecting the quality of returns with the moral evaluation of punishment is a complicated formulation and raises the important theme of deterrence.

On November 18, 2007, a front-page story in the *New York Times* posed a provocative question in its title: "Does Death Penalty Save Lives? A New Debate."[63] Really an old debate, reformulated by several recent studies, the focus of the article was on the question of the role of the death penalty in deterring violent crime. Deterrence functions as a justification for capital punishment in ways that might align with Boltanski and Thevenot's "industrial" world, where expertise (in this case, social scientific) is recognized as the superior common principle, or it might align with their "civic" world, where the greatest end is the common good. As Randall Collins writes: "Executions are now to be humane and relatively painless, and are carried out in private; their justification is generally held to be of a rational, educative, warning nature, not passionate vengeance."[64]

Deterrence as justification is marked off from both exclusively moral justifications and from vengeance, though it rests on its own utilitarian morality. A favorite hypothetical scenario recalled by those claiming deterrence as a justification of torture is that of the "ticking time-bomb." In this scenario, a public official (military or intelligence agency) must decide whether torturing a terrorist suspect will effectively elicit information to save large numbers of people from an impending terrorist attack. Certainly, the *manifest* conceptualization of torture is that it is, in fact, a tool for information gathering and not a punishment for past behavior. In a lengthy *New Yorker* magazine interview heavily bearing on questions of interrogation techniques, former National Intelligence Director Michael McConnell claimed, "it was not difficult to evaluate the truthfulness of a confession, even a coerced one."[65] But even those general supporters of the Bush administration's "war on terror" campaign, such as Senator John McCain, have refuted the effectiveness of torture to elicit information. Former FBI Special Agent Jack Cloonan is emphatic on this point, claiming that "it is the testimony of terrorists we tortured after 9/11 who have provided the most unreliable information, such as stories about a close connection between al-Qaeda and Saddam Hussein."[66]

While substantively different, there is a structural analogy here between the deterrence argument in debates about capital punishment and arguments about the effectiveness of torture to elicit information that might preempt the loss of lives. In both cases, with all their identified flaws of logic and empirical evidence to the contrary, they nevertheless serve a mythical function of asserting industrial and civic justifications.

National Values and National Identity: Past Meets Present

In the most recent events and decisions regarding the status of the death penalty in the United States, the related, though distinct, discourses of revenge and of retribution are put forward with great diffidence (although Scalia's statement that they are talking about executions, not surgery, may implicitly evoke sentiments of punishment as revenge).[67] While there are reasons for this that are internal to the various social and legal forces mobilizing around capital punishment, I propose a supplementary reason: much of the energy fueling the discourses of revenge and of retribution has migrated to the public arena contexts of the "war on terror" and its deployment of torture.

Torture seems pretty clearly threatening to an American self-understanding as harbinger of freedom, democracy, and civil rights. Of course, this self-understanding does not, for a minute, abandon its claim to power and must always invoke the name of power, even and especially when attesting to its values. Tom Ridge, secretary of the Department of Homeland Security between 2003 and 2005, recently weighed in on waterboarding and did so by precisely linking the "softness" of human rights values with American power. Ridge stated: "One of America's greatest strengths is the *soft power of our value system* and how we treat prisoners of war, and we don't torture. . . . And I believe, unlike others in the administration, that waterboarding was, is—and will always be—torture. That's a simple statement."[68] Various senators participating in the Mukasey confirmation hearings of the Judiciary Committee also attempted to get clarity on this apparent contradiction between American national values and torture.

Senator Durbin, in particular, pushed on this point and referred to previous testimony by Mukasey to set up an implicit conflict between the effectiveness justification and the question of American values:

> One of the things which we talked a lot about was this issue of torture, and you said at one point, quote, "There's a whole lot between pretty please and torture," and you suggested that coercive techniques short of torture are effective. . . . [W]ill you now acknowledge that it is illegal and inconsistent with our values as a nation to subject detainees to cruel and inhuman and degrading treatment?

To which Mukasey responded: "It is unlawful to subject detainees to cruel, inhuman and degrading treatment, there's no doubt, and I don't think that's inconsistent with what I said."[69]

Despite what seemed to be some clarity in this response, the embedded report of an alternative discourse by Mukasey in private to Senator Durbin, a discourse less guarded and cautious (where the world of interrogation between "pretty please" and torture is left to the imagination), points to a subtext that it might be useful to engage analytically. Such a subtext might constitute one of what Carol Greenhouse, following James Scott, terms "hidden transcripts." These transcripts do not only circulate in totalitarian, authoritarian, or colonial contexts: "In liberal democracies too, perhaps, we can seek hidden transcripts at the junctures where the powerful must conceal their own resentment of their role and their constant need for political justification, as well as their internal divisions where these arise from crucial structural contradictions."[70] Thus:

> Senator Durbin: I also asked you about Guantanamo. You referred to it—a colorful phrase. You referred to it as, quote, "a fright wig" used by critics of the administration, and defended Guantanamo on the grounds that detainees receive, quote, "Three hots and a cot, health care better than many Americans, and taxpayer-funded Korans."
>
> Mr. Mukasey: I admit I have not visited but I have spoken to people who have. Is—my feeling is pretty much what I told you in a rather pungent, conversational way. I don't think people are mistreated there.[71]

> Senator Durbin: We had questions yesterday about the issue of torture under the Geneva Conventions. The techniques which have been attributed to this administration involve painful stress positions, threatening detainees with dogs, forced nudity, waterboarding—that is simulated drowning—and mock execution. When we had the judge advocate general testify, I asked point blank whether they believed that these techniques violated the Geneva Conventions. They said yes. . . . What is your opinion?
>
> Mr. Mukasey: They—I mean I'm certainly not in a position here to argue with a judge advocate general's view that they violate the Geneva Conventions, and that, whether used against us or against anybody else, they would. That said, I think we have to recognize that when we're talking about coercive methods of interrogation, this is not a matter of choosing pleasant alternatives over unpleasant alternatives. . . . It's a choice among bad alternatives. . . . What the experience is of people in the Judge Advocate General's Corps . . . with captured soldiers, captured military people from enemies we fought in the past, may very well be far different from the experience that we're having with unlawful combatants who we face now. It's a very different kind of person.[72]

Without bearing too hard on the phrase, "a very different kind of person," I contend that one subtext of this discourse on torture in the context of the "war on terror" is ultimately that of race. Here the necessary reference is to the previous form of tolerated torture in the United States, the pervasive and persistent lynching of African American men after the Civil

War. Of course, here is where torture and the "death penalty" become fatally fused. No American discourse about these acts and their political meaning can separate and compartmentalize the issues.

A number of scholars across a range of disciplines—from sociology to political science, to criminal justice, to law—have identified and characterized the massive system of lynchings in the United States from the late 1880s to the 1960s as a specific mode of racial repression. Such scholars as Charles Ogletree, David Garland, Carol Steiker, and Loic Waquant have empirically described and theoretically analyzed the terror and persistence of these forms of executions, including both mob executions and those that were "executions sanctioned by the forms of judicial process absent the substance of judicial fairness."[73]

Scholars such as Stuart Banner, in his detailed accounting of the history of the death penalty in the United States,[74] have shown that capital punishment has cast a wide and shifting net in terms of specified crimes and target populations. Nevertheless, and especially after the Civil War, the specific targeting of African Americans for both illegal lynching (with the acquiescence, if not participation, of officials of the law) and legal executions is significant. And there seems to have been a crossover effect. The lasting impact of these only relatively recently extinct forms of torture and social control is documented in sociological studies of the contemporary distribution of capital punishment across diverse states in the United States. A recent study published in the *American Sociological Review* provides evidence that "states with the largest black populations and the most substantial inclinations to use vigilante violence in the past now are more likely to impose the death penalty."[75]

In 1987, the Supreme Court heard the case of *McCleskey v. Kemp*, in which an African American petitioner claimed that his Fourteenth Amendment rights had been violated because of the racially discriminatory way in which capital punishment was carried out in the United States. The plaintiff's argument was based largely on a social scientific study, the Baldus study, which argued, via the use of statistical analysis, that the combination of black defendant and white victim was the one most likely to be subject to the death penalty. By a 5–4 majority, the Court ruled that an argument made on the basis of statistics alone, without evidence of discriminatory intent in an actual case, is not sufficient to prove that capital punishment as practiced violates the Fourteenth Amendment. Since that time, other studies have found similar patterns, and a recent study of the imposition of the death penalty in Harris Country, Texas, released to the public in May 2008, found, among other things, that death was more likely to be imposed against black defendants than white defendants.[76]

Thus the history of racial violence, the fit between states with greatest numbers of multiple lynchings and greatest numbers of contemporary death sentences, and the persistence of racial discrimination in death sentences is one element accounting for the exceptionalist quality of American capital punishment. This perduring history may also help us interpret the disheartening prevarications about, and justification of, torture.

Various executive, legislative, and judicial acts have established, defined, and redefined categories of enemies in post-9/11 America. The category of "unlawful enemy combatant" (codified in the Military Commissions Act of September 2006) stands out for its active utilization and its negative definition. These unlawful enemies are understood to have engaged in hostilities against the United States or its allies, but not as "members of regular forces of a State party engaged in hostilities against the U.S."; and not as "members of a militia, volunteer corps, or organized resistance movement belonging to a State party engaged in such hostilities, which are under responsible command, wear a fixed distinctive sign recognizable at a distance, carry their arms openly, and abide by the law of war"; and not as "a member of a regular armed force who professes allegiance to a government engaged in such hostilities, but not recognized by the United States."[77]

One of the signal consequences of falling under the category of "unlawful enemy combatant" (termed significantly by the Bush White House as "alien unlawful enemy combatant") is that of the loss of basic legal, military, and human rights. The *Hamdan v. Rumsfeld* case in June 2006 had explicitly taken up some of these questions of rights, specifically those designated in the Uniform Code of Military Justice and the Geneva Conventions, as described earlier.

Thinking in this context about the prevarications over basic rights, it is important to recollect the principles of distinction and proportionality engaged by the laws of war, principles designed to make clear distinctions between civilians and combatants, for example, and to guarantee basic human rights in all wars. Nevertheless, Jochnick and Normand reveal the elasticity of the concept of "military necessity," a concept they claim can always trump humanitarian rules of law. They also highlight the history of distinctions and decisions in matters of humanitarian initiatives in warfare often being made on the basis of race. Writing about the 1899 Hague Peace Conference, Jochnick and Normand note: "Britain and the United

States also cast the lone dissenting votes to the proposed ban on dum dum bullets, which expand inside the body to cause permanent, disfiguring wounds. Britain, which manufactured the bullets in India and used them in colonial wars in Africa, argued that dum dum bullets were necessary to disable tenacious 'savages.'"[78] And a recent article about the history of "the water cure" (what is now called waterboarding) by U.S. forces in the Philippines in the early years of the twentieth century recounts Senate testimony by military officials characterizing Filipinos as "a semicivilized people, with all the tendencies and characteristics of Asiatics, with the Asiatic indifference to life."[79] This historical mechanism of dehumanization has not, it seems, entirely disappeared.

What I am suggesting is that the current "war on terror" with its adamant justifications of "extreme interrogation" has engaged its own forms of racism. Scholars such as Amy Kaplan and Susan Willis have analyzed the particular "symbolic economy" of Guantanamo and extraterritorial sites of rendition in these terms, drawing connections between the image of the enemy combatant and that of immigrants, for example.[80] This is a symbolic economy that provides a ground for thinking and talking torture.

One final reference here will serve as a bridge between the racist discursive environment for the torture debates and the specter of the public torture lynchings of African Americans. In the oral arguments of *Hamdan v. Rumsfeld*, a series of questions revolved around the lawfulness of the military tribunals established to try the "unlawful enemy combatants" by the Bush administration. The petitioner in that case was precisely claiming that, under the Geneva Conventions, the tribunals were not lawful. In a series of questions between the government's lawyer, General Clement, Justice Scalia, and Justice Kennedy, the appropriateness and timing of such challenges to the lawfulness of tribunals is debated. At one point, Justice Kennedy asks: "Is that—is that true? If a group of people decides they're going to try somebody, we wait until that group of people finishes the trial before the Court—before habeas intervenes to determine the authority of the tribunal to hold and to try?" The following dialogue is striking in its rhetorical references and resonance:

> General Clement: With, with respect, Justice Kennedy, this isn't a "group of people." This is the President invoking an authority that he's exercised in virtually every war we've had. It's something that was recognized in the Civil War, something in the World War II that this Court approved.

Justice Kennedy: I had thought that the historic function of habeas is to—one of its functions—is to test the jurisdiction and the legitimacy of a court.

General Clement: Well, but—habeas corpus generally doesn't give a right to a pre-enforcement challenge. . . .

Justice Scalia: To a forum that is prima facie properly constituted. I mean, it—this is not a—you know, a necktie party. Where it parades as a court, and it's been constituted as a court, we normally wait until the proceeding's completed.[81]

The *Oxford English Dictionary* defines "necktie party" as U.S. slang for a lynching or hanging (now chiefly historic). Notwithstanding the awkward manner in which Scalia lurches up to that phrase, the underground connection between the history of lynching in the United States and the judicial apparatuses set up by executive fiat in the "war on terror" must give pause.

Conclusion: Convergences between the Present Histories of Capital Punishment and Torture

When the state engages its monopolized violence, it necessarily identifies and categorizes its targets and victims—in war, in capital punishment, in any imposition of pain such as torture. From the death penalty to torture, one unbroken strand of the U.S. use of violence is the story of racial categorization and racism. Privileged categories of individuals are either nearly immune to state violence or are protected by rings of recognized rights. Citizens—specifically, wealthy white citizens—have historically been less victimized by state violence in its various forms. Might it be that we are living in a period of transition, subject to multiple influences and movements, when the emotional energy of the culture of state violence is migrating away from capital punishment (with its fixation on African Americans) and toward torture (with its fixation on Arabs qua Islamic fundamentalists qua terrorists)? This may be the unacknowledged link between the death penalty and torture in the United States. In each case, the legacy, if not the practice, of racism maintains the hold on support for the death penalty and ("necessary") torture. If the death penalty in the contemporary United States is a contemporary performance of an American racial caste system, then the decline of the death penalty concomitant with the rise of (thinkable) torture against fundamentalist Islamicists (mostly Arabic) might not be an accidental contingency of separate historical forces but, rather, a reflection of a single mechanism. The United States, for peculiar reasons linked to its own sovereignty anxieties, may need an actively suppressed and marginalized group at any time.[82]

It takes a greatness and complexity of vision for a nation-state to identify and reject cruel and unusual punishment and torture in all of its aspects and arenas. From waterboarding to capital punishment, from prison beatings to decades-long incarceration and detention, prisoners and detainees may be said to be cruelly treated on many fronts. A recent *New York Times* interview with 70-year-old Texas death-row inmate Jack Harry Smith ends with him being asked about the prospect of an imminent date for his execution. He responds: "[A] life sentence is a whole lot worse—it's torture."[83] Michael McCann and David Johnson make the point, in their essay in this volume, that preoccupation with torture, Guantanamo, and rendition has diverted attention from the more familiar, everyday violence in American prisons and police stations. This may be true, but such differential practices of state violence ought not be counterposed and placed in competition with each other for attention. The United States may be at a critical juncture in its tolerance of state violence and torture in the name of the state. It is the obligation of the public to be vigilant in its identification of such actions and conditions and in making the connections across domains and issues, so that we can do justice to the complexity and greatness of an alternative vision.

NOTES

1. "U.S. Announces Criminal Inquiry into C.I.A. Tapes," *New York Times*, Jan. 3, 2008, p. A1, and "States Hesitate to Lead Change on Execution Method," *New York Times*, Jan. 3, 2008, p. A1. The second article ends with a quotation by one of this volume's authors, Professor Deborah Denno, who speaks strikingly to the issue of methods and their appearances, or representations: "States have adopted a process that appears humane because it looks like medical treatment, Professor Denno said. But looks can be deceiving, she added" (p. A16).

2. "General Clears Army Officer of Crime in Abu Ghraib Case," *New York Times*, Jan. 11, 2008, and "Administration Is Rebuffed in a Ruling on Deportation," *New York Times*, Jan. 11, 2008, p. A17.

3. "Hanging and Amputation Find Favor in Iran Courts," *New York Times*, Jan. 11, 2008, p. A3.

4. Leon Shaskolsky Sheleff, *Ultimate Penalties: Capital Punishment, Life Imprisonment, Physical Torture* (Columbus: Ohio State University Press, 1987), p. 9.

5. Bob Woodward and Scott Armstrong, *The Brethren: Inside the Supreme Court* (New York: Simon and Schuster, 1979), p. 218. Thanks to Nikki Beisel for this reference.

6. Austin Sarat, ed., *The Cultural Lives of Capital Punishment* (Stanford: Stanford University Press, 2005), p. 1.

7. For the concept of "discursive surround," see Robin Wagner-Pacifici, *Discourse and Destruction: The City of Philadelphia vs. MOVE* (Chicago: University of Chicago Press, 1994), pp. 5–10.

8. Transcripts selected include recent (2007–2008) news articles and op-ed pieces from the *New York Times*; the transcript of the October 17–18, 2007, Senate Committee on the Judiciary confirmation hearings for Michael Mukasey, nominee for attorney general of the United States; oral arguments for the Supreme Court cases *Hamdan v. Rumsfeld* (2006) and *Baze v. Rees* (2008); the Supreme Court *Baze et al. v. Rees* opinion; the State of New Jersey Office of the Governor December 17, 2007, news release regarding elimination of the death penalty in New Jersey; and the *New Yorker* magazine January 21, 2008, interview with Michael McConnell, National Director of Intelligence.

9. Steven Hilgartner and Charles Bosk, "The Rise and Fall of Social Problems: A Public Arenas Model," *American Journal of Sociology* 94 (1988): 53–78.

10. Ibid., p. 54.

11. Ibid., p. 61.

12. David A. Snow, E. Burke Rochford, Jr., Steven K. Worden, and Robert D. Benford, "Frame Alignment Processes, Micromobilization, and Movement Participation," *American Sociological Review* 51, no. 4 (1986): 464–81. For a critique of Snow and Benford along these lines, see Myra Marx Ferree, "Resonance and Radicalism: Feminist Abortion Discourses in Germany and the United States," *American Journal of Sociology* 109, no. 2 (2003): 304–44.

13. Luc Boltanski and Laurent Thevenot, *On Justification: Economies of Worth*, trans. Catherine Porter (Princeton, N.J.: Princeton University Press, 2006), p. 14.

14. Ibid., p. 38.

15. "[W]e discuss defenses to an allegation that an interrogation method might violate any of the various criminal prohibitions discussed in Part II. We believe that *necessity* or self-defense could provide defenses to a prosecution." John Yoo, "Memorandum to William J. Haynes II, General Counsel for the Department of Defense. Re: Military Interrogation of Alien Unlawful Combatants Held Outside the United States," March 14, 2003, Office of Legal Counsel, U.S. Department of Justice, Declassified March 31, 2008, p. 2; italics added. .

16. Lawrence Wright, "The Spymaster," *New Yorker*, Jan. 21, 2008, pp. 42–59, at p. 53.

17. Boltanski and Thevenot's ideas about situational beings who are considered to be irrelevant when the justificatory world simply doesn't recognize them is also applicable here. Boltanski and Thevenot, *On Justification*, p. 216.

18. Max Weber, *From Max Weber: Essays in Sociology*, ed. Hans Heinrich Gerth and C. Wright Mills (New York: Oxford University Press, 1958), p. 77. On the pacification process, see Norbert Elias, *The Civilizing Process: Power and Civility*, trans. Edmund Jephcott, vol. 2 (New York: Pantheon, 1982), p. 235.

19. Paul Kahn, *Sacred Violence: Torture, Terror and Sovereignty* (Ann Arbor: University of Michigan Press, 2008) p. 113; italics added.

20. Leon Shaskolsky Sheleff makes a similar point about the essential political nature of state violence, including capital punishment. Sheleff, *Ultimate Penalties*, p. 12.

21. For example, Elaine Scarry, *The Body in Pain: The Making and Unmaking of the World* (New York: Oxford University Press, 1985), and Randall Collins, *Violence: A Micro-Sociological Theory* (Princeton, N.J.: Princeton University Press, 2008).

22. Kim Lane Scheppele, "The International State of Emergency: Challenges to Constitutionalism after September 11," unpublished ms., 2007, p. 5.

23. Ibid., p. 1. See also Gordon Silverstein, "Balancing National Security and Civil Liberties," *American Bar Association Focus on Law Studies* 22, no. 2 (2007): 1–17, at 2.

24. Scheppele, "International State of Emergency," 25–30.

25. I am using Max Weber's concept of the "ideal type" here, a concept described by Wolfgang J. Mommsen as "basically nomological in nature; that is, they do not possess reality in any sense . . . nor do they have a normative status of any sort . . . [rather] . . . [t]hey are intended to measure the discrepancy between a particular segment of empirical reality and the constructed norm." Wolfgang J. Mommsen, *The Political and Social Theory of Max Weber* (Chicago: University of Chicago Press, 1989), pp. 123–24.

26. Chris Jochnick and Roger Normand, "The Legitimation of Violence: A Critical History of the Laws of War," *Harvard International Law Journal* 35, no. 49 (Winter 1994): 3.

27. Scarry, *Body in Pain*, p. 63.

28. Kahn, *Sacred Violence*, p. 58.

29. Ibid., p. 176. See also Meyer Kestnbaum, in his historical sociological description of modern warfare, which highlights risk in his recitation of the Clausewitzean factors of real war. Meyer Kestnbaum, "Mars Revealed: The Entry of Ordinary People into War among States," in *Remaking Modernity: Politics, History and Sociology*, ed. Julia Adams, Elisabeth S. Clemens, and Ann Shola Orloff (Durham, N.C.: Duke University Press, 2005), p. 262.

30. Execution victims may not be completely powerless to salvage or redeem moral personhood, however, according to scholars like Philip Smith, in

"Executing Executions: Aesthetics, Identity, and the Problematic Narratives of Capital Punishment Ritual," *Theory and Society* 25, no. 2 (April 1996): 235–61, at 236.

31. *Hamdan v. Rumsfeld*, No. 05-184, sec. 31, pp. 3–25.

32. Rosa Ehrenreich Brooks, "War Everywhere: Rights, National Security Law, and the Law of Armed Conflict in the Age of Terror," *University of Pennsylvania Law Review* 153 (December 2004): 675.

33. Carol Steiker, "Capital Punishment and American Exceptionalism," *Oregon Law Review* 81 (Spring 2002): 97.

34. Paul Kahn, "American Exceptionalism, Popular Sovereignty, and the Rule of Law," in *American Exceptionalism and Human Rights*, ed. Michael Ignatieff (Princeton, N.J.: Princeton University Press, 2005), pp. 198–222.

35. Greta Proctor, "Reevaluating Capital Punishment: The Fallacy of a Foolproof System, the Focus on Reform, and the International Factor," *Gonzaga Law Review* 43, no. 211 (2006–2007): 4 (on-line version).

36. Military Commissions Act, Public Law 109-366—October 17, 2006, 120 Stat. 2607.

37. Explanation of Position by Robert S. Hagen, Deputy Representative to the United Nations Economic and Social Council, on the Moratorium on the Use of the Death Penalty, in the Third Committee of the General Assembly, November 15, 2007, United States Mission to the United Nations website, USUN Press Release No. 309 (2007). Thanks to Kevin Kish for pointing out this overt contradiction.

38. Quoted in Christopher Einolf, "The Fall and Rise of Torture: A Comparative and Historical Analysis," *Sociological Theory* 25, no. 2 (2007): 101–21, at 102.

39. Memorandum for Alberto R. Gonzales, Counsel to the President. Re: Standards of Conduct for Interrogation under 18 U.S.C. 2340–2340A, Office of Assistant Attorney General, Washington, D.C., Department of Justice, August 1, 2002. Available at http://www.washingtonpost.com/wpsrv/politics/documents/cheney/torture_memo_aug2002.pdf.

40. Kim Lane Scheppele, "Hypothetical Torture in the 'War on Terrorism,'" *Journal of National Security Law and Policy* (University of the Pacific, McGeorge School of Law) 1 (2005): 285–340, at 298; italics added.

41. Ibid., p. 300.

42. Yoo, "Memorandum to William J. Haynes II, " 38.

43. In 2005, for example, Germany refused to extradite Mohammed Ali Hamadi to the United States to face charges of killing a Navy diver in the 1985 hijacking of a TWA airplane, on the grounds that he might face the death penalty. Nevertheless, as Kathryn King notes: "Viewed as functional inroads, the increasingly frequent decisions of the US Department of State and of the US military not to seek the death penalty as a condition of a European government's granting an American extradition request appear to constitute a widening

incursion into America's historic disregard for European opinion about the practice of capital punishment." Kathryn F. King, "The Death Penalty, Extradition, and the War against Terrorism: US Responses to European Opinion about Capital Punishment," *Buffalo Human Rights Law Review* 9, no. 161 (2003): 12.

44. Another recent focus of discussion about capital punishment was the December 2006 execution of Saddam Hussein. For reasons of space, I am not able to include this event in my analysis, but this event raises important issues that are explicitly linked to current practices of punishment for crimes against humanity, war crimes, and genocide.

45. The subject may have been thought closed, but not the practice. Christopher Einolf claims that, despite its formal abolition, "the practice of torture actually increased in the 20th century over the 19th." Christopher Einolf, "The Fall and Rise of Torture: A Comparative and Historical Analysis," *Sociological Theory* 25, no. 2 (2007): 101–21, at 101.

46. *Baze v. Rees*, at sec. 3, pp. 10–18.

47. Ibid., at sec. 11, pp. 14–17.

48. Ibid., at sec. 21, p. 24 to sec. 22, p. 4.

49. Max Weber, "Politics as a Vocation," in *From Max Weber: Essays in Sociology*, ed. H. H. Gerth and C. Wright Mills (New York: Oxford University Press, 1958). Paul Kahn highlights a completely different understanding of the essence of state power in contemporary *jus cogens* claims: "The sources of contemporary jus cogens claims have been, first of all, an idea of the ultimate moral value of the pre-political individual, and increasingly, an idea of an apolitical nature. A state has value, on this view, just to the degree that it furthers the norm of human dignity or preserves a natural environmental order. The *state becomes a means to ends that are defined apart from politics.*" Kahn, "American Exceptionalism," p. 220; italics added.

50. Carl von Clausewitz, *On War*, trans. from the German by J. J. Graham (Harmondsworth: Penguin, 1968), p. 119.

51. *Baze v. Rees,* at sec. 48, pp. 4–20.

52. *Baze et al. v. Rees*, Commissioner, Kentucky Department of Corrections, et al., No. 07-5439, argued January 7, 2008—decided April 16, 2008 (Roberts et al., JJ., concurring), p. 2.

53. Ibid. (Scalia, J., concurring).

54. In chap. 8 in this volume, Jürgen Martschukat draws attention to the purposive pain in historical executions.

55. Greta Proctor writes: "These debacles cast serious doubt on the presumed infallibility of scientific evidence. . . . A jury's misplaced reliance on erroneous evidence is most problematic where the punishment is ultimate and irrevocable—capital trials." Proctor, "Reevaluating Capital Punishment," p. 2.

56. *Baze v. Rees*, at sec. 27, p. 22 to sec. 29, p. 4; italics added.

57. *Baze et al. v. Rees* (Roberts et al., JJ., concurring), p. 1.

58. Scott Shane and Mark Mazzetti, "Tapes by C.I.A. Lived and Died to Save Image," *New York Times*, Dec. 30, 2007, p. A8.

59. Michael Mukasey, Senate Judiciary Committee Confirmation Hearings, October 18, 2007, Morning Session, p. 24 (downloaded transcript).

60. Adam Goldman, "ACLU: Pentagon Documents Highlight Interrogation Methods," *Associated Press*, April 30, 2008, available at http://hosted.ap.org/dynamic/stories/d/detainee_abuse_report?site=fltam&section=us.

61. Editorial, "A Pause from Death," *New York Times*, Dec. 20, 2007.

62. *Baze et al. v. Rees*, at pp. 11, 17 (Stevens, J., concurring).

63. Adam Liptak, "Does Death Penalty Save Lives? A New Debate," *New York Times*, Nov. 18, 2007, p. A1.

64. Randall Collins, "Three Faces of Cruelty: Towards a Comparative Sociology of Violence," *Theory and Society* 1, no. 4 (1974): 415–40, at 431.

65. Quoted in Wright, "Spymaster," at 52.

66. Jack Cloonan, "No Torture, No Exceptions," *Washington Monthly*, Jan.–Mar. 2008, available at http://www.washingtonmonthly.com/features/2008/0801.cloonan.html.

67. Austin Sarat, *When the State Kills: Capital Punishment and the American Condition* (Princeton, N.J.: Princeton University Press. 2002).

68. Quoted in Eileen Sullivan, "Waterboarding Is Torture," *Associated Press News Service*, Jan. 18, 2008; italics added.

69. Mukasey, Senate Judiciary Committee Confirmation Hearings, October 17, Afternoon Session, p. 12.

70. Carol Greenhouse, "Hegemony and Hidden Transcripts: The Discursive Arts of Neoliberal Legitimation," *American Anthropologist* 107, no. 3 (2005): 356–68, at 360.

71. Mukasey, Senate Judiciary Committee Confirmation Hearings, October 17, Afternoon Session, p. 12.

72. Ibid., October 18, Morning Session, p. 24.

73. Stuart Banner, quoted in Carol Steiker, "Capital Punishment and American Exceptionalism," *Oregon Law Review* 97, no. 81 (2002): 97–130, at 123.

74. Stuart Banner, *The Death Penalty: An American History* (Cambridge: Harvard University Press, 2002).

75. David Jacobs, Jason Carmichael, and Stephanie Kent, "Vigilantism, Current Racial Threat, and Death Sentences," *American Sociological Review* 70, no. 4 (2005): 656–77, at 671.

76. Scott Phillips, "Racial Disparities in the Capital of Capital Punishment," *Houston Law Review* 45 (2008): 807–40.

77. Military Commissions Act of 2006, at sec. 5, p. 16, to sec. 6, p. 8.

78. Jochnick and Normand, "Legitimation of Violence," p. 8.

79. Quoted in Paul Kramer, "The Water Cure," *New Yorker*, Feb. 25, 2008, p. 5 (downloaded version).

80. Amy Kaplan, "Where Is Guantanamo?" *American Quarterly* 57, no. 3 (2005): 831–58. See also Susan Willis, "Guantanamo's Symbolic Economy," *New Left Review* 39 (May–June 2006): 123–31.

81. *Hamdan v. Rumsfeld*, at sec. 44, p. 20 to sec. 45, p. 18.

82. On these peculiarities of sovereignty, see Austin Sarat, quoted in Steiker, "Capital Punishment and American Exceptionalism," p. 117.

83. Quoted in Ralph Blumenthal, "After Hiatus, States Set Wave of Executions," *New York Times*, May 3, 2008, pp. A1, A15.

10

||||||||||||||||||||||||||||||||||||||||||||||||||

Making Difference
Modernity and the Political Formations of Death

Peter Fitzpatrick

> I am against the death penalty but the issue of its aboli-
> tion is not a closed discourse, it's a matter which seeks
> itself, which is still looking for itself.
> —Jacques Derrida, seminar on Time and the Death
> Penalty, University of Trieste, November 16, 2000

To continue seeking in Derrida's epigraphic terms may seem to contradict
the telos of an unswerving "road to abolition," but to continue seeking is,
rather, to intimate an open, perhaps a more sinuous, road. Bluntly, self-
styled "modern" political formation both sustains and counters the death
penalty, and it does so in a way, along a road, that is antinomic yet constituent of the formation itself. It is the contrary dimensions of the antinomy as they combine in different realized forms that either diminishes the
death penalty or sustains it. And even as the antinomy leaves the road to
abolition open, it still provides the abolitionary "matter which seeks itself,
which is still looking for itself."[1] The antinomy, in short, is generative. We
are not dealing here with an aporia. We are not, to adopt its Greek meaning, without a road. Nor are we without the intimation of a terminus, a
coming to the "matter which seeks itself."

The argument for such an intimation proceeds this way. Without
some transcendent resolution, a resolution disallowed by modernity, a
political formation as a realized form of the antinomy cannot fully accommodate both of its opposed dimensions. One of those dimensions,
as we shall see, is a formative force of hyperdeterminacy, of quasi-tran-
scendent self-constitution, a determinacy that would take all possibility

of relation into itself and thence assume a confident competence to deal death. The other dimension, the opposed formative force, carries an ultimate openness and responsiveness to life that is imperative for our being-together in modernity. This dimension irreducibly denies the death penalty.[2] To effect *modern* political formation, so the argument continues, the dimension that would sustain the death penalty would have to give way to the dimension countering it. The conclusion then becomes this: modern political formation and the death penalty are incompatible. Adhering to the death penalty reveals, to adapt an enviable title, that we have not yet been modern.[3]

As if to compensate for that overschematic opening, in the first section of this chapter I seek questioning orientations of formation and antinomy in some of the recent literature on the death penalty. In the second section, I amplify those orientations, bringing them together in an account of the political formation of modernity. The constituent dimensions of that formation are then differentiated in the next section, and differentiated in a way that reveals how the "sovereign" affirmation of one dimension embeds the death penalty and denies the modernity of the formation.[4] This outcome entails more than a regret for a modernity not yet achieved. The actual political formation necessarily implied by adopting the death penalty is shown to be continuedly impossible.

Orientations

The three orientations to be derived from the recent literature on the death penalty can be abruptly called exceptionalism, sovereignty, and death. As for exceptionalism, the standard pronouncement is that, of a collection of countries usually described as democratic and western, the United States stands alone in not having abolished the death penalty. Perhaps the most spectacular recent eruption of debate on exceptionalism comes with an issue of *Punishment and Society* in 2005, in which David Garland strikingly dissented from two recent instances of the genre and was responded to no less demonstratively.[5] The detail is not of immediate concern, but the general orientation would sharply set something distinctive of the United States which sustains the death penalty against an essential similarity between the United States and other western countries, the difference between them being only an "American tardiness in enacting full legal abolition" because of certain institutional peculiarities.[6]

My promiscuous intent is to adopt both orientations implicitly and to extend them explicitly to a third that would contradict each by denying the premise of abolition in western countries, or in "Europe" to adopt the more common locus of comparison. Jon Yorke's revisionist analysis of the death penalty in Europe, focusing mainly on the regime of the European Convention for the Protection of Human Rights, reveals that, far from the death penalty's being quite abolished, "[i]t is merely suspended; at a greater distance from some states, but it is tentatively hovering and its shadow is close over others."[7] And any sanguine expectation that there may still be a discernable road to abolition is dampened in the observation that "[i]t is difficult to pinpoint a general theory to suggest why the death penalty was renounced."[8]

The next orientation to be touched on is considered more extensively. It concerns the remarkable, not to say astonishing, status of modern sovereignty in its relation to the death penalty. Some of the most perceptive, even oppositional, analysts of the death penalty accord sovereignty the intrinsic, even constituent power to impose the death penalty.[9] A variation extends this to a power over life—a biopower or, in Achille Mbembe's terms, a necropower.[10] Here my concern is with orientations, and with disturbing them, and for now I will do no more than qualify the mantric reliance on authorities supporting this notion of sovereignty, and then amplify the disturbance by considering what could be called the Foucault question.

Taking two of the canonical authors summarily invoked, I start with Thomas Hobbes. Certainly Hobbes does recognize capital punishment and, as with punishment generally, for Hobbes it is something imposed by a sovereign, and Hobbes's sovereign Leviathan has unlimited power—although it should be noted in a preliminary way that Hobbes accords this Leviathan so empowered the status of a god even if a "mortal god."[11] Closer inspection reveals a Leviathan who conforms to Hobbes's dictum that "God made Kings for the People and not People for Kings," and reveals also a Leviathan who depends on a natural sociality and owes primal duties to the people.[12] More pointedly as regards the death penalty, and superordinate as Leviathan may be, Leviathan is still a creation of the human drive to preserve and enhance life, and if the sovereign Leviathan should seek, no matter how "legitimately," to take life away, the sovereign can be resisted to the utmost.[13] In short, one could say, along with James Martel, that "the project in *Leviathan*" is "one that does not so much build authority and sovereignty as call it into question."[14]

Inexcusably, doubtless, Immanuel Kant can be accommodated just as briefly, and he will be required to produce the same questionable conjunction of sovereignty, deism, and the people, even if less robustly than does Hobbes. Notoriously, for Kant, the sovereign's power to exact capital punishment would extend to a situation where "[e]ven if a civil society were to be dissolved by the consent of all its members (e.g., if a people inhabiting an island decided to separate and disperse throughout the world), the last murderer remaining in prison would first have to be executed."[15] Soon after something of a qualification supervenes. If the accomplices to a murder, who as such "must suffer death," were so many "that the state, in order to have no such criminals in it, could soon find itself without subjects [without a people], . . . then the sovereign must also have it in his power . . . to assume the role of judge (to represent him) and pronounce a judgement that decrees for the criminals a sentence other than capital punishment."[16] This seems apt since Kant introduces the section of *The Metaphysics of Morals* where these scenarios unfold with some recognition of their demotic dependence. There, in the beginning, we find that the members of society "in a civil condition . . . are united for giving law" and a "*state (civitas)* is a union of a multitude of human beings under laws of right."[17] What all of this may import for the sovereign authority to deal, or not to deal, death remains moot because "a people" can neither inquire into the origin of that authority nor "judge otherwise than as the present head of state (*summus imperans*) wills it to do."[18] The "law" sustaining such supreme authority assumes the status of a secular theology, it being a law "so holy (inviolable) that it is already a crime even to call it in doubt *in a practical way*, and so to suspend its effect for a moment," it being likewise a practical imperative to regard this law as if it came from a divine source.[19]

My remaining questioning of sovereignty's death comes by way of the Foucault question. This is a question prompted by numerous recent engagements with Michel Foucault on the death penalty, a question of whether the death penalty has a place in his rendition of modern society.[20] Here we can begin to connect sovereignty with some basis for considering the claimed exceptionalism touched on earlier. Foucault could be seen, with justification, as necessarily opposed to the death penalty. For him, modern society with its tentacular powers, disciplinary power and "biopower," displace a society that sovereignly depended on the power to deal death.[21] And, indeed, Foucault did indicate that the operative effect of such powers in modern society was incompatible with the death penalty.[22] Matters are more intriguingly mixed, however.

The main source for Foucault's setting disciplinary powers and such against deathly sovereign assertion is the final part of the first volume of *The History of Sexuality*.[23] He begins this part by noting that, "for a long time, one of the characteristic privileges of sovereign power was the right to decide life and death. In a formal sense, it derived no doubt from the ancient *patria potestas* that granted the father of the Roman family the right to 'dispose' of the life of his children and his slaves," this right being "absolute and unconditional."[24] The extravagance and inaccuracy of this assertion can be ignored because Foucault merely contrasts it with the conditioned power of the monarchical sovereign. For such a sovereign, the power to deal death was central, but it could only be exercised in war or through law. Then he notes the shift from this sovereign power to threaten and effect death from afar, as it were, to new forms of disciplinary power and biopower "utterly incongruous" with it, powers that minutely invest "life," constituting and regulating a "population" and its members.[25] That change does not entirely displace the sovereign "right to death"; rather, there is "a parallel shift in the right of death, or at least a tendency to align itself with the exigencies of a life-administering power and to define itself accordingly."[26] That defining did nonetheless mark, for Foucault, an essential shift:

> As soon as power gave itself the function of administering life, its reason for being and the logic of its exercise . . . made it more and more difficult to apply the death penalty. How could power exercise its highest prerogatives by putting people to death, when its main role was to ensure, sustain, and multiply life, to put this life in order? For such a power, execution was at the same time a limit, a scandal, and a contradiction. Hence capital punishment could not be maintained except by invoking less the enormity of the crime itself than the monstrosity of the criminal, his incorrigibility, and the safeguard of society. One had the right to kill those who represented a kind of biological danger to others.[27]

This, however, was a matter of the death penalty adjusting to a mode of power on which it has been made contingent. It is as if the death penalty is carried forward with a sovereignty that endures for reasons no longer germane to it, a sovereignty that finds its own continuance now in the role it plays in support of the newly predominant powers.[28]

These were powers "whose highest function was perhaps no longer to kill, but to invest life through and through."[29] Their formative force was conjointly individualizing and totalizing, oriented toward both minute particularity and total comprehension.[30] Yet we also find that this same mixture remains capable at an extreme of unleashing "murderous power, or in other words, the old sovereign right to take life," Foucault instancing "Nazi society" where that deathly power was accorded ultimate effect, thus rendering the state under Nazism "an absolutely suicidal State."[31] Yet further, uncontainable "life," says Foucault "constantly escapes" these new powers that would encompass and administer it.[32]

Bringing this closer to a concern with political formation and modernity, and Foucault again:

> [W]hat might be called a society's 'threshold of modernity' has been reached when the life of the species is wagered on its own political strategies. For millennia man remained what he was for Aristotle: a living animal with the additional capacity for political existence; modern man is an animal whose politics places his existence as a living being in question.[33]

This same threshold of modernity sees the correlate entry of a "critical ontology," one entailing "a permanent critique of ourselves" and "a permanent creation of ourselves."[34] All of which imports a "governing" of oneself.[35] This responsibility for and as ourselves is made imperative by the death of God, by the elevation of a transcendent point of resolution that is apart from ourselves—something clung to by Kant, for example.[36] Not that the lineaments of the deity disappear and there is some "finally delivered judgement of his nonexistence," but, rather, we are left reliant on "the now constant space of our experience, an experience that is enduringly shaped by the death of God."[37]

With an accumulating obviousness, I come now to the third and final orientation derived from recent literature on the death penalty: that to do with death—with death as apposed to life or complicit with it. Here, and for quite a while after, my generative companion is Jacques Derrida (the more extensive engagement with him will come shortly, and after an introduction by way of his acknowledged progenitor, Maurice Blanchot). As with Foucault, we again face a seeming contradiction at the outset. Derrida's conspicuous and sustained opposition to the death penalty, asserted both politically and philosophically, is at one with a poststructural rejection of any fixedly surpassing predetermination. We cannot, for example, find the death penalty to be inexorable by resorting to a predetermining Freudian drive fixated on cruelty or death.[38] Yet it seems that Derrida would have it that, "[i]n order to maintain an essential aspect of its sovereignty, the state must reserve the right to impose the penalty of death, at least in exceptional cases."[39] In a more moderated vein, he sees the death penalty as, besides war, "the best emblem of the sovereign power of the state over the life and death of the citizen."[40] Yet in a further and now crucial moderation, Derrida reassures us that "one cannot place the death penalty in question in a radical, principled, unconditional way without contesting or limiting the sovereignty of the sovereign," that same "sovereignty, without which the death penalty has no chance."[41] This is a sovereignty that, for Derrida, is "the heritage of a barely secularized theology," it being itself "a theological phantasm or concept."[42] That same questioning, then, would extend to "the political theology of the death penalty" to "the *welding* of ontology" to this theology in a way that has "held together . . . the *political.*"[43] The stakes are suddenly even more momentous, and I now leave these orientations derived from the literature and approach them from another and cohering direction.

Laws of Death

My next concern is with law. This is not just a disciplinary indulgence. Law embeds modern political formation—a claim that I consider here shortly. And it is through law after all that the death penalty is imposed. The affinity between law and death is often noted. For Foucault the conjunction of "law, death . . . and sovereignty" was axiomatic, and in modernity law is still for Foucault "armed . . . *par excellence*" by death.[44] Walter Benjamin, furthermore, would equate the death penalty with "law itself in its origin, in its very order."[45] Instances could be multiplied, but Mitchell Dean aptly summarizes a common view in which law is a "principal instrument" of sovereignty, whence it is "backed up by coercive sanctions ultimately grounded in the right of death of the sovereign."[46]

I return to that formulation shortly, but let me move on for now by way of Blanchot's ostensibly disparate writings on law and death. On one side, as it were, the law in *The Madness of the Day* describes herself as "the angel of discord, murder, and the end."[47] Elsewhere Blanchot finds: "The law kills. Death is always the horizon of the law."[48] However in yet another elsewhere, and in the company of Saint-Just of all people, we find a different law, one that must "never . . . encroach upon life itself," must never entail endowing a sovereign with "the right to death."[49] The horizon of death now becomes one at which law stops short in an inability to take life.

There follows the crux, and it comes as a distinction between the law and laws: "the law is always above any particular law."[50] So death for Blanchot can be seen as the horizon of the law in quite another way. Here the horizon does not simply contain but, rather, connects incipiently or integrally with what is beyond. The horizon thence becomes not only the condition and quality of law's contained and distinct existence but also an opening onto all that lies beyond and is other to that existence. It is in this way that, for Blanchot, death "raises existence to being," that "death becomes being."[51] This death "is man's possibility, his chance, it is through death that the future of a finished world is still there for us."[52] And this is death as a liberated "nothingness," a nothingness that "is the creator of the world in man."[53] Death as horizon here is not only the end but also the beginning, the opening to and making possible of a coming from being to existence: death is "the Other."[54]

For death as this horizon of the law, however, what we have with Blanchot is not now an explicit affinity between death and law but, rather, parallel descriptions. So, law for Blanchot is (also) that which is quite lacking in fixity, quite uncontained and unsubordinated, a self-affirmation made "without reference to anything higher: to it alone, pure transcendence."[55] This law takes its instituted existence from a being beyond. "Let us grant," says Blanchot, "that the law is obsessed with exteriority, by that which beleaguers it and from which it separates via the very separation that institutes it as form, in the very movement by which it formulates this exteriority as law."[56] Such law is the same as what Blanchot would also see as *the* law, as the law of the law, see as "a responsibility . . . towards the Other" that is "irreducible to all forms of legality through which one necessarily tries to regulate it," and which ultimately "cannot be enounced in any already formulated language."[57]

Returning to Derrida now for a constituent relation between this "exterior" law beyond determinacy and law in its instituted existence, I rely on various works of his but initially on "Force of Law." In "Force of Law" Derrida would want to "make explicit or perhaps produce a difficult and unstable distinction between justice and *droit*, between justice (infinite, incalculable, rebellious to rule and foreign to symmetry)" on the one hand and, on the other, "the exercise of justice as law or right, legitimacy or legality, a . . . calculable apparatus . . . , a system of regulated and coded prescriptions."[58] The distinction, to emphasize, is "unstable" for the two sides are always in protean combination. So justice for Derrida imports an unlimited responsiveness to the other, an "other" that extends to an illimitable alterity or otherness. Such an unlimited responsiveness of justice is impossible "in itself," always beyond attainment. To be made possible, in the sense of becoming existent, and given operative force, justice must be "cut" into, reduced, and in a certain sense denied.[59] For Derrida, the legal decision cuts into and enacts justice, even while denying justice as illimitably responsive. In this, "law is the element of calculation."[60] Law, in the legal decision, can never be "presently and fully just."[61] So, rather than starkly and simply attributing a dissipating "force" to justice, Derrida would see it as dependent on the determinate presence effected by the legal decision. Derrida would go as far as to find in law, and elsewhere, some reductive ability to contain responsiveness, to ensure that "the aleatory margin . . . remains homogenous with calculation, within the order of the calculable."[62]

Yet, if law is necessary for justice, justice is also necessary for law. The bringing of law to bear, the legal decision, the very call for such decision— these all involve a responsiveness that cannot be contained. Not only is it a matter that "no existing, coded rule can . . . guarantee absolutely" what will be brought to bear or decided, but also neither the bringing to bear nor the decision can ever fully saturate its own context, can ever "provide itself with the infinite information and the unlimited knowledge of conditions, rules or hypothetical imperatives that could justify it."[63] Law must ever inchoately respond to an uncontainable justice, to a justice that "exceeds law but at the same time motivates movement, history, and becoming of juridical rationality."[64] Yet law's rendering of justice is incipiently coextensive with it, so much so that "justice" cannot be peremptorily aligned with justice as virtue, as the Good, for "justice is always very close to the bad, even to the worst, for it can always be reappropriated by the most perverse calculation."[65] So, although "justice exceeds law and calculation," law has also and somehow to be conceived as "exceeding" justice.[66] We have to calculate, "incalculable justice *commands* calculation," and for this we must "negotiate the relation between the calculable and the incalculable." This imperative "does not *properly* belong either to justice or law. It only belongs to either realm by exceeding each in the direction of the other."[67] What will prove central to my argument, then, will be this negotiation and the dissonance it involves, a dissonance in which law and justice are mutually constituent yet distinct and able to exceed each other. What is involved here is not, and cannot be, a negotiation aimed at securing a deal or some surpassing compromise. Law and justice—or, put another way, the determinate and the responsive dimensions of law—each retains a distinct ultimacy.[68]

It is from this divide that modern law's relation to sovereignty is generated. If law is to be illimitably responsive, it must be quite unrestrained, never bound to anything before it. It must, says Derrida, "be without history, genesis, or any possible derivation."[69] Yet law's unrestrained responsiveness, its lack of any confining ties to the past or to anything else, its vacuity or nothingness, result in its not having any enduring content of its own. It always depends for its very content and for much of its force on some power apart from itself. "Law itself," says Jean-Luc Nancy, "does not have a form for what would need to be its own sovereignty."[70]

There is point, then, to the jurisprudential perception of law's constituent dependence on such a sovereignty apart. Yet, with law's refusal of any primal attachment, this dependence, this taking of content from such as sovereign or society, has always to subsist with that opposed jurisprudential tradition elevating law's autonomy. That autonomy is "founded" in the illimitability of law, in law's insistent inability to be contained by any of the powers on which it depends for its content and for much of its force. And, no matter how seemingly abject law's borrowings, it will autonomously endow these with its own content. This content will often differ markedly from the contributed contents. Also, law will not simply absorb and re-create the contents of a given sovereignty or of a given society. It will, in its responsiveness, take on many and diverse sovereign or social configurations. And even where law determinately elevates one such configuration over another, this is neither to elevate the included pervasively nor to exclude the other finally.

So far, then, we have components of an ontology that awaits, in Derrida's terms, "*welding*" to a sovereign theologic that has "held together . . . the *political* (at least where it is dominated by a thought of the *polis* or the sovereign state)," all of which is signaled by Derrida as entailing a questioning of the death penalty.[71] In a summary way, these components in or as law can be seen as law's determinate existence for one, its responsiveness to justice or alterity being the other. It is such responsiveness and the vacuity of content it presupposes that impel the divide in law's relation to death and to the death penalty. Law's vacuity of content, its lack of ipseity, renders it reliant on sovereign assertion apart from it—an assertion that, repeating Derrida's claim, can be the "sovereignty without which the death penalty has no chance."[72] Thence we have law's constituent and, as it turns out, vicarious relation to death as terminal. That same vacuity, however, imports law's utter openness, its illimitable responsiveness to life, its being of death where death is a making possible—death, in Blanchot's terms now, as "the Other."[73] This law, the law of the law—still with Blanchot—is "irreducible to all forms of legality through which one necessarily tries to regulate it" and, ultimately, "cannot be enounced in any formulated language."[74]

Modernity and Political Formations of Death

Blanchot's conclusion is hardly propitious if some measure is to be ascribed to political formations of a death that, borrowing now from Françoise Dastur, "exposes us to the immeasurability of something we can never experience."[75] It is time to return to the measuring intimated in the orientations toward the death penalty described and disturbed earlier. Three possible measurings can be extracted from these orientations: an insistence of the people, a secular theology seemingly necessary for conceiving of a surpassing sovereignty, and the challenge posed to sovereignty by a modern governing of life. Each of these is now considered in turn and cumulatively.

The People

My tendentious concern here, still with Derrida's help, is to constitute a "people" that is effective but immune to any preoriented containment, whether in the cause of the death penalty or of any other.[76] Letting an instance carry the argument for now, there is a certain declaration made "in the Name and by the authority of the good People of these Colonies," and made by their "Representatives of the United States of America." This demotic scene can be generalized to become one of the constitutive contributions required characteristically of "the people" in modern political formation. Inevitably, then, we come to a classic conundrum: "the people" create the polity, yet, as Lindahl incisively notes, "the people" is incapable of coming together to constitute itself as a political unity and from there institute a political and legal order; rather, they come to be a people through the creation of that order.[77] So this very people, in a feat of what Derrida would call "fabulous retroactivity,"[78] is a creation of what it is taken as creating, a creature of the law.

The formative dimensions of this law can be discerned in Jean-Jacques Rousseau's rendition of the classic conundrum just considered: for a people to be "formed . . . the effect would have to become the cause; the social spirit which must be the product of social institutions would have to preside over the setting up of those institutions; men would have to have already become before the advent of the law that which they became as a result of the law."[79] The dimensions of such a law are those of any law, of the law delved into in the last section. It is the law combining its achieved determinacy with a responsiveness to the ever-originating possibility beyond that determinacy. Perhaps most obviously, the people is a creation of what could be called laws of immediate formation, such as the constitution, laws to do with immigration and citizenship, electoral laws, laws to do with mental capacity, and laws providing the definitive processes of demotic assertion. In even more encompassing terms, however, it is law that provides the continuate normative terms of the people's being-together. The lawgiver for Rousseau generates social "bonds" that are "lasting": "Laws are, properly speaking, only the conditions of civil association."[80]

Mapping these dimensions of law now onto the political formation of "the people," despite its elusive quality, political appeals to the people in such as the Declaration of Independence often assume a widespread demotic purchase, yet they are not perceived as deception. And political appeals generally to "the people" are not confined to a determinate people within a particular polity—to those who have the vote, for example. It would not be considered an adequate or even an apt taking account of "the people" to claim that the people were taken account of in part— that part who could vote, or that part in existence when a putative social contract was entered into centuries before, and so on. Yet "the people" is also taken to be capable of partition and to have some correspondence to rendition in part. As Giorgio Agamben would confirm, "[t]he people is neither the all nor the part, neither the majority nor the minority. Instead, it is that which can never coincide with itself, as all or as part, that which infinitely remains or resists in each division."[81]

In short, and this interim conclusion will be elaborated on shortly, "the people" is an essentially unresolved condition—"beyond the current state of . . . definition," to borrow from Derrida[82]—a condition mediating between "its" determinate emplacements and "the people" beyond such emplacement, including "its" alterity, an alterity importing the possibility that "its" determinacy can be ever otherwise. And, when used in situations similar to that in the Declaration of Independence, like all good origins, such as the myth of origin, the concept of "the people" has to accommodate not just some specific originary conjunction of the determinate and what is beyond it but also their conjoining continuously. The origin has iteratively to endure as the origin of who or what "we" are now, to this day, as Derrida would have it.[83] Further, this accommodation is something rightful, the correlate of that "rectitude" found in the declaration. With its irresolution and its incipience of alterity, the people cannot be rendered in a set factuality. Its composition is of the ever-originating law.

I now approach the essence of this law of political formation by way of another antinomy taken from Derrida, that between the unconditional and the conditioned. I begin with an instance, one where Derrida explicitly invokes the law, that relating to "hospitality," including a "cosmopolitanism" reworked by Derrida in terms of this hospitality.[84] Derrida advances an unconditional "law" of hospitality that is "transgressive, outside the law, like a lawless law, *nomos anomos*, law above the laws and law outside the law."[85] That is, as it were, one side of the antinomy. The other would be applied laws of hospitality, laws which "limit and condition . . . *the* law of hospitality":[86]

[E]ven while keeping itself above the laws of hospitality, *the* unconditional law of hospitality needs the laws, it *requires* them. This demand is constitutive. It wouldn't be effectively unconditional, the law, if it didn't *have to become* effective, concrete, determined, if that were not its being as having-to-be. It would risk being abstract, utopian, illusory, and so turning over into its opposite. In order to be what it is, *the* law thus needs the laws, which, however, deny it, or at any rate threaten it, sometimes corrupt or pervert it. And must always be able to do this.

For this pervertibility is essential, irreducible, necessary to. The perfectibility of laws is at this cost. And therefore their historicity. And vice versa, conditional laws would cease to be laws of hospitality if they were not guided, given inspiration, given aspiration, required, even, by the law of unconditional hospitality. These two regimes of law, of *the* law and the laws, are thus both contradictory, antinomic, and inseparable. They both imply and exclude each other, simultaneously. They incorporate one another at the moment of excluding one another, they are dissociated at the moment of enveloping one another.[87]

For emphasis now, and returning to the other side as it were: "Only an unconditional hospitality can give meaning and practical rationality to a concept of hospitality. Unconditional hospitality exceeds juridical, political, or economic calculation. But no thing and no one happens or arrives without it."[88] Without it, "we would have no concept of hospitality in general and would not even be able to determine any rules for conditional hospitality (with its rituals, its legal status, its norms, its national or international conventions)."[89] Yet, to repeat somewhat, the unconditional is nothing without instantiation, without the conditioned. In all, "[p]olitical, juridical, and ethical responsibilities have their place, if they take place, only in this transaction . . . between these two hospitalities, the unconditional and the conditional."[90]

Taking one further instance of the antinomy between the unconditional and the conditional—one of pointed relevance to the concerns of this collection, that to do with forgiveness—after noting several conditioned encapsulations of forgiveness (he instances amnesty, acquittal, "some political therapy of reconciliation"), Derrida goes on to assert:

> [I]t must never be forgotten . . . that all that refers to a certain idea of pure and unconditional forgiveness, without which this discourse [of forgiveness conditioned] would not have the least meaning. What complicates the question of 'meaning' is . . . : pure and unconditional forgiveness, in order to have its own meaning, must have no 'meaning,' no finality, even no intelligibility.[91]

If, however, and Derrida would add, "one wants, and it is necessary, forgiveness to become effective, concrete, historic," it must become conditional and, presumably, thence have meaning; but "[t]hese two poles, *the unconditional and the conditional,* are absolutely heterogeneous, and must remain irreducible to one another. They are nonetheless indissociable."[92] Being so indissociable, and with one of the two constituent elements having no meaning, leaves the not-inconsiderable challenge of a meaning that has to have no meaning if it is to carry meaning. And still in a less than encouraging vein, Derrida has in a broadly cognate context spoken of "an impossibility of substantializing."[93]

How, then, can some quiddity be attributed to what "is" this impossible combining? Staying with the cognate, Derrida can be taken as offering a lineament of substance with the invocation of "what lets singular beings (anyone) 'live together.'"[94] What this "what" may be could then be conceived, minimally, as a negative ontology—using the phrase somewhat more positively than is usual. If there were no unconditonality, albeit made effective, there could be no "living together," no being together. In the absence of the pure unconditional, the existence of any togetherness would be a terminal stasis. Its truth would be, as Nancy would have it, "the truth of death," death of the terminal, enclosing variety.[95] Looked at another way, and adapting Foucault now, the very line or limit that marks out a conditioned determinacy is created by an unconditionality that "incessantly crosses and re-crosses" that line or limit.[96]

Returning to our instances, perhaps an obviousness to the unconditional now emerges. It is not simply a matter that unconditional hospitality is desirable because it facilitates sociality, although it does do that. Rather, it is imperative for sociality. The holding back from such hospitality, the containing of some part of being together as immune to an engaging hospitality, would require a totalized comprehension, both to hold the part in an ungiving stasis and to predetermine its relation or possible relation to everything else.[97] That would entail a further appearance of "the truth of death." One could say all of that about any Derridean unconditionality, but there are further and poignant reasons to do so with being together when it comes to forgiveness. Hannah Arendt now: "Without being forgiven, released from the consequences of what we have done, our capacity to act would, as it were, be confined to one single deed from which we could never recover: we would remain the victim of its consequences forever."[98] And, still with Arendt, our ability to act in the continuate responsiveness of being together depends on unconditional forgiveness: "Only through . . . constant mutual release from what they do can men remain free agents, only by constant willingness to change their minds and start again can they be trusted with so great a power as that to begin something new."[99]

Other exemplars of Derridean unconditionality could be explored,[100] but I return now to the people and to law, claiming that status for both of them. The way is eased by Derrida's finding that we are "caught up" in a sociality that is something moving yet a bond, a sociality that is "a law, perhaps the very essence of law," a law that is "prior to all organized *socius*, all *políteia*, all determined 'government,' *before* all 'law.' . . . Let's get this right: prior to all *determined* law, *qua* natural law or positive law, but not prior to law *in general*."[101] Here Derrida can be taken as fusing the people and law along the dimensions of unconditionality and the conditioned. As we saw, "the people" could be conceived as both an illimitable preexistent, or unconditional, and as determinate, as conditioned. Likewise with law. Although law was also configured in terms of unconditional justice and conditioned law, law itself in any instantiation constituently combined the unconditional and the conditioned.

Finally, in this section on the insistence of the people, we reach an aptly concluding question of what insistence, what force the people can bring to bear. Perhaps it is only some sovereign activating force of the conditional that combines formatively with a quiescent unconditional. As we saw in this section, and by way of a negative ontology, there could be no formed conditional in the absence of the unconditional. That could still leave the positively formative force to the conditional. Yet we also saw that unconditional hospitality and unconditional forgiveness were imperative if there is to be a formed and a sustained sociality. However, that does not bring us to the point where the people itself would have a positively formative force as unconditional. Such a force can be discerned in a return to Derrida's invocation of "what lets singular beings (anyone) 'live together,'" beings in their unconditional singularity and prior to any conditioned constitution.[102] If such beings were simply singular yet came to live together, along with the commonality that would entail, the only available commonality would be one in which they were definable and completely the same as each other. Singularity would be lost. Singularities in common, then, require and generate a commonality that is apart from them, a commonality conditioned yet responsive to singularity—that is, illimitably responsive. The law again—and again in constituent concordance with the people.

Secular Theology

Moving on now to the second measuring derived from the orientations toward the death penalty surveyed at the outset, that being a secular theology seemingly necessary to conceive of a surpassing sovereignty, allow me again to consider the ur-instance of a certain declaration. What it declares into existence is not simply the people of law. The people is also an amply acknowledged endowment of God. There would seem to be two gods involved, or the two dimensions of the monotheism of the Abrahamic religions, the Christian being the operative one here. The first dimension invokes "the Laws of Nature and of Nature's God," which laws "entitle" a people to a "separate and equal station." This would seem to be the god of deism, a god of nature, a god already instructed by Malebranche not "to disturb the simplicity of his ways,"[103] a god whose constituent laws are enduringly determinate and knowable as such. It would seem to be the same god invoked as a "Creator" that endows people with "certain unalienable Rights," including the right to "Life," rights that impel them to form "Government" so as to secure these rights.

When it comes to the formative and performative declaration itself, however, a more evident theism is invoked. This resort is to "the Supreme Judge of the world" who is appealed to "for the rectitude of our intentions," the intentions of "the Representatives" who "declare, that These United Colonies are, and of Right ought to be Free and Independent States." Judging and being the store of rectitude require qualities akin to those of the other god of monotheism, the god of revelation and nature confounded, a god of alterity, a god ranging beyond any determinate, any existent order.

Occidental political formation in modernity, if not of modernity, has combined these imperatives in neodeific terms. Nietzsche's prescient madman, in announcing the death of God to his uncomprehending audience, speculated on what "sacred games" we would now have to invent in order to secure atonement, at-one-ment.[104] Nietzsche provided one answer with the "new idol" of the sovereign nation-state.[105] As we saw earlier with Derrida, and as the classical sources of Hobbes and Kant at least intimated, sovereignty was "the heritage of a barely secularized theology," it being itself "a theological phantasm or concept."[106] Like its monotheistic antecedent, the sovereign nation-state combines a determinate existence with an unconstrained efficacy, a self-enclosing with indefinite extension, the existent combined acquisitively with what is ever beyond it.

The stark counter to such hyperdeterminacy is that sovereignty is and has to be unconditional.[107] Sovereignty joins other mediate matter where the impossibility (yet necessity) of combining the unconditional and the conditioned is accommodated. So, forgiveness, law, and so on as mediate between the unconditional and the conditioned can be neither of these definitively, yet they are of both. Likewise with sovereignty. Of course, sovereignty is usually associated with the making conditioned in and as itself, with bringing what is beyond into a unified and surpassing assertion. It is, to take the first of what will soon be several borrowings from Derrida's *Rogues*, the very force of an achieved ipseity.[108] Yet, departing from Derrida momentarily, there is also an antithetical sovereignty. This is a sovereignty "opposed to mastery or domination."[109] It is a sovereignty that for Georges Bataille is nothing.[110] Nancy, explicitly following Bataille, would also find that "sovereignty is nothing" and would add emphatically that it is "bare," an "empty place."[111] And Nancy, furthermore, would equate the "nothing" of sovereignty with "the *cum*, the *with*" of being-with, of community, a "*with* deprived of substance."[112].Such a sovereignty is necessarily deprived of a fixity of conditioned substance if it is to accommodate the illimitable unconditionality of our being together. This, then, is a sovereignty, returning to Derrida now, of the "absolutely" open, a sovereignty that "engenders like a generative principle of life."[113]

How, indeed, could sovereignty be conceived of otherwise if it is to secure the commitment of "subjects," a commitment to all that is to come in and as its "rule"? If it were confined to a conditioned ipseity, it would subject only those who were thoroughly subordinated by its presently looming force, by its felt factuality. Without more, the merely conditioned will always lack, will always deliquesce, when facing what transformatively comes to it from beyond its conditioned existence. Sovereignty, sovereign being, must constituently combine its unconditionality with its conditioned existence. There must be, as it were, and as Derrida would have it, a taking turns between these two imperatives.[114]

The Life of Sovereignty

We come now to the third and final measuring derived from the initial set of orientations around the death penalty. This involves the challenging terms of sovereignty's relation to the governing of life.

The standard sovereignty of surpassing determinacy, being incapable of sustained realization, can only be, in Derrida's terms, a phantasm—more particularly, "a theological phantasm."[115] That theology entailed, as we saw, sovereignty's taking on the dimensions of an occidental monotheism, dimensions that could be rendered now in profane terms as the conditioned and the unconditional. The operative problem with this phantasm is that its ultimately surpassing determinacy can only seek to contain the illimitability of unconditional life by being ramped up to a position of quasi-transcendence.[116] With the determinate existence of sovereignty thus set self-sufficiently apart from the constituent unconditional, a phantasmic sovereignty is left as something of a pure phenomenon.[117] It is here that law reenters. In its unrestrained responsiveness, in what could now be seen as "its" unconditonality, "law itself does not have a form for what would need to be its own sovereignty," as Nancy discerned.[118] With occidental political formation, the paradigm of law is the law "of" the national or imperial sovereign. Thence law is a dependent creation of the sovereign. Yet the opposite is (also) the case. The law is the vicarious receptivity of sovereign unconditionality, of life as living together. Should the sovereign as pure phenomenon be so receptive in and as itself, it would deliquesce.

Thus far we have two sovereignties. One is a surpassing sovereignty. This is a sovereign hyperdeterminacy that can take life. It depends for this, and more generally for its very constitution, on a transcendent reference, on a quasi-deific self-exaltation. This was, and is, a sovereignty associated with death as terminal, as an end. It was a sovereignty that Foucault, as we saw, considered a mere survival from previous ages, a sovereignty that was subordinate and accessory to a new biopower elevating the governing of life. However, Foucault also rather vaguely saw sovereignty as playing a more integral and seemingly significant part in this new situation.[119] This part would appear to be more in accord with a sovereignty which, for Derrida, as we noted a little earlier, "engenders like a generative principle of life."[120] Relating this, in turn, to death, and as we just saw also, this is a sovereignty that is "absolutely" open, "nothing."[121] The end for such a sovereignty, its determinate affirmation "for the time being," its determination, is of death as the incipient opening to alterity, as the dying to what determinately is and as an opening to what can ever be otherwise. This necessary ability, necessary if sovereignty is to be ongoing, is starkly opposed to the hyperdeterminacy of an occidental sovereignty in the modern period. That opposition is, as we saw, overcome by law's taking on that necessary receptive ability. Understandably enough, this is a law that sovereignty seeks to subordinate to itself, to make its own creation, something that is ultimately impossible because of the very dependence of sovereignty on the illimitable law.

All of which is little more than summary of much of the argument so far. It could be taken further and set toward a conclusion by noting with Derrida that sovereignty "is undivided, unshared, or it is not;" yet he would ask: "What happens when . . . [sovereignty] divides? When it must, when it cannot not divide?"[122] The seeming opposites merge when Derrida talks about ipseity in terms of "the sovereign and reappropriating gathering of self in the simultaneity of an assemblage or assembly, being together or 'living together,' as we say."[123] As with Nancy's equation of sovereignty and the "with" of our being-with, sovereignty here becomes a manner of being, of being together.[124] This manner of being combined, as we have just seen, an unconditional, an illimitable sovereignty with the sovereignty that was delimited and conditioned. With such a manner of being neither the unconditional nor the conditioned, while each retains a necessary difference, can have a surpassing ultimacy. Each depends on the other for its existence. And neither can occupy a position that is enduringly apart from the other. Likewise with law, whether as sovereignty's complement or as the constitution of the people, law was, as we saw, the combining of its conditioned determinacy with its responsiveness to the unconditional, a combining in which each was necessary for the other but in which each was also and imperatively distinct from the other.

The stark alternative and the most telling expedient here is the simple claim to the totality, the attempted bringing of all life within a determinate comprehension, within a pervasive presupposition. What is so telling about this expedient is that, in its inexorable failure, there is the overwhelming intimation of unconditionality, the unconditionality of life of living together. Instancing Nazism, Foucault found it "an absolutely suicidal state," as we saw earlier. [125] Or, as Nancy put it, the truth of this condition would be "the truth of death," death as terminal.[126] A point is always reached when there is no ongoing. Nor is such an outcome securely sui generis. Given the source of the pathology—the occidental subordination of the unconditional to a determinate appropriation of life—then, as Lacoue-Labarthe and Nancy conclude, it is not "possible to simply push [Nazism] aside as an aberration, still less as a past aberration"; and even if "Nazism does not sum up the West, nor represent its necessary finality," still it belongs to "the history in which our own provenance lies."[127] Modern imperialism exemplifies a like solipsism even if one somewhat blunted, as Arendt points out, by an unavoidable regard for diversity.[128]

Yet even if—with imperialism, occidental sovereignty, the death penalty—the claim is to hold life in determinate part only, a total comprehending of life is still imported for, repeating somewhat, the part and everything that would ever relate to it would have to be held in a totalizing comprehension.[129] Whether in terms of negative ontology or in terms of the positive constitution of a living together, this claimed comprehension was, as we saw, entirely incompatible with modern political formation.

Conclusion

The road to abolition mapped out here, in following the trajectory of modern political formation, is found to be an open road. Unlike Oedipus, no resolving riddle was found in the road and, going on that precedent as well as on the argument of this chapter, if it were found, it would have best been avoided. Still, there are clear markers, measurings along the way, indicating what direction the road takes in its orientation toward abolition. Indeed, the cumulation of these markers quite undermines that sovereignty still affirmed as the generative basis of the death penalty.

What the journey also indicates are certain characters of political formation likely to sustain an obdurate retention of the death penalty. The perceptive may discern that all along I have been addressing a particular political formation, and the perceptive would be right. A sovereignty heightened by imperial self-elevation to a position of perceived predomination in the world is unlikely to question the "classic" conjunction of sovereignty and the power or "right" to deal death. Neither would a sovereignty whose quasi-theological transcendence is suscitated by a civil religion. No more propitious would be a sovereignty that sets its "executive" power increasingly and interminably above the law, the law embedded in life, in living together. Still, the recent accentuations of these traits does sharpen the stakes involved.[130]

NOTES

Thanks to Austin Sarat for unconditional generosity and for yet more provocation; thanks to Ben Golder and Jon Yorke for an abundance of insight and references; and thanks to Carol Steiker, Jordan Steiker, and Timothy Kaufman-Osborn for invaluable comments on a previous version of this chapter.

1. See the report by Stefano Crosara, "I'm Against the Death Penalty," *Trieste Contemporanea: La Revista* 6 (2000), available at http://www.triestecontemporanea.it/pag20-e.htm (last accessed June 6, 2008).

2. The pervasive concern in this chapter with the difference between dimensions of political formation and how this difference is made reflects the faint irony of my title, "Making Difference." The phrase is, of course, derived from judicial incantations that the penalty of death makes a difference in conducting cases since "[t]here is a heightened need for fairness in the administration of death" (per Justice Harry Blackmun in *Callins v. Collins* 114 S. Ct. 1127, 1132)—an injunction observed recurrently in the breach.

3. Bruno Latour, *We Have Never Been Modern*, trans. Catherine Porter (London: Harvester Wheatsheaf, 1993).

4. Adam Thurschwell, "Ethical Exception: Capital Punishment in the Figure of Sovereignty," *South Atlantic Quarterly* 107, a special issue under the title "Killing States: Lethal Decisions/Final Judgements," ed. Austin Sarat and Jennifer Culbert ((2008): 571.

5. David Garland, "Capital Punishment and American Culture," *Punishment and Society* 7 (2005): 347. The main targets are James Q. Whitman, *Harsh Justice: Criminal Punishment and the Widening Divide between America and Europe* (New York: Oxford University Press, 2003), and Franklin E. Zimring, *The Contradictions of American Capital Punishment* (New York: Oxford University Press, 2003). For an extensive account of theories of American exceptionalism, see Carol S. Steiker, "Capital Punishment and American Exceptionalism," *Oregon Law Review* 97 (2002): 97.

6. Garland, "Capital Punishment," 356.

7. Jon Yorke, "The Changing Relationship of Sovereignty and the Death Penalty: A Conundrum for the Council of Europe," MS 2 (on file with the author). The death penalty is "abolished" in Article 1 of Protocol No. 6 to the Convention. Article 2 excepts the use of "the death penalty in respect of acts committed in time of war or of imminent threat of war." With the extensive conception of "war" and of such "imminent threat" being advanced of late, abolition becomes attenuated. For details of a sympathetic turning toward the "abolished" death penalty by the federal government in Canada, see the site of the Canadian Coalition Against the Death Penalty at http://www,ccadp.org/can-con.htm (last accessed June 2, 2008).

8. Yorke, "Changing Relationship," MS 6.

9. Thurschwell, "Ethical Exception"; Kyron Huigens, "Derrida on the Death Penalty," available at http://www.cardozo.yu.edu/life/winter2001/derrida/ (last accessed January 9, 2008). Cf. Austin Sarat, "Capital Punishment as a Legal, Political, and Cultural Fact: An Introduction," in *The Killing State: Capital Punishment in Law, Politics, and Culture*, ed. Austin Sarat (New York: Oxford University Press, 1999), 4–5, and Austin Sarat, *When the State Kills: Capital Punishment and the American Condition* (Princeton, N.J.: Princeton University Press, 2001), 17. All of which is, of course, not to deny, as Bataille has it: "A real or unreal existence (a person, a god, or a state), by threatening others with death, heightens within itself its transcendent nature." Georges Bataille, *On Nietzsche*, trans. Bruce Boone (London: Continuum, 1992), 177.

10. Achille Mbembe, "Necropolitics," trans. Libby Mientjes, *Public Culture* 15 (2003): 11.See also Giorgio Agamben, *Homo Sacer: Sovereign Power and Bare Life*, trans. Daniel Heller-Roazen (Minneapolis: University of Minnesota Press, 1998).

11. Thomas Hobbes, *Leviathan* (Chicago: Encyclopedia Britannica, 1952), 100 (chap. 17), 145 (chap. 28).

12. For the quotation, see Thomas Hobbes, *A Dialogue Between a Philosopher And a Student of the Common Laws of England* (Chicago: University of Chicago Press, 1971), 61 (chap. 15). For a conspectus relating to *Leviathan*, see Peter Fitzpatrick, *Modernism and the Grounds of Law* (Cambridge: Cambridge University Press, 2001), 93–95, 105–7. See also Hobbes, *Leviathan*, 86 (chap. 13), 94 (chap. 15), and Thomas Hobbes, *The Elements Of Law Natural And Politic* (Whitefish: Kessinger, n.d.), 61 (chap. 17 para. 2).

13. Hobbes, *Leviathan*, 90 (chap. 14), 115 (chap. 21); Thomas Hobbes, *De Cive* (Whitefish: Kessinger, n.d.), 26 (chap. II, para. xviii). Cf. Hobbes, *Leviathan*, 101 (chap. 18).

14. James R. Martel, "Strong Sovereign, Weak Messiah: Thomas Hobbes on Scriptural Interpretation, Rhetoric and the Holy Spirit," *Theory and Event* 7:4 (2004): 9 (para. 20), available at http://muse.jhu.edu/login?uri=/journals/theory_and_event/voo7/7.4martel.html. See also James R. Martel, *Subverting the Leviathan: Reading Thomas Hobbes as a Radical Democrat* (New York: Columbia University Press, 2007), chap. 2.

15. Immanuel Kant, *The Metaphysics of Morals*, trans. Mary Gregor (Cambridge: Cambridge University Press, 1996), 106 (*6:333*).

16. Ibid., 107 (*6:334*).

17. Ibid., 89–91 (*6:311–12, 314*); his emphasis.

18. Ibid., 95 (*6:318*).

19. Ibid., 95 (*6:319*); his emphasis.

20. Thurschwell, "Ethical Exception," 573–74, 577–79.

21. Ibid. What could be seen in a couple of ways as the most spectacular instance in Foucault's work comes with his sharp setting of disciplinary power against the torture and execution of the failed regicide, Damiens. Michel Foucault, *Discipline and Punish: The Birth of the Prison*, trans. Alan Sheriden (Harmondsworth: Penguin, 1979), 3–6.

22. Michel Foucault, *Foucault Live (Interviews, 1966–84)*, trans. John Johnston (New York: Semiotext(e), 1989), 165.

23. Michel Foucault, *The History of Sexuality*. Vol. 1: *An Introduction*, trans. Robert Hurley (Harmondsworth: Penguin, 1981), 135–59.

24. Ibid., 135.

25. Ibid., 89.

26. Ibid., 136.

27. Ibid., 138. Cf. Whitman, *Harsh Justice*, 94–95. Perhaps for the United States one could add "the impact of victim impact" (Zimring, *Contradictions*, 57); and perhaps even the currently intense engagement with questions of lethal injection as a biopolitical concern with what is left of a life. For more, see Timothy Kaufman-Osborn, chap. 7 in this volume.

28. Michel Foucault, "Governmentality," in Michel Foucault, *Power: Essential Works of Foucault 1954–1984*, vol. 3, trans. Robert Hurley and others (London: Penguin, 2001), 218; Michel Foucault, *"Society Must Be Defended"*: *Lectures at the Collége de France, 1975–76*, trans. David Macey (London: Allen Lane, 2003), 241.

29. Foucault, *History of Sexuality*, 139.

30. Ibid., 149–50; Michel Foucault, "The Political Technology of Individuals," in Foucault, *Power*, 417.

31. Foucault, *"Society Must Be Defended,"* 260.

32. Foucault, *History of Sexuality*, 143; Michel Foucault, "Georges Canguilhem: Philosopher of Error," *I and C* 7 (1983): 51, 60. This resonates with the generative excess of "resistance," which, for Foucault, both exceeds and goes to constitute formations of such power. For example, Foucault, *History of Sexuality*, 95–96. Or, borrowing the pith from Deleuze, "the final word on power is that *resistance comes first*." Gilles Deleuze, *Foucault*, trans. Seán Hand (London: Continuum, 1999), 74; his emphasis.

33. Foucault, *History of Sexuality*, 143.

34. Michel Foucault, "What Is Enlightenment?" trans. Catherine Porter (amended), in Michel Foucault, *Ethics: Essential Works of Foucault 1954–1984*, vol. 1 (London: Penguin, 2000), 313, 314, 316.

35. For example, Michel Foucault, "Technologies of the Self," in Foucault, *Ethics*, 225, 249. The momentous point is taken here as surviving the more commonly attributed view that for Foucault we, ourselves, were utterly subordinated to and constituted by the disciplines and such. Cf. Jon Simons, *Foucault and The Political* (London: Routledge, 1995), 3.

36. Michel Foucault, "Preface to Transgression," in Michel Foucault, *Language, Counter-Memory, Practice: Selected Essays and Interviews*, trans. Donald F. Bouchard and Sherry Simon (Ithaca, N.Y.: Cornell University Press, 1977), 30–31.

37. Ibid., 31–32.

38. Jacques Derrida, "Psychoanalysis Searches the States of Its Soul: The Impossible Beyond of a Sovereign Cruelty," in Jacques Derrida, *Without Alibi*, trans. Peggy Kamuf (Stanford, Calif.: Stanford University Press, 2002), 274, 276. See also Foucault, *History of Sexuality*, 150.

39. Huigens, "Derrida on The Death Penalty."

40. Derrida, "Psychoanalysis Searches," 245.

41. Jacques Derrida, "Capital Punishment, Another 'Temptation of Theodicy,'" in *Pragmatism, Critique, Judgement: Essays for Richard J. Bernstein*, ed. Seyla Benhabib and Nancy Fraser (Cambridge, Mass.: MIT Press, 2004), 197, 201.

42. Jacques Derrida, "The University Without Condition," in Derrida, *Without Alibi*, 207; Jacques Derrida, "A Discussion with Jacques Derrida," *Theory and Event* 5 (201): para 49, available at http://muse.jhu.edu/journals/theory_and_event/v005/5.1derrida.html.

43. Derrida, "Capital Punishment," 204; his emphasis.

44. Foucault, *History of Sexuality*, 144, 148.

45. A synopsis provided by Jacques Derrida, "Force of Law: The 'Mystical Foundation of Authority,'" trans. Mary Quaintance, in Jacques Derrida, *Acts of Religion* (New York: Routledge, 2002), 276. For Benjamin, see Walter Benjamin, "Critique of Violence," in Walter Benjamin, *One Way Street and Other Writings*, trans. Edmund Jephcott (London: New Left Books, 1979), 140. The configuration of law–death–certainty is trenchantly traced in the jurisprudence of the Supreme Court in Jennifer L. Culbert, *Dead Certainty: The Death Penalty and the Problem of Judgment* (Stanford, Calif.: Stanford University Press, 2008).

46. Mitchell Dean, *Governmentality: Power and Rule in Modern Society* (London: Sage, 1999), 105. And there is Locke's famed dictum: "Political Power then I take to be *a Right* of making Laws with Penalties of Death." John Locke, "The Second Treatise of Government," in John Locke, *Two Treatises of Government* (New York: Cambridge University Press, 1960), 308; original emphasis.

47. Maurice Blanchot, *The Madness of the Day*, trans. Lydia Davis (Barrytown: Station Hill, 1981), 16. "Well," Blanchot's protagonist responds, "that's more than enough to get us both locked up." Ibid.

48. Maurice Blanchot, *The Step Not Beyond*, trans. Lycette Nelson (Albany: State University of New York Press, 1992), 25.

49. Maurice Blanchot, *The Infinite Conversation*, trans. Susan Hanson (Minneapolis: University of Minnesota Press, 1993), 225. See also Maurice Blanchot, "Literature And the Right to Death," in Maurice Blanchot, *The Station Hill Blanchot Reader: Fiction and Literary Essays*, trans. Lydia Davis (Barrytown: Station Hill, 1999), 376.

50. Blanchot, *Infinite Conversation*, 225.

51. Blanchot, "Literature And the Right to Death," 391–92.

52. Ibid., 392.

53. Ibid., 398–99.

54. Maurice Blanchot, *The Writing of the Disaster*, trans. Ann Smock (Lincoln: University of Nebraska Press, 1995), 19.

55. Blanchot, *Step Not Beyond*, 25.

56. Blanchot, *Infinite Conversation*, 434.

57. Maurice Blanchot, *The Unavowable Community*, trans. Pierre Joris (Barrytown: Station Hill, 1988), 43.

58. Derrida, "Force of Law," 250.

59. Ibid., 252.

60. Ibid., 244.

61. Ibid., 252.

62. Jacques Derrida, "Psyche: Inventions of the Other," trans. Catherine Porter, in *Reading de Man Reading*, ed. Lindsay Walters and Wlad Godzich (Minneapolis: University of Minnesota Press, 1989), 25.

63. Derrida, "Force of Law," 251, 255.

64. Jacques Derrida, *Rogues: Two Essays on Reason*, trans. Pascale-Anne Brault and Michael Naas (Stanford: Stanford University Press, 2005), 150.

65. Derrida, "Force of Law," 257.

66. Ibid.

67. Ibid.; his emphasis.

68. However, some seemingly contrary resolution of this dissonance by way of negotiation is suggested by Derrida in Jacques Derrida and Jean-Luc Nancy, "Responsabilité—du sens à venir," in *Sens en tous sens: Autour des travaux de Jean-Luc Nancy*, ed. Francis Guibal and Jean-Clet Martin (Paris: Galilée, 2004),

179–80. I am grateful to Pablo Ghetti for this reference. See also the use of "compromises" in Jacques Derrida, "The Deaths of Roland Barthes," trans. Pascale-Anne Brault and Michael Naas, in *Philosophy and Non-Philosophy Since Merleau-Ponty*, ed. Hugh J. Silverman (London: Routledge, 1988), 266–67. Cf. Jacques Derrida, *Negotiations: Interventions and Interviews 1971–2001*, trans. Elizabeth Rottenberg (Stanford, Calif.: Stanford University Press, 2002), 12–14. And specifically on law as noncomprizable, see Derrida, "Force of Law," 257, 270.

69. Jacques Derrida, "Before the Law," trans. Avital Ronell, in Jacques Derrida *Acts of Literature* (New York: Routledge, 1992), 191.

70. Jean-Luc Nancy, *Being Singular Plural*, trans. Richard D. Richardson and Anne E. O'Byrne (Stanford, Calif.: Stanford University Press, 2000), 131.

71. Derrida, "Capital Punishment," 204.

72. Ibid., 197.

73. Blanchot, *Writing of the Disaster*, 19.

74. Blanchot, *Unavowable Community*, 43.

75. Françoise Dastur, *Death: An Essay on Finitude*, trans. John Llewelyn (London: Athlone, 1996), 4.

76. For the idea of the political being insinuated here, see Philippe Lacoue-Labarthe and Jean-Luc Nancy, *Retreating the Political*, trans. Simon Sparkes (London: Routledge, 1997), chap. 6.

77. Hans Lindahl, "Constituent Power and Reflexive Identity: Towards an Ontology of Collective Selfhood," in *The Paradox of Constitutionalism*, ed. Martin Loughlin and Neil Walker (Oxford: Oxford University Press, 2007), 19.

78. Jacques Derrida, "Declarations of Independence," in Derrida, *Negotiations*, 50.

79. Jean-Jacques Rousseau, *The Social Contract*, trans. Maurice Cranston (London: Penguin, 1968), 86–87 (Book II, chap. 7).

80. Ibid., 87 (Book II, chap. 7); Jean-Jacques Rousseau, *The Social Contract and Discourses*, trans. G. D. H. Cole (London: Dent, 1986), 212 (Book II, chap. 6). The switch in translations is because the latter is more accurate here. The reliance on Rousseau in the setting of my overall argument is not consonant with his strained approval of the death penalty. Ibid., 208–10 (Book II, chap. 5).

81. Giorgio Agamben, *The Time That Remains: A Commentary on the Letter to the Romans*, trans. Patricia Dailey (Stanford, Calif.: Stanford University Press, 2005), 57.

82. Jacques Derrida, "Autoimmunity: Real and Symbolic Suicides—A Dialogue with Jacques Derrida," in *Philosophy in a Time of Terror: Dialogues with Jürgen Habermas and Jacques Derrida*, Giovanna Borradori (Chicago: University of Chicago Press, 2003), 120.

83. Derrida, "Declarations of Independence," 50 and 50–51. See also Bonnie Honig, "Between Decision and Deliberation: Political Paradox in Democratic Theory," *American Political Science Review* 101 (2007): 1, 3.

84. Jacques Derrida, *Of Hospitality*, trans. Rachel Bowlby (Stanford, Calif.: Stanford University Press, 2000), and Jacques Derrida, *On Cosmopolitanism and Forgiveness*, trans. Mark Dooley and Michael Hughes (London: Routledge, 2001), 1–24. Cf. Friedrich Nietzsche, *Twilight of the Idols*, in *Twilight of the Idols/The Anti-Christ*, trans. R. J. Hollingdale (Harmondsworth: Penguin, 1968), 37.

85. Derrida, *Of Hospitality*, 79.

86. Derrida, *On Cosmopolitanism*, 17; his emphasis.

87. Derrida, *Of Hospitality*, 79 and 81; his emphasis.

88. Derrida, *Rogues*, 149.

89. Derrida, "Autoimmunity," 129.

90. Ibid., 130.

91. Derrida, *On Cosmopolitanism*, 45.

92. Ibid., 44–45; his emphasis.

93. Derrida, *Negotiations*, 36. See also John D. Caputo, "Without Sovereignty, Without Being: Unconditionality, the Coming God and Derrida's Democracy to Come," *Journal for Cultural and Religious Theory* 9 (2003): 9, 9, and 12. See also the text at note 57 above.

94. Derrida, "Autoimmunity," 130.

95. Jean-Luc Nancy, *The Inoperative Community*, trans. Peter Connor, Lisa Garbus, Michael Holland, and Simona Sawhney (Minneapolis: University of Minnesota Press, 1991), 12.

96. Foucault, "Preface to Transgression," 34.

97. Jacques Derrida, *Spurs: Nietzsche's Styles*, trans. Barbara Harlow (Chicago: University of Chicago Press, 1979), 125. I am especially grateful to Ben Golder for this reference.

98. Hannah Arendt, *The Human Condition* (Chicago: University of Chicago Press, 1958), 237.

99. Ibid., 240. See also Nasser Hussain and Austin Sarat, "Toward New Theoretical Perspectives on Forgiveness, Mercy, and Clemency: An Introduction," in *Forgiveness, Mercy, and Clemency*, ed. Austin Sarat and Nasser Hussain (Stanford, Calif.: Stanford University Press, 2007), 2–3. Cf. Jacques Derrida and Elisabeth Roudinesco, *For What Tomorrow . . . A Dialogue*, trans. Jeff Fort (Stanford, Calif.: Stanford University Press, 2004), 163–64. See, generally, Richard J. Bernstein, "Derrida: The Aporia of Forgiveness?" *Constellations* 13 (2006): 394–406.

100. For example, the necessity of the unconditional gift for the movement of economy. Jacques Derrida, *Given Time: 1. Counterfeit Money*, trans. Peggy Kamuf (Chicago: University of Chicago Press, 1994).

101. Jacques Derrida, *Politics of Friendship*, trans. George Collins (London: Verso, 1997), 231; his emphasis. See also Jacques Derrida, "Nietzsche and the Machine," in Derrida, *Negotiations*, 241.

102. Derrida, "Autoimmunity," 130.

103. Patrick Riley, *The General Will Before Rousseau: The Transformation of the Divine Into the Civil* (Princeton, N.J.: Princeton University Press, 1986), 40.

104. Friedrich Nietzsche, *The Gay Science*, trans. Josefine Nauckhoff (Cambridge: Cambridge University Press, 2001), 119–20. For this etymology of atonement, see "Atone" in Walter W. Skeat, *A Concise Etymological Dictionary of the English Language* (New York: Capricorn, 1963), 30. My thanks to the late Hans Mohr.

105. Friedrich Nietzsche, *Thus Spoke Zarathustra*, as reprinted in *The Portable Nietzsche*, trans. Walter Kaufmann (New York: Viking, 1954), 160–61.

106. Derrida, "University Without Condition," 207.

107. Cf. Michael Naas, "*Comme si, comme ça*: Phantasms of Self, State, and a Sovereign God," *Mosaic* 40, no. 2 (2007): 1.

108. Derrida, *Rogues*, 12 (for example).

109. Lacoue-Labarthe and Nancy, *Retreating the Political*, 116.

110. Georges Bataille, *The Accursed Share: An Essay on General Economy*, Vols. 2 and 3, trans. Robert Hurley (New York: Zone, 1991), 207–11.

111. Nancy, *Being Singular Plural*, 36, 137.

112. Ibid., 36; his emphasis.

113. Derrida, *Rogues*, 136, 138.

114. Ibid., 6–18.

115. Derrida, "University Without Condition," 207.

116. Cf. Gilles Deleuze and Félix Guattari, *What Is Philosophy?* trans. Graham Burchell and Hugh Tomlinson (London: Verso, 1994), 45.

117. Naas, "Phantasms of Self," 5.

118. Nancy, *Being Singular Plural*, 131.

119. For example, Foucault "Governmentality," 202, 218, 219, 220.

120. Derrida, *Rogues*, 138.

121. Ibid., 136; Bataille, *Accursed Share*, 207–11.

122. Jacques Derrida, "Provocation: Forewords," in Derrida, *Without Alibi*, xix–xx.

123. Derrida, *Rogues*, 11.

124. Nancy, *Being Singular Plural*, 36, and text above note 112.

125. Foucault, "*Society Must Be Defended*," 260.

126. Nancy, *Inoperative Community*, 12.

127. Philippe Lacoue-Labarthe and Jean-Luc Nancy, "The Nazi Myth," trans. Brian Holmes, *Critical Inquiry* 16 (1990): 291, 312. See also Nietzsche, *Gay Science*, 199, and Friedrich Nietzsche, *On the Genealogy of Morals*, trans. Doulas Smith (Oxford: Oxford University Press, 1996), 134–35.

128. Hannah Arendt, *The Origins of Totalitarianism*, new ed. (San Diego: Harcourt Brace, 1958), 124–28.

129. On the death penalty and its relation to the setting apart, see Michel Foucault, "Against Replacement Penalties," in Foucault, *Power*, 460. Although one could argue with Foucault that death as irretrievable still makes a difference, his emphasis on incorrigibility as the objectionable criterion for setting apart should give pause to advocates of imprisonment for the whole of a life as an alternative to the death penalty.

130. Michael McCann and David T. Johnson, chap. 5 in this volume. See also Sangmin Bae, *When the State no Longer Kills: International Human Rights Norms and Abolition of Capital Punishment*, (Albany: State University of New York Press, 2007), chap. 5.

About the Contributors

JAY D. ARONSON is Assistant Professor of Science, Technology, and Society in the History Department at Carnegie Mellon University. His research and teaching focus on the interactions of science, technology, law, and human rights in criminal justice and post-conflict resolution contexts. His first book, titled *Genetic Witness: Science, Law, and Controversy in the Making of DNA Profiling*, examines the development of forensic DNA analysis in the American legal system. He received his Ph.D. in History of Science and Technology from the University of Minnesota and was both a predoctoral and postdoctoral fellow at Harvard University's John F. Kennedy School of Government.

SIMON A. COLE is Associate Professor of Criminology, Law and Society at the University of California, Irvine, where he teaches a course on capital punishment. He received his bachelor's degree in History from Princeton University and his Ph.D. in Science and Technology Studies from Cornell University. He is the author of *Suspect Identities: A History of Fingerprinting and Criminal Identification* and a coauthor of *Truth Machine: The Contentious History of DNA Fingerprinting*. He is a member of the American Judicature Society Commission on Forensic Science and Public Policy.

DEBORAH W. DENNO is the Arthur A. McGivney Professor of Law at Fordham Law School. She has published books and articles concerning a broad range of areas relating to criminal law, including the death penalty. For nearly two decades, she has written on, and testified in state and federal courts about, the constitutionality of lethal injection and electrocution. In 2007, she was selected as one of the *National Law Journal*'s "Fifty Most Influential Women Lawyers in America."

PETER FITZPATRICK is Anniversary Professor of Law at Birkbeck, University of London, and Honorary Professor of Law in the University of Kent. In 2007 he was given the James Boyd White Award by The Association for the Study of Law, Culture and the Humanities. He has taught at universities in Europe, North America, and Papua New Guinea and published many books on legal philosophy, law and social theory, law and racism, and imperialism, the latest one being *Law as Resistance: Modernism, Imperialism, Legalism*. Outside the academy he has been in an international legal practice and was also in the Prime Minister's Office in Papua New Guinea for several years.

BERNARD E. HARCOURT is the Julius Kreeger Professor of Law and Criminology at the University of Chicago and the director of the Center for Studies in Criminal Justice. His writings and teaching bridge empirical and social theory in the criminal justice domain. He is the author of *Against Prediction: Profiling, Policing and Punishing in an Actuarial Age*; *Language of the Gun: Youth, Crime, and Public Policy*; and *Illusion of Order: The False Promise of Broken-Windows Policing*. He has also taught at Harvard Law School, New York University School of Law, the École des Hautes Études en Sciences Sociales in Paris, Université Paris X–Nanterre, and Université Paul Cézanne Aix-Marseille III.

DAVID T. JOHNSON is Professor of Sopciology and Adjunct Professor of Law at the University of Hawaii. He is the author of *The Japanese Way of Justice: Prosecuting Crime in Japan*, which received best book awards from the American Society of Criminology and the American Sociological Association, and coauthor (with Franklin E. Zimring) of *The Next Frontier: National Development, Political Change, and the Death Penalty in Asia*.

TIMOTHY V. KAUFMAN-OSBORN is the Baker Ferguson Professor of Politics and Leadership, as well as the chair of the faculty, at Whitman College. He is the author of several books and numerous articles on topics including capital punishment, the discipline of political science, feminist theory, and American pragmatism. He has served as president of the Western Political Science Association, as well as the American Civil Liberties Union of Washington, and he recently completed a term on the Executive Council of the American Political Science Association.

JÜRGEN MARTSCHUKAT is Professor of History at Erfurt Unversity in Germany. His research interests are the cultural history of violence and the death penalty in Europe and the United States. He is the author of *Inszeniertes Töten: Eine Geschichte der Todesstrafe vom 17. bis zum 19. Jahrhundert* [Performances of execution in German history, capital punishment from the 17th to the 19th century] and *Die Geschichte der Todesstrafe in Nordamerika* [History of capital punishment in North America], as well as of other publication on the cultural history of the death penalty.

MICHAEL MCCANN is Gordon Hirabayashi Professor for the Advancement of Citizenship at the University of Washington. He is the author of *Rights at Work: Pay Equity Reform and the Politics of Legal Mobilization* and (with William Haltom) *Distorting the Law: Politics, Media, and the Litigation Crisis*. McCann is also editor and lead author for *Law and Social Movements*; and co-editor, with David Engel, of *Fault Lines: Tort Law as Cultural Practice*.

CHARLES J. OGLETREE, JR., is the Jesse Climenko Professor of Law at Harvard University and Founding and Executive Director of the Charles Hamilton Houston Institute for Race and Justice. He is a co-editor (with Austin Sarat) of *From Lynch Mobs to the Killing State: Race and Death Penalty in America* (NYU Press) and author of *All Deliberate Speed: Reflections on the First Half-Century of* Brown v. Board of Education.

MICHAEL L. RADELET is Professor and Chair, Department of Sociology, University of Colorado–Boulder. He served for 22 years on the faculty at the University of Florida (including five years as Chair of the Department of Sociology) before moving to Boulder in 2001. Radelet's research on capital punishment focuses especially on the problems of erroneous convictions, racial bias, public opinion, and medical involvement.

AUSTIN SARAT is William Nelson Cromwell Professor of Jurisprudence and Political Science at Amherst College. He is a co-editor (with Charles J. Ogletree, Jr.) of *From Lynch Mobs to the Killing State: Race and Death Penalty in America* (NYU Press) and the author of numerous books, including *Mercy on Trial: What It Means to Stop an Execution*.

CAROL S. STEIKER is the Howard and Kathy Aibel Professor of Law at Harvard Law School. Before joining Harvard's faculty, Steiker served as President of the *Harvard Law Review*, as a law clerk to Justice Thurgood Marshall, and as a staff attorney for the D.C. Public Defender Service. A specialist in criminal justice issues, Steiker is the author of numerous scholarly works regarding criminal law, criminal procedure, and capital punishment. She also continues to litigate criminal defense issues and to work on law reform projects as a consultant to nonprofit organizations and as an expert witness in state legislatures and Congress.

JORDAN M. STEIKER is the Judge Robert M. Parker Chair in Law at the University of Texas School of Law. He also serves as the Co-Director of the law school's Capital Punishment Center. Steiker's scholarship focuses on capital punishment law, federal habeas, and constitutional law. In addition to his academic work, Steiker has represented numerous death-sentenced inmates in state and federal court.

ROBIN WAGNER-PACIFICI is the Gil and Frank Mustin Professor of Sociology at Swarthmore College. Her work examines critical social and political events, analyzing their trajectories into and out of violence, and includes analyses of terrorist kidnappings (*The Moro Morality Play: Terrorism as Social Drama*), urban police actions (*Discourse and Destruction: The City of Philadelphia vs MOVE*), extremist groups in standoffs with law enforcement (*Theorizing the Standoff: Contingency in Action*), and military surrenders at the conclusion of war (*The Art of Surrender: Decomposing Sovereignty at Conflict's End*). Recently, she published work on policy documents of state strategy, "The Innocuousness of State Lethality in an Age of National Security," *South Atlantic Quarterly*, 2008.

Index